Daniel Will-Harris

WordPerfect 5 Desktop Publishing in Style

the expert's guide to WordPerfect & graphic design

PEACHPIT PRESS
Berkeley, CA

WordPerfect 5: Desktop Publishing in Style

Peachpit Press
1085 Keith Avenue
Berkeley, CA 94708
415/527-8555

Art Direction by Toni Will-Harris

Portions of this book have appeared in *Personal Publishing, Compute!* and *Computerland* magazines.

Library of Congress Cataloging-in-Publication Data
Will-Harris, Daniel
WordPerfect 5: Desktop Publishing in Style
Includes index
1. Desktop Publishing 2. Microcomputers
3. Typesetting 4. Graphic design
I. Title
Z253.W47 1988 070.5'72

0 9 8 7 6 5 4 3
Printed and bound in the United States of America
ISBN: 0-938151-04-5

This book is dedicated to our parents.

Acknowledgments

I want to thank my wife Toni, a respected writer, editor, and publication consultant in her own right (usually on my left). When we met, she was Editor-in-Chief of our college newspaper, and she still edits everything I write (no matter how hard I try to sneak it past her). She wrote a majority of the design chapter in this book and compiled the reading list, glossary, and index in the Appendix. She also designed most of the example pages and provided art direction for the entire book. While I could have done this book without her, it wouldn't have been any fun (but there probably would have been a little less shouting).

I would also like to thank Louise Domenitz at Bitstream, Mary Brunger and all the crew at WordPerfect, Harley Haas and the gang at LaserMaster, Dr. Robert Fenchel and Scott Taylor at SoftCraft, Rhonda Aldrich, Mark Evanier, Susan Harrison, and Rhoda Wasserman. A special thanks to Rowby Goren and Karen Linden.

Contents

Introduction !

The myth and the reality

DTP in the real world

Your favorite word processing program (or the one your boss forces you to use), WordPerfect, is about to take you to the deep, dark regions of desktop publishing. While some people would like you to believe that desktop publishing is as simple as pressing a few buttons, it isn't. The uncharted territory of desktop publishing is fraught with confusing lingo, dangerous pitfalls, and an intimidating thing called *graphic design.*

WordPerfect is a remarkable program. It's the first PC word processor that combines excellent word processing with a wondrous amount of desktop publishing power. Desktop publishing is simply a way to make printed matter more attractive and effective, and WordPerfect does that better than any other PC word processing program.

You may be at home with WordPerfect's word processing, but now you'll be confronted with horrifying details like fonts, points, rules, grids, readouts, gutters, hairlines, kerning, layout, leading, serif, sans-serif, sidebars, widows, orphans, and other frightening characters. It's a jungle out there.

But never fear! This book will guide you through it, making sure you don't step in anything messy or fall prey to cannibalistic dealers trying to sell products you don't need. You'll not only discover how to navigate your way around a page like a pro, but you'll find the best way to present information, and learn the exact codes necessary to create the many examples you'll find on these pages. This book will show you how to make your publications as professional-looking as possible, without having to spend more time and money than is necessary.

If this book seems different from some of the others you may have looked at, that's because it is. It's not a rehash of the instruction manual (if that's what you're looking for, there are many such books available). In my millions of hours spent consulting and training people to use new programs, I've learned that most people are bored and frustrated with dry, technical manuals (I know I was when I started reading computer books, and I haven't forgotten it).

If you're at all like them, you want a book that you can readily comprehend. This book is written in terms you can understand. The fields of desktop publishing, graphic design, and typography all have separate vocabularies that you'll need to learn. You'll pick up the jargon along the way, without being assaulted and confused by it right from the start. You'll find the definitions for all these new terms in the glossary of this book.

I've written this book so you can feel as if a friend has come over to explain desktop publishing with WordPerfect to you. For some, the tone of my explanations may be too casual, but although the tone may be casual, the information is not. I cover techniques that are not contained in the WordPerfect documentation, or other books about the program, and have attempted to present this material in as accurate, detailed, and lively manner as possible.

Before we get any further, how about a little straight talk? I know this is dangerous, and everyone has warned me that you should be careful about telling readers the truth, but (call me Cher), I can't abide dishonesty, at least about desktop publishing.

While desktop publishing is truly a revolution in the way printed communications are created, as in any revolution, it's jammed packed with hype. I have one simple rule about DTP: it's not whether you *can* do something with a program, but whether you'd *want* to. Call it the "sequin" effect. Sequins are dazzling, but would you wear them if you had to sew them on yourself?

So you have to be cautious. To this end, I'm going to tell you exactly what you can and *can't* do. I've seen advertisements that show dazzling pages, actually created with a product. But such jimmied, round-about, time-consuming measures were required to create the finished page, that it's not really honest. Yes, you *can* create a page like that with the program, but would you really *want* to? Do you have the time, patience and expertise to manage it?

I've tried to avoid such convolutions in this book. However, I've become such a WordPerfect junkie that I too have found myself using and abusing every one of its tricks (and a few of my own), finally extracting a single correct page after about 20 trial and error prints. Rather than resorting to that, I've tried to make everything in this book something you'd *want* to do, rather than just something you *could* do.

Even without resorting to trickery, WordPerfect provides a vast array of features, some not even feasible in expensive dedicated desktop publishing programs, including Ventura and PageMaker. Using a PostScript printer, WordPerfect can rotate type, and includes special effects such as outline and shadow for fonts. Fonts can be pre-downloaded to LaserJets, so the print time can be quicker than even speedy Ventura. And WordPerfect's ability to print graphics in draft mode is something I've yearned for in a page composition program.

It's easy to install fonts (you get a whole slew of superb fonts free from Bitstream). In addition, WordPerfect uses files from many graphics programs, has excellent typography and is still one heck of a word processing program, with features ranging from search and replace, to footnotes, tables of contents, indexes, and a document compare feature that's a godsend for writers and editors.

Most of us equate desktop publishing with the final page emerging from the printer, with type and graphics perfectly positioned. No more rubber cement and X-Acto knives (or whatever you used to cut and paste). But it isn't a sin to use the old tools; some effects you may not be able to achieve with your current system, such as upside down type, or scanned artwork at an angle.

If you're working with a super-ambitious design and actually need to cut and paste, there's no need to feel guilty—it's okay. Do as much as you can with what you have on-screen, and then do the rest by hand—after all, this is still a free country (last time I checked). Producing a great looking document is what matters, and using whatever tools are available makes sense.

So come along with me and discover new ways to make your documents more attractive, effective, and — who knows — maybe even fun. ❖

1

Getting it all together

System configuration

Before you can get the most desktop publishing power out of WordPerfect, you have to make sure your system is set up properly. If it's not, you're going to waste a lot of time feeling sorry for yourself, something society now deems unattractive. And so...

First, a few conventions so that we understand each other. I was confused when I first started reading (and cursing) computer books, because I didn't understand the conventions. I'd see directions like "12n," but I didn't know I was supposed to replace the n with something of my own choosing. I just kept entering "12n" and couldn't figure out why things didn't work. My wife Toni took this approach one step further the first time she sat down at a computer. When the software provided her with a list (or menu) and a prompt which read "Type Your Choice," she dutifully typed the words "Your Choice" and wondered why nothing happened.

In this book I try to have as few conventions as possible. If you see letters in bold like this: **BOLD**, it means you type these letters on your keyboard (no, type them on your microwave keypad... sheesh, what does he think we are, gerbils?).

If you see CONTROL-F1, it means you hold down the **CTRL** key first, and keep holding it while pressing the key marked **F1**. Do not type the words CONTROL-F1, or press a dash between the Control and the F1 key (if you do, other people will snicker at you, as they did when I did such things lo those not-so-many years ago). If you see the word [ENTER], it means you press the key marked **ENTER** (or sometimes **RETURN**) on your keyboard. If you understand the concept, read on. If you don't, join me in the department of redundancy department and I'll repeat myself, so you won't be confused.

- INSTANT REPLAY: ALT-F8 means press the **ALT** key and keep holding it while pressing the key marked **F8**. SHIFT-F1 means hold down the **SHIFT** key while pressing the key marked **F1**.

Keystrokes look like this:

SHIFT F10 OFF ITALIC [ENTER]

In the keystroke font, notice that the zeros are tall and thin and the alphabet letter "O" is very round. Also notice that the number one is indicated by a small serif at the top of its stroke, and the alphabet letter "I" has no serif.

❖ *Keyboard*

If you have a keyboard with the function keys along the left hand side, you're going to have an easier time using WordPerfect than if the function keys are along the top. This is because you can press SHIFT, CONTROL and ALT at the same time with one hand. The function keys along the top require both hands for three-quarters of WordPerfect's commands.

I would like to put a curse on the head of whoever designed the so-called "enhanced" keyboard because it is illogically, un-ergonomically, and unproductively designed. If you like it, ignore this little outburst; if you don't, think about getting a new keyboard. I'm not joking. Keyboards with the function keys on the left make life with WordPerfect much easier. Since you don't use a mouse with WordPerfect 5, you're going to be spending a lot of time with the function keys.

```
Setup

     1 - Backup

     2 - Cursor Speed                  50 cps

     3 - Display

     4 - Fast Save (unformatted)       No

     5 - Initial Settings

     6 - Keyboard Layout               DTP.WPK

     7 - Location of Auxiliary Files

     8 - Units of Measure



Selection: 0
```

The ever-popular Setup Menu.

◆ Help

It's also reassuring to know that WordPerfect has an excellent built-in help system. If at any time you need help with a particular feature, press **F3** and then the key where the feature is located. If you don't know or can't remember where a particular feature is located, just press the first letter of the name of the feature (for help with underlining, you would press the letter u).

❖ *On your mark . . .*

Depending on your hardware, WordPerfect has certain limitations. So before you go any further, make sure WordPerfect is installed properly.

- Press **SHIFT-F1** and go into the WordPerfect SETUP menu. This will allow you to make sure WordPerfect is set up in the best way possible for your computer and monitor.
- Press **DG** and make sure that WordPerfect is installed for the type of monitor and graphics card installed in your computer.

WordPerfect will automatically know what type you are using, unless you have installed something exotic (like a high-resolution or full page monitor). If you have, find it listed on the menu and select it; otherwise, you will be unable to use the graphic preview function. If WordPerfect can't figure it out, here are a few hints: If your screen is black and white, black and green or black and amber, chances are you have either a text-only screen or a Hercules-compatible graphics card. The Hercules card is the most popular and reasonably priced monochrome graphics card for PCs.

If you have a text-only graphics system, you're not going to be able to experience the thrill of seeing your pages on-screen, just the way they'll print. Nor will you be able to effectively edit graphics on-screen. You will be missing out on two of WordPerfect's most fun-filled (and useful) new features. If you're serious about desktop publishing with WordPerfect, you should seriously consider purchasing a Hercules-compatible graphics card. These cards will work with almost any monochrome monitor and cost under $200.

If you have a color monitor, you will probably be using either CGA or EGA. If your text is grainy, you're using CGA. If it's sharp, you're probably using EGA 640x350. EGA is much sharper for both text and graphics. If you're using an IBM PS/2 computer Model 30 or below, you'll probably want to use EGA 640x350. If you've got your nose pressed to a PS/2 Model 50 or above, you'll have VGA graphics, and want to select VGA 640x480. If you don't see your particular graphics system listed, call WordPerfect's 800 support number.

- To ensure that WordPerfect displays in the way I'll describe, press **AY**, then **SY**, and press **[ENTER]**.
- To make sure that WordPerfect saves your files automatically, and backs them up in case of trouble, press **BTY5**, press **[ENTER]**, then press **OY**, and press **[ENTER]**.

While still in setup, I suggest you select a character such as the double chevron, ALT-174 (on the keypad), to indicate carriage returns.

One last point and then we're ready to move onto the printer. Unlike normal word processing which relies on lines and columns to tell you where you are on the page, desktop publishing needs more accurate units of measure. WordPerfect is able to measure in inches, centimeters, points (72 points=1 inch) and old-fashioned lines and columns.

For desktop publishing, you should set your units to either inches or centimeters, whichever is easiest for you to understand. Unless you are a real techie-type, or have a strong typesetting background, you would not want to measure everything in points.

- Press **UD"S"** (press the quote marks here) and hit return twice to leave the set-up menu. That wasn't too hard now, was it?

❖ Get set . . .

Now we turn to what might possibly be the single most important piece of hardware. In the trade it's winsomely called your "Output Device," but that always sounds too anatomical to me; and besides, in English it's simply known as your printer.

The type of printer you have (or have access to) determines what kind of pages you can produce with WordPerfect. WordPerfect can print using anything from a dot-matrix printer (costing under $200), to a Linotronic phototypesetting machine (costing upwards of $50,000). Naturally, the more expensive printer gives you more expensive-looking pages—true typeset quality, in fact.

For the best desktop publishing results, a laser printer is required. That doesn't mean you need a very expensive laser printer, but it does mean that you can expect to shell out at least $1,500... which some people might consider very expensive. If you can't afford a laser printer, I'll cover some ways to beg, borrow, steal, or rent time on someone else's printer.

◆ Printers

Laser printers fall into two main categories: LaserJet compatibles and PostScript printers. PostScript printers are the most expensive because they contain many typefaces built-in. You can print any of these typefaces at any size, and also use many special effects, such as outline and shadow.

The LaserJet II is the most popular laser printer and much less expensive than a PostScript printer. But it comes with almost no fonts (just Courier and a tiny line printer font), and no special effects. However, WordPerfect comes with a program called Bitstream Fontware, and two typefaces, Times Roman and Helvetica (aka Dutch and Swiss), that allow you to create type up to 144 point (2 inches) tall.

Whichever kind of laser printer you have, the best way to connect it to your computer is with a parallel cable. Parallel cables are faster and infinitely easier to install than serial cables. If you must use a serial cable, be aware that it will take far longer to print, especially if you want to print graphics or use a LaserJet compatible with Fontware fonts for WordPerfect. You may also need a specially configured serial cable.

If you have any kind of PostScript printer, install WordPerfect's QMS-PS/800/810 printer driver. The QMS is a PostScript printer, and all PostScript printers share the same commands. You can live without Fontware fonts for WordPerfect, unless you want to purchase other Fontware fonts that are not built-in your printer.

The LaserJet comes in several models, the oldest and least powerful being the plain LaserJet. This printer uses only cartridge fonts which are no larger than 14 point. The next step up is the LaserJet Plus, which has enough memory to use the Fontware fonts, but only up to 30 point (less than 1/2 inch) tall. The LaserJet II has the same abilities as the LaserJet Plus, but you can add extra memory, enabling you to use larger fonts and produce more complex graphics.

If you have a LaserJet or compatible, here's what you will need to do. If you are using a plain LaserJet, find out what kind of font cartridge is on your printer (it will be sticking out the front of the machine), and install WordPerfect for that particular cartridge. If you are using a LaserJet Plus or Series II, find out what cartridges you have, and how much memory your printer has.

If you have at least 512K of memory (as all LaserJet Plus and Series II printers do), you will want to install Fontware on your hard disk. The Fontware installation program is easy to use if you follow their instructions carefully (that's why step-by-step instructions are not repeated in this book). However, here are a few words of advice.

If you only print portrait pages (tall), choose "Portrait Only" in the installation. This will save time and tremendous amounts of disk space. If you need both Portrait and Landscape (wide), then select both.

Create Dutch and Swiss fonts in Medium, Bold, Italic, and Bold-Italic in the following sizes: 8, 10, 11, 12, 14, 18, 24, 30 point. If you have more than 512K, also install fonts in 36, 48, and 72 point.

I hope you're sitting down, because this will take as much as 8 hours on an XT-type computer, about half that on an AT-type computer, and even less on a '386. It's a lot of computer time, but remember that these fonts would cost $400 if you had to buy them. You got them free with WordPerfect, so try not to complain too much.

❖ GO!

While Fontware is making fonts, sit down and read the rest of this book... starting with this little aside about bugs.

◆ Is it a bug or a feature? Only her programer knows for sure.

No software is perfect, and any program as large (two and a half times bigger than 4.2) and complex as WordPerfect 5 is bound to have a few problems. I know, I feel like I've personally experienced the challenge of all of them.

It's next to impossible to make any software bug free because you may fix two bugs, but create another one (a bug you don't know you've created until some crabby user tells you about it).

The beta version of WordPerfect 5 was excellent, except that you couldn't print and edit at the same time. Somehow, in fixing this and other minor bugs, they came up with some rather major ones. This is not meant to scare you, only to advise you that there are known bugs so you won't think you're doing something wrong.

The very first release of WordPerfect 5 was dated 5/5/88, and perhaps you have one. To find out the date of your software, start the program, then press **F3** (the Help key). The date will appear in the upper right corner of your screen. If you requested the Bitstream Fontware package, WordPerfect may have included their latest release of the software.

If the date of your program is 5/5/88, as a registered owner you should have received an upgrade dated 1/3/89. If not, call WordPerfect (800-321-3349 or 800-541-5096) *immediately* and have them send you an update. I believe they may be charging a nominal fee for this, as well as for the Fontware kit.

Many improvements have been made in the program since the 5/5/88 release, and the step-by-step examples in this book won't work properly with that release because it lacks some of these refinements. If you have the version dated 1/3/89, most of the bugs will have been fixed.

There have been so many updates of the program that it sometimes creates difficulties when you try to use a file created with an earlier version of the program. It's a tendency of new users to think that they've hit a bug when they've actually just made a mistake. (I know, because I still do it.) Of course, sometimes they have hit a bug. If a feature doesn't seem to work, the best thing to do is call WordPerfect tech support. If your problem has been reported as a bug, they'll tell you; if not, they'll try to help you to do it right.

The 4/29/89 release is important because it supports the LaserMaster line of printer controllers (printer disk #19), and some other printer devices previously not supported. However, this version has a bug in the Fixed Line Height with multiple fonts. This adversely affects files with more than one font size on a line, such as raised caps. If you aren't using a LaserMaster, you might want to stick with the 1/3/89 version, since it is virtually bug-free and the fixed line height works well.

WordPerfect is trying out a *Software Subscription Service* for those who want to automatically receive all interim releases and software upgrades. If you call 801-222-1400 and give them your credit card number, or send them a $200 deposit, they will see that you receive the latest material as it's released.

And now, as they say in the movies: lights, camera, action!

2

Conquering new frontiers

or What, me worry?

There's no need to worry about all this newness, as long as you know what you're getting into. One advantage of using WordPerfect as a desktop publishing program is that you already know its word processing features. In general, desktop publishing consists of two parts: word processing and formatting. In this chapter, I'll explain what some of WordPerfect's new desktop publishing features can do, and take you on a guided tour of them.

◆ Appearance

Allows you to select attributes such as super and sub-script, underline, italic, small caps, shadow, outline, redline and strikeout. Whether or not you can use these features depends on what your printer can do.

◆ Color

Lets you mix and select colors for type (if your printer is capable of printing in more than one color).

◆ Columns

WordPerfect's column feature has been improved so it works with any font. You can create newspaper style columns, where text "snakes" from the bottom of one column to the top of another, or parallel columns, which let you put paragraphs of information side-by-side.

> WordPerfect's column feature has been improved so it works with any font.
> You can create newspaper style columns, where text "snakes" from the bottom of one column to the top of another. You can also use parallel columns, which let you put paragraphs of information side-by-side.
> You can create newspaper style columns, where text "snakes" from the bottom of one column to the top of another. Or parallel columns, which let you put paragraphs of information side-by-side.
> WordPerfect's column feature has been improved so it works with any font.
> WordPerfect's column feature has been improved so it works with any font.
> You can create newspaper style columns, where text "snakes" from the bottom of one column to the top of another. Or parallel columns,

◆ Fonts

Allows you to specifically select different fonts, or styles of type, and sizes, depending on your printer's capabilities.

◆ Graphics

WordPerfect now lets you mix text with graphics. WordPerfect automatically wraps text around graphics for professional-looking results. The graphics can be from paint-type programs such as PC Paintbrush, draw-type programs such as Harvard Graphics, spreadsheet graphs from Lotus 1-2-3, and many other programs (a complete list is in WordPerfect's Reference Manual Appendix). The Graphics feature also lets you draw lines (often called "rules" in publishing), boxes, and sets quotes out in what is called "read-outs" or "pull quotes." This feature is also useful for keeping tables of information correctly formatted when text around them moves.

◆ Kerning

Kerning is a feature that adjusts the spacing between pairs of letters in tiny amounts so that they look their best.

◆ Leading

WordPerfect calls this feature "Line Height," but in publishing it's called leading (pronounced ledding), and means the white space between lines of text. WordPerfect will adjust this automatically (based on the size of type you choose), providing the right amount of space for any size font. You can also set this manually.

◆ Print

WordPerfect's printing function has been so drastically redesigned over time that it's like new. In addition to printing, this feature includes a "View Document" mode; this shows you on-screen almost exactly what your document will look like, complete with text in different sizes, and graphics, when it is printed. The print feature also allows you to print fast "proof[|]" copies of your pages without graphics, or with graphics at a lower resolution than normal. This is a valuable feature which saves time when you are checking your pages for accuracy.

◆ Size

Lets you choose different sizes of type automatically, such as *Small, Large,* or *Extra Large.* These sizes are based upon the size of your body text, the main portion of your document.

◆ Style

Microsoft Word users have been gloating about this feature for years, and with good reason. Style sheets let you create what most other programs call "Tags." (WordPerfect doesn't call it this, but everyone else does.) These tags can be applied to your text, speed formatting, and make it much easier to create consistent documents.

Here's an example: let's say you have a file where all the subject headings in your 100-page document are to be printed in 18-point Times Roman. You (or more likely your boss or client) decide that all the subject headings need to be in 14-point Helvetica. Using old WordPerfect, you would have to go through all 100 pages and make the change on each subhead. Using Styles, you change one style, such as the subhead, and every subhead you marked with that style is automatically updated. Because you can share style sheets between more than one file, they too can be updated automatically. Style sheets can contain any formatting command, text and graphics boxes, but not graphics files.

◆ Typographic controls

Because you are no longer just printing, but typesetting, features such as Word and Letterspacing, and Justification limits allow you exceptional control on exactly how your type will appear. If you don't want to get into all that, WordPerfect's built-in settings attempt to give you the best-looking type possible.

◆ Units of measure

This is an important new feature because of "proportionally spaced fonts." In the past, you were probably used to "monospaced fonts," such as Courier or Elite. In monospaced fonts, every letter takes up the same amount of space: the letter "i" takes up as much room as the letter "M." But now you will be using the same kind of fonts used in typesetting, and they are proportionally spaced so that each letter takes up just the amount of space it needs. Proportionally spaced fonts are easier to read, look better, and let you put more information on a page than monospaced fonts.

But proportionally spaced fonts can complicate matters. No longer can you line things up by using the space bar, it simply will not work. When using proportional fonts, *tabs* become vital. Tabs are "absolute" measurements, which means that a tab set at 5" will always be at 5", no matter what precedes it. You will now use tabs to align columns of numbers, or indent paragraphs.

What does this have to do with WordPerfect's new "Units of Measure" feature? Glad you asked. In the past, WordPerfect measured only in lines and spaces, but now it can measure in lines and spaces, inches, centimeters and points (there are 72 points to an inch). When you use inches or centimeters (whichever is easiest for you to understand) WordPerfect will display your exact location on the page.

If you've ever seen those old Italian Hercules movies from Italy, you've learned a valuable lesson about proportional fonts: "Never believe what you see" (on-screen). Sometimes when using tabs, things may not appear to line up on-screen, but they will be in the right place; a quick check in the lower right corner of the screen will show you where you really are.

◆ Margins

If you're used to setting margins such as "10 and 70," get ready for a shock. These same margins would now be 1" and 1". Why? Because now instead of measuring across the page, you have to measure in from the edges of the paper. Margin settings of 1" and 1" mean that your text will begin 1" from the right edge of the paper, and end 1" from the left edge of the paper. The same applies to top and bottom margins.

◆ View document

WordPerfect's View Document feature (formerly known as the "Preview"), allows you to see, on-screen, almost exactly what your page will look like, including graphics. View allows you to perfect your page before you print it. You can see your entire page on-screen at once, in full size, at twice its real size, or even with facing pages. You cannot edit in View mode.

◆ So what?

So now you know what WordPerfect's desktop publishing features are. Big deal. The point is to learn how to use them, and even at times how to abuse them, or at least force them to do exactly what you want them to do.

Unlike the WordPerfect Workbook (which uses pre-designed forms that make it appear easy but neglect to show you how to do it yourself), the following chapter will take you through a step-by-step example from start to finish.

❖ *Preparation*

Desktop publishing entails more than just producing a publication with a computer. Careful preparation will save you a lot of time and aggravation in the long run. With WordPerfect, it's easy to try out many diverse styles within a single document. However, users are sometimes so excited with the ease and speed the program offers (after the initial hair-pulling), that they forget about design and content, and just concentrate on getting it done fast. This is where a little homework and planning will pay off.

No matter what software/hardware combination you use, the first time you create any publication, it's going to take longer than you think. Some people purchase a program, and without really spending the time to learn how it works, try to produce their company newsletter with it. It takes them days longer than it should, and they get very frustrated and blame the program.

The importance of planning in advance cannot be overly stressed. Simply reviewing the tutorial or manual is not always enough. Sometimes the pressure of deadlines does not allow for experimentation before you actually have to produce a publication. Inevitably, you will waste time later on learning the program when you are on deadline producing your first publication.

Try to create a style sheet for your publication before you have to produce a finished product. If possible, take some old word processing files and try to recreate a previous publication to familiarize yourself with WordPerfect's new features. If you follow this advice, you will be thoroughly prepared, confident, and ready to begin desktop publishing.

◆ Ready or not

If you do your homework in the graphic design chapter, you'll be ready to play. I say play, not because you're necessarily going to have loads of fun, but because you're going to experiment, and experimentation is the basis of play. Repeat that line at parties, it never fails. In the following chapter we're going to take one page and do it a couple of different ways, demonstrating how WordPerfect allows you to be both flexible and consistent. Here we go.

3

Follow my example

Steps will be taken

Now I'm going to show you, step-by-everloving-step, how to create a desktop published document with WordPerfect. During this example, you'll use almost all of WordPerfect's new features.

It's important for you to complete these examples because they're going to take you through the basics (and in some cases the complexities) of creating a desktop published page with WordPerfect. Each of the other examples in this book is accompanied by a chart that shows the keystrokes required to recreate the page yourself. The charts will make more sense and be easier to follow if you've completed these examples.

The two examples we'll cover in this chapter will provide you with a solid foundation for understanding WordPerfect's new features. The first example is fast and simple, and the second is more complex. You may not understand all the steps as you are doing them, but just keep following along and it will start to make sense (really, it will. This is also known as the *learn by doing* method).

We're going to be using the Bitstream Dutch and Swiss fonts that I suggested you make in Chapter 1. You'll need Dutch 10, 12, 14, 24, 30 and Swiss 12 and 24 point bold. For more information about installing these fonts, see Chapter 7. If you are in a hurry and haven't made the fonts, you may attempt the examples, but I warn you, if you substitute fonts, the spacing may not be accurate, and your examples will not match the ones in the book.

◆ Font note for PostScript users

If you are using a PostScript printer, you will not need to make Fontware fonts. Substitute Times Roman for Dutch, and Helvetica for Swiss. WordPerfect does not list each size separately for PostScript printers the way it does for LaserJets. To select the size you want, move the cursor to the font you want and press **[ENTER]**. WordPerfect will then ask for the size you want. Enter the number, such as 10 or 12, and press **[ENTER]** again. PostScript fonts are narrower than LaserJet fonts, so your text will appear shorter than the text in the finished examples.

❖ *General instructions*

Make sure the units of measurement are set to inches, with **SHIFT-F1 U**. Otherwise, when I say "type 1.75," you may be entering 1.75 centimeters, or 1.75 points, or 1.75 WordPerfect units, none of which are even remotely close to 1.75 inches.

Before you do any formatting, you'll have to retype the text in the simple example. Don't do any formatting, just type the text. Using the exact same text will simplify matters, as I sometimes have to tell you where to go (on the page) in accordance with the text in my example.

Make it easy on yourself. After you've typed the simple example text, load that file and then immediately save it under a different name. This will allow you to use the same unformatted text for the complicated example. (The text for these two examples is also available on *Will-Harris Designer Disk #5*; see the order form in the Appendix for complete details.)

If it seems as if you have to go through a lot to produce a page that looks so simple, you're right. You must tell WordPerfect what type of font you want, margins, columns, graphics, tabs, tables. That's a lot of information. At first, it's bound to be a slow and perhaps even confusing process, but once you start to understand the features, you can produce pages such as these in anywhere from 5 to 20 minutes, depending on your speed.

Once you've created this format, you can use it over and over again in a fraction of the time it took to produce it. You can insert new text, or new graphics, while retaining your original layout. So think of this as a worthy investment of time, rather than as a practice exercise.

Unlike the desktop publishing examples in the *WordPerfect Workbook*, you will be formatting this page yourself. The only completed files are the graphics we'll take from the disks that were included with WordPerfect.

Putting together a page is rarely straightforward, even when you are well-prepared with thumbnail sketches and dummies (Edgar Bergen had a well-prepared dummy, but that's another book). It's a process of give and take; you try something, it doesn't quite appear quite right, so you change it. With that in mind, this step-by-step example isn't always linear. One change affects another change, creates new problems, and requires more adjustments all around.

Just as in real life, this example won't be perfect the first time through. We'll make a lot of changes until the page looks the way we want.

- I find that it's helpful to work with Reveal Codes on when you're creating complicated files. This enables you to see exactly where you are, and what you've entered.

- These examples assume that you have a hard disk called C: and a floppy called A:. You should be working on drive C. It doesn't matter what directory you are in.

Just one warning: be patient. Plan on spending at least a couple of hours working with each example. If you get tired, save the file as it is, and then start up again when you're ready, from wherever you left. Mastering these new features will take time and practice, and there's only so much you can comprehend in one sitting. Don't worry if you don't understand everything the first time around. Just do it and let it seep into your unconscious like so much Lady Clairol or Grecian Formula.

- One iron-clad guarantee: experimenting with these examples won't be as bad as having a root canal, or passing a kidney stone.

❖ Simple example

A full page in 10 easy steps. Well, 10 steps more or less (maybe 11).

The first step is to open a new file. Start WordPerfect and say hello to the blank screen. (This may be one of the few times that it won't talk back to you.)

◆ Reveal codes

First you need to turn Reveal Codes on by pressing

ALT-F3

If you haven't already initialized the printer, do so now. If you have, don't type this next line. If you don't know what I'm talking about, follow this instruction anyway. Press

SHIFT-F7 I

This will ensure that the printer is ready for action. The Bitstream downloadable fonts will be sent to the printer, even as you are working on this example. You don't have to stop and wait for them to finish.

Select the printer you are going to use. In this case, we're going to use the printer driver that contains the Bitstream Dutch fonts I asked you to create in Chapter 1. If you haven't created them, I'm disappointed in you, but I'll live. You, on the other hand, aren't going to be able to accomplish much without them. To select the printer, press

SHIFT-F7 S

Move the cursor to the name of the printer file you created with the Dutch fonts, then press

S

You should now find yourself at the print menu. The name of the printer you selected should be next to the words "Select Printer."

◆ Retrieving a file

Now we're going to retrieve the text file you typed for this example. Press

SHIFT-F10

and type the name of the file you are going to use for text. Press

[ENTER]

Mama Rowby's Blue Ribbon Pies

Any way you slice it, we're #1

This last year has been one of great change for Mama Rowby and her family of fine foods. Corporate Raider/Pond Scum Walter Scanlan tried to wrest the company away from the family that has owned and operated it with such great care for lo these past five years, and if it hadn't been for the great spirit of loyalty among management and employees, Mama Rowby's Pies would have become just another corporate conglomerate, instead of the caring, loving, gold mine it is.

Last year pie consumption skyrocketed the world over, partly due to our massive advertising campaign, and the "Miss Cutie Pie" competition, co-hosted by Morgan Fairchilde (desperate to overcome her image as being someone who'll go to the opening of a drawer). Even more important, Mama Rowby is now making mince meat of the competition.

To keep employee morale up during the recent corporate nightmare, Mama decided to institute a "pie-a-day" plan, whereby employees could take home a pie a day. Productivity skyrocketed (as did the bathroom scales of our employees).

This coming year, Mama Rowby is introducing a blitz of new flavors coming out the wazoo. These are revolutionary flavors that will blow the lid off the pie market. Everything from the new "California Cuisine," including "Linguini and Clam Meringue," and "Cactus Ice Cream."

Another hot new line will be retailed under the Cajun Queen moniker, and will include "Blackened Red Cherry," and "Fruit-Slaw Jumbalya." The sleeper of the new trio will be "Dr. Ruth's Good Pies," packaged with illustrated instructions for unorthodox uses. These flavors will be offered in only soft and safe fruits, such as Banana and Cherry.

This fall, Mama will be starring in her own syndicated cooking show where she and her guests (Dr. Ruth is at the top of the list) will help solve world problems and promote "Peace Through Pies." The show is pre-sold in 175 of the largest markets, and will be a perfect platform for increasing customer awareness of "Pie Possibilities," as well introducing new products. Because of Reagan's FCC deregulation (first seen on Saturday morning TV), Mama will sponsor her own show--a first in the syndication market. Dr. Abiner Goren, noted pet psychologist, has said that this unity of information will help to relieve much of the stress that modern television viewers are subjected to, as well as do "Darn good business."

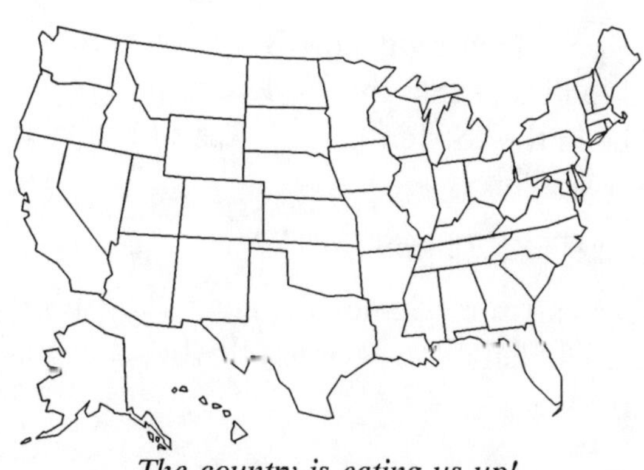

The country is eating us up!

You need no justification to turn off justification for this example. Press

SHIFT-F8 L J N F7

You also need to set the initial font for this document. This is the font WordPerfect will use for everything, unless we tell it otherwise. We're going to choose Dutch Roman 12 point.

SHIFT-F8 D F

Move the cursor to **Dutch Roman 12pt (ASCII) (Port) (FW)**. This means that the font is Dutch, 12 points tall, the ASCII symbol set, portrait orientation, and made by Fontware. Be careful to choose ROMAN 12pt and not BOLD 12pt or ITALIC 12pt.

◆ Creating a paired style

We're going to create only one style for this page. Since this book is called *Desktop Publishing In Style,* I would be remiss if I didn't include a style, even in a simple example like this.

This is a paired style, placed at the top of the file. I call this type of style a "topper," because (you guessed it) it's always at the top of the file. As you'll see in Chapter 10, *Styles,* this type of style makes it easier to change the document from a simple report such as this, to a full-blown newsletter, in the least amount of time.

The opening half of the style contains margin commands, while the closing half contains column and tab definitions, and a line height setting. I'm going to create the style now. Won't you join me? (Don't give me any lip, just follow along.) Press

ALT-F8 C N Topper [ENTER] C

The only thing on-screen right now is a [Comment] code. Anything you enter before the code will appear in the "Style:On" part of the style, and anything after the code will be in the "Style:Off" half. Let's just place a margin setting in the first half of the style. Press

SHIFT-F8 L M .75 [ENTER] .75 [ENTER] F7

Move the cursor past the [Comment] code. Now it's time to add another return, so that there's a blank line between the headline and the two columns. Press

[ENTER]

Now we're going to set up columns. Press

ALT-F7 D D .3 [ENTER][ENTER] C

◆ Setting tabs

We want the paragraphs to be equally indented on both columns, and so we're going to set tabs. Press

SHIFT-F8 L T [HOME][HOME] [LEFT ARROW] CONTROL-END 1.05 [ENTER] 4.7 [ENTER] F7 F7

Just one more step: set the line height (the white space between the lines of text). Press

SHIFT-F8 L H F .2 [ENTER] F7 F7 F7 F7

◆ Applying a style

Now that we've created the style, we're going to apply it to the file. Brace yourself, excitement like this doesn't happen every day (every other day, maybe).

To use this style, we're going to block the headline, and then apply the style. Turn on the block by pressing:

ALT-F4

Move the cursor to the "T" of "This last year..." To apply the style, press

ALT-F8 O

The headline still takes one column, but the body text is now in two columns.

◆ Creating a user-defined box

Are we having fun yet? And you were going to fritter the night away being sociable! Now you get to put in that lovely map of the US of A instead.

Move the cursor so that it's right after the [Style On:Topper] by pressing

[HOME] [HOME] [UP ARROW]

We're going to create a User-defined box by pressing

ALT-F9 U C

Faster than you can say the immortal Dick Shawn catch phrase, "Suck on a shoe," you've created a user-defined graphics box. We need to make it a page type box and center it at the bottom of the page. Let's do that now, shall we? Press

T A V B H M C

Here's an instant memory tip: just think of "TAV BHMC" (Tav Bhamuc is one of Dickens' all-time favorite characters. You know, the travelling tea salesman in "Oliver with a Twist." Stop that moaning now, it only took a few seconds of your time and at least **I** enjoyed it. Some jokes you do for yourself—others you should just keep to yourself.)

◆ Retrieving a graphic

Let's retrieve the graphic now. Check that the Fonts/Graphics disk is in Drive A and press

F A:USAMAP.WPG [ENTER]

Voila! You've got a graphic. Now how about a caption? Press

C [BACKSPACE] SHIFT-F6 CONTROL-F8 A I **The country is eating us up!** F7 F7

◆ Placing a horizontal line

Almost finished, cross my heart. Now we're going to place the horizontal line on the page. Press

ALT-F9 L H H C L 2.79 [ENTER] [ENTER]

Then put some space between the line and the headline by pressing

[ENTER][ENTER]

You should now see two returns after the graphic line, and before the headline. If you don't, you obviously missed the boat at some point in our journey (luckily for you, this will not translate into bad karma in your next life, unless you come back as a computer).

My, this desktop publishing sure makes a person hungry. Go get some chocolate chip cookies, then come back. If anyone asks what you're doing, just say "following instructions."

◆ Making a headline extra large

Back so soon? We have only one more little thing to do, and we get to do it three whole times. We're going to make the headline extra large, the #1 line large.

Move the cursor to the "M" of Mama Rowby and turn block on by pressing

ALT-F4

Move the cursor to the line that says "Blue Ribbon Pies" and go to the end of the line by pressing:

[END]

We're going to make the headline extra large, or 24 point. Press

CONTROL-F8 S E

The words may not appear any different on-screen, but they will in View Document and on paper. Now, move the cursor to the "A" of "Any way you slice it." We're going to block this entire line and enlarge it. Press

ALT-F4 [END] CONTROL-F8 S L

◆ Creating raised caps

We're in the home stretch. We're going to make the "T" of "This" very large, so that it becomes a "Raised Cap." Move the cursor over to the "T" of "This last year." Block it by pressing

ALT-F4

And pat it and mark it with a "B" and put it in the oven for... no, no, wrong book. Cover the "T" with the block by pressing

[RIGHT ARROW]

To make the "T" into a raised cap, press

CONTROL-F8 S V

◆ Centering a headline

If the headline isn't already centered, do that now. Go to the top of the file by pressing

[HOME] [HOME] [UP ARROW]

Turn block on

ALT-F4

And move the cursor so it covers the entire headline. Tell WordPerfect to center the blocked text. Press

SHIFT-F6 Y

◆ View document

Now, at last, we can take a look-see at this masterpiece with View Document. Press

SHIFT-F7 V

If you can't see the entire page, press **3**, if you can see the page but can't read the text, press **1**. If you're totally confused and thinking of ways to exchange this book for something else like "Larry: the Stooge in the Middle," don't press your luck. Take it again from the top—it has worked for other people. Who knows, it just might work for you.

◆ To print

If it looks something like my example, congratulate yourself. Now, print it, quick, before it melts. No, it won't really melt. I'm kidding. (Geez, lighten up, will you?) To leave View Document and go to the Print menu, press

F1

Make sure that your printer is plugged in and connected to your computer. It's showtime, folks. Press

P

The computer will emit some hard-disk noises, and then the lights on the printer should start flashing. The page should emerge victoriously from the printer in anywhere from 1 to 5 minutes, depending on the speed of your printer.

I don't know about you, but I'm tired. Take the rest of the day off.

❖ Complicated example

Now that you've been hooked by the first example, let's move on to the hard stuff. As usual, the first step involves retrieving a file. Remember how the *General Instructions* on page 16 told you to save the simple example text file under a different name before you started putting codes into it? This is where that file will come in handy. Start WordPerfect.

◆ Turn reveal codes on

To turn Reveal Codes on, press

ALT-F3

Select the printer you are going to use. In this case, we're going to use the printer driver that contains the Bitstream Dutch fonts. Press

SHIFT-F7 S

Move the cursor to the name of the printer file you created that contains the Dutch fonts, and then press

S F7

You should now be at the print menu, and the name of the printer you selected should be next to the words "Select Printer."

◆ Retrieving a file

Now let's retrieve a text file. (Can you say "Retrieve?" I knew you could.) Press

SHIFT-F10

Type the name of the file you are going to use for text. (If your text contains a table, as this one does, make sure you use tabs, and not spaces, between each column of numbers. If you use spaces, the column will never line up when using a proportional font, such as Dutch.) Press

[ENTER]

◆ Font default

Now you need to set the Initial (default) font for the file. This font will be used for all body text, headers, footers, and captions, unless we specify otherwise. Press

SHIFT-F8 D F

Move the cursor to **Dutch Roman 10 pt** The name of the font will also indicate whether it uses ASCII for Roman-8 symbols, and whether it's portrait or landscape. If you created ASCII symbol fonts, the complete name will be **Dutch Roman 10pt (ASCII) (PORT) (FW).** The (FW) stands for Fontware. Select this font by pressing

[ENTER] F7

◆ Open style

Now we'll create a topper style which contains important global formatting commands. (Doesn't "Global" sound important?) I had wanted to create a paired style as in the first example, but WordPerfect kept giving me trouble about margins. Even though I'd set margins after the comment, it wouldn't place them in the style. Whatever the problem was, I came up with a new approach. Create two styles: one for the very top, and one containing the horizontal line, the requisite number of returns, and the column definition. Press

ALT-F8 C N TOPPER [ENTER] T O C

◆ Setting margins

Set the margins. We'll use a seven-tenths of an inch margin on the top and bottom, and a half-inch margin on each side. Let's first set the top and bottom margins. Press

SHIFT-F8 P M .7 [ENTER] .7 [ENTER] [ENTER]

Now we're going to set the left and right margins. Press

L M .5 [ENTER] .5 [ENTER] F7 F7 F7

Mama Rowby's Blue Ribbon Pies

Vol 1. No. 1.

Any way you slice it, we're #1

Mama takes a big bite out of the pie market

This last year has been one of great change for Mama Rowby and her family of fine foods. Corporate Raider/Pond Scum Walter Scanlan tried to wrest the company away from the family that has owned and operated it with such great care for lo these past five years, and if it hadn't been for the great spirit of loyalty among management and employees, Mama Rowby's Pies would have become just another corporate conglomerate, instead of the caring, loving, gold mine it is.

Last year pie consumption skyrocketed the world over, partly due to our massive advertising campaign, and the "Miss Cutie Pie" competition, cohosted by Morgan Fairchilde (desperate to overcome her image as being someone who'll go to the opening of a drawer). Even more important, Mama Rowby is now making mince meat of the competition.

To keep employee morale up during the recent corporate nightmare, Mama decided to institute a "pie-a-day" plan, whereby employees could take home a pie a day. Productivity skyrocketed (as did the bathroom scales of our employees).

This coming year, Mama Rowby is introducing a blitz of new flavors coming out the wazoo. These are revolutionary flavors that will blow the lid off the pie market. Everything from the new "California Cuisine," including "Linguini and Clam Meringue," and "Cactus Ice Cream."

Another hot new line will be retailed under the Cajun Queen moniker, and will include "Blackened Red Cherry," and "Fruit-Slaw Jumbalya." The sleeper of the new trio will be "Dr. Ruth's Good Pies," packaged with illustrated instructions for unorthodox uses. These flavors will be offered in only soft and safe fruits, such as Banana and Cherry.

This fall, Mama will be starring in her own syndicated cooking show where she and her guests (Dr. Ruth is at the top of the list) will help solve world problems and promote "Peace Through Pies." The show is pre-sold in 175 of the largest markets, and will be a perfect platform for increasing customer awareness of "Pie Possibilities," as well introducing new products. Because of Reagan's FCC deregulation (first seen on Saturday morning TV), Mama will sponsor her own show--a first in the syndication market. Dr. Abiner Goren, noted pet psychologist, has said that this unity of information will help to relieve much of the stress that modern television viewers are subjected to, as well as do "Darn good business."

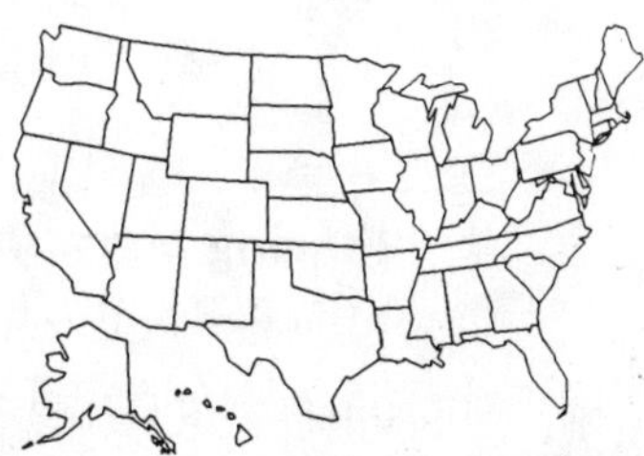

	WA	AK	TW	MA	NY	CA
Cherry	.50	.55	.83	1.24	1.86	**2.78**
Apple	.70	.77	1.16	1.73	2.60	**3.90**
Coconut	.30	.33	.50	.74	1.67	**1.67**
Pecan	1.10	1.21	1.82	2.72	4.08	**6.13**

◆ Creating a column style

Now we need to create the column style. Press

C N Columns [ENTER] T O C

The column style starts with the horizontal line, includes three returns, and has a column definition. Press

ALT-F9 L H [ENTER] [ENTER] [ENTER] [ENTER]

ALT-F7 D N 3 [ENTER] D .25 [ENTER] [ENTER] C F7 F7

◆ Creating a headline style

For good measure, let's create a headline style, making the text Swiss 24 point bold. Press

C N Headline [ENTER] C CONTROL-F8 F

Move the cursor to "Swiss Bold 24pt" and press

S F7 F7 F7

So much for creating styles. Now move to the very top of the file by pressing

[HOME] [HOME] [HOME] [UP-ARROW]

And turn on the Topper Style by pressing

ALT-F8

Move the cursor to "Topper" and press

O

◆ Placing a graphics box

Now let's place the first graphic, located in the upper right-hand corner of the page. We're going to use a "User-Defined" box because it has no border around it. Press

ALT-F9 U C

We need to tell WordPerfect where to place this box. WordPerfect's default will put graphics along the right margin. In this case, we want them along the left margin. Press

H L

◆ Sizing a box

We will also set the size of the box. The box should only be a half inch high. We'll set the height, and WordPerfect will figure out the width when we retrieve the graphic. Press

S H .5 [ENTER]

◆ Retrieving a graphic

Now we're going to retrieve the graphic. Rather than type the name, we're going to use **F5**, the List Files key. Press

F F5 A: [ENTER]

Move the cursor to the file called **AIRPLANE.WPG** and press

R

After the file has been loaded, you'll notice that the size is 1.83" wide, by .5" high.

◆ Reducing a graphic

Let's reduce the graphic by 10%. First, go into graphic edit mode by pressing

E

The graphic should appear on-screen. If it doesn't, you may have set up WordPerfect incorrectly for the type of graphics your computer has. Consult the Getting Started Chapter in the WordPerfect manual, or the "Setup" section in the reference manual.

◆ Rotating a graphic

Notice the number between the parentheses in the lower right-hand corner of the screen. This should read 10%. If it doesn't press the **INS** key until it does. As long as we're here, let's play with the graphic. If you press the + key (next to the cursor or number-pad), you'll see that the graphic rotates 45 degrees (it's doing a nose dive.) To pull the plane up before it goes downs in flames, press the **minus** key (next to the cursor or number-pad). The graphic will rotate 45 degrees in the other direction, returning it to where as it was.

◆ Enlarging a graphic

Now,let's zoom in on the plane itself. Press

[INS][INS][INS]

until the number in the lower right-hand corner reads "25%." Now let's increase the picture by 125%. Press five times

[PgUp]

Now we need to move the picture to the right. Press 20 times

[RIGHT ARROW]

Now we need to move the picture down. Press 20 times

[DOWN ARROW]

We have now zoomed in on the plane. We decide that this was a mistake and want to return the picture to its original state. Press

CONTROL-[HOME]

and the picture will return to its normal size. Enough fun and games. Press

F7 F7

A box will appear on-screen that displays the approximate dimensions of the graphic we just created.

◆ Replacing a graphic

But wait! We hold an impromptu staff meeting and decide to insert a new graphic file in this same graphics box. Sure, the plane is cute, but maybe just a little too cute. What were we thinking? But, at least it won't be difficult to change. Let's take care of that right now before anyone grabs an eyeful of our handiwork and pokes fun at us in front of our coworkers. Press

ALT-F9 U E 1 [ENTER]

Quick, it's time to replace the current graphic with one called AWARD.WPG. Don't worry, no one will ever be the wiser. Press

F A:AWARD.WPG [ENTER] Y

Because this graphic is a different size, it is now too small. Let's size it again. We'll instruct WordPerfect to make the new graphic 1" high. Press

S H 1 [ENTER] F7

WordPerfect has automatically calculated how wide the graphic should be and come up with .76"

◆ Enlarging a headline

Now we want to increase the size of our headline. This will be the banner/logo of our publication. Our body text is Dutch, and our headlines are Swiss for contrast, but this is not a headline, it's a logo. (It's not a gang, it's a club). We could use some fancy display or headline typeface (such as Broadway) to match our company logo. But in this case, we'll only use Swiss and Dutch, so the logo will be Dutch.

The reason we're not using "Appearance Extra Large" to enlarge the type in this logo is that when you use a 10 point base font, Extra Large will give you a 24 point font. We want a 30 point font, so we'll have to choose it specifically. If we were using a 12 point base font, Extra Large would give us a 30 point font. Let's select a new font. Press

CONTROL-F8 F

Move the cursor to **Dutch Bold 30pt** (ASCII) (Port) (FW), and press

[ENTER]

When you selected this font, WordPerfect automatically adjusted the line spacing so that lines of text wouldn't print over each other. We chose a bold base font, so it will print bold, even without using WordPerfect's bold feature. If we used the bold feature, the bold font would print in an even darker shade.

But because of this font change, WordPerfect is now formatting the rest of the file for this large font. We need to change the font. Put the cursor on the "s" of "Pies," then press

[RIGHT ARROW] CONTROL-F8 F

Move the cursor to **Dutch Roman 10pt** and press

[ENTER] F7

◆ Aligning text

Make sure that Reveal Codes is still on. (Some people turn it off so they can see more of their page. They think I won't notice.) Move the cursor so that it is on the "A" of "Any way you slice it..." We're going to make this flush right, so press

ALT-F6

and the text jumps to the right margin.

◆ Applying italics

Let's use italics on that "Any way you slice it" line. Turn block on by pressing

ALT-F4

Move the cursor to the end of the line by pressing

[END]

To turn on italics for the block, press

CONTROL-F8 A I

The line is now in italics. Let's re-block it and increase it to Large (or 12 point). Press

ALT-F4 CONTROL-[HOME] CONTROL-[HOME] CONTROL-F8 S L

◆ View document

Getting curious? Let's use View Document to see how it looks. Press

SHIFT-F7 V

If you've carefully followed instructions, you should see this something on-screen which looks like the printed example.

◆ Enlarging view

You probably can't read any of the type on this full page on-screen view. For a closer look, press

1

You're now seeing the page in 100% view. For a still closer look, press

2

You're now seeing the page in 200% view. This is as close as you can get without getting the pie in your face. Let's return to full page view. Press

3

We still haven't finished this puppy. Let's go back to work. Press

F7

◆ Applying a column style

Now it's time to place three columns in the body text. Move the cursor to the "B" of "Blue Ribbon" and press

[DOWN ARROW]

Turn on the column style by pressing

ALT-F8

Move the cursor to "Columns" and press

O

Extra space will appear under the headline, and the text will be set in three columns.

◆ Applying a headline style

We need to use that headline style on the headline. Block the entire headline by pressing

ALT-F4

Apply the headline style and press

ALT-F8

Move the cursor to "Headline," and press:

O

We want the rest of this column to be blank, and so place the cursor after the [Style Off:Headline] code and press

CONTROL-[ENTER]

The remaining text will jump to the second column, leaving the rest of the first column blank. Ahh, white space.

◆ Turning justification on

We didn't want our headline justified, but we would like our text justified. Time to turn on justification. As annoying as hyphenation can be, we'll have to turn it on for an accurate idea of how our text fits on the page.

Justification without hyphenation can result in extremely unattractive type, and you wouldn't want that, would you? I didn't think so. Since both justification and hyphenation are in the same menu, we can turn both of them on simultaneously. Press

SHIFT-F8 L J Y Y A F7

It's always smart to get in the habit of adjusting as many features as you can when you're on a particular menu. This saves a lot of keystrokes.

◆ Hyphenation

Whenever WordPerfect asks you to hyphenate, press **ESC** if you want it to place the hyphen where it recommends, or move the cursor to where you'd like the hyphen and then press **ESC**. WordPerfect sets a hyphenation range, so you may not be able to move the cursor to the precise location you desire. If you don't want the word hyphenated, or can't move the cursor to wherever you want it, press **F1** to tell WordPerfect not to hyphenate that word.

If you get really sick and tired of having WordPerfect pester you about so many words, press **F7** to temporarily turn hyphenation off. Hyphenation will remain off only through your next cursor move or command, and then will turn itself back on.

Let's go back into View Document to see how the page is progressing. Press

SHIFT-F7 V

It's getting there, isn't it? If we didn't have the table at the bottom, we could stop right now. But you paid $21.95 for this book and I'm here to see that you get your money's worth. By the end of this example (and certainly by the end of the book), you'll know more about desktop publishing with WordPerfect than you ever dreamed of (even in your worst nightmare).

◆ Blocking & copying a table

Before we proceed any further, let's take care of that table at the bottom. We've already placed a graphic in a graphics box, but now we're going to put a table in a table box.

Since we want this "graphic" table to span several columns, we're going to create it as a page type graphic. To ensure that it prints on this page, and not the next, we'll place this code at the top of the page, right after the margins.

First we're going to block our table and copy it, then create a table box, and then paste the table into the box.

Move the cursor to the beginning of the table. To turn the block on, press

ALT-F4

Move the cursor so that it covers the entire table, and then press

CONTROL-F4 B M

The table will disappear, but it's not gone forever. WordPerfect has put it in a special magic place, and will drop it back onto the page as soon as you press return. As a convenient reminder, WordPerfect says, "Move cursor, press **Enter** to retrieve."

Now that the table is safely tucked away, let's hope that it said its prayers, and create that table box.

◆ Creating a page type graphic box

Go to the top of the file, and press

[HOME] [HOME] [HOME] [UP ARROW]

To ensure that the table box is the correct size, we have to check that the cursor is after the two margin codes, so press

[RIGHT ARROW] [RIGHT ARROW]

Before we create the table, we're going to set the options. We'll have a single line above, and a thick line below. The table is will contain a 10% gray background. Press

ALT-F9 T O B N N S T G 10 [ENTER] [ENTER]

Now we're ready to create the table of "States." Press

ALT-F9 T C

We need to tell WordPerfect what type of box this is, where it will be on the page, and how large it will be. Let's start with what type of box it is. This is a page type box, so it can span the two columns of text. Press

T A

WordPerfect automatically places this box on the top of the page, flush with the right margin, and makes it 3.25" square. First, let's move it to the bottom of the page by pressing

V B

◆ Placing a box

Next, let's tell WordPerfect how wide this box is. This box will stretch all the way across the page, from the left margin to the right margin. When you create a page-type box, you can place it on the page based on margins, columns, or exact numerical measurements. We're going to make it flush with both the left and right margins by pressing

H M B

Now, we can finally edit the contents of the box itself. Press

E

Don't worry, our text is still there. The [ENTER] that we hit when creating the table options didn't count. Now we're going to press

[ENTER]

Zippity do dah, here's our table. (Zippity do dah may be a registered trademark of the Walt Disney Company—I'm sure it belongs to either them or possibly Apple.)

Make sure there are no extra returns at the top of the table. If there are, your table will be larger than the one in the example.

◆ Changing fonts

Let's make the entire table Swiss 12pt bold. Press

CONTROL-F8 F

Move the cursor to "Swiss 12pt Bold" and press

S

◆ Setting tabs

And now, without further ado, it's tab time! We'll employ one set of tabs for the headings, and another for the numbers. First, we need to clear the existing tabs by pressing

SHIFT-F8 L T [HOME] [HOME] [LEFT ARROW] CONTROL-END

Now we're going to set the new tabs. The first one will be a right aligned tab, and we'll tell WordPerfect to set the rest of them 1" apart and right aligned as well. Press

1.88 [ENTER] R 1.88,1 [ENTER] F7 F7

Now move the cursor to the first space of the second line (in this case, right on the "C" of "Cherry"). We're going to set decimal tabs here by first clearing the old ones, and then setting the new ones by pressing

SHIFT-F8 L T [HOME] [HOME] [LEFT ARROW] CONTROL-END

1.66 [ENTER] D 1.66,1 [ENTER] F7 F7

◆ Search & replace for tabs

Here's a really neat tip on how to whip tables into shape. Even though we've set these tabs to be right aligned and decimal, WordPerfect uses one type of codes for regular tabs, and another for aligned tabs, and so text may not line up correctly.

What's a mother to do? (It's easier than you think.) Did you know that you could perform a search and replace on just a block? Well, you can. Did you know that you could search for tabs and replace them with Aligns? Well you can (you learn something new every day). First, block the table by pressing

ALT-F4

Move the cursor so that the block covers the entire table. Now it's time to search for tabs and replace them with Align codes. Press

ALT-F2 N [TAB] F2 CONTROL-F6 F2

In a flash (or a flush, depending on the speed of your computer and the length of the table), WordPerfect will replace those nasty old tabs with new-fangled Aligns, and the table will look like a million bucks, even if your numbers don't.

Leave the table box by pressing

F7 F7

I don't know about you, but that trick alone was worth the $21.95. Hey, here's an idea. Find someone who's struggling with 1-2-3 and WordPerfect and offer to help them out. Charge them $22.95 (or have them buy you an expensive lunch—it's all spelled out in Chapter 16) and you're a dollar ahead already. No, please, I don't accept commissions.

◆ Moving around in view document

Golly Gee Willikers, this page looks mighty unique to me. But then, I'm near-sighted. Let's sneak another peek through the magic mirror of View Document by pressing

SHIFT-F7 V

Go into 100% mode by pressing

1

Did you know that you can move around the View Document screen with any cursor movement keys (including gray **[+]** or gray **[-]**, the "Screen Down" and "Screen Up" keys)? You can also jump to any page by pressing **CONTROL-HOME**, and then typing in a page number. Will wonders never cease? (Yes they will, probably around 5 pm.)

You're spending altogether too much time looking at View Document (stop it or you'll go blind). Press

F7

◆ Measuring a table

Three more things and we'll call it a day, a week, or a marsupial—whichever you prefer. First, let's put a vertical rule between the headline column and the body text.

Move the cursor to the "M" in "Mama takes..." We're going to create a vertical line running from this line down to the table. WordPerfect will automatically start the vertical rule at the current line, but unless we intervene, it will print the line to the bottom of the page, right through the table.

First, let's look at the "States" table to see how tall it is. Press

ALT-F9 T E 1 [ENTER]

We can see that it's 1.4" high. That's all we needed to know. Press

F7

To quickly return to the "M" of "Mama takes," press

CONTROL-[HOME] CONTROL-[HOME]

◆ Creating a vertical rule

Now we're going to create that vertical rule. Press

ALT-F9 L V

We need to tell WordPerfect where to place the rule on the page. We're going to select Between Columns, and then tell WordPerfect to place it to the right of column 1. Press

H B 1 [ENTER]

Now we're going to set where the line begins vertically. When we choose Vertical Set, WordPerfect will insert our current location on the page (which should be 2.09"). Press

V S [ENTER]

Next let's tell WordPerfect how long to make the line. WordPerfect has automatically calculated 8.15" as the distance to the bottom of the page. We don't want to print over the table, and so we're going to subtract 1.4" (the height of the table), and end up with 6.75. Press

L 6.75 [ENTER] [ENTER]

Viola! the vertical rule is in place.

Two more to go. You can see the light at the end of the tunnel, the wind's at your back, and the only obstacle between you and immortality is death. You look Death in the face and say, "The word 'scared' isn't in my vocabulary." Death responds with a snappy "What about the word 'stupid?'" Death has very bad breath, and what's worse, you (and I) cannot keep up this level of witty repartee much longer.

You snap back to reality and experience something akin to psychic whiplash. You ponder the inevitable existential questions, then decide to just finish the example and drown reality in Heavy Belgian Chocolate ice cream (Steve's, of course).

◆ Creating a user-defined box

Move the cursor to the end of the text (in this case, after "business"). Put a blank line after the text. Press

[ENTER]

Now we're going to create another User-defined box with its horizontal position both left and right, so it fills the column by pressing

ALT-F9 U C H B

◆ Loading a graphic

It's that time again. Time to load a graphic file. We know the name, so we won't bother using list files this time. Make sure the Fonts/Graphics disk is in drive A and press

f A:USAMAP.WPG [ENTER] F7

We've already had more than our share of fun playing with graphics, and besides if you mirror the map of the US, we might be branded as pinko troublemakers.

There. The page is finished at last. Well, a drop cap wouldn't hurt. Then people will be sure you've done the page in Ventura. They'll think you must be pretty well-off to be able to afford Ventura and, boy, you sure know how to use it. Little will they suspect that you've been using a word processing program all along.

Ah, what the hay—if you're game, I'm game. Drop caps can be tricky, but they look fab (some even say gear).

◆ Creating a drop cap

To create a drop cap, we need to set some special options. We don't want to change the User-defined box that contains the captivating map of the US, and so lets make this a Text Box.

Move the cursor to the "T" in "This last year," in the first paragraph of the story. We're going to delete the letter T. Press

[DEL]

First, we have to set the options. We don't want any lines around the box, no border space inside or out, and a background of 0% black (otherwise known as white). If you skip this option, your Drop Cap will not work worth beans. Press

ALT-F9 B O B N N N N

O 0 [ENTER] 0 [ENTER] 0 [ENTER] 0 [ENTER]

I 0 [ENTER] 0 [ENTER] 0 [ENTER] 0 [ENTER]

G 0 [ENTER] [ENTER]

That seems like a lot to suffer through, but just remember how much time and money you'll save, and how you'll get to spend it on trips to the Virgin Islands, genuine diamond jewelry, cheesecake...

◆ Creating a text box

Now let's create the Text Box that will contain the drop cap itself. Press

ALT-F9 B C

We'll align it with the left margin by pressing

H L

Now we're going to type the text of the box. First we'll change the font, and then we'll type the letter "T." Press

E CONTROL-F8 F

Move the cursor over to **Dutch Roman 30pt** and press

S T F7

◆ Sizing a box

Now for the hard part—sizing the box. Let's use the on-screen measurements to help us. WordPerfect would size the box for us, but it overcompensates and makes the box too large for our purposes.

Put the cursor *on* the letter T. Look at the measurement. Mine says 3.08. Press the **[RIGHT ARROW]** key and check the measurement again. Mine says 3.35. Subtract the first number from the second and you get .27. If you come up with another figure, your math is as bad as mine is.

(In fact, I received my worst grade ever in math. I should have flunked the class, but my mother threatened the teacher and he gave me a "C." It's a true story. My mother is a master of threats, not to mention a master of baking. Until she was 40, all she'd ever baked was a chicken, then she decided to open a bakery. Who can explain these things? Now she's this master baker, and bakes huge, glamorous wedding cakes that make Martha Stewart's look paltry. Anyway, this has nothing to do with anything except that it's undeniable proof that being able to use WordPerfect is not genetic. My mother can't even operate a clock radio.)

Back to the drop cap. We've learned that it's .27 wide, and since we know it's 30pt high, we already know how tall it is. Let's get out of here and size this box, complete this example, and do something more interesting (like have some dessert). Press

F7 S B .3 [ENTER]

Before we enter 30pt for the height of the box, I have to add something. Don't worry—it has nothing to do with my family, it has to do with this drop cap.

(By now, you probably feel like you know my family intimately, and I haven't even told about my sister who lived in a tee pee or my brother who could argue about the fact that it was daylight outside. I'm only telling you this because it should shed some light on the way I think, and creating a drop cap in WordPerfect is a study in problem solving).

We could enter 30pt for the height of the box, but we want to make the box to be a bit smaller than that, so the text will flow neatly around it. This always calls for some experimentation. I started with 30pt and it was too large.

WordPerfect automatically gives us 12.2 leading with 10-point Bitstream body text. (With 10-point PostScript or other soft fonts, WordPerfect gives you 11-point leading, but Bitstream added extra leading and the improvement is noticeable on the page.) I only know this because I spent hours investigating it. Sometimes I wonder if it's really such a good way to spend one's time.

Since the drop cap will be two lines high, I tried 24 point for the height of the box. It was still a bit too big. I tried 22 point (.3") and it was perfect.

If you make the box too narrow, the letter will print with a hyphen after it. If the box is too short, the letter won't print at all. So we've settled on .3". Press

.3 [ENTER] [ENTER]

Now let's squeeze some juice from the fruits of our labor. Press

SHIFT-F7 V

◆ Printing

A page like this may take some time to display on-screen. On my Victor AT, it takes about 15 seconds. There it is, it looks terrific, and now it's time to print. To leave View Document and go to the Print menu, press

F1

Make sure the printer is plugged in, and connected to the computer. It's showtime. Press

P

The page should pop out of the printer in anywhere from 1 to 5 minutes, depending on the speed of the computer and printer.

I don't know about you, but it's times like this when I'm proud to be an American: happy to be alive, and overjoyed that someone had the sense to invent computers.

One final thought. Maybe using WordPerfect is genetic, after all. My father is always the first one on our block to buy the latest gadget and figure it out. Maybe I acquired those genes from him. No, that doesn't hold up—he's a great wood carver and I can't even carve a turkey. Well, I still think everything is genetic. Surely weight is. (But the members of my family aren't "fat"—we're just larger than life.)

4

Show & Tell

Examples of applications

This chapter shows you the types of applications you can realistically expect to create using WordPerfect. Each example is accompanied by a brief summary of the specific fonts, software, and hardware used to produce the example, as well as the WordPerfect codes used for that example.

The examples range from the first page of a newsletter to three pages of an annual report. Don't try to make a brunch reservation at *My Old Dutch Pancake House*, or list your house with *HomeFinders*—they are figments of my imagination. The material in these examples is intended primarily for your enjoyment, but it's possible to pick up some useful information along the way, too. Also take a look at Chapter 16, *1-2-3 Publishing*, for an example (with codes) of a financial report.

◆ Style sheets on disk

For novice desktop publishers, predesigned style sheets can be a big help. I have assembled the WordPerfect style sheets I used to produce these examples, and they are available on a disk. My *Designer Disk 5* contains many practical tips about the basics of graphic design and shows how to quickly modify a style sheet. Users can load in their own text and graphic files, and instantly tailor any element of the page layout to fit their individual document (see *Designer Disks* ordering details in the Appendix).

❖ *Codes dissected*

Don't be intimidated by what looks like a ton-o-codes. When you look the codes for each example, it may seem like there are millions of them, and they seem impossible to decipher.

But if you take them code by code, you can put these pages together in less time than you think. And remember, once you've created these pages, you can use the design (and all those WordPerfect codes) over and over again with new text and graphics.

I'll admit deciphering this stuff is not unlike reading the Rosetta Stone, but I include a Rosetta Stone/WordPerfect translation chart on the inside back cover of this book that shows each code, what it does, and what keys you have to punch to get it. Refer to this if you want to recreate any of the examples, and it will give you the exact keystrokes you need.

❖ *Flavor of the month*

WordPerfect codes come in two flavors; the first (I'll call chocolate) displays all the information you need to know about them, and the second flavor (vanilla) is cryptic: it shows you the code, but not the variables inside.

➻ Here's an example of a chocolate code:

[Col Del:3,1",3",3.25",5.25",5.5",7.5"]. This is a column definition code. The first number tells you how many columns, the next numbers tell you the margins of the columns. In this case, the margins of column one are 1" on the left and 3" on the right. Column two's margins are 3.25 on the left and 5.25 on the right. Column three's margins are 5.5" on the left, and 7.5" on the right. Got it?

Remember, most codes display their information in the same order as you've entered it on-screen. Here's an example: [VLine:1.25",2.19",7.81",0.01",100%] This is a vertical line, and the first number if the first menu choice on the screen, Horizontal Position. The second number is the second menu item, Vertical Position. The third number is the third menu item, Length of Line. The fourth is, not surprisingly, the fourth menu item, Width of Line. And last (and who knows, maybe least) is the fifth number and its matching menu item, Gray Shading.

From this one code we can tell that the Horizontal Position is 1.25", the vertical position is 2.19" from the top of the page, the line is 7.81" inches long, .01" inches wide, and is 100% solid black.

- When point sizes are listed in fonts, it means that this specific font was the default font for that file.

◆ A double dip of vanilla, please

- Here's an example of a vanilla code: [Fig Opt]. This code can contain up to 18 different variables, and so the code doesn't show them all. If you want to see what the settings are, you have to put your cursor below the code, and go into the menu where the code was created, in this case, **ALT-F9**.

If you want to recreate these examples, please make sure that your Initial codes (**SHIFT-F1 I I**) in the setup menu don't include any Figure, Table, Text, or User Box options, as this will change your results. I've based the examples in this book on the standard WordPerfect defaults and only mention those variables that I've changed from the default.

Because of the sheer number of variables, it would take a book the size of the *Encyclopedia Britannica* to include them all. When there are vanilla codes, I've included the keystrokes necessary for any important variables in brackets like this < >, and any special explanations in brackets like this {}. If you see anything between in < > brackets, remember that these don't appear on-screen; they aren't the keystrokes to access the command, they are keystrokes you type from within the menu to select the correct variables. If you see anything between {} brackets, please don't type it, just use it as reference to explain what the codes are doing.

I use figures whenever possible because then it's easy for me to search for them. I only use more than one kind of box when I need one kind to have certain attributes, such as lines around or an outside margin, and others to have different attributes.

This sounds much more complicated that it really is, but I've tried to make the instructions as clear as possible.

- You'll see a lot of "Advance" codes, often set to .1". I use these to make small adjustments in line height that make a big visual difference. Hitting the return to add extra white space between a headline and text for instance, usually adds more space than you really wanted. Using the advance code is the best way to make elements fit precisely. It's so good, I've put it in my soft keyboard so that I can press just one key to advance up or down in .1" increments.

And remember, don't hit return unless there is a [Hrt] code.

- Here's an example for a mysterious code:

[Fig Opt]<BAAAA> This made sure that the borders around a figure were dashed lines. All the other defaults remain the same. (Please, whatever you do, don't see this code and think you're supposed to make a noise like a sheep.)

Even if you don't want to follow these babies code for code (and I don't blame you a bit if you don't), you can still use them as design examples, and get a good idea of what WordPerfect is capable of when you put your mind and fingers to it.

◆ LaserJet examples

- All opening and closing quotes are made with double accent marks such as ' and '. Dashes use **ALT-196.**

◆ PostScript examples

- opening quotes use **CONTROL-V 4,32**, closing quotes are **CONTROL-V 4,31**, and dashes are **CONTROL-V 4,34**.

If an example is shown for a PostScript printer, it doesn't mean you can't reproduce it on a LaserJet. The only two exceptions to this involve WordPerfect's inability to print graphics in landscape orientation on a LaserJet, and the LaserJet's inability to rotate type, thereby prohibiting the printing of portrait and landscape fonts on the same page. All other effects, including outlines, shadows and gray type could be produced on a LaserJet, using Font Effects from SoftCraft. The PostScript examples will be first.

❖ Newsletter — Astral Travel

Experience Level: Advanced

- **Fonts** Bitstream Bodoni 14pt, for PostScript
- **Graphics** MGI Publisher's PicturePak-CGM, Sales/Marketing
- **Printer** QMS-PS 810

Notes: When using a PostScript printer, graphics are opaque. WordPerfect prints in the order they are placed on the page. So in this case, the gray type was on the page after the passport graphic, and so it printed over the graphic. If I had placed gray type after the "TRAVEL" headline, it would have printed gray over the black type.

```
[VLine:1.1",Full Page,9",1w",100%][VLine:Right Margin,Full Page,9",1w,100%][L/R
Mar:1.25",1"][T/B Mar:1",0.75"]
[Fig Opt]<BNNNN>
[Figure:1;SA0209.CGM;]<TA V2 HMC S .75 E 3 10>
[Txt Opt]<BNNOO I 0 0.05 0>
[Text Box:1;;]<TA VT HMC SW 1.75>[HRt]
[HRt]  {Press [HRt} 8 more times}
[AdvToLn:3.86"][Cntr][Ln Height:0.23"]
[Font:Bodoni Book (WP PostScript) (FW) 125 pt]
 [Color:90%,90%,90%]ASTRAL[Color:Black][C/A/Flrt][HRt]
[Cntr][C/A/Flrt][Cntr][Ln Height:Auto][AdvToLn:3.62"]
[Font:Bodoni Book (WP PostScript) (FW) 125 pt]TRAVEL
[Font:Bodoni Book (WP PostScript) (FW) 14 pt]
[AdvUp:0.5"][C/A/Flrt][HRt]
[Col Def:3,1.25",3.79",3.99",4.79",4.99",7.5"][Col On]
[Tab Set:0",0.5",1",1.5",5.24"]
[Figure:2;;]<TA V5.21 HC2B SH 4>
[Figure:3;SA0195.CGM;]<TA V5.21 HC2C SW.4>
[Figure:4;SA0194.CGM;]<TA V7.78 HC2C SW.6>
[VLine:Column 1,5.21",5.04",1w,100%]
[VLine:Column 2,5.21",5.04",1w,100%]
```

by Swami Macdonaldo

ASTRAL TRAVEL

Love to travel but hate to leave home? That's where **Astral** Travel comes in: to give you the vacation of your dreams (or perhaps literally, in your dreams). Unlock your imagination with the exclusive **Time**Travel network—even the past and future are within your reach.

Let Mark Twain take you steamboating on the Mississippi. Thrill to the Bermuda Triangle at midnight. Help Cleopatra invent the practical joke, and play it on Marc Anthony. Ride a dolphin to Atlantis, a Blue whale to the coast of Mexico, or just take Shamu for a ride around the tank. See the Leaning Tower of Pisa before it leaned. Watch the Divine Sara perform. See how your grandchildren will turn out. Anything's possible!

London
City
of
Dreams

Paris
City
of
Light

Ain't no mountain high enough, ain't no valley low enough, nothing is ever out of the question, nothing is ever out of your reach. The only limit is your own imagination. Ask Shirley McClaine, she'll tell you: there's nothing like it. **Astral**Travel operates 24 hours a day, for everything from a daydream to a full night's dream. But rest assured, you'll never have a nightmare.

AstralTravel will make sure you'll see the world like you've never seen it before.

They're out-of-this world!

❖ *Invitation — Sleepwalker's Ball*

Experience Level: ***Intermediate***

- **Fonts:** Palatino, Adobe, 14 pt
- **Printer:** QMS-PS 810

Notes: Most invitations are not a full page like this, so you might want to have the printer reduce the page. Reducing the page by 50% will increase the resolution to 600 dpi, the resolution of some commercial typesetting machines. This invitation is designed to be folded in half right above the line "DayDreamer Alliance." If you have enough money in your budget, you could print the "Z's" and the large "T" in a second color. You might also consider using Galliard Italic, an excellent choice for formal invitations. The gray "ZZZZZ's" at top of page are inside the first figure box, which also provides the double line around the page.

```
[Just On][Comment][Hyph On][L/R Mar:1",1"]
[Fig Opt]<BDDDD>[Figure:1;;]<TA VF WN>
[L/R Mar:1.5",1.5"][Font:Palatino Italic 14 pt]
[AdvToLn:5.5"][Cntr]The DayDreamers Alliance[C/A/Flrt][HRt]
[Cntr]Presents[C/A/Flrt][HRt]
[HRt]
[Font:Palatino Italic 30 pt][BOLD][Cntr]A Sleepwalking Ball[C/A/Flrt][bold][HRt]
[Font:Palatino Italic 14.4 pt][AdvDn:0.1"][Cntr]February 30, 1989,
8 p.m.[C/A/Flrt][HRt]
[HRt]
[Font:Palatino Italic 30 pt][BOLD][Cntr]A Sleepwalking Ball[C/A/Flrt][bold][HRt]
[Font:Palatino Italic 14 pt][AdvDn:0.1"]
[Cntr]February 30, 1989, 8 p.m.[C/A/Flrt][HRt]
[HRt]
[HRt]
[Ln Height:0.25"][Usr Opt]<O 0000 I 0000 G0>
[Usr Box:2;;]<TP HL SB 1.3 2 E [Flsh Rt]
[Font:Palatino 157 pt]T[C/A/Flrt]>o sleep, p
erchance to dream...
{Here are the codes for the gray Z's:}
[L/R Mar:1",1"][Ln Height:1"][AdvDn:0.7"][HRt]
[Color:99%,99%,99%][Font:Palatino Bold Italic 300 pt]z[AdvDn:0.4"][Color:98%,98%,98%]
[Font:Palatino Bold Italic 200 pt]z[AdvDn:0.4"]
[Font:Palatino Bold Italic 150 pt]z[AdvDn:0.4"]
[Font:Palatino Bold Italic 100 pt][Color:96%,96%,96%]z
[AdvDn:0.4"][Font:Palatino Bold Italic 80 pt]
[Color:94%,94%,94%][AdvDn:0.2"]z[AdvDn:0.4"]
[Font:Palatino Bold Italic 60 pt]
[Color:90%,90%,90%][AdvDn:0.2"]z[Color:Black]
```

Z Z Z Z Z Z

The DayDreamers Alliance
Presents

A Sleepwalking Ball

February 30, 1989, 8 p.m.

To sleep, perchance to dream... a somnambulist's heaven. Come wearing your favorite bedtime ensemble and be lulled by the sounds of Sam and his All-girl Sandman Band. Enjoy a buffet, scientifically formulated to provide sweet dreams. See you there—and don't let the bed bugs bite!

R.S.V.P Essential
Produced by REM Associates

Contact: Rip
212-555-2121

❖ Book — Babies in Space

Experience Level: ***Easier than it looks.***

- **Fonts:** ITC Avant Garde, Adobe, 9 pt
- **Graphics:** Baby, Dynamic Graphics, Four Seasons, edited with PC Paintbrush Plus; Astronaut, Publisher's PicturePak-CGM, Sales/Marketing
- **Printer:** QMS-PS 810

Notes: Once again, here's a page that looks hard, but isn't. It's all done with parallel columns. Type a sidehead, press CONTROL-ENTER, then type your text. When you want another sidehead, press CONTROL-ENTER, and repeat the process until you get good and tired of it. The graphic figure box is in the narrow left column, and the CONTROL-ENTER is directly after it. If you want to use Fontware ITC Avant Garde from Bitstream, remember, while the package includes four weights, it lacks an italic (or in this case, Oblique. Don't ask me, I just write about it.) If you wanted italics, you'd have to use a program like SoftCraft's Fontware Installation program to "oblique" the characters.

```
[W/O Off][HZone:10%,10%][Hyph On][T/B Mar:0.75",1"]
[L/R Mar:0.75",0.75"][Fig Opt]<BNNNN>
[Figure:1;BABY.PCC;]<TA V .8 HMR SH 1.5>
[T/B Mar:1.75",0.75"][HRt]
[Font:ITC Avant Garde Gothic Demi 30 pt][Color:80%,80%,80%]
Chapter 1[Color:Black][HRt]Babies In Space
[Font:ITC Avant Garde Gothic Book 14 pt]
[Flsh Rt]NASA's Toddlers[C/A/Flrt][HRt]
[HRt]
[Tab Set:0", every 0.5"][Ln Height:0.18"]
[Font:ITC Avant Garde Gothic Book 9 pt]
[Col Def:2,0.75",2.75",3.25",7.75"]<TP>[Col On]
[Style On:sidehead]A chilling tale of[SRt]
infants out of[HRt]
control: dirty[SRt]
diapers and[SRt]
weightlessness.[HRt]
Ick, Pooey.[HRt]
[Style Off:sidehead][HRt]
[HRt]
[Figure:2;SA0235.CGM;]<TP HB>[HPg]
Dirty Work. That's what NASA called their five year project...
```

Paired Style for Sidehead

```
[Ln Height:0. 22"][Font:ITC Avant Garde Gothic Book 14 pt] [Comment]
```

Chapter 1
Babies In Space

NASA's Toddlers

A chilling tale of infants out of control: dirty diapers and weightlessness. Ick, Pooey.

Dirty Work. That's what NASA called their five year project, *Infanta.* A mission designed to see how babies would fare in deep space. Dr. Albert Gonquin, head of the Juvenile division of NASA, could take it no longer; he leaked the story to the press, and the rest is history. What would drive a bunch of normally sane guys gaga enough to think they could raise a bunch of space cadets from seedlings?

It started in 1987. The space program was in shambles, and the country had begun to forget the dream of space for the sport of TV Evangelist scandals. NASA's budget was being trimmed to a quarter of Tammy Fay Baker's mascara allowance, and heads were going to roll.

It was while he was staring at his pink slip that Al got the idea. He was absentmindedly humming the Don McClean refrain "and babies float by, just counting their toes," and there it was, as clear as a super nova. "I figured we needed a gimmick that would get more publicity than the three billion dollars NASA spent hiring Bill Blass to design haute couture space suits."

"The whole idea kind of started as a joke. We'd say that someone had left a baby in the unmanned rocket launcher, and it was accidentally sent into orbit. I told a pal, and pretty soon the whole theory spread out of control, until the head of NASA approached me, asking how much my 'baby' would cost."

The scam, I mean plan, was to specially train a group of infants for the rigors of space travel. They could fly to the farthest reaches of the galaxy and still be alive to tell about it when they got back to Earth. None of this "suspended animation" hooey—this was practical, and the country would be hooked for years. Just imagine, the sight of those little babes bobbing around the high-tech cabin. You can't buy publicity like that (and I know, I've tried).

Less than nine months after the initial joke, an entire new top-secret division was working on the intricacies of the plan. Robots had to be constructed with electronic breasts. Specially absorbent disposable diapers were a high priority. The PR division was working more feverishly than any part of NASA. Polls were conducted: "Do you think babies should be brought up in space?" and other cleverly veiled questions were being asked to tourists at DisneyWorld by people in dwarf costumes. Disney already had the TV rights to this ultra event.

Gentlemen, we have achieved poopoo

Zero Hour, 6 AM. Six toddlers (three Adams, three Eves), were packed into foil-covered bassinets, hurtling towards the future at light speed. Jane Pauley stopped chatting with the author of a diet book

❖ Catalog — Babs Ryan Originals

Experience Level ***Intermediate***

- **Fonts:** Palatino, Adobe 12 pt
- **Graphics:** Dynamic Graphics, Desktop Art Artfolio, edited with PC Paintbrush Plus
- **Printer:** QMS-PS 810

Notes: This design requires pictures that are all approximately the same width; they can vary in height, however. The subheads use Palatino Bold Italic which is then bolded, creating extra bold subheads. If you use the bold attribute on fonts that are already bold, WordPerfect prints the characters several times, shifting slightly each time, and this creates extra bold type. The picture on the bottom was edited heavily in PC Paintbrush so that it would match the style and shape of the two other graphics.

The text also has a lot of "hand justification." This means I've pressed return (and in this case, also an indent), so that the lines would end the way that looked best, rather than the way WordPerfect broke them. Hand justification can make a big difference in the appearance of a page, but can be used only when type is set flush left (ragged right).

```
[L/R Mar:1.25",1"][T/B Mar:0.75",0.5"]
[Font:ITC Avant Garde Gothic Book 30 pt]Babs Ryan Originals[HRt]
[HLine:Left & Right,6.25",0.05",100%][HRt]
[AdvDn:0.1"][Font:ITC Avant Garde Gothic Book 12 pt]
Fashion for the Well[-] Heeled Broad[Font:Palatino 12 pt][HRt]
[HRt]
[Tab Set:3.58",3.9",4.4",7.3"][Tab][Style On:subhead]
[Flsh Rt]A Little Night Music[Style Off:subhead][C/A/Flrt][HRt]
[Col Def:3,1.25",3.5",4",5.85",6.15",7.5"]<TP>[Col On]
[Fig Opt]<O 0000 I 0000>
[Figure:1;ERTE.PCC;]<TP HB>[HPg]
[Ln Height:0.19"][HRt]
[Style On:drop cap]E[Style Off:drop cap]asy does it...
```

Paired Style for Subheads

```
[Flsh Rt][Wrd/Ltr Spacing:Optimal,150% of Optimal]
[Font:Palatino Bold Italic 14 pt][BOLD] [Comment]
```

Paired Style for price listings

```
[Font:Palatino 10 pt][Ln Height:0.16"] [Comment]
```

Babs Ryan Originals

Fashion for the Well-Heeled Broad

A Little Night Music

Easy does it—you don't want to be placed under Fashion arrest. This design is sure to keep you out of the clutches of the Style Patrol.

Colors	*Price:*
Wine	$429.95
Burgundy .	$329.95
Claret	$239.95
Maroon . . .	$199.95
Puce	$129.95
Rust	$109.95

Straws in The Wind

The latest hats are breezy and romantic. We've got two of the most enchanting patterns this side of the Rockies—non-flammable too!

Colors	*Price:*
Cream	$155.50
Eggshell . .	$135.99
Beige	$122.16
Tan	$114.44
Ostrich . . .	$109.95
Sand	$107.97

A Breath of French Air

He'll fall head-over-heels when he sees your tresses wrapped up in this little satin chapeaux—ooh la la.

Colors	*Price:*
Peach	$122.50
Turquoise .	$155.99
Puce	$122.16
Baby Puke .	$144.44

❖ *Flyer — Cooking School*

Experience Level: ***Easy***

- **Fonts:** Palatino 12pt, Zapf Dingbats - Adobe PostScript
- **Graphics:** MGI Publisher's PicturePak-CGM, Sales/Marketing
- **Printer:** QMS-PS 810

Notes: This design is really ridiculously easy. It's just three columns, with a thick black line at the top of each. I've created a style that selects the dingbat font, and this makes it easier to globally change size or placement on the line. It's easy to go overboard with dingbats because they're fun, but keep them under control so they add zest, but don't clutter the page.

This same page could easily be done on a LaserJet, *without* the graphic (you could paste it in by hand). Since that graphic will probably be your company logo anyway, you'll probably have plenty of copies ready for paste up anyway.

Because this is a three-fold flyer, the backside of this flyer could be portrait, segmented into three blocks the same size as each of the folds. One segment would contain the mailing and return address, and the other two would available for more sales pitch material, maps, etc.

```
[Ln Height:0.19"][Par Num Def][Paper Sz/Typ:11" x 8.5",Standard]
[L/R Mar:0.5",0.5"][T/B Mar:0.7",0.5"]
[Col Def:3,0.5",3.63",3.93",7.06",7.36",10.5"]<D .3>
[Col On][HLine:Left & Right,3.13",0.2",100%]
[VLine:Column 1,Full Page,7.3",1w,100%]
[VLine:Column 2,Full Page,7.3",1w",100%][HRt]
[HRt]
[VRY LARGE][ITALC][AdvDn:0.1"]I Even Burn Water[vry large] [italc][HRt]
[Fig Opt]<BNNNN PBI>{The caption contains an [AdvUp:2.5"] code to move the text to the middle of the graphic rather than below it}
```

Paired Style for Dingbats:
[Font:ITC Zapf Dingbats 16 pt][Comment]
Paired Style for Headlines:
[BOLD][Ln Height:0.5"][EXT LARGE][Comment]
Paired style for subhead:
[Ln Height:0.22"][LARGE][Comment]
Paired style for schedule:
[Font:Palatino 10 pt][Comment]

"I Even Burn Water"

Cooking Classes for the Hopelessly Inept

"After being banished from Home Ec, I didn't think I would ever learn how to cook—But CFC taught even me!"

And we can teach you, too. Klutz after klutz has been cured, using our patented CRC *Klutz-Control-System*.

Our staff of highly trained professional "Cooking Counsellors" will not only teach you how to cook, but how to enjoy it! It's almost like being a Stepford Wife! Or if your a man, a Stepford Husband! (Girls can't resist men who cook.)

Classes include:

- Boiling Water 101
- Parboiling Just About Anything!
- Tips For Buttering Toast
- Miracle "Whip It Good"
- Blow Torch Browning
- Microwave Madness!

"My husband was going to leave me for this teenager who worked at KFC. You taught me the true meaning of shake and bake, and saved my marriage!"

Watch your life improve dramatically as you explore the basics of food preparation. You'll learn how to be a cheap date, or a good homemaker.

If you're in a hurry, we offer a special classes for the overworked Executive: *Defrosting Debriefings!*

✲ SCHEDULE OF CLASSES ✲

Course	*Begins*	*Fee*
❶ Defrost 101	May 23, 2 4-hour classes	$90.00
❷ Boiling Water	October 19, 12, 2-hour classes	$285.00
❸ Klutz Control	October 29, 9, 6-hour classes	$1,250.00

Cooking for Klutzes
123 Microwave Dr.
Amana, PA

☎ 800-555-BURN

❖ *Form — Runsheet*

Experience Level: ***Advanced to make, easy to use***

- **Fonts:** ITC Avant Garde, Adobe, 14 pt
- **Printer:** QMS-PS 810

(This page could also easily be produced on a LaserJet, provided you created landscape fonts with Fontware first.)

Notes: This is the runsheet we used while putting together this book. The form is a lot of fun because the form prints at the same time your information does. The secret is in the Advance codes. The styles for the form are placed into the header, so they automatically print on every page. The end of Topper3 contains [AdvToLn:0.9"] which moves WordPerfect back to the top of your page. When you watch the page draw in View Document, you see WordPerfect draw the entire form, then move back up to the top of the page and put in your information.

Topper3 looks like a billion codes, but in actuality, you only have to create one line, delete it, and then paste it back 13 times. The settings are the same for all 26 boxes. These figures boxes create the ballot boxes along the right side of the page, and if you don't want them, then all you need is the horizontal lines.

IMPORTANT: Once you save this as a style sheet you can use it over and over, but you must do it correctly. Topper1 is the first code in the file. Topper 2 and Topper 3 are both placed in a header that prints on every page. Once you do that, you can type all the information you want. The titles will not display on-screen, but they will print.

The Up/Down/Star Dingbats are a form of visual shorthand you create with paired styles. Rather than having to write GREAT, GOOD, or UH-OH, you can simply apply one of these styles. These are optional, but fun. Interestingly, WordPerfect can access the entire set of dingbats, something Ventura Pulisher can't do.

I've used Avant Garde because it looks so open and modern, but Dutch/Times Roman or Swiss/Helvetica would also work fine. The codes continue on the next page after the example.

This is the complete file:
[Open Style:Topper1][Header A:2]

HEADER
[Open Style:topper2][Open Style:topper3]

Open Style for TOPPER1
[Paper Sz/Typ:11" x 8.5",Standard][T/B Mar:0.5",0.3"][L/R Mar:0.5",0.5"]
[Font:ITC Avant Garde Gothic Book 14 pt][Ln Height:0.5"]
[TabSet:1.5",3",3.75",6.5",7",8.5"][Wrd/Ltr Spacing:Normal,Normal]

Open Style for TOPPER2 (In Header)
[Font:ITC Avant Garde Gothic Book 14 pt]
[Paper Sz/Typ:11" x 8.5",Standard][T/B Mar:0.5",0.4"]

RunSheet Project: BAM! Page 5

Author	Title	Size	Head/Info	P#	Artwork	Format/Status	
DWH	Minnie Mouse	4p	Minnie's Night of Hell	27	Cartoons	WP ▲	☐ IN ☐ OUT
TWH	Mickey Mouse	2p	Mickey's Torment	32	Photo	WP ▲	☐ IN ☐ OUT
KLL	Vance the Pig	3p	My Romance with Vance	18	Trotters	WP ✪	☐ IN ☐ OUT
SR	Lucille Ball	4p	I Loathe Lucy	12	Dumps	MW ▼	☐ IN ☐ OUT
							☐ IN ☐ OUT
							☐ IN ☐ OUT
							☐ IN ☐ OUT
							☐ IN ☐ OUT
							☐ IN ☐ OUT
							☐ IN ☐ OUT
							☐ IN ☐ OUT
							☐ IN ☐ OUT
							☐ IN ☐ OUT

[L/R Mar:0.5",0.5"][HLine:Left & Right,10",0.1",100%][HRt]
[AdvDn:0.1"][LARGE][BOLD]Run[bold]Sheet[large][Tab][Tab][Tab][Tab]
[AdvToPos:3.75"]Project: BAM![Flsh Rt]Page ^B[C/A/Flrt][HRt]
[HLine:Left & Right,10",0",100%][HRt]
[Ln Height:0.25"][AdvDn:0.1"][TabSet:1.5",3",3.75",6.5",7",8.5"]
[VLine:1.4",1.07",6.93",0",100%][VLine:2.9",1.07",6.93",0",100%]
[VLine:3.65",1.07",6.93",0",100%][VLine:6.4",1.07",6.93",0",100%]
[VLine:6.9",1.07",6.93",0",100%][VLine:8.4",1.07",6.93",0",100%]
[BOLD]Author[Tab]Title[Tab]Size[Tab]Head/Info[Tab]P#[Tab]Artwork
[Tab]Format/Status[bold][HRt]

Open Style for TOPPER3 (In header)
[AdvToLn:1.32"][HLine:Left & Right,10",0",100%][HRt]
{This is where the repeat begins}
[Flsh Rt][SMALL][Figure:1;;]<TC VB SB 14p 14p> IN [Figure:2;;]<TC VB SB 14p 14p>
OUT[small][C/A/Flrt][HRt]
[HLine:Left & Right,10",0",100%][HRt]
{Enter the above, then cut from [Flsh Rt] to the [HRt] after the [HLine] and paste it 13 times. This will give you figure numbers up to 26. After you paste them all in, enter the following:}
[AdvToLn:0.9"]{If you forget this Advance code, the whole thing won't work}
Paired Style for Up Triangle Dingbat
[Font:ITC Zapf Dingbats 14 pt][129n:12,115][Comment]
Paired Style for Down Triangle Dingbat
[Font:ITC Zapf Dingbats 14 pt][129n:12,116][Comment]
Paired Style for Star Dingbat
[Font:ITC Zapf Dingbats 14 pt][129n:12,74][Comment]

❖ Poster — Lincoln

Experience Level ***Couldn't be easier***

- **Fonts:** New Century Schoolbook, Adobe 18 pt
- **Graphics:** DG Desktop Art, edited with PC Paintbrush Plus
- **Printer:** QMS-PS 810

Notes: This looks tricky, but it isn't. When using a PostScript printer, the shadow type is opaque, which means that it prints white on top of any kind of graphic. The 18 point rotated text along the edge of the page is in a text box, and rotated using ALT-F9 2.
[Figure:1;ABE.PCC;]<<TA VF WN>
[Text Box:1;;]<TA VF HMR SB 1 9 WN E ALT-F9 2>
[W/O Off][HRt] [L/R Mar:1.2",1.2"][HRt]
[Font:New Century Schoolbook Bold 72 pt]
[SHADW]Happy[HRt] Birthday[shadw][HRt]

Happy Birthday

A Fourth of July Celebration at the Lincoln Memorial

❖ *Storyboard — ASPCA*

Experience Level: ***Easy***

- **Fonts:** Helvetica Narrow, Adobe PostScript, 12 pt
- **Graphics:** Add your own with a scanner, draw them in PC Paintbrush, or paste them in manually.
- **Printer:** QMS-PS 810

Notes: This is a presentation storyboard. You'd be out of your mind to use this to develop a storyboard, but it makes a very sharp presentation once you've already polished the storyboard the old-fashioned way (pencil and paper).

This design uses one paired style, called SHOT. This includes an automatic paragraph number, and automatic flush right for the shot.

Because these are parallel columns, make sure you don't accidentally delete at [HPg] codes between columns when you are editing. If you do, press **CONTROL-[ENTER]** to put in a new Hard Page code, and start the next column.

If you are going to use the two column introduction at the top of the page, type all your text and see how many lines it is. Divide that number in half, and place a Hard Page at the end of the half-way point. In this case it was six lines long, so I put a Hard Page code in after three lines.

To create more pages of boxes: Block a single box, then press CONTROL-F4 BC and copy it as many times as you want (that way you don't have to set the size over and over again).

If you aren't going to print graphics on the page, you can easily do this page on a LaserJet, but at the time this book was done, WordPerfect did not support landscape graphics for the LaserJet. The codes for this example continue on the next page after the example.

```
[Fig Opt]<C [BOLD]1[bold] O 0000 1 .1 .1 .1 .1>
[Paper Sz/Typ:11" x 8.5",Standard][T/B Mar:1",0.25"]
[L/R Mar:0.5",0.5"][Wrd/Ltr Spacing:200% of Optimal,200% of Optimal][Font:Helvetica
Narrow 16 pt][Ln Height:0.16"]
[HLine:Left &Right,10",1w",20%]
S•T•O•R•Y•B•O•A•R•D[Tab]FOR: A.S.P.C.A.
[Flsh Rt][Wrd/Ltr Spacing:Optimal,Optimal]DATE: 6/2/90[C/A/Flrt]
[Font:Helvetica Narrow 10 pt][HRt]
[Col Def:2,0.5",5.4",5.6",10.5"]{For intro text}[HRt]
[Col On]We see two teenage girls in poodle skirts fussing with their hair... {For Storyboard
itself}
[Col Def:4,0.5",2.85",3.05",5.4",5.6",7.95",8.15",10.5"]<TP D .2>
[Tab Set:0.9",3.45",6",9",9.55"][Col On]
[Figure:1;;[Box Num]<TP HB SH 1.76>
[Style On:SHOT] ... ][BOLD]EMMA:[bold] Hey,
Karen, what's that on your[SRt]
```

S•T•O•R•Y•B•O•A•R•D FOR: A.S.P.C.A.

DATE: 6/2/90

We see two teenage girls in poodle skirts fussing with their hair. We see only the back of KAREN's head, and EMMA is watching her try out a new fad. Her face belies a feeling of repulsion.

As they speak, we see the shadow of a giant creature looming outside the window, and hear subtle crunching noises of a mutant Gerbil, seeking revenge on Madison Avenue for promoting this new fad.

1 *TWO SHOT*

EMMA: Hey, Karen, what's that on your hair?
KAREN: It's dreamy, isn't it?

2 *CU - EMMA*

EMMA: I'll say, I've never seen anything quite like it!
ANNOUNCER: It's new.

3 *CU - BACK OF KAREN'S HEAD*

KAREN: Isn't Johnny gonna flip?
EMMA: I'll say!

4 *CU - KAREN'S LIPS*

ANNOUNCER: It's cool.
KAREN: He just loves this kind of thing.

5 *MCU - KAREN TURNS TO WINDOW*

EMMA: All guys do!
ANNOUNCER: It's what you've been waiting for.

6 *TWO SHOT - BOTH TURN TO WINDOW*

KAREN: Don't cha just love it?
EMMA: I'll say...

7 *WIDER REVEAL- KAREN TURNS*

After a pause
EMMA: But, what is it?
KAREN: Beats me...

8 *SLOW FADE*

ANNOUNCER: It's a Gerbil
EMMA: They don't use real poodles in these skirts, do they?
*The shadow blocks all light from the window, as we **FADE***

hair?[HRt]
[BOLD]KAREN: [bold]It's dreamy, isn't it?[HPg]
Paired Style for SHOTS
[BOLD][Par Num:Auto][bold][FlshRt][SMALL][ITALC]
[Comment]
[AdvDn:0.1"][small][italc][C/A/Flrt]

❖ *Sign — Time Management*

Experience Level: ***Really Easy***

- **Fonts:** ITC Avant Garde, Adobe PostScript, 14pt
- **Printer:** QMS-PS 810

Notes: Try it. You'll like it.

[Just Lim:60,120][Paper Sz/Typ:11" x 8.5",Standard][Just On]
[Txt Opt]<BTTTT>[Text Box:1;;]<TA VF WN>{Box around page}
[HRt]
[HRt]
[HRt]
[HRt]
[HLine:Center,2.88",0.2",20%][HRt]
[HRt]
[Font:ITC Avant Garde Gothic Demi 30 pt]
[Cntr][OUTLN]The Fallacy of[outln][C/A/Flrt][HRt]
[Font:ITC Avant Garde Gothic Demi 36 pt][Cntr]Time Management[C/A/Flrt][HRt]
[L/R Mar:2.25",2.25"][Font:ITC Avant Garde Gothic Book 14 pt]
[Ln Height:0.22"][Hyph On][AdvDn:0.1"]While the organization of...

The Fallacy of Time Management

While the organization of material is important, when it is left until the last minute, nothing can be organized because there is not enough time. Organization requires time, and saving time requires organization.

If there is not enough time to organize, there will seldom be logic. Without logic and organization, there can be no judgement. If there is no judgement, then nothing is accomplished. If nothing is accomplished, then there is no reason for organization, and without organization why manage time?

So take a nap.

❖ Overhead projection — GoCo

Experience Level: ***Easy***

- **Fonts:** Helvetica Bold, Adobe PostScript, 36 pt Zapf Dingbats
- **Graphics:** Gem Draw, printed to disk in HPGL format
- **Printer:** QMS-PS 810

Notes: The second line of gray type is 70,70,70, and the third line is black. Replace "GoCo DTP" and the graphic with your own company name and logo, and use them at the top of all slides for increased name recognition.

If you don't have a graphic logo, you can put a box around the page, your company name, and the line under it all in a header so they will automatically repeat on every page. (Beat them over the head with your name. "How did those half moon marks get on his forehead and hands?")

```
[Tab Set:3.5",4"][Paper Sz/Typ:11" x 8.5",Standard]
[T/B Mar:1.25",1"][Figure:1;;]<TA VF WN>{Box around the page}
[T/B Mar:1.75",1.25"][L/R Mar:1.75",1.75"]
[Font:Helvetica Bold 36 pt][Usr Opt][Flsh Rt][OUTLN]GoCo DTP
[Usr Box:1;ZULU.HPL;][outln][C/A/Flrt][HRt]
[HLine:Left & Right,7.5",0.05",100%][HRt]
[HRt]
[ITALC]Choose any two[HRt]
[SMALL](all three not available as a package)[small][italc][HRt]
[HRt]
[Ln Height:0.5"][Color:90%,90%,90%]
[Style On:dingbat]~[Style Off:dingbat]Cheap[HRt]
[HRt]
```

Paired Style for Dingbats

```
[Tab][Font:ITC Zapf Dingbats 36 pt][Comment][Indent]
```

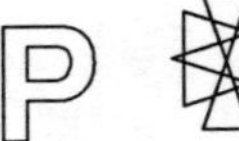

Choose any two

(all three not available as a package)

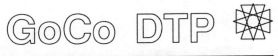

 Cheap

 Fast

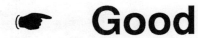

 **Good**

❖ Outline — WordPerfect 5 DTP in Style

Experience Level: **Intermediate**

- **Fonts:** Palatino 12pt - Adobe PostScript
- **Graphics:** SpinFont from SoftCraft, with Bitstream Zapf Calligraphic (Palatino)
- **Printer:** QMS-PS 810

Notes: The double outline effect was created by selecting a bold base font, then using both outline and bold attributes. Because the font is already bold, WordPerfect prints the characters several times, shifting to the right each time, in tiny increments.

[Tab Set:2", every 0.4"][T/B Mar:1“,0.75"][L/R Mar:1.5",1”][Just Off]
[Fig Opt]<BNNNN>[Font:Palatino 12 pt][Usr Opt]<BSSSS>
[Usr Box:1;;]<TA VF WN>{Box around the page}
[Figure:1;DPIS2.TIF;]<TA VT SW 1.5>
[L/R Mar:2",1.75"][T/B Mar:1“,1”]
[HRt]
[HRt]
[HRt]
[HRt]
[HRt]
[HRt]
[HRt]
[Ln Height:0.55"][Font:Palatino Bold Italic 40 pt]
[Cntr][BOLD][OUTLN]with[outln][bold] WordPerfect
[Font:Palatino 12 pt][Ln Height:0.2"][C/A/Flrt][HRt]

Paired Style for Outline Numbers:
[Cndl EOP:6][HRt]
[HLine:Left & Right,4.75",0.05",10%][HRt]
[AdvDn:0.1“][VRY LARGE][BOLD][Par Num:Auto][Indent]
[Comment]

Paired Style for Chapter Titles:
[VRY LARGE][BOLD][SM CAP][Comment]
Each numbered line:
[Tab][Par Num:Auto][Indent]

with WordPerfect

Introduction: This is the book that's going to blow the lid off the word processing/desktop publishing industry—and isn't that just what we've all been waiting for? Desktop publishing puts the power and responsibility of designing pages and formatting documents into the hands of the people. This book will show them how to make these publications as professional as possible, without having to spend more time and money than doing it the old fashioned way.

---

1. Getting it together

1. System Configuration
2. What kind of printer?
3. Make LJ fonts.
4. PostScript vs. LaserJet.

---

2. Steps will be taken

1. Follow my example
   - a. Concept/Market.
   - b. Writing.
   - c. Designing.
     - I. Selecting font.
     - II. Choosing graphics.
   - d. Assembling with WP commands.
     - I. Sharing the styles with other docs.
     - II. Re-using the format.

LaserJet examples

❖ *Promotional piece — Desktop Publishing in Style*

Experience Level: ***Intermediate (easier than it looks)***

- **Fonts:** Bitstream Korinna, 12 pt
- **Graphics:** MGI Publisher's PicturePak-CGM, Finance/Administration
- **Printer:** Hewlett-Packard LaserJet II

Notes: The graphic of the pen is line art, so WordPerfect was able to rotate and mirror the image so it faced into the page on each corner. Bitstream's Korinna is a wonderful font, so sharp it looks typeset right out of the printer; decorative and suitable for this type of promotional material.

```
[W/O Off][L/R Mar:1",0.75"][Hyph On][T/B Mar:0.75",0.75"] [HZone:10%,10%][Font:ITC
Korinna Regular 11pt (Port) (FW)]
[Usr Box:1;FI0172.CGM;]<TA VT HML SW 1>
[Usr Box:2;FI0172.CGM;]<TA VB HML SW 1 E R 0Y>
[Usr Box:3;FI0172.CGM;]<TA VT HMR SW 1 E R 180 N>
[Usr Box:4;FI0172.CGM;]<TA VB HMR SW 1 E R 180 Y>
[Font:ITC Korinna Kursiv Regular 11pt (Port) (FW)]
[AdvDn:0.1"][AdvDn:0.1"]
[Font:ITC Korinna Kursiv Ex Bold 18pt (Port) (FW)]
[Cntr]Daniel Will[-]Harris[C/A/Flrt][HRt]
[Font:ITC Korinna Regular 36pt (ASCII) (Port) (FW)]
[Cntr][Ln Height:0.5"]WordPerfect Desktop[C/A/Flrt][HRt]
[Cntr]Publishing in Style[C/A/Flrt][HRt]
[AdvDn:0.1"][Just On][Tab Set:1.25",4.75"]
[Col Def:2,1",4.25",4.5",7.75"][Col On]
[Txt Opt]<BNNTO I .1 .1 .1 .1>
[Text Box:1;;]<TA VC HC1-2C>
[Ln Height:0.18"][Font:ITC Korinna Regular 11pt (Port)(FW)]
[VLine:Column 1,2.35",1.65",0.01",155D00%]{Top vertical line}
[VLine:Column 1,7.03",3.21",0.01",155D00%]{Bottom vertical line}
[VRY LARGE]J[vry large]ust when you thought...
```

Daniel Will-Harris

WordPerfect Desktop Publishing in Style

Just when you thought it was safe you go back into the computer section of a bookstore, you see it—yet another book about WordPerfect. But wait a sec, this isn't just another book for people who have the program, but (mysteriously) not the manual.

This practical and amusing guide offers sound advice on everything from important technical information such as undocumented features that make publishing easier and more efficient, to a comprehensive graphic design guide with font examples and page layouts for many business applications.

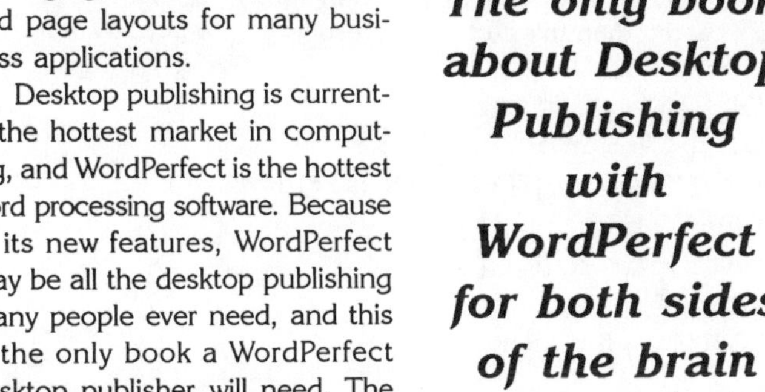

The only book about Desktop Publishing with WordPerfect for both sides of the brain

Desktop publishing is currently the hottest market in computing, and WordPerfect is the hottest word processing software. Because of its new features, WordPerfect may be all the desktop publishing many people ever need, and this is the only book a WordPerfect desktop publisher will need. The WordPerfect manual is sketchy, and actually fails to mention many advanced DTP features. It contains no in-depth examples of how to use the DTP commands, or even clues about many features.

If it can be done with WordPerfect, Daniel Will-Harris will show you how. This book stresses honest, practical desktop publishing—not art director hype.Beginners will learn all they need to know about both WordPerfect and graphic design. Advanced users learn tricks not covered in the manual, or any other books, including hidden commands and highly complex page formatting.

Third party programs that expand WordPerfect's scope are extensively covered, including graphics software, font installation programs, and fonts.

Capsule reviews of monitors and printers are also included. The book specifically covers all aspects of using WordPerfect with either a LaserJet or PostScript printer, going into great detail about what each can and can't do.

Packed with design tips, this book graphically shows how to get professional results with WordPerfect. Full page examples are supplied for the 25 most commonly produced documents, including advertisements, books, brochures, calendars, catalogs, charts, directories, documentation, flyers, forms, invitations, invoices, letterheads, magazines, menus, newsletters, presentations, proposals, reports, and resumes, with all the codes required to recreate them.

No other book about WordPerfect will:

- Reveal secret commands which not even WordPerfect technical support personnel are aware of. (Author beta-tested WP5.)
- Show you full page examples (not teensy-weensy sketches), and all the codes necessary to recreate them yourself.
- Contain specific information for every command from bullets to word spacing.
- Present technical information in an entertaining and amusing way.
- Give detailed information about graphics software for enhancing WordPerfect pages.
- Explain simple tricks to get around major LaserJet deficiencies.
- Be written by an author with as much hands-on WordPerfect experience. The author is a regular contributor to many computer publications and writes a monthly column for a major desktop publishing magazine.

❖ *Magazine — Trends in Type*

Experience Level: ***Easy***

- **Fonts:** Bitstream Zapf Humanist (Optima headlines), Zapf Elliptical (Melior) 12pt
- **Printer:** Hewlett-Packard LaserJet II

Notes: This page design is simple and looks good with almost any typeface. I used this as the test page each time I created fonts with Fontware, and everything looked good in this format. Melior looks especially serious, if not a little dry.

As you can see, sometimes WordPerfect's letter spacing leaves something to be desired, especially in the narrow columns next to the readout. Still, I'd rather have extra letterspacing than huge rivers of white between words, because it gives the page an overall even tone, whereas rivers make the page look blotchy.

```
[Wrd/Ltr Spacing:Optimal,105% of Optimal]{WordPerfect was setting Melior too tight, so
that the letters were almost on top of each other. this code tells WordPerfect to put 5% more
space between the letters}
[Just Lim:60,120][Hyph On][W/O Off][Tab Set:1.25",4.62"]
[Usr Opt]<I .25 .25 .1 .1>[Usr Box:1;;]<TA V 5.9 HC1-2C SW3>
[Font:Zapf Humanist Roman 14pt (Port) (FW)][Cntr]TRENDS IN TYPE[AdvDn:0.1"]
[HLine:Center,1.53",0.03",100%][C/A/Flrt][HRt]
[AdvDn:0.1"][Font:Zapf Humanist Bold 30pt (Port) (FW)]
[Cntr]Putting your best face forward[C/A/Flrt][HRt]
[Font:Zapf Humanist Bold 12pt (ASCII) (Port) (FW)][HRt]
[HRt]
[BOLD]By Daniel Will[-]Harris, Dt.P.[AdvDn:0.1"][bold][HRt]
[AdvUp:0.1"][Col Def:2,1",4.12",4.37",7.5"]<d .25>[Col On]
[Just On][Fig Opt]<BNNNN O 0000 I0000>
[Figure:1;;]<TP HL: SB .25 .35>{Drop Cap}
[Ln Height:0.18"]ypestyles, like clothing styles, go in...
```

TRENDS IN TYPE

Putting your best face forward

By Daniel Will-Harris, Dt.P.

Typestyles, like clothing styles, go in and out of fashion. There's such a variety of printed matter that, like any other kind of fashion, there's always room for the pendulum to swing between the trendy and the outre. This is the kind of thing art directors get paid to think about, but for the typical desktop publisher, font fashions may be a revelation. As Bill Blass says about clothing, certain typestyles "just look right now."

Except for the terminally trendy, desktop published documents should go out of their way *not* to look like desktop publishing. Typefaces can be modern without being extreme, stylish, but not overdesigned or faddish.

For the past few months, the trend for popular type has been leaning towards extremes. The two hottest typefaces now are very sans serif and very serif. In the sans serif corner, Futura Extra Black (and the entire Futura family) are #1 among the avant garde (the people, not the typeface). The type is overwhelming, yet elementary, heavy yet plain, and impossible to miss. As Buster Poindexter says, it's hot, hot, hot.

Of course the trendiest magazines have started using Futura Extra Black. But unfortunately, some of them teamed it with Univers, a combination that Allan Haley, noted authority on type and a VP at ITC, says you should "avoid like the plague."

At the serif end of the spectrum, the type de jour is Galliard. It's simple yet baroque, classic yet flashy, readable yet verging on caricature, especially in the italics. It's today's replacement for Palatino. It's not quite as readable or efficient as Palatino, but it's so "late Eighties." New trends are defined by their radical extremes, and in the future I won't be surprised if the move away from classical faces continues, with even more extravagant faces becoming the norm.

Post-modern neoclassical is becoming dated, and Russian Expressionism looks like the next big thing. If you don't want to have to redesign your publications every year (as some imprudent publishers do), you should think about using more suitable font combinations. Consider a makeover that's more classic, and you won't have to redesign it every 12 months. The combination of Baskerville for body copy and Franklin Gothic for headlines, raised caps, and captions is a well-balanced choice, and one which will retain its clean, distinctive look for a long time.

This year nostalgia is out, except for maybe Fifties nostalgia. A popular theory holds that whatever people remember from their childhood becomes

> When you get hooked on type, you get hooked in the gills, or possibly the Gill Sans. You won't see words in quite the same way again.

❖ *Advertisement — Hollywood Screenwriters*

Experience Level: ***Easy***

- **Fonts:** Bitstream Bodoni, 14pt
- **Graphics:** Arts & Letters
- **Printer:** Hewlett-Packard LaserJet II

Notes: There's not much to say except that this was very simple. The only problem was that the 7/11/88 release of WordPerfect categorically refused to print this graphic in high or even medium quality. WordPerfect would do all sorts of interesting, but unfortunately strange things with the graphic, and it didn't look as I had intended.

I thought it might work better on a PostScript printer, but the filmstrip wouldn't print at all. I always try to remember, "If you're handed a lemon, make lemon-aid," so I left it at low resolution and just printed it anyway. This is a good example of what can happen (or not happen, as the case may be). You just have to forgive WordPerfect its little weaknesses as you'd have it forgive you, and get on with it.

The square bullets are simply graphics boxes. I created the first one, then blocked it and copied it four more times so I didn't have to create it from scratch each time.

One more item: I used View Document (a lot) to make sure that my text wasn't running into the horizontal lines.

```
[Usr Box:1;FILM.CGM;]<TA VF WN>
[L/R Mar:2",2"][Cntr][Font:Bodoni Book 14pt (Port)(FW)]
[C/A/Flrt][AdvDn:0.1"][HRt]
[Font:Bodoni Bold 36pt (ASCII) (Port) (FW)][Cntr]"Tinsel! Glamor![C/A/Flrt][HRt]
[Cntr]Excitement!"[C/A/Flrt][HRt]
[Font:Bodoni Book 18pt (ASCII) (Port) (FW)][Cntr]If you can type with at least two
fingers,[C/A/Flrt][HRt]
[Cntr]you can have a lucrative career as[C/A/Flrt][HRt]
[Cntr]a Hollywood screenwriter![C/A/Flrt][HRt]
[Cntr](That's what producers think)[Font:Bodoni Book 14pt (Port)(FW)]...

[Fig Opt]<BNNNN O0000 G100>
[HRt]
[Tab][Tab][Figure:1;;]<TC VB SB .1 .1>  Power Breakfasts[HRt]
[Tab][Tab][Figure:2;;]<TC VB SB .1 .1>  Taking a Meeting[HRt]
[Tab][Tab][Figure:3;;]<TC VB SB .1 .1>  Using a Car Phone[HRt]
[Tab][Tab][Figure:4;;]<TC VB SB .1 .1>  Schmoozing at Parties[HRt]
[Tab][Tab][Figure:5;;]<TC VB SB .1 .1>  Smooth[-]talking Temperamental Stars[HRt]
[HRt]
```

"Tinsel! Glamor! Excitement!"

If you can type with at least two fingers,
you can have a lucrative career as
a Hollywood screenwriter!
(That's what producers think)

In just three easy lessons, Big Bucks Screenwriting School will teach you the secrets of

- Power Breakfasts
- Taking a Meeting
- Using a Car Phone
- Schmoozing at Parties
- Smooth-talking Temperamental Stars

If you successfully complete this course (and thousands have), you can reminisce about the Strike of '88 with the rest of your fellow writers and remember how David Letterman called the producers "money grubbing scum!"

Have lunch at the famous restaurants, meet movie stars, shop on Rodeo Drive, watch helplessly as know-nothings hack your script to pieces...enjoy all the perks the big-time writers enjoy.

Don't delay! Call Today!

800-BIG-BUCKS

Big Bucks Screenwriters School, Hollywood, Cal

❖ Directory — Astral Travel Agents

Experience Level: ***Easy***

- **Fonts:** Swiss. Galliard, Bitstream
- **Graphics:** Scanned from a Dover Pictorial Archive book with a Hewlett-Packard ScanJet and GEM Scan software
- **Printer:** Hewlett-Packard LaserJet II

Notes: Once you set it up, this design is automatic. Each listing is surrounded with a listing style that contains the line above and a block protect code to insure that listings are broken between columns or pages. This makes them easier to read, and adds extra white space so the page doesn't become confusing.

While it's unusual to make the names flush right, it sets them apart from the rest of the text, without taking up much space. While the body text is Swiss/Helvetica, you might want to use Swiss/Helvetica Condensed for the headings. Without the big headline, you could easily do a page like this with just a font cartridge. If you don't use graphics, make sure to leave even more extra white space.

```
[Open Style:Topper;]
[VLine:Column 2,Full Page,10",0.01",100%]
[Footer A:2;[Font:ITC Galliard Italic 11pt (ASCII) (Port) [HRt]
[Fig Opt]<BNNNN>[Figure:1;STARGIRL.IMG;]<TP HB> [HRt][HRt]
[Style On:headline][Flsh Rt]American{one space} [C/A/Flrt][HRt]
[Flsh Rt]Association{one space} [C/A/Flrt][HRt]
[Flsh Rt]of Astral{one space} [C/A/Flrt][HRt]
[Flsh Rt]Travel Agents{one space} [C/A/Flrt][HRt]...[HPg]
[Style On:ENTRY;[HRt]
[Block Pro:On][HLine:Left & Right,2.2",0.01",100%][HRt]
[HRt][Style On:name]Ellen Aires[Style Off:name][C/A/Flrt][HRt]
1-800-555-8768[HRt]
[ITALC]Specialty:[italc] A hard hitting approach[SRt]
to the Zen of software. Takes[SRt]
travellers on a wild adventure[SRt]
[ITALC]Travel Tip:[italc] Always bring enough[SRt]
leading.[HRt]
[BOLD][bold][Style Off:!][HRt]
[Style On:!][Style On:name]Carol T. Download[Style Off:name][C/A/Flrt][HRt]
```

Paired Style for each Entry

```
[HRt]
[Block Pro:On][HLine:Left & Right,6.5",0.01",100%][HRt]
[HRt]
```

American Association of Astral Travel Agents

Ellen Aires

1-800-555-8768
Specialty: A hard hitting approach to the Zen of software. Takes travellers on a wild adventure through a CRT, dodging electron beams and leaving footprints on the sands of Times Roman.
Channels: Gutenberg, Zapf.
Travel Tip: Always bring enough leading.

Carol T. Download

800-555-4328
Specialty: Running with the "in" crowd.
Channels: Janes, including Jane Austin, Jane Meadows, Jane Jetson.
Travel Tip: When in doubt, guess.
Motto: Don't ask me.

Thomas Filum

800-111-1111
Specialty: Impressionistic Relativity. Leads tours through Paris, circa 1900.
Channels: Serat, Monet, Van Gogh.
Travel Tip: Plimsoles and Bandaids.
Motto: Give me a foot and I'll walk a mile.
Rates: Works too cheap.

Robert E. Lee

800-555-2347
Specialty: Darwinian treks.
Channels: Ben Franklin, Anton Mesmer.
Motto: You can't direct it if you don't respect it.

Bruce Lekec

800-555-7147
Specialty: Excursions into hand-held calculators. Claims 2+2 do not equal 4 (especially on Parisian hotel bills figured with Pascal). Averages a C++
Travel Tip: Always sleep in crepe-soled shoes are as they are non-conductive.
Motto: It's not a bug, it's a feature.
Rates: 2+2 in the fourth dimension.

Sue Marie Harrysun

(Sue) SUE-SUDIO
Specialty: Whisks participants back and forth over the international date line until they get younger.
Channels: Grace Kaeko Kelly Fugitami, Sara Bernhardt.
Motto: Me Habla Japanese

Isaiah Sheven Louis

800-555-5555
Specialty: Astrologer/stock broker, Tao Jones Stock Exchange. Renaissance man, shameless self-promoter.
Channels: Anything for an audience.
Travel Tip: Don't leave home without me.
Motto: Say it with *cash.*

Fred Noodnick

c/o Rosali & Alana's Fungi Factory.
Specialty: Playwrights of the late 20th century. Also dabbles in the healing powers of swing music and the dead languages of China.
Channels: Walt Whitman, Paul Whiteman, Chairman Mao.
Motto: Don't follow a fad, be one.
Rates: The current market price of a leather sofa.

John Tomorrow

800-555-2121
Specialty: All inclusive holidays into harmonic scales; A Flat minor a must.
Channels: Fats Waller.
Travel Tip: It don't mean a thang if it ain't got that swang.
Motto: Be hip, or be gone, real gone.

Sven Wrath

800-555-6792
Specialty: Spys and Smiley faces. Takes side trips into the pseudo-Jungian imagery of undercover ABC affiliates.
Channels: Noah Webster, Hearst.
Travel Tip: It's only worth doing if it can't be done.
Motto: I'd rather be sailing.

AAATA, "Triple A Service with some T&A to spare." Also incorporating the Universal Society of Astral Paranormals (USAP)

[Comment][Block Pro:Off]

Paired Style for Name:
[LARGE][BOLD][Flsh Rt] [Comment]
Open Style for Topper
[Open Style:3 col w/rul;[T/B Mar:0.5",0.5"][L/R Mar:0.75",0.75"]
[Col Def:3,0.75",2.95",3.15",5.35",5.55",7.75"]<D .3>
[Col On][VLine:Column 1,Full Page,10",0.01",100%]
[VLine:Column 2,Full Page,10",0.01",100%]
Open Style for Vertical intercolumn rules on following pages
[VLine:Column 1,Full Page,9.65",0.01",100%][VLine:Column 2,Full Page,9.65",0.01",100%]

Footer:
[Font:ITC Galliard Italic 11pt (Port) (FW)]Membership Roster Page ^B[Flsh Rt]December 1990[C/A/Flrt]

❖ *Flyer — Estate Finders*

Experience Level: ***Complex***

- **Fonts:** Bitstream Galliard, 11 pt
- **Graphics:** Both scanned from 1920's periodicals using a Hewlett-Packard ScanJet and GEM Scan software
- **Printer:** Hewlett-Packard LaserJet II

Notes: Notice how different this example looks from the "HomeFinders" example that follows, even though the layout is almost identical (but flopped). While it should have been straightforward to create three columns, the first two narrow and the last wide, for some reason this page was a pain. The text kept wanting to run around the graphic, one letter at a time. The "HomeFinders" example was much easier to do.

[Hyph On][T/B Mar:0.9",1"][Footer A:2; ...]
[Fig Opt]<BNNNN>[Figure:1;MANSION.IMG;]<TP HR SH 1 WN>
[Font:ITC Galliard Italic 14pt (ASCII) (Port) (FW)]Investment Information[HRt][AdvToLn:1.2"]
[Font:ITC Galliard Italic 36pt (ASCII) (Port) (FW)]{Yes, spaces}
EstateFinders [HRt]
[Font:ITC Galliard Italic 14pt (ASCII) (Port) (FW)][AdvUp:0.1"]
[Flsh Rt]"A Person's Home is their Castle"{Yes, more spaces}[C/A/Flrt]
[HRt]
[AdvUp:0.1"][HLine:Left & Right,6.5",0.01",100%][AdvToLn:1.93"]
[Just On][Font:ITC Galliard Roman 11pt (ASCII) (Port) (FW)]

EstateFinders

"A Person's Home is their Castle"

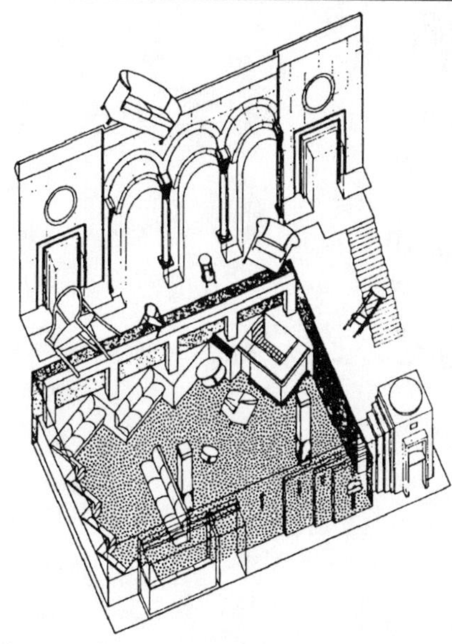

Post-Modern Luxury: Geo-Classical splendor on 12,000 acres, with 19 Bedrooms, 47 Bathrooms, 25 Fireplaces. Tennis Court, Pool/Lagoon.

Schools

Yale University is only 20 minutes away by Lear Jet. No public schools are located within the city limits, although personal tutors are plentiful, cheap, and exceptionally well-dressed.

Neighbors of Note

Ron & Nancy
Malcolm Forbes
Bob Hope
Abiner & Puppy
Donny Trump
Merv Griffini

You deserve it. Just imagine 12,000 carefully manicured acres with all the amenities. Based on the original drawings for Versailles, this magnificent estate is fully furnished--you won't have to do a thing. Everything that can be made out of marble has been, from the floors to the many sunken bathtubs, replete with anatomically correct marble statuary.

Envision unparalleled luxury with no expense spared--including a staff of nine young, blonde, Swedish au pair girls with 5 years still left on their indentured servitude.

This stunning property includes bulletproof windows, and a fully stocked bomb-type shelter, fortified to resist uzis and small armored tanks. The entire neighborhood has been walled and surrounded by moats. Ex-jewel thieves have been hired to design the security systems, then mysteriously disappeared, assuring the highest possible safety. A private police force of 44 is on guard 24 hours a day, and requires a low monthly maintenance fee of just $120,000.

Play tennis on the tournament-grade clay courts, or bowl in Howard Hughes own alley, brought in it's entirety from Las Vegas, and complete with those famous Kleenex dispensers.

And what a pool! Because it's almost a mile wide, you can swim, fish, yacht, cavort with dolphins, or simply relax, as the private hydro-electric plant provides all the energy, with enough left over to sell back to the power company.

The guest house consists of an authentic Scottish castle, imported stone-by-stone and set in it's own island in the middle of the pool. Or if you prefer a tropical flavor, there's always the Polynesian Village, stocked with happy natives who don't even know they're not still in Polynesia. Your own little bit of the islands, without ever leaving home.

Even Aaron Spelling would be jealous!

[Fig Opt]<BNNNN O .1 .1 .01 .1>
[Figure:2;FLYCHAIR.IMG;]<TA V 1.93 H M L SW 3>
[Hyph Off][AdvDn:0.1"][Font:ITC Galliard Bold 14pt (Port) (FW)] ...]
[Col Def:3,1",2.25",2.5",3.8",4.05",7.5"][Col On]
[Ln Height:0.18"][Style On:subhead][Just Off]Schools[HRt]
Paired Style for Subhead (as in "Schools/Neighbors")
[Ln Height:Auto][Font:ITC Galliard Italic 18pt (Port) (FW)]
[Just Off] [Comment]

Paired Style for Raised Cap
[Font:ITC Galliard Italic 36pt (ASCII) (Port) (FW)] [Comment]
Footer:
[HLine:Left & Right,6.5",0.01",100%][AdvDn:0.1"][HRt]
[Cntr][Font:ITC Galliard Italic 11pt (ASCII) (Port) (FW)]1 Park Place, El Mirage, California, 90342 (213) 555[-]8768[C/A/Flrt][HRt]

❖ Flyer — Home Finders

Experience Level: ***Intermediate***

- **Fonts:** Bitstream Serifa, 12 pt, Bitsream Slate Extra Bold
- **Graphics:** Top & Footer: Created in PC Paintbrush; Spanish House scanned from 1920's magazine using a Hewlett-Packard ScanJet and GEM Scan software
- **Printer:** Hewlett-Packard LaserJet II

Notes: Once this format is setup, it's easy to change the text and graphic and use it over and over again. The trickiest thing on the page is the subhead "Vital Statistics," centered over the second two columns. The only way to do this is to make it part of the caption and then center it. WordPerfect was being finicky, and didn't want to let me insert a lot of codes in the caption, but it would let me do this.

[Hyph On][L/R Mar:1.25",0.75"][T/B Mar:0.75",0.75"]
[Footer A:2; ...][Figure:1;HOUSE.PCC;]<TA VT HML SH 1>
[Fig Opt]<O 0 0 .5 0>[Figure:2;BUNGALO.WPG;]<TA V2 HMR SH2>
[HRt]
[AdvUp:0.05"][HRt]
[Font:Slate Extra Bold 36pt (Port) (FW)]HomeFinders
[Flsh Rt][Font:Serifa Roman 11pt (Port) (FW)][BOLD]HomeWork Sheet[bold][C/A/Flrt][HRt]
[AdvUp:0.1"][Font:Serifa Roman 11pt (Port) (FW)]"We don't find houses, we find [BOLD]Homes[bold]"[HRt]

HomeFinders

HomeWork Sheet

"We don't find houses, we find **Homes**"

The Great American Dream of owning your own home is still possible for first-time buyers.

We at **Home**Finders are dedicated to finding homes that you can afford, no matter what the cost. If we can't find you a home, we guarantee that one of our trained professionals will make you realize that you really didn't want a house after all.

Of course, because we look for low-priced homes, most of them are fixer-uppers (which means they aren't fit for man nor beast). But never mind about that—you want a house, you'll get a house. You want plumbing bills, you'll get plumbing bills (and every other kind of bill, too).

This house is much too nice for the likes of you. Still, drool over this: 2 bedrooms and a half bath. Close to shopping, the kitchen window faces the K-Mart loading dock!

This Week's Hot Home!

This little Spanish bungalow would make the perfect home for a growing family. The second floor is merely a false front to impress the neighbors. But there's plenty of room for expansion, should you want to add a real second story!

The house was built in 1942, just as building supplies were being rationed. But the developer was smart, and you'd never even know that the plumbing was made out of the hoses from his 1932 Model T. Custom-built doesn't even begin to describe this little enchilada.

Talk about local color! The tile roof was made of local mud and seepage from the famed LaBrea Tar Pits, some of which are located in your own backyard (and after big rains, your master bedroom). With a little loving care, elbow-grease, and a lot of cash, this could be the house of your dreams (or nightmares).

PRICE: **$197,500**

Vital Statistics

Bedrooms	2
Bathrooms	1/2
Fireplace	NO
Garage	NO
Pool	NO
A/C	NO
Central Heat	NO
Carpet	NO
Appliances	HA!
Ghosts:	Does the word "Amityville" ring a bell?

SCHOOLS

Nursery:
Norman Bates Sunshine School (Accredited)

Elementary:
Benedict Arnold Lower School

High School:
Lizzie Borden Memorial Correctional Center

Alta Mira was incorporated in 1911, and has since become famous for it's frozen yogurt stands; 72 of them at last count.

This property is located not far from the Monda Vista Mile of Cars, with the largest assortment of used cars in the West.

The major employer is Asphalt Associated, and 55% of the locals are involved in tar collection.

[HLine:Left & Right,5.44",0.01",100%][HRt]
[HRt]
[HRt]
[HRt]
[HRt]
[Just On][Col Def:3,1.25",4.37",4.62",6.1",6.35",7.75"][Col On]
[Style On:drop cap]T[Style Off:drop cap][Style On:firstpar]he Great American Dream of[SRt]
owning your own home is still[SRt]
possible for first[-]time buyers. [HRt]
[Style Off:firstpar][Ln Height:0.16"]

Footer:
[HLine:Left & Right,6.5",0.01",100%][AdvDn:0.1"][HRt]
[Figure:1;HOUSE.PCC;]<TP HR SH .33>
[Flsh Rt]321 Main Street, Alta Mira, Ca 90342
(213) 555[-]1342[C/A/Flrt][HRt]
Caption:
[AdvDn:0.1"][ITALC]This house is much too nice for the likes of...
[Font:Serifa Bold 11pt (ASCII) (Port) (FW)][Cntr]Vital Statistics[C/A/Flrt]

Paired Style for Raised Cap
[Font:Slate Extra Bold 36pt (ASCII) (Port)(FW)] [Comment]
Paired Style for Firstpar (First Paragraph)
[LARGE][Ln Height:0.22"] [Comment]
Paired Style for Subhead
[HLine:Left & Right,3.12",0.01",100%][HRt]
[Ln Height:Auto][Font:Serifa Bold 18pt (ASCII) (Port) (FW)][BOLD] [Comment]

❖ *Proposal — Making It Count*

Experience Level: ***Intermediate***

- **Fonts:** Bitstream Zapf Humanist (Optima) 12pt
- **Graphics:** MGI Publisher's PicturePak-CGM, Finance/Administration
- **Printer:** Hewlett-Packard LaserJet II

Notes: You might want to use the single coin graphics as bullets. Each level of bullets could be a smaller denomination of coin.

[W/O Off][Hyph On][T/B Mar:1",0.75"][L/R Mar:1.25",0.7"]
[Fig Opt]<BNNNN>[Figure:1;FI0146.CGM;]<TA VB HMR SB .3 .3>{Coin at bottom}

Making it Count

■ Time, Money and Computers

(or how to use one to save the other two)

"Time is Money." One of the great cliches of all time. Another popular and pervasive myth, is that if you throw enough money into computers, you somehow create extra time from the ether; sit down in front of a machine and you will instantly work harder and produce more.

The hype that surrounds computers makes you think if you have enough money you can buy time. This fiction is somehow comforting. The truth is that computers *aren't* inherently efficient and productive.

They *are* inherently frustrating, maddening, and difficult. They require much thought and concentration, something not in vogue this year. They also require effort, also unpopular.

And the results? The results are that you work just as hard, but in different ways. At first it's far harder to do something on a computer than to do it by hand. You try to tell the machine to do something, but it doesn't understand what you mean, so you have to learn its language as well as your own.

But after enough trial and error, after enough tension and stress, computers start to pay off. They do what you want. If you leave it at that, you will save time from there on in, until the machine breaks, which it inevitably will.

But if you get hooked, if you get reeled in—that's it. You'll spend hours, days, weeks, months, years, learning new things, experimenting, discovering. And it's wonderful. You have fun in ways you never knew existed.

However, if you're not careful, it can hit you. The desire to learn how to do things you have no intention of ever using, just to learn them. You've never been near a spreadsheet, but you find yourself in a store buying a spreadsheet program, learning what statistical formulas are, even though you don't believe statistics.

And then you're lost. You spend all your time in the quest to master software, to know its ins-and-outs, and you forget that you originally got the computer so you'd never have to retype anything ever again.

Therein lies the danger. Not with the fun. But with forgetting what you originally obtained a computer to do. With forgetting everything but the computer.

Then slowly, almost imperceptibly, the unthinkable happens. Before you know it, you've become:

A SLAVE TO TECHNOLOGY.

```
[Font:Zapf Humanist Roman 14pt (ASCII) (Port) (FW)]
[Wrd/Ltr Spacing:Optimal,200% of Optimal][ITALC]
Cash in the Real World[italc]
[Wrd/Ltr Spacing:Optimal,Optimal][AdvUp:0.1"][HRt]
[HLine:Left & Right,6.55",0.1",100%][Tab Set:3.33",5.7"][HRt]
[HRt]
[Font:Zapf Humanist Bold 30pt (ASCII) (Port) (FW)][Flsh Rt]
Making it Count[C/A/Flrt]
[HRt]
[Font:Zapf Humanist Roman 14pt (ASCII) (Port) (FW)]
[Col Def:3,1.25",2.75",3",5.3",5.5",7.8"][Col On][HRt]
[HRt]
[HRt]
[HRt]
[Figure:2;FI0143.CGM;]<HB>[AdvUp:0.2"][Figure:3;COINS.WPG;]<HB>
[HPg][Ln Height:0.19"][Usr Opt]<G100>
[Usr Box:1;;]<TC VB SB .1 .1>{This is the square bullet}
[Font:Zapf Humanist Bold 18pt (ASCII) (Port) (FW)]
Time, Money[HRt]and Com-puters[Ln Height:0.22"][HRt]
[Font:Zapf Humanist Italic 14pt (ASCII) (Port) (FW)](or how to use one[HRt]
[Ln Height:0.19"][Font:Zapf Humanist Roman 12pt (ASCII) (Port) (FW)][Just On][AdvDn:0.2"]
[VLine:Column 1,3.13",7.21",.01c,100%]"Time is Money...
```

❖ *Cover pages — Butterfly*

Experience Level: ***Easy***

- **Fonts:** Bitstream Galliard, 14 pt
- **Graphics:** Dynamic Graphics Desktop Art, Four Seasons, edited with PC Paintbrush Plus
- **Printer:** Hewlett-Packard LaserJet II

Notes: This graphic is bitmapped at only 75 dpi. Because the resolution is so low, there's no sense to print the page with graphics quality set to high. If it's going to be jagged, you might as well make the most of it. Actually, this should have been either smoother, or more jagged. If the picture of the butterfly had been line-art, I could have scaled it to any size without a loss of quality.

```
[Fig Opt]<BOOOO>{Oooh, Scary} [Figure:1;BUTTERFL.PCC;]<TA VF WN>{This is the
box around the page}[HRt]
[HRt]
[HRt]
```

This year we'll

Sting Like A Bee

BFD International

Annual Report

1989

[Cntr][Font:ITC Galliard Bold 14pt (ASCII) (Port) (FW)]
[Wrd/Ltr Spacing:Optimal,150% of Optimal]
This year we'll[C/A/Flrt][HRt]
[HRt]
[Cntr][BOLD][Font:ITC Galliard Italic 36pt (ASCII) (Port) (FW)]Sting Like A Bee[C/A/Flrt][bold][HRt]
[Font:ITC Galliard Bold Italic 18pt (ASCII) (Port) (FW)][HRt]
[Wrd/Ltr Spacing:Optimal,Optimal][Cntr]BFD International[C/A/Flrt][HRt]
[Font:ITC Galliard Italic 18pt (ASCII) (Port) (FW)]
[Cntr]Annual Report[C/A/Flrt]
[HRt]
[Cntr]1989[C/A/Flrt][HRt]
[HRt] {*Press [HRt five more times)*
[Tab Set:3",5.5"][AdvDn:0.1"][Font:ITC Galliard Bold 14pt (Port) (FW)]
[Tab]CEO's Statement[Align]3[C/A/Flrt][HRt]
[Tab]Big Bucks[Align]5[C/A/Flrt][HRt]
[Tab]Takeover Attempts[Align]7[C/A/Flrt][HRt]
[Tab]Five Year Plan[Align]9[C/A/Flrt][SPg]

❖ *Report/Newsletter — BFD International*

Experience Level: ***Intermediate***

- **Fonts:** Bitstream Futura Light, Condensed, & Extra Black, 11 pt
- **Graphics:** Harvard Graphics
- **Printer:** Hewlett-Packard LaserJet II

Notes: Even without the chart, these pages are sharp. Business-like without being dull, stylish without being overly-trendy. They have a subtle insouciance, not unlike a spicy little Diverstrimeiner. Anyway it's a good example of how pages can be interesting even without graphics, and how something as simple as a header can bring continuity, style, and increased corporate (or personal) awareness to a document. Don't try to figure the graph out, it means nothing (no, it means less than nothing as it's really the wrong kind of graph to use). But what the hay, it's impressive.

[T/B Mar:1",0.25"][W/O Off][HRt][HLine:Left,2.04",0.05",100%][HRt]
[HRt]
[Font:Futura Extra Black 72pt (ASCII) (Port) (FW)]BFD[HRt]
[AdvUp:0.3"][Font:Futura Light 11pt (ASCII) (Port) (FW)]
[BOLD][Wrd/Ltr Spacing:Optimal,220% of Optimal]International
[Wrd/Ltr Spacing:Optimal,Optimal][bold][HRt]

5 Year Plan

'89

[HLine:Left & Right,6.5",0.05",20%][HLine:Left,2.04",0.05",100%][HRt]
[HRt]
[Flsh Rt][Font:Futura Condensed Medium 18pt (Port) (FW)]
[Wrd/Ltr Spacing:150% of Optimal,150% of Optimal]5 Year Plan[C/A/Flrt][Wrd/Ltr Spacing:Optimal,Optimal]
[Font:Futura Condensed Medium 14pt (ASCII) (Port) (FW)][HRt]
[HRt]{23, don't count 'em, 23 returns in all}
[Flsh Rt][Font:Futura Extra Black 72pt (Port) (FW)]'89[C/A/Flrt][HRt]
[AdvUp:0.2"][HLine:Right,1.71",0.05",100%][HPg]

❖ *PAGE 2*

[Font:Futura Light 12pt (ASCII) (Port) (FW)][T/B Mar:1",1"]
[Hyph On][Header A:2;]{See below for complete header}[Just On]
[Col Def:2,1.5",3.9",4.15",7.5"][Col On][Tab Set:1.75",4.63"]
[Fig Opt]<BNNEO>
[Figure:1;US-THEM.CGM;]<TA VB HC2B>{graph}
[Style On:heading][BOLD]Take The Money & Run[bold][HRt]
[Style Off:heading][HRt]

Take The Money & Run

By B. Friedreich Dunn, CEO

Let's face it, greed is hip. Ron & Nancy have made conspicuous consumption the Eighties replacement for Jimmy and Rosalyn's unpopular social consciousness and civic responsibility.

And why not? It works. Who wants to think about the homeless when they can think about remodelling their home? Who cares about the needy when they need a new VCR?

All those poor, sick people are downers; sitting around on the street, making things so dirty you don't even want to take the Mercedes out anymore.

So we at BFD have the alternative. Cocooning is the hot buzz word at the moment, and who better than us to capitalize on it, and wring every last cent possible from this burgeoning market.

This year we've created two wholly-owned subsidiaries: *BFD-TV* and *Serf-City*. The first is dedicated to the new breed of Americans who can entertain themselves at home. They bring back the American ideal of self-sufficiency.

BFD-TV is a combined cable channel, and video tape delivery service. The customer doesn't even have to decide what they want to watch. First, our computerized *Personality-Probe* runs a battery of psychological tests on the customer. Not only does the customer not have to make the difficult decision as to what they want to watch, our system even knows when they want to watch.

The cable arm of *BFD-TV* provides an eclectic mix of programming, consisting of whatever we could get the cheapest. Of course, we are heralding this programming mix as "MacroTV" a clinically-designed system that stimulates, educates, and decorates.

Serf-City is an entirely new concept in personal services. While we live in a "service economy," it seems that good service is hard to find.

For about the same amount as you'd pay monthly on a Range Rover, Serf-City provides a 24-hour hotline. Anything a client wants (within legal limits), we'll get for them.

In our test market, Serf-City was deemed "Indispensable" by 75 percent of the users within the first month. Everything from groceries to plastic surgeons—all the necessities of life are brought to your door within 30 minutes (or you pay nothing). You can't buy time, but you can buy convenience: someone to go to the dry

Celebrate! We've made "Them" look like dog food!

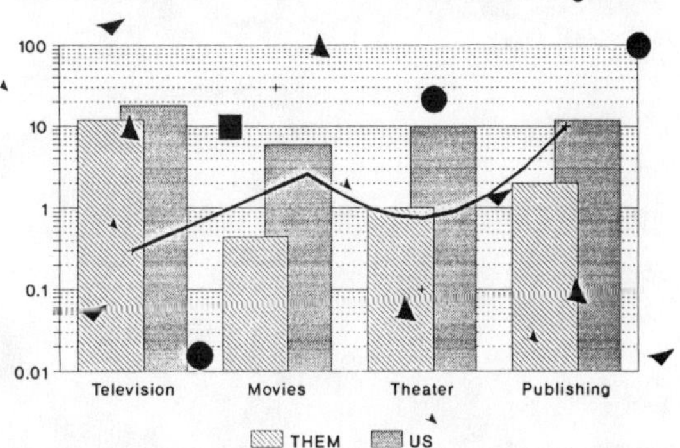

❖ PAGE 3

Everything was automatic, except for the readout, which is text in a graphics figure box. The ruling lines were set with the Figure Options on page 2.

HEADER: {This contains the company logo which automatically prints on each page}
[L/R Mar:0.75",1"][HLine:Left,0.85",0.03",100%][HRt]
[AdvDn:0.15"][Font:Futura Extra Black 30pt (ASCII) (Port) (FW)]BFD[HRt]
[AdvUp:0.15"][Font:Futura Light 11pt (ASCII) (Port) (FW)]International
[Flsh Rt][Font:Futura Condensed Medium 14pt (Port) (FW)] Page ^ B[C/A/Flrt][HRt]
[HLine:Left,0.85",0.03",100%][HLine:Left & Right,6.75",0.03",20%][HRt]
[VLine:1.25",2.19",7.81",0.01",100%]

Paired Style for Heading
[HLine:Left,1.88",0.03",100%][AdvDn:0.1"][HRt]
[Font:Futura Condensed Medium 18pt (ASCII) (Port) (FW)] [Comment]

cleaner, someone to massage your feet, someone to read bed-time stories to you, whatever.

Serf-City has the potential to change the way people live, and certainly change the way we live (as it requires minimal overhead, yet has maximum profit potential).

Last year it was "excellence," this year it's profits. Wait until you see what we've got up our collective sleeves for the next five years. Huge unjustified profits.

Last, but certainly not least, this year we will launch a new line of personal accessories. The cornerstone to this entire product line is called ''Orb.'' Developed by a noted Dutch psychiatrist (in co-operation with Jackie Collins), *Orb* is the ultimate personal codicil.

Fundamentally, the product is as simple as baby food for adults. The product helps adults to re-live their childhood, but it's also great for commuters, because it doesn't spill. What's more, it's better for your teeth than sucking your thumb.

Orb doubles as a flask or canteen. It can be used be used to sprinkle vinegar on salads. Unbreakable and dishwasher safe, *Orb* helps improve the reflexes and instills a feeling of relaxation and security. Deluxe models are packaged with a small blue blanket.

So much for our plans. As always, or overriding goal, our main ambition, the thing that guides us through those brutal union-bashing sessions is *Money*. People talk about it like it's a dirty word. You're not supposed to admit you like it, you're not supposed to admit you want it, and whatever you do, don't admit that you like making it.

Balderdash. You can like it, you can want it, and you can enjoy making it. But if you're smart, the thing you'll enjoy most is making the most of it.

Something for Nothing, was our motto this year. ''Value for Money'' is passe, but according to our market research, that's what *everyone* wanted. We at BFD were ready to give it to them.

Unfortunately, our demographics sucked the big one, and while the supply was there, the demand wasn't. What went wrong? That's what we asked ourselves all spring. The answer came in the form of my 12 year old daughter. ''Dad, have you lost your marbles? Everyone wants it, but everyone also knows you can't get it. Who'd be taken in by such hype?'' Who indeed? We were. Seeing how Melissa saw right through our $250,000 PR firm's supposed findings, we thought we'd promote her to VP of Marketing. After all, she was exactly the market we were going for: pre-teens, teens, and other minimal IQ individuals.

Melissa's first edict was that we had to hire someone ''neato'' to be our spokesman. Barry Manilow was ruled out immediately with

❖ Invoice — Classical Accoutrements

Experience Level: **Intermediate**

- Fonts: Bitstream Zapf Calligraphic (Palatino) 12 pt
- **Graphics:** Publisher's PicturePak-CGM, Sales/Marketing
- **Printer:** Hewlett-Packard LaserJet II

Notes: Here's another lemon/lemon-aid page. I wanted thin dotted lines between all the columns and the one after "unit price" wouldn't print for love, money, or threats of bodily harm. I made it a solid line and not only did it print, it looked better. I also included the somewhat complex Item/Description part of the page (including vertical rules) in a style, so it wouldn't be so easy to mess up. The style contains an "Advance to Line" code to insure it's always at the right place on the page for the vertical rules. This page successfully used WordPerfect's math feature to do the calculations. I don't recommend using WordPerfect as a database for invoices, however. I keep a separate database, and then use WordPerfect's mail merge to print out snappy look invoices.

[Figure:1;;]<TA VF WN>[L/R Mar:1.25",1.25"]
[T/B Mar:1.25",1.25"][Fig Opt]<BNNNN PAO>
[Figure:2;SA0128.CGM;]<TP HR SW 2.5>{The company address is a caption above the graphics box}
[Style On:form]I n v o i c e[Style Off:form][HRt]
[HRt]
[Style On:form]Date:[bold][sm cap][Style Off:form][Date:3, 1,4][HRt]
[HRt]
[Style On:form]Invoice #:[Style Off:form] 880771[HRt]
[HRt]
[Tab Set: 4.5]

Open Style for Items
[AdvToLn:5.5"][Tab Set:2",4",5",6.25"][VLine:6.1",5.5",4.25",1w,100%]
[VLine:1.9",5.5",4.25",1w,20%][VLine:3.9",5.5",4.25",1w,20%]
[VLine:4.9",5.5",4.25",1w,20%][VLine:6.15",5.5",4.25",1w,20%]
[LARGE][BOLD][SM CAP]Item[Tab]Description[Tab]Quan
[Tab]Unit Price[Flsh Rt]Amount[C/A/Flrt][sm cap][bold][large][HRt]
[HLine:Left & Right,6",0.05",100%][Tab Set:2",4.25",5.55",6.85"][HRt]
[HRt]

Paired Style for Form (Headings on Form)
[LARGE][BOLD][SM CAP] [Comment]

INVOICE

DATE: Jan. 2, 1989

INVOICE #: 880771

TERMS: Due Yesterday

CLASSICAL ACCOUTREMENTS
710 N. BUPKISS PKWY.
HELEN OF TROY, PA 15219
412-555-1206

BILL TO:
Wilton Veneer
MetroSpace Inc.
2117 Placido Domingo Place
Newbury, CT, 10101
(201) 555-5555

SHIP TO:
Erica Kane
17 Glen Mar Oaks
Pine Valley, PA, 20123
(407) 555-2333

ITEM	DESCRIPTION	QUAN	UNIT PRICE	AMOUNT
			Discount 10%	
435S	Eschucian Plate	1	$327.50	$294.75
123B	Side Chair	3	$755.22	$2,039.09
876R	Warhol Xeroxes	4	$12,112.95	$43,606.62
	TOTAL			**$45,940.46**

❖ Catalog — Robot-a-Rama

Experience Level: ***Easy***

- **Fonts:** Bitstream Amerigo, 12pt
- **Graphics:** Left: MGI Publisher's PicturePak-CGM, Finance/Administration; middle & right: Metro Image Base
- **Printer:** Hewlett-Packard LaserJet II

Notes: This is an extremely easy page to do, and it's good for catalogs or listings that have long descriptions. While the captions don't all look like they're the same length, I've added an extra return on the second one so WordPerfect considers it the same length. If you don't do that, the columns underneath won't all start on the same line.

```
[Hyph On][T/B Mar:1",0.75"][L/R Mar:1.25",1"]
[Footer A:2;[HLine:Left & Right,6.25",0.01",100%]
[Just Off][Font:Bitstrm Amerigo Bold 48pt (Port) (FW)]
[Wrd/Ltr Spacing:Optimal,160% of Optimal]
[Cntr]Robot[-]a[-]Rama
[Font:Bitstrm Amerigo Roman 11pt (ASCII) (Port) (FW)]
[Wrd/Ltr Spacing:Optimal,Optimal][C/A/Flrt][HRt]
[HRt][AdvUp:0.2"]
[Col Def:3,1.25",3.16",3.41",5.33",5.58",7.5"]<TN D .25>
[Col On][VLine:Column1,2.04",8.02",0.01",100%]
[VLine:Column 2,2.04",8.02",0.01",100%]
[Figure:1;FI0249.CGM;]<TP HB SH 1.97>
{Caption has [AdvDn:0.1"]}
[Ln Height:0.16"][Style On:Raised Cap]B[Style Off:Raised Cap]ig News!
```

Paired Style for Raised Cap

```
[Font:Bitstrm Amerigo Bold 24pt (ASCII) (Port) (FW)] [Comment]
```

Open Style for Paragraph Indents

```
[AdvRgt:0.5"]
```

Robot-a-Rama

The Original, the Classic, the One and Only FiFi, as French as an android gets.

Big News! Robo-Fax announcess three new models, guaranteed to knock the socks off Robo-cops.

That's right—not one, not two, but three new house-keeping automatons to choose from.

Fifi is our original model, now **priced to sell, sell, sell.** She cooks, cleans, and tickles humans with her simulated ostrich feather duster.

FiFi may be getting a little long in the transistor, but she's a proven design, kind of like the Dodge Dart of the Android set.

FiFi was the **winner of the 1997 Antarctica World's Fair** Household Robotics competition. Rumor has it that she was modeled after Catherine Denuve, and that's why her head constantly tilts to one side.

She may be a little on the homely side, but you weren't going to take her out dancing... were you?

LaWanda, a hot little number (actually serial # 5117).

Ultra feminine. Now here's an android to take dancing! There'll be a hot time in the old town tonight when you bring home LaWanda to LaBamba.

LaWanda is specially engineered to withstand extensive shimmying and shaking without breaking.

PlayDroid magazine called LaWanda **"A hot little number in lycra and stainless steel."**

She's a combination drill-sergeant/belly-dancer, and is pre-programmed to kill intruders.

While LaWanda is a little lax on the dustballs, she'll keep you hopping. A few of our beta testers have stated that it's hard to keep up with her, but we didn't hear any complaints.

Andrew Roid, the latest thing in male models. Anatomically correct.

You know a good man's hard to find, but who needs a man when they can have our latest robotic model. He kills scary insets, does household repairs, and doesn't complain about your hair or your cooking. *What more you could want?*

Reliability? You may never have met a male before who was reliable, but Andy's been programmed to run for years without routine maintenance. We guarantee you won't even have to raise his hood for the first 12 months or 12,000 miles.

Power? You got it. Able to leap tall buildings, move heavy refrigerators, even act as a nautilus machine/expert trainer.

Handling? Your wish is his command—it's easy to wrap him around your little finger.

Price? Less than you think for. All with a full 90 minute warranty.

❖ *Documentation — Pie Throwing*

Experience Level: ***Easy***

- **Fonts:** Bitstream Hammersmith (Gill Sans) 12 pt
- **Graphics:** Scanned from Dynamic Graphics paper clip-art using a Hewlett-Packard ScanJet and GEM Scan software
- **Printer:** Hewlett-Packard LaserJet II

Notes: This page uses parallel columns and is genuinely easy to create. Instead of graphics, you could use keystrokes (with SoftCraft's wonderful KeyCap font) or make the first column wider and use this area for screen dumps. While I've used Hammersmith (Gill Sans) for headlines and subheads in this book, it is an extremely popular typeface for body copy as well, especially in England and Europe. It's a sans serif font with a lot of character, modern without being cold.

```
[Fig Opt]<BNNNN>[Just On][T/B Mar:1",0.75"]
[L/R Mar:1.25",0.75"][L/R Mar:0.75",1.25"]
[Footer B:4;[Open Style:footer]
[Par Num Def][Just Lim:60,110][Style On:Headline]Pie throwing for fun & profit[Style
Off:Headline][HRt]
[HRt]
[Ln Height:0.19"][Col Def:2,0.75",1.75",2",7.25"][Col On][Style On:sidehead]
[LARGE]R[large]eady[HRt]
[HRt]
[Figure:1;BAKERR.PCC;]<TP HB>[HRt]
[HRt]
[HRt]
[Style Off:sidehead][HPg]
```

Paired Style for Headline

```
[Font:Hammersmith Roman 36pt (ASCII) (Port) (FW)] [Comment]
```

Paired style for Headline

```
[Font:Hammersmith Roman 36pt (ASCII) (Port) (FW)][BOLD]. [Comment]
```

Paired style for Sideheads

```
 [HLine:Left,1",0.01",100%][HRt][JustOff]
[Wrd/Ltr Spacing:150% of Optimal,150% ofOptimal]
[Font:Hammersmith Italic 18pt (ASCII) (Port)(FW)] [Comment]
```

Paired style for Readout

```
[Ln Height:Auto][AdvDn:0.1"]
[Font:Hammersmith Roman 14pt (ASCII) (Port) (FW)]
[Comment]
[AdvDn:0.1"][Ln Height:0.19"]
```

4. Pie throwing for fun & profit

Ready

Pie throwing is a classic piece of schtik, invented by Cleopatra as a way to pass the time when Marc Anthony was away. It became a favorite of Greek playwrights, and its first known inclusion in dramatic form was in Aristophanes' "The Birds." Pie throwing in film and television reached its apex with Laurel & Hardy, and later, Soupy Sales.

First, you must obtain a pie. The cream variety is preferable to the fruit variety, for several of the reasons listed below.

- It is lighter, and more easily maneuverable.
- It makes a stronger visual impression.
- It is easier to clean up.
- It doesn't stain clothing.
- Cream is more fun to lick off of one's face.

Throwing a pie is a lot like throwing a tantrum, only requiring choreography and a keener aim.

Aim...

When choosing a subject to be the recipient of a pie in the face, you are looking for someone who won't object too much.

1. The subject will be the object of much speculation about his/her level of sportsmanship, so try to choose someone who doesn't have a proven track record of getting even.
2. This person should not be a direct superior with the power to hire and fire (unless, of course, this is no longer a problem, and is in fact, the catalyst for the episode. In that case, go for it—what have you got to lose?).

WARNING: Choose your subjects carefully. Not all personality types react positively to pie attacks. Never, under any circumstances, throw a pie at the President, or President elect. Secret Service agents will wrestle you to the ground, and besides getting a lot of unwanted media attention, your FBI file will expand by leaps and bounds. The Vice President however, is fair game.

Fire!

PIE VELOCITY AND TRAJECTORY

Peanut Butter has a velocity of 120% and a -25° angle correction is advised. Mud pies have a velocity of 77% and a +16° angle correction is needed. Key Lime pie, always a big favorite with the menfolk, has a velocity of 82% and requires a +13° angle correction. Be sure to adjust the trajectory, depending on what kind of pie you are using. If using a cream pie, not as much velocity will be necessary as if using a fruit pie.

Different pies will create different stains, and require different methods for removal of those stains. The easiest stain to remove is created by the Lemon Chiffon pie, and is easily removed with lemon dishwashing liquid. Banana Cream pie stains can be removed with white wine, and Blueberry pie stains are impossible to remove.

[Font:Hammersmith Roman 11pt (ASCII) (Port) (FW)]
Open style for Footer
[HLine:Left & Right,6.5",0.05",100%][HRt]
[AdvDn:0.1"][Font:Hammersmith Roman 11pt (ASCII) (Port) (FW)]Pie Throwing Manual[Flsh Rt] ^ B

❖ *Menu — Dutch Pancake House*

Experience Level: ***Easy***

- **Fonts:** Weaver Graphics BG (Benguiat) 14pt, Weaver Dingbats
- **Graphics:** Corner border: Arts & Letters; Pancake: Metro Image Base
- **Printer:** Hewlett-Packard LaserJet II

Notes: Type the entire menu, then center it at once by blocking it, then pressing SHIFT-F6. Benguiat is a beautiful typeface, perfect for short pieces of text such as this. Don't use it to set the type for an entire book or magazine, though.

[L/R Mar:1.25",1"][Fig Opt]<BNNNN>
[Figure:1;CORNER4.CGM;]<TA VT HML SW 1.5 WN>
[Figure:2;CORNER4.CGM;]<TA VT HMR SW 1.5 WN>
[Figure:3;CORNER4.CGM;]<TA VB HML SW 1.5 WN>
[Figure:4;CORNER4.CGM;]<TA VB HMR SW 1.5 WN>
[Figure:5;PANCAKE.WPG;]<HC SW 2>[HRt]
[HRt] {*Press [HRt eight more times*}
[BOLD][Font:Benguiat 30pt (SF) (LF)][Cntr]M[Style On:dingbat] u
[Style Off:dingbat] E [Style On:dingbat]u[Style Off:dingbat] N
[Style On:dingbat]u[Style Off:dingbat] U[C/A/Flrt][bold][HRt]
[Font:Benguiat 14pt (SF) (LF)]
KES[C/A/Flrt][large][bold][Wrd/Ltr Spacing:Optimal,Optimal][HRt]
[AdvDn:0.1"][Cntr]Ham & Cheese $4.75[C/A/Flrt][HRt]

Paired Style for dingbat (diamonds)
[Font:Zapf Dingbats 14pt (SF) (LF)][AdvUp:0.06"]
[Comment]
[AdvDn:0.06"]
{The advance moves the dingbats up so they print in the middle of the line, rather than on the baseline.}

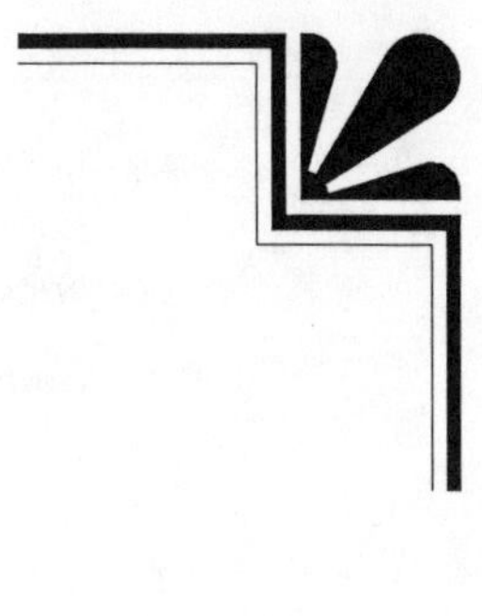

M ◆ E ◆ N ◆ U

SAVORY PANCAKES

Ham & Cheese $4.75
Gouda or Edam, your choice

Smoked Sausage $4.50
With that farm-fresh flavor

SWEET PANCAKES

Apple $3.75
Warm, cinnamon-spiced apples

Blueberry $3.75
Fresh blueberries, direct from Maine

Raspberry $3.75
Ripe, luscious red berries

Met slagroom (whipped cream) add $1.50

My Old Dutch Pancake House

We reserve the right to serve refuse to anyone.

❖ Brochure — Travel

Experience Level: ***Challenging/Painful***

- **Fonts:** Weaver Friz Quadrata 12pt (SoftCraft LaserFonts Manager installed the fonts, and created the outline and shadow versions of this font)
- **Graphics:** MGI Publisher's PicturePak-CGM, Sales/Marketing
- **Printer:** Hewlett-Packard LaserJet II

Notes: This is a very complicated, very busy layout. It took a long time to figure out and perfect. I almost didn't use it in this book because it was verging on "sequin," but if you like this kind of look, here's proof that you can get it. If you were going to use this over and over, it would be worth the investment, as you'd only need to insert new text and graphics. If you wanted to use photos, you could scan them (use TIF format for photos) or just leave spaces and have the printer insert the halftones.

The "Astral Travel" logo uses the Option Printer Word Spacing function to an extreme, with a different amount of space between each letter, starting at 200% and working it's way down to 100% by the end of "Travel." Very over the top.

I haven't included the specs for all the pictures because this book is too long as it is. All are figures with no lines around. Mt. Rushmore and the cruise ship have wrap turned off.

```
[W/O Off][T/B Mar:0.5",0.5"][T/B Mar:1",0.25"][L/R Mar:1",0.5"]
[Fig Opt]<BNNNN>[Figure:1;SA0199.CGM;]<TP HR SH .95>
[HRt]
[Font:Friz Quadrata 30pt (SC)][OUTLN]
[Wrd/Ltr Spacing:Optimal,200% of Optimal]Astral
[Wrd/Ltr Spacing:Optimal,150% of Optimal][outln][SHADW]T
[Wrd/Ltr Spacing:Optimal,140% of Optimal]r
[Wrd/Ltr Spacing:Optimal,130% of Optimal]a
[Wrd/Ltr Spacing:Optimal,120% of Optimal]v
[Wrd/Ltr Spacing:Optimal,110% of Optimal]e
[Wrd/Ltr Spacing:Optimal,Optimal]l[shadw]
[Wrd/Ltr Spacing:Optimal,Optimal]Agents[HRt]
[Font:Friz Quadrata 14pt (SC)]SUMMER BULLETIN[HRt]
[Font:Friz Quadrata 11pt (SC)]Vol. 1. No. 33
"Literally, the Vacation of Your Dreams"
{Spaces, yes spaces to move date to the right}August 8, 1988
[Font:Friz Quadrata 11pt (SC)][HRt]
[HLine:Left & Right,7",0.01",100%][HRt]
[HRt] {Press another [HRt]
[Col Def:4,1",2.5",2.7",5.3",5.4",5.9",6.1",8"]<TP>[Col On]
[Style On:Sidehead]Straighten[HRt]up and Fly[SRt] {Continued...}
```

Astral Travel Agents

SUMMER BULLETIN
Vol. 1. No. 33 "Literally, the Vacation of Your Dreams" August 8, 1988

Straighten up and Fly Right

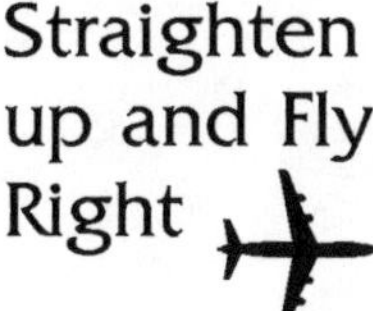

Airports. Reservations. Certain Restrictions may apply. Customs. Long flights with crying babies. Lost luggage. These are a few of the things that make travel, something that ought to be a pleasure, a pain.

That's where we at **Astral**Travel come in: to give you the vacation of your dreams (or perhaps literally, in your dreams).

We supply everything you'll need, from maps of the area, to lists of the best places to eat. There's never an accommodation problem because you never stay overnight!

Astral-Travel: Your passport to a world of potential

Astral travel is fast and easy. And don't worry about safety—time tested by Yogi's over the last three thousand years, at last you'll get exactly what you want—without ever leaving home.

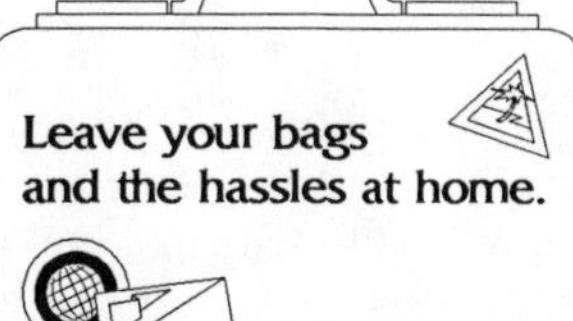

Leave your bags and the hassles at home.

There's more than one way to see the sights. How about from the inside of Teddy Roosevelt's nose? Or from an orbit of 25,000 miles above the Earth?

Travel back to ancient Rome and learn the true meaning of "Lorem ipsum dolor sit."

AstralTravel will make sure you'll see the world like you've never seen it before.

Whether it's by stream of consciousness or steam train, Astral-Travel's the only way to fly!

You're the top with Astral-Travel!

Fully guided **Astral**Tours start at only $50 per hour once you've completed our $450 weekend training seminar (includes a vegetarian lunch for both days, and a **AT** beach towel for meditation).

In as little as six hours, Frequent Flyers can start to earn bonus trips to all those out-of-this-world places.

Sea the USA!

Let Mark Twain take you steamboating on the Mississippi. Thrill to the Bermuda Triangle at midnight. See Davy Jones in his locker. Ain't no mountain high enough, Ain't no valley low enough, nothing is ever **out of the question,** nothing is ever **out of your reach.** The only limit is your own imagination. Ask Shirley McClaine, she'll tell you, there's nothing like it.

Around the World in 80 ways

Ride a dolphin to Atlantis, a Blue whale to the coast of Mexico, or just take Shamu for a ride around the tank. **Astral**Travel is open 24 hours a day, for everything from a daydream to a full night's dream. But rest assured, you'll never have a nightmare.

AstralTravel is a fully bonded member of the AAA, the Astral Agent's Association

Paired Style for Sideheads
[Font:Friz Quadrata 18pt (SC)][Comment]
Open Style for Captions
[Font:Friz Quadrata 9pt (SC)][Comment]

❖ *Price List — KidStuff*

Experience Level: ***Easier than it looks. Intermediate***

- **Fonts:** Bitstream Cooper Light 11pt, Bitsream Cooper Black
- **Printer:** Hewlett-Packard LaserJet II

Notes: The giant exclamation point on the right consists of a WordPerfect graphics box with a 100% blackground, and a 30 point Cooper Black period. The bullets are also 30 pt Cooper Black periods, shifted up .06" by a style. The KIDstuff logo combines 30 pt Cooper Black for the "KID" with 36 pt Cooper light for the "stuff"

[T/B Mar:1",0.75"][L/R Mar:1",0.75"]
[Fig Opt]<G100>Figure:1;;]<TA VT HMR SB .2 7.5 WN>
[Fig Opt]<G0>[Figure:2;;]<TA V8.4 HMR SB .2 .3 WN>
[L/R Mar:1.25",1.25"]
[Footer A:2; ...]<LH [ENTER] [ENTER]>
[Font:Bitstream Cooper Black 30pt (ASCII) (Port) (FW)]
[Flsh Rt]KID[Font:Bitstream Cooper Light 36pt (Port)(FW)]
stuff[Font:Bitstream Cooper Light Italic 18pt (Port)(FW)][C/A/Flrt][HRt]
[Flsh Rt]What's New![C/A/Flrt]
[Open Style:line][AdvUp:0.1"]
[Font:Bitstream Cooper Light 11pt (ASCII) (Port) (FW)]
[Tab Set:1.48",7.25"][Col Def:3,1.25",3.08",3.33",5.16",5.41",7.25"]
<TP D .25>[Col On][Style On:Name]

Paired Style for Name
[Ln Height:0.27"]
[Font:Bitstream Cooper Black 30pt (Port)(FW)]
[AdvUp:0.06"].[AdvDn:0.06"]
[Font:Bitstream Cooper Bold 18pt(ASCII) (Port) (FW)]
[Indent][Comment]
Open Style for Line (horizontal rules between products)
[HRt]
[HLine:Left & Right,6",0.01",100%][HRt]
[HRt]
[AdvDn:0.1"][AdvUp:0.1"]

KIDstuff

What's New!

• Barbi's Alfred Hitchcock Theatre

Enter Barbi's world of terror and the unknown. This horrific set includes Norman Bates and Brian DePalma dolls!

Quantity	Price
1	$33.50
5	$33.00
10	$23.50
25	$23.00

• Sticky Wickets

A fun way for kids to clean up their room. Sticky Wickets attract dustballs but are safe for pets!

Quantity	Price
1-10	$3.99
11-25	$2.99
REFILLS:	
10 per pack	$1.50

• Little Baby Peabrain

A perfectly charming but perfectly stupid little doll. Perfect for those pretend custody battles, and make believe surrogate parenthood!

Quantity	Price
1-10	$19.99
11-25	$17.99
26-100	$15.95

• CLOSE OUT!

Big sellers from past seasons we can't give away anymore. Yours for a song, even in Quantity 1!

SpaceSlime	$ .99
Nefarious Nutballs	$ .49
Dinky Little Dora	$1.25
Electro-Shock Experiment Kit	$4.99
Michael Jackson Makeup	$2.55
Ed Meese "Blinded Justice Kit"	$4.99
Piranha Pals	$1.99
Mary Hart Leg Waxing Set	$3.55

KIDstuff
(213)-555-1122

"Where great toys are *child's play!*"
Prices good through March 1990

❖ Resume — F. Scott Fitzgerald

Experience Level: ***Intermediate***

- Fonts: Pacific Data Products “Z” Font Cartridge, Tms Rmn 12pt
- Printer: Hewlett-Packard LaserJet

Notes: Here’s an example of how good a page can look with only relatively small font cartridge fonts and no graphics or artwork. The gray bar over the years is a WordPerfect User-defined box with wrap off, and the dotted lines are .1" tall graphics boxes inside a style.

```
[T/B Mar:1.5",1.5"][L/R Mar:1.25",1“][Font:Tms Rmn 14pt Bold (Z)]
[Wrd/Ltr Spacing:200% of Optimal,200% of Optimal]
F. Scott Fitzgerald[Font:Tms Rmn 12pt (Z)]
[Wrd/Ltr Spacing:Optimal,Optimal][HRt]
 [AdvDn:0.1“][HLine:Left,3.5",0.01”,100%][HRt]
[Font:Helv 12pt (Z)][AdvDn:0.1“]RESUME
[Font:Tms Rmn 12pt (Z)][HRt]
[Flsh Rt][ITALC]481 Laurel Avenue[C/A/Flrt][HRt]
[Flsh Rt]St. Paul, Minnesota[C/A/Flrt][HRt]
[Flsh Rt](330) 555[-]0924[C/A/Flrt][italc][HRt]
[Open Style:Horizontal[HRt]
[Col Def:2,1.5",3",3.25",7.25"][Col On]
[Style On:Subhead]Experience[Style Off:Subhead][HRt]
[HRt]
[Usr Opt]<G10>[Usr Box:1;;]<TA V3.25 HML SB.6 4.57 WN>
[AdvDn:0.1“][LARGE]1930[HRt] 1937[large][HPg]
```

Open Style Horizontal (for long solid lines:)

```
[AdvDn:0.1“][HLine:Left &Right,6.25",0.01”,100%]
[AdvDn:0.1“][HRt][HRt]
```

Paired Style for Subheads:

```
[Font:Helv 14pt Bold (Z)][Comment]
```

Paired Style for dotted lines

```
[Usr Opt]<BNNNO O0000.2>[Usr Box:1;;]<TP HR SB4.25 .1> [Comment]
```

F. Scott Fitzgerald

RESUME

481 Laurel Avenue
St. Paul, Minnesota
(330) 555-0924

Experience

1930 1937	Organized and conducted year-round social events for regular members of Hearst's International. Also arranged holiday programs and other fund raising drives for the beautiful and the damned.
1926 1929	Booked travel arrangements for yachting tours, museum days, seasonal picnics, and special "Rented is the Night" theater parties for Charles Scribner's Sons.
1922 1925	Extensively toured Europe, visited Babylon again. Researched and provided source material for quarterly newsletter listing new resorts and villas this side of paradise.
1917 1920	Entered military service. Member of the Army horse guards; aide-de-camp to Commanding General Monte Montgomery. Honorable discharge, 1920.

Education

Graduated Princeton University, 1917.

References

Jay Gatsby, East Egg, Long Island.
Dorothy Parker, Algonquin Hotel.

❖ *Calendar — Bunny Run Preschool*

Experience Level: ***Easier than it looks***

- **Fonts:** Bitstream Futura Light, Condensed, Extra Bold, 11 pt
- **Graphics:** Dynamic Graphics Desktop Art, Education; edited with PC Paintbrush Plus
- **Printer:** Hewlett-Packard LaserJet II

Notes: This really isn't that hard. It's simply seven parallel columns and a style. The style creates the extra-black date numbers, and a CONTROL-ENTER at the end of each day takes you to the next day. The only thing to remember is that no day can be longer than 6 lines. If you didn't use such big numbers, or used smaller body text, you could have more lines per day. The gray bar behind the date is the Redlining feature. On PostScript printer, redlining gives you gray text, rather than a gray overlay.

```
[T/B Mar:0.5",0.5"][L/R Mar:0.3",0.3"][FigOpt]<BNNNN>
[Figure:1;PAGE05ED.PCX;]<TP VL SH 1.4>
[Font:Futura Extra Black 30pt (ASCII) (Port) (FW)]
[Flsh Rt]Bunny Run Pre[-]School [C/A/Flrt][HRt]
[Font:Futura Condensed Medium 14pt (ASCII) (Port) (FW)]
[Flsh Rt]for Troubled Teens   [C/A/Flrt][HRt]
[HRt]
[Flsh Rt][REDLN]  S E P T E M B E R   1 9 9 9   [C/A/Flrt][redln][HRt]
[HRt]
[L/R Mar:0.3",0.3"][Font:Futura Light 11pt (ASCII) (Port) (FW)]
[Col Def:7,0.3",1.21",1.46",2.37",2.62",3.54",3.79",4.7",
 4.95",5.87",6.12",7.03",7.28",8.2"][Col On]
[Style On:Day of Week]Monday[HPg]
Tuesday[HPg]
Wednesday[HPg]
Thursdsay[HPg]
Friday[HPg]
Saturday[HPg][Col On]
[VLine:Column 1,2.63",7.86",1w,30%][VLine:Column 2,2.63",7.86",1w,30%]
[VLine:Column 3,2.63",7.86",1w,30%][VLine:Column 4,2.63",7.86",1w,30%]
[VLine:Column 5,2.63",7.86",1w",30%][VLine:Column 6,2.63",7.86",1w,30%]
[Ln Height:0.16"][Style On:#]1[Style Off:#][HRt]
School[SRt]
Begins--[SRt]
Psychologist[SRt]
on call[HPg]
[Style On:#]2[Style Off:#][HRt]
```

Bunny Run Pre-School

for Troubled Teens

SEPTEMBER 1999

Monday	Tuesday	Wednesday	Thurdsay	Friday	Saturday	Sunday
1 School Begins—Psychologist on call	**2** Nursery School dropouts on Parade	**3** Wet Nurse Round-up. Rabies Shots for all	**4** De-Weaning Training	**5** Basketball Practice-Prayer Meeting	**6** Fun with Inner Tubes! Keg Parties were never like this before!	**7** Save the Streptococci Campaign begins in Cafeteria
8 Let's all Wear A Wig Day!	**9** The 1 Minute Scuba Diver Visits (if he's still alive)	**10** RTD Bus Dodging! Don't forget your helmet!	**11** Cat Cleaning day! Bring a cat to our Tabby-mat!	**12**	**13** **Saturday the 14th Strikes Back** screens in Room 13	**14** Help the folks at Home: enforced chores, 3 credits
15 Kelp Massage for all 4th graders—wear swim trunks and goggles	**16** Out-Run a Shark at lunch! Win a Month's supply of ear-wax!	**17**	**18** Annette Funicello bares all!	**19** Rehearsals for 1st grade production of "Long Day's Journey into PooPoo"	**20** Trip to the Museum of Scouring Powder (bring Lunch and a dirty sink)	**21**
22 Rummage through Mommie's purse. Most embarassing secret wins a prize!	**23** Milk Monitor Elections today! Payola suggested	**24** Rummage through Daddy's underwear drawer. More prizes!	**25** Betting pool on Principal's trial closes at 5pm, PST	**27** Verdict in on Principal. Will he be convicted of embezzlement or return triumpant?	**28** *Gouda and Gherkin* day. The Famous Pop Duo performs at lunch	**30** Sweat-Sock extravaganza. Wear nothing but your best dress sweat socks!
31 Hey, what's going on here? This month only has 30 days	**Info:**	Our Motto: Bunny Run, Where the Turf meets the Smurfs	Did you change your underwear today?	Have you hugged your cleaning woman today?	Mucilage Eaters Club meets Tuesdays at 3 Paste Power!	

Nursery[SRt]
[Style On:#]2[Style Off:#][HRt]
Nursery[SRt]
School[SRt]
dropouts on[SRt]
Parade[HPg]
[Style On:#]3[Style Off:#][HRt]
Wet Nurse[SRt]
Paired Style for Day of Week
[Font:Futura Condensed Medium 14pt (ASCII) (Port) (FW)] [Comment]
Paired Style for # (big date number)
[Font:Futura Extra Black 30pt (Port)(FW)] [Comment]

Daniel Will-Harris

May 23, 1989

[L/R Mar:1",1"][Usr Opt]<G100>[Usr Box:1;;]
<TP VT HML S .1 .1>
[Usr Box:2;;]<TP VB HML S .1 .1>
[T/B Mar:1",0.5"][T/B Mar:1",0.75"][Usr Box:3;;]<TP VB HML S .1 .1>[Usr Opt]<G0>[Usr Box:4;SPLAT!.CGM;]<TP VB HMR S .1 .1>
[T/B Mar:1",0.75"][T/B Mar:1",0.65"]
[Footer A:3;[Cntr] ...]<type your return address>
[Fig Opt]<BNNNN>[Figure:1;DWH.CGM;[AdvDn:0.1"]<Insert your graphic logo. Use caption for your name. I've used Bodoni 14 point bold.>
[Font:Bodoni Bold 14pt (ASCII) (Port) (FW)] ...][Header A:4; ...]<the header contains the four user boxes so they will print on every page>[HRt]
[HRt]
[HRt]
[HRt]
[HRt]
[HRt]
[HLine:Center,2",0.03",100%][HRt]
[HRt]
[HRt]
[Cntr][Date:3 1, 4][C/A/Flrt][Ln Height:0.19"][HRt]
[Comment]<This should contain a note to yourself, telling you where to start typing the body of the letter>[L/R Mar:1.5",1.5"]

<NOTE: The DWH graphic was created in Freelance Plus. The Splat! is from Arts & Letters. The default font is Bitstream Fontware Bodoni 12 point. The page was printed on a Hewlett-Packard LaserJet II>

Box 480265, Los Angeles, CA 90048

5

Communicating by design

Graphic design basics

You're probably eager to delve into the technical wonders of WordPerfect, but don't get too excited just yet. Contrary to popular belief, you don't start desktop publishing by turning on your computer. You begin long before you even sit down at your computer. (This is the point where, if this was a movie, the screen would get all foggy and wavy and you'd know you were in for a flashback, or some other piece of information vital to understanding the plot...)

In order to become an accomplished desktop publisher with WordPerfect, you need to know a few things about graphic design. People expect magazines to have a certain appearance, while books have another look, and the more your publication resembles what people have come to expect, the more acceptance it will receive. All the sophisticated hardware and software in the world won't produce a truly effective (much less professional) document, newsletter, or other publication without a working knowledge of design fundamentals.

Remember that your number one concern is to *communicate.* It doesn't matter how flashy your publication looks if it doesn't get your message across. Don't risk readability for design. I'd rather have someone say, "I read it," than "Oh, doesn't that look hip, doesn't that look modern, doesn't that look pretty..." Remember architect Louis Sullivan's advice: "Form follows function."

However, don't be intimidated by this unfamiliar design territory. If you're not the artistic type, that's okay. You don't have to be able to draw to design a newsletter or flyer. You're not going to be drawing pictures; you're going to be putting type and artwork together, constructing an inviting, readable format, and that's something anyone can learn to do.

❖ Understanding the basics

The process of composing a page in order to attain a specific appearance is called "layout." Page layout simply refers to the arrangement of type and graphics. The most effective arrangement will attract the reader's attention and make the page easy to read.

All printed material, no matter how simple or elaborate, has to go through a layout process. A specific typestyle has to be chosen. That type has to be sized; the headlines are one size, the body text another. For a magazine or newspaper, one needs to decide about where to place an article on the page: at the top, the middle, or the bottom? Column widths have to be chosen—how many columns should be on the page? Should all the type be set at the same width? What about graphics? Should photos be one or two columns wide? Should they be boxed with a border? What about captions? Should they be set in bold, or italic, or in a different size than the body copy? All these choices have to be addressed with even the most elementary layout.

If wrestling with these types of decisions is foreign to you, don't be afraid. Once you understand the basics, it will be easier, but you will have to think in a way that may be new to you. If you have always focused on the meaning of words, start paying attention to the format of the words. Print is a highly visual medium, and you must notice how words "look."

What some books about desktop publishing, and many advertisements (especially Apple's), conveniently forget is that the whole idea is to produce documents which *don't* look desktop published. If you already know what you want beyond a shadow of a doubt, you can go directly to the step-by-step examples. If there are any shadows lurking in the corners of your mind, illuminate them here.

◆ Decisions, decisions

Your first step is to decide what kind of publication you are going to create. Even if your publication is already designed and you just want to produce it using WordPerfect, invest some time ensuring that your design is as fine as it can be. This entails more than simply deciding what kind of typefaces you'll use, or how many columns you want. You can't arrive at design decisions until you first answer some eternal questions.

Who is this publication intended for? Who will be reading it? Are they within your organization or outside of it? Have they ever heard of you before? Are they already interested in your organization, or do they have to be sold?

What do you want them to know? What's the single most important point you want them to remember/learn after reading your publication? Do you want to excite them? Warn them? Sell them? Calm them? The appearance of your publication can contribute to all of this.

What do they expect? People see so many publications that they have developed certain expectancies. Most news magazines have a certain look, and newsletters have a basic format. You don't have to be a slave to tradition, but you should realize that if your design doesn't bear some resemblance to the type of publication you're creating, you'll have to work harder to get your message across.

How much time/money do you have at your disposal? Your budget will dictate the limits on your hardware, graphics software, fonts, electronic clip-art, number of pages, printing and mailing costs, and most importantly, *time.*

How much material do you have? Do you have tons of text and no graphics, or pictures and no text? Do you have 20 pages of material to fill an eight-page issue? Do you have one page of material for an eight-page issue? Answer each of these questions and then find other publications similar to the type you are doing, and study them for type, graphics, layout. Are they easy to read? Are they attractive, or do they look like junk mail? Do you want to read them, or do you have to force yourself to read them? Compare what they did with what you want to do. Learn from their mistakes. If you weren't able to answer these questions, you didn't fail; you just need to learn some new ways of looking at all this.

All the great masters learned to paint by copying paintings they admired. Only after careful study did they attempt to paint on their own. See how your text and graphics would fit into someone else's format. Don't be afraid to let yourself be influenced by others who have gone before you. *Plagiarism is the sincerest form of flattery.* Actually, I don't believe in plagiarism (nepotism, or any other inconvenient "ism"), but being *influenced* by some other publication is fair and honest.

If you must use a design almost verbatim, give credit to the original designer or publication. Then you can join the likes of film director Brian DePalma, who claims that his Alfred Hitchcock-like films are an "homage" to the master. He doesn't pretend he invented the genre—he gives credit where it's due, and still manages to bask in the limelight, and/or cash the checks.

Of course, as composer Andrew Lloyd Webber well knows, critics may complain that your work is derivative, may even accuse you of plagiarism; still, most people respond to something familiar with a sense of "Oh, what a catchy tune..."

❖ *Fashion vs. style*

You may not have noticed, but graphic design has ever changing fashions, much the way clothing does. And like clothing, as soon as a fashion comes into widespread use, a new one has to be cooked up to make the old one obsolete, forcing people to spend even more money. But, there's a difference between fashion and style. Fashion comes and goes, but style never changes. There are classic clothes, and there is classic graphic design.

The art directors at Apple (or Apple's ad agency) are responsible for years of cutesy, cartoony pages which came to be equated with "desktop publishing." Their commercials were filled with serious looking executives, oohing and aahing over silly-looking pages; giant type, giant graphics, and graphs which resembled animals.

It was all very cute and all very impractical. Graphs in the shape of trout are all fine and good if you work in a seafood restaurant with a large, full-time art department, but for the most part they trade clarity for cute. And, worst of all, they are terribly hard to take seriously.

Now I clearly don't equate serious with important, but an awful lot of people do, and you aren't producing your pages for me, you're producing them for... *them.* It doesn't mean you can't have fun, it doesn't mean you can't introduce wit, it just means that the material should come first, the cute, second. Flash is certainly a legitimate way to attract attention, but once you have someone's attention, you don't want them to concentrate on the flash, but on the substance.

Just as in fashion, there's something called *classic* design. Pages that illuminate the text with a judicious mix of graphics and white space. They don't overpower the text, they add to it. The design of the page leads the reader's eye to the most important points, without calling attention to itself.

Jan White's *Editing by Design* is one of the bibles of classic design; it stresses design as a way to add to the text, not compete with it. (In fact, I was going to mention it in my introduction, but I wanted you to buy this book first. It does get the full treatment in the recommended reading list in the Appendix, though.)

Classic design doesn't come out and scream anything, but nudges, prods, and subtly guides the reader. Subtle doesn't mean wimpy—it means quietly, without making a spectacle of itself. And as with anything else, it's far more difficult to be subtle than to indulge in over-kill (one of my favorite pastimes).

If your publication is a flash in the pan, something which needs to say "now," just remember that it won't be long before people look at it and it will say "then." Check out some old magazines (especially the ads), and see how quickly they become dated. Classic pages don't show their age—they're useful for years, and keep repeating your message, day after day, year after year.

◆ What's a person to do?

So how can you decide what to do? As my wife Toni loves to tell me, "Put yourself in the other person's shoes." What do *you* want to see? What would persuade *you?* What would inform *you?*

While everyone in the world is not going to share your personal taste, it's a reasonable starting point. If you find something attractive, chances are other people will too.

But remember, the best page design results from having a reason for everything. That sounds awfully clinical and fairly obvious, but it's important to bear in mind. Everyone in the traditional publishing arena was scared to death of desktop publishing, because they thought the layman would use hundreds of different typestyles on a single page. While that hasn't happened in the extreme, there has been a notable proliferation of brain-dead pages.

Some people go wild when designing pages for the first time; they try to use too many different elements for no other reason except that they're available. When you ask the novice designer why there's a big picture above a story when the two are clearly not related, he's likely to say, "I don't know, I hadn't thought about it, it looked good there...," or some equally flimsy response.

Every professionally designed page you've seen in your life was designed for a reason: to grab your attention, to convey a specific message, to distract you from something else. And it's important to sit down and think about what really attracted you to the page in the first place.

◆ Subliminal messages

Now for the psychological slant: *why* do you like what you do? We often fail to notice just what specifically catches our eye. Mental associations are very powerful persuaders. IBM has an established corporate image which runs through every piece of printed material they produce. If you've ever studied their print advertisements, you'll notice that they always use the same typestyle, and usually the same ad layout: a big picture on top, with copy running along the bottom.

You may have also seen, but not realized, that smaller companies have often copied this format, right down to the typeface. At first you may look at their ad because you think it's from IBM. But even once you realize that it's not (and not everyone will), you will still link their company or product with IBM.

While it's illegal to use IBM's logo (or even their name without proper trademark disclaimers), there has yet to be any kind of "look and feel" case for printed pages, unless an actual name or logo was involved. If you want your magazine to look like *Time* magazine, go right ahead. Measure it, study it, use the same typefaces. You're not going to create any kind of image on your own, but people are immediately going to identify the look of the page with something they've seen before, something respected.

❖ *Does anyone need so many typefaces?*

There were, at last count, more typefaces than I could count. There are literally thousands of typefaces for the English language alone. While only a fraction of these are currently available, hundreds of old favorites and new typefaces keep materializing for desktop publishers each year. Commercial typesetting equipment and font companies, such as Bitstream and Compugraphic, promise that it won't be long before the entire library of fonts used by commercial typesetters is available for desktop publishing. (Gee, doesn't that sound like something you'd hear at a World's Fair? Me, I'm still waiting for the picture phones AT&T promised me in 1964. Whatever happened to AT&T?)

A colleague and friend, Allan Ayars, insists that the world could survive with only Times Roman and Helvetica. While he understands that variety is the spice of life, he still sighs in despair when he sees a new, but uninspired typeface. "The world needs a new typeface like it needs a new brand of toothpaste," he tells me. He refers to these useless, spineless imitations as *Upchuck #3,* as if to say it's a new variation on the ever-popular *Upchuck #1.* This is not unlike the soon to be released *Friday the 13th,* Part 17: *The Snoozing,* as opposed to the thoroughly original and hysterical *Saturday the 14th Strikes Back.*

Sometimes, when the face is uninspired, derivative or just plain ugly, I agree. Still, those simple 26 letters can take on countless, imaginative, distinctive forms. And even the minor difference between two typefaces can have a marked impact on a publication's appearance.

◆ Two of a kind, or behind the times

Even with the hundreds of typefaces available, certain ones dominate the scene. Times Roman and Helvetica are used for a large percentage of all printed materials. You could get by with just these two if you had to, because they typify the two basic styles of type, serif and sans serif.

A serif is the little doo-jiggy that sticks out at the ends of letters. Okay, okay, you've paid good money for this book and you deserve a better explanation than that. Allen Haley, a noted authority on type and Vice President of ITC (no relation to AT&T), put it this way: "A line crossing the main strokes of a character. It may take on many varieties." Satisfied? Sans serif type doesn't have any extensions at the ends of the letters. Here's a visual example.

Times Roman SERIF

Helvetica SANS SERIF

Many studies indicate that serif type, such as Times Roman, is much easier to read than sans serif type, such as Helvetica. The serifs are supposed to lead the eye from letter to letter. Other studies show that we read not letter by letter, but word by word, and the shape of words in serif type is more quickly recognizable. While no study is conclusive (do 8 out of 10 dentists really prefer sugarless gum for their patients who chew gum? Has anyone really asked this question of all dentists, or did they ask just 10 dentists?) you can perform a taste-test of your own. Print a page in Dutch (Times Roman), or Swiss (Helvetica), and compare the two. Depending on how wide the columns are, how long the lines of type are, and how much leading there is between the lines of type, one should be easier to read than the other—it's up to you.

What you'll find is what the latest studies have found: if you grew up reading serif types (as most Americans have), then you'll find serif types easier to read. If you grew up reading sans serif types (as many Europeans have), then you will find sans serif faces easier to read. (See the two full-page examples at the end of this chapter which illustrate these two typefaces and how to avoid some design mistakes.)

Sans serif type appears to be more modern because it is more modern. Sans serif typefaces started appearing early in the 20th Century. Some are more readable than others. Personally, the only sans serif types I can stand to read for any length of time are Gill Sans and Optima. Optima is technically sans serif, but it has a tapered design similar to a serif. Optima is not only one of the most readable sans serifs, it's also one of the most attractive.

For a newsletter, choosing a single type for the body copy, such as Times Roman, and a contrasting type such as Helvetica for headlines and subheadings allows for an effective combination. In general, serif fonts like Times Roman are easier to read when set in long columns of text than a sans serif font such as Helvetica would be. If you're not sure about which two fonts will work well together, don't mix them at all—use one font for both your text settings and your headings.

◆ Font follows function

More important than these awe-inspiring technical considerations is how the appearance of fonts dominates, influences, and guides the style of a publication, whether it be a letter, magazine, or a book.

Fonts are more than just letters and numbers. They're powerful symbols, with strong connotations. Their ability to stimulate your memory is often as powerful as their capacity to transmit ideas through language.

The next time you leaf through a magazine, consider how you recognize certain advertisements simply by the kind of typeface used. You don't have to stop and read the letters that form the company or product name; you instantly recognize the product or company just by the shape of the words.

In my first book, *Desktop Publishing with Style,* I said (and I quote—I mean who better to steal from than myself?): "Choosing a typeface is like choosing a mate: it says a lot about what you like or dislike, and communicates it to the rest of the world. While divorcing yourself from a typeface is less painful than from a human being, once people get used to associating you or your business with that typeface, it can cause more than a little confusion when you change to something new. People might stop and think, 'What else have they changed? Are they under new management?'" (I couldn't have said it any better myself—though many have tried, including a writer friend of mine while proofing this paragraph: "A face is literally a *face*—the face your publication shows to the world.")

❖ *Role playing*

Desktop publishers should be aware that the typeface they choose makes a statement about what they want to convey. They must be positive that the typeface matches the message they want to get across. If you're not sure about what will look best, it's perfectly acceptable to study other publications and see what they use.

I've played one of those "first-thing-that-comes-to-mind" games with some common typefaces. In general, if a font is suitable for body copy, it will work well in smaller sizes. Fonts that function as headlines are also known as display faces, and are attractive in large sizes. Type can be as decorative as any kind of illustration, and can communicate emotions as well as words. Here are some examples.

Times Roman — **Solid,** *practical,* ***unpretentious***

Effective for body copy and headlines. Newspapers, books, magazines, just about anything. Everyone uses it, and with good reason. It doesn't have a very distinct image, but it's efficient and easy-to-read. If you use Times Roman, also known as Dutch, for headlines, these typefaces work well for body text: Amerigo, Avant Garde Gothic, Benguiat, Bookman, Cooper Light, Friz Quadrata, Futura, Gill, Helvetica, Optima, Souvenir, and Univers.

Helvetica — **Serious,** *modern,* ***impersonal***

Suitable for signs, headlines, etc. I would hate to read a novel or even a magazine set in Helvetica, but reports or very businessy applications have a "serious" appearance when set in Helvetica. Also known as Swiss, as headline type it works well with these fonts as body text: Benguiat, Bodoni, Bookman,

Century Schoolbook, Cooper Light, Friz Quadrata, Garamond, Goudy Old Style, Korinna, Melior, and Palatino.

Helvetica Narrow — **Dense,** *compact,* ***condensed***

May sometimes be hard to read. Good for one column headlines, subheads, price lists, and catalogs. Not for body copy unless you're really sadistic. As a headline font it works well with the same fonts that work with regular Helvetica.

ITC Avant Garde — **Modern,** *geometric,* ***worldly***

Avant Garde is perfect for advertisements, signs, headlines. This font takes up a lot more space than Times Roman, and although graphic and striking, it's difficult to read when set in long stretches of text, as for a book. As a headline font it works well with body text set in Benguiat, Bookman, Century Schoolbook, Cooper Light, Goudy Old Style, Korinna, Melior, Palatino, and Souvenir.

ITC Bookman — **Offbeat,** *friendly,* ***casual***

(A little shy, but with a terrible temper lurking underneath.) Bookman is acceptable for body copy, but it's better for headlines because it's more interesting in larger sizes. Brochures, advertisements, short blocks of text (but not too small). As a headline font it works well with these text faces: Avant Garde Gothic, Cooper Light, Friz Quadrata, Futura, Gill, Helvetica, Kabel, and Souvenir.

New Century Schoolbook — **Studious,** *unassuming*

Century is appropriate for both headlines and body copy. Books, newsletters, semi-informal publications. As headline type, it works well with body text set in Amerigo, Avant Garde Gothic, Cooper Light, Friz Quadrata, Futura, Gill, Helvetica, Kabel, Optima, and Souvenir.

Palatino — **Formal,** *elegant,* ***classical***

Suitable for body copy and headlines. Books, magazines, reports, advertisements, brochures, menus. Use the italics for very elegant invitations. A more formal alterative to Zapf Chancery, it is also known as Zapf Calligraphic. As a headline font, it works well with body text set in Amerigo, Avant Garde Gothic, Friz Quadrata, Futura, Gill, Helvetica, Kabel, and Optima.

Courier — **Old fashioned,** *official*

Useful as body copy and headings for reports, legal documents, office correspondence, memos. This is what you use if you're going for that "typewritten" look. Some people seem to feel that letters printed in Courier have a more personal appearance. I think they are the antithesis of desktop publishing, clumsy and old-fashioned.

*ITC Zapf Chancery — **Calligraphic,** flowing, **handmade***

Ideal for invitations and announcements, it's also suitable for advertisements, business cards, logos, etc. Most effective in sizes above 14 point, and in short doses. Can be formal, but somehow isn't truly elegant.

Zapf Dingbats ✂☎✇✈☛✍✏➲☆★➽✪❄➳▲▼❤❦➮➧

Fun, silly, novel. An entire alphabet of symbols, not text. Eye-catching accents such as arrows, stars, fun bullets. Has many possible applications, but use judiciously. A little goes a long way.

This selection of headline fonts does not cover every single font available, but these are some of the most popular (and not coincidentally, included in most PostScript printers). For many applications, you won't really *need* fonts other than these, but you may *want* them.

❖ *Making the right choice*

Standard typefaces such as Times Roman and Bookman have been employed effectively for years as "body copy" (the main text part of a document). These typefaces are easy to read and do not strain the reader's eye when used for books or newspapers. More flamboyant, attention-grabbing "display" typestyles, such as Cooper Black and Futura Black are utilized for headlines, advertisements, or brochures.

Futura Black

ABCDEFGHIJKLMNOPQRSTUVWXYZ
abcdefghijklmnopqrstuvwxyz 1234567890&!$

Cooper Black

ABCDEFGHIJKLMNOPQRSTUVWXYZ
abcdefghijklmnopqrstuvwxyz 1234567890&!$

If you are aiming for a modern, slick, up-to-the-minute look for a publication, you may want to choose from the sans serif family of fonts, such as Helvetica, Futura, and Avant Garde for headings. If you want an elegant, polished appearance for your pages, you'll probably choose a serif typeface such as Galliard, Korinna, or Palatino. These dignified faces are also appropriate for formal invitations and announcements.

If you are producing a newsletter about schools, you might take a look at New Century Schoolbook, because that's the typeface used in so many "See Jane Run" books. I happen to despise New Century Schoolbook (I guess it reminds me of grade school), but it's a free country and you can choose whatever typeface you (or your boss, wife, or client) likes. The text of this book is set in Bitstream Goudy Old Style, and the headings are Bitstream Hammersmith (a.k.a. Gill Sans).

A serious financial newsletter calls for a dependable, trustworthy font, such as Times Roman or Century Schoolbook. It would lose credibility if it were set in a decorative, lush font, such as Korinna or Benguiat. And it would look foolish if it were set entirely in Tiffany.

Benguiat

ABCDEFGHIJKLMNOPQRSTUVWXYZ
abcdefghijklmnopqrstuvwxyz 1234567890&!$

Korinna

ABCDEFGHIJKLMNOPQRSTUVWXYZ
abcdefghijklmnopqrstuvwxyz 1234567890&!$

Tiffany

ABCDEFGHIJKLMNOPQRSTUVWXYZ
abcdefghijklmnopqrstuvwxyz 1234567890&!$

These three art nouveau-flavored fonts were all designed by Ed Benguiat for the International Typeface Corporation. Korinna was actually designed in 1904, but Benguiat is responsible for adding the first true italic design for Korinna, and enlarging the font into a family suitable for typesetting. Tiffany is a combination of two typefaces designed about 80 years ago: Ronaldson and Caxton. Benguiat blended them together and created a font with long, graceful serifs and strong weight contrast between the thin and thick strokes. These fonts are useful for short blocks of text copy, advertising, and display type.

Just be sure that the font you select is appropriate for the publication or printed material you're creating. And remember that other people's connotations will influence their unconscious reaction to your publication. Take another look at Chapter 4, *Show & Tell,* for more examples of typefaces, and how they can be used in various publications.

❖ *Measuring up or get to the point*

Once you've determined which typeface is most appropriate for your document, you'll need to know some specifics about applying the type to the page.

You may be used to measuring fonts in pitch. A 10-pitch font is generally larger than a 12-pitch font, because 10-pitch signifies that you can print 10 characters in an inch. Pitch is a horizontal measurement, but proportionally spaced fonts, the kind you'll be using for desktop publishing, are measured in points.

- Points are a vertical measurement (72 points= 1 inch).

- A 10-point font is roughly 10 points high, from the tip of the descenders (found in letters such as g, j, p, q, y) to the top of the ascenders (found in letters such as b, d, f, h, l). A 12 point font will be about 20% larger than a 10 point font.

- Text set in any size below 10 point is fine print; 10 and 11 point are standard sizes for body copy; 18 to 30 point is standard for headlines, and any size larger than 30 is used for very important headlines (such as those on the cover of the *National Enquirer*).

Not all 10-point fonts are the same size, however. Font size is actually determined by the designer of the font. That's why 10-point Helvetica is larger than 10-point Times Roman. (Try this bit of trivia at your next cocktail party; your friends will be impressed and bored at the same time—maybe they'll even leave.)

While points are a vertical measurement, the width of a line of text is measured traditionally in "picas." WordPerfect offers you the option of measuring in inches, centimeters, or points, and it's advisable to use what you're most familiar with.

Just as it makes little sense to have 12 inches to a foot, there are six picas to an inch, and twelve points to a pica. This makes a pica one-sixth of an inch, and a point one-seventy-second of an inch. A standard column width is about 12 picas, or two inches.

◆ Between the lines or beside the point

The amount of white space between the lines of type is called leading, and should always be at least one point larger than the size of the type. If you're using 11-point type, a leading of 12 or 13 would result in maximum readability. This is written as 11/12 and referred to as eleven over twelve.

Leading can also make an enormous difference in how a page looks. Pages seem gray and hard to read when not enough leading is used. Too much white space between lines of text can also be confusing, in that it's difficult to follow a sentence from line to line. (Notice how easily you're following these sentences?)

◆ Sizing up the situation or what's my line length?

When you are calculating the width of columns, there are several details to consider, such as page size, type size, and the size and number of photos or other artwork that you will be using. Columns should be neither too narrow nor too wide. For a newsletter, it's best to divide the page into two, three, or even four columns if you're using 10-point type on a standard letter size page.

A single column wider than 42 picas (about 7 inches) is not very easy to read. Readers forget which line they're on with a very wide column, and may get lost starting a new line of text (that's why there are so many people in analysis). Using a single column can be very effective and attract attention if the column is only about 24 picas wide, has a wide expanse of white space on either side of it, and has a generous amount of leading between the lines, such as 11 over 14 or 15.

Columns with lines shorter than about 10 picas (an inch and a half), may also confuse the reader. The fewer times your eye has to pause, the faster you can read a line. Narrow columns can break up a sentence's structure until it no longer makes sense, and the same sentence must be read over and over until it does. For an 8 1/2 by 11 inch page, the optimum line length for normal body copy (10 to 12 point type) is between 12 and 36 picas. (See the two full-page examples at the end of this chapter which illustrate these principles.)

◆ Alignments

➜ There are four basic kinds of alignment for text.

Justified type is aligned on both the left and right sides, forming even, solid blocks of text. This book is set with justified text, as are these lines of text.

With **flush left** type, also known as "ragged right," the left margin lines up flush, or straight, but the right margin is ragged, with each line of type a slightly different length.

Flush right type lines up flush on the right side of a column of type. This is not as common as flush left or justified, but it is still used for headlines, readouts, etc.

Centered type is at an equal distance from the margin or column edges. Centered text is not usually set in paragraph form or used for anything with columns (such as a newsletter), although individual lines of type may be centered. Headlines are often centered, as are announcements and invitations.

◆ Set it your way

Both justified and ragged right text settings have their place in publications. While most newspapers, books, and magazines are justified, an increasing number of publications are setting text ragged right. The ragged margins provide a page with a more informal (or less pretentious) appearance. The major drawback with unjustified columns of type is that extremely uneven line lengths may be created—very long lines can be followed by very short ones. These shapes are hard for the reader's eye to follow, and result in an undesirable visual impact. You can always hyphenate ragged right columns to improve unbalanced lines, but if the columns are too narrow, it won't be of much help.

If you like the look of vertical rules (lines) between columns on a page, then you may prefer ragged margins where the rules can act as a kind of justification. Justified type and rules can be a bit much unless there's plenty of white space, but once again, this is not etched in stone.

Justified type is suitable for every type of publishing. The uneven spacing between words that can occur with justified type may be particularly evident in short lines, but for the most part, justification adds a neat, orderly appearance to a page. When it's used properly, justification adds crispness, geometry, and a sense of pleasing formality to a page. The choice is yours.

◆ Deep in the heart of texes

If you justify type, it's an absolute necessity to hyphenate as well. Otherwise, paragraphs will have big, ugly, gaping spaces running through them; these gaps are called "rivers." Hyphenation allows words to be divided, and by keeping part of a word on a line, there are fewer oversize gaps in the lines. Letterspacing, adjusting the amount of space between each letter within a word, is another way to avoid those ugly and embarrassing gaps. (See the "bad" example at the end of this chapter.)

An additional ingredient for cooking up appealing type involves adjusting the space between individual pairs of letters. This feature is called kerning, and is most noticeable with larger typesizes. But remember, everything is relative. Kerning is more vital on a phototypesetting machine than it is on a laser printer. If you plan to send the finished product through a Linotron or other typesetter, kerning can improve the outcome.

❖ *Gridlock*

One of the main concepts in graphic design is the "grid." While this may be useful, the concept is bandied about like it's the holy grail, the be-all and end-all. "Use the grid," some design gurus claim, and everything will fall into place automatically.

Designers have grappled with this concept for years. I would see examples of a five-column grid, but the page looked like three columns. It didn't make any sense. One day I was working with a corporation headquartered in Denmark, and while they didn't speak English very well (their slogan was: "Personal Planning, making your life come true, faster"), their "Corporate Identity" book spoke to me. Their entire corporate identity was based on a 45-millimeter small square. Every

This is a three-column grid. Don't be intimidated by it. It is nothing but a geometrical pattern that divides the page into shapes that are supposed to make page layout easier. However, your material may not fit into a grid format;
don't feel bad. Use your imagination, and arrange your material to communicate effectively without being tied to some arbitrary grid.

component of their design system was based on this square, this *grid;* it was a *unit* around which everything revolved.

Squares and rectangles are convenient shapes for interpreting a grid, and in some cases, you can use circles and triangles. The great architect Frank Lloyd Wright used a grid for all his buildings. It creates a certain rhythm and order.

In essence, a grid is a unit of measure (which can be anything you decide on) that you use as the basis for your design. If your grid is a one-inch square, then your page will be designed with one-inch blocks, or *even* increments of one inch such as 1/4, 1/2, 3/4, 1 1/2, 2, etc. (or, for you decimal fans, .25, .5, .75, 1, 1.25, 1.5, 1.75, 2).

You might design a page with one-inch margins, three two-inch columns (twice the grid size), 1/4-inch gutters between columns (one quarter the grid size), 12-point body copy type (since there are 72 points per inch, 12 point is an even 1/6th of 72 point), 36-point headlines (1/2 of 72 point), etc. The grid acts as a tool which allows all the elements to work together harmoniously.

That's the good news. The bad news is that the grid doesn't always function as it should. Just because you work in increments of a grid doesn't guarantee that your page will always have the correct appearance, and more importantly, doesn't mean that the information you have will fit onto that page.

The grid is a tool, not a rule. Strict adherence to the grid can fast lead to visual boredom. Use it to help you make decisions, but don't become a slave to it.

❖ Creating a style

Review some of your favorite publications, and note how, while each page is different, there are obvious similarities in style—a header or footer that ties material together, a certain way of boxing readouts, a different typeface (usually italics) for captions than for regular text. These design elements provide a publication with its own unique, easily recognizable style.

A "readout" is typesetting or newspaper terminology for text which is set in a bigger size and positioned within an article to highlight an intriguing phrase or emphasize a particular point. It offers you another opportunity to grab the reader's attention and keep it on the page. Readouts are often used to enhance visual interest when you lack photos or other artwork, and can be thought of as another type of graphic element. They are also handy when you simply need to fill up a page when the text runs short. Magazine terminology refers to this technique as a "callout" or "pull quote." As long as you use them effectively, you can call them whatever you like. Chapter 11, *Graphics*, has many examples of readouts. Here is just one, taken from Dorothy Parker.

Brevity is the soul of lingerie

Developing a standard page structure will help you organize your words and pictures so they will be consistent throughout your work. While different page layouts within a single piece can add variety, it's easy to overdo it so that the reader is no longer sure what he's reading.

The message you're trying to get across is the most vital element. Your page design should lead the reader's eye to the most important items first. Headlines should not only illuminate the subject, but should be placed so that they sit directly above the article itself; otherwise, the reader won't be able to match the article with the headline, will become confused, and eventually find something better to do. Variety and contrast are instrumental in creating a pleasant texture on a page, and they can be achieved by using several different graphic techniques. A large capital letter, either raised or dropped, at the beginning of a paragraph will attract attention and serve as an invitation to begin reading.

◆ Tools of the trade

Gray columns of type in long rows will be more appealing to readers if you break them up with subheads or set the first few words of a paragraph in boldface. Using different sizes and variations of a single typeface for headlines adds contrast while still retaining a sense of consistency and interest. All these elements provide visual clues to amplify the meaning of the words. Some of these design choices have a subliminal effect, and many readers remain largely unaware that they are being manipulated by graphic design. Would-be desktop publishers need to begin noticing and applying these techniques to their own publications.

While WordPerfect allows you to have many different typefaces, borders, boxes, graphics, and screens on a single page, using them simultaneously is a surefire way to make a page unintelligible. In effective graphic design, every element is on the page for a reason. If you can't come up with a reason why that 2-point border is going to help the reader notice or understand the material inside it, lose it; otherwise, it will just be a distraction.

There are many options you must deal with when designing any publication. What paper size will your printed piece be, and what about the margins? Most laser printers require some sort of margin—approximately half an inch because of their paper transport mechanisms—on all sides, and are unable to print all the way to the edges of the paper. Printing presses also require a margin—usually about a quarter inch—but in either case, the paper can be trimmed after printing so that the margin is not apparent.

◆ Less is more

If you are just beginning, try to keep page composition simple and clean. Avoid mixing too many different typefaces and using unnecessary rules (lines), which only serve to muddle the reader.

Rules are meant to separate, and they are not merely ornamental. Do not use them to divide material incorrectly. It is hardly ever advisable to put a full ruled line under a headline; this separates the title from the material and defeats the purpose of the headline. This may seem obvious, but it's a mistake novices often make. Beginners think that by adding lines, boxes, and flashy fonts, their publication will seem professional. Unfortunately, just the opposite result is achieved. If you want a ruled line to deliberately separate the elements on a page, place the line below the end of one article and above the headline of the other. A *kicker*, however, does look good with a thin ruling line under it. Kickers are a few words, usually aligned flush left, that appear just above a headline to amplify and help get attention for that headline.

Keeping it simple doesn't mean it has to be spartan, but you should try to keep the design subtle. Whether you're creating a newsletter, invitation, or advertisement, the purpose is to communicate your message. If readers spend too much time oohing and aahing over the lines, typefaces, graphics, and boxes, they are not spending their time reading. And, what's the point of trying to make your product attractive if it's hard to read at the same time?

❖ Design tips and hints

Page composition can be very complex when you're juggling several unrelated items on the same page. The reader must be able to follow a section of text easily from its beginning to its end. To accomplish this, there are a few practices you should try to avoid. (Take a look at the "bad" example at the end of this chapter to see what a page that ignores these tips looks like.)

- Don't mix typefaces of body text within a document or publication. Don't set one article in Times Roman and the other in Helvetica (or if you do, please remove this book from your bookshelf).
- Don't mix sizes of body text. Body text should always be the same point size.
- Don't mix too many different typefaces in one publication.
- Don't use too many "swash" or special effects fonts, such as drop caps or raised initial caps. Also do not use outline and shadow fonts to excess.
- Don't set lengthy blocks of text in italic, bold, or all capital letters.
- Don't begin an article without a headline.
- Don't place smaller headlines above larger ones. The most important material and the biggest headline should be at the top of a page.
- Don't have more white space below a headline than above it.
- Don't use the same font, size, and style (such as Helvetica 24-point bold) for every headline. Headline weights and styles should be varied, such as Helvetica 30-point bold for an article at the top of a page, and 24-point italic for one further down the page.
- Don't place two articles directly side by side, so that their headlines bump up against each other.
- Don't place advertisements in the middle of the page (floating among articles as if they were illustrations).
- Don't box text without using enough white space around it (so that the border is too close to the type).
- Don't use a flamboyant typeface for a serious document.

❖ Headlines

Headlines are usually set in upper and lowercase letters, since this is generally simpler to read than headlines set in all caps. Headlines in all caps may serve a purpose at times, but not on a regular basis. Readers recognize words not only by how they are spelled, but by the shapes they form. Words in all caps form rectangular blocks and are harder to recognize as specific words, thus slowing down a fast reader and discouraging a slow one.

The purpose of a headline, or large display type, is to attract the readers' attention, convey a quick message, and persuade them to read the text that follows. Headlines are read more often than the material underneath them—that's where the power to influence enters in. An effective headline should compel a reader to want more information.

Headlines can be placed above text, either flush left, flush right, or centered, depending on your design. Headlines should extend across the full width of the column they are in, because a short headline leaves a white space that resembles an unintentional hole.

All material requires some sort of identification, including articles that are continued from one page to another. A simple "continued from page 3" in 8-point type is not an acceptable substitute for a headline. When readers turn to that inside page looking for the continuation of the "Dolphins Speak to Researcher" article, they need some kind of help to find it. It may just be one or two words from the original headline, such as "Dolphins Speak," or even just "Dolphins," if the story now fits in one column.

- The headline should always be placed near the beginning of the article instead of floating too far above it. Place white space above a headline, not below it (except when it is at the top of the page).

- Don't place two articles right next to each other, beginning on the same line. This will create "bumping heads." The headlines will run together, and will be confusing and hard to read (this is also referred to as "tombstoning").

❖ *Tips for handling newsletter design problems*

If an article does not fill an allotted space, there are several steps you can take to correct the problem. Don't simply enlarge the type or change the leading—the article will stand out, but for the wrong reason, and that's not how to draw attention to an article. It is usually possible to change the layout, making it more horizontal, or to eliminate the problem by moving artwork around. More often than not there will be several ways a layout can be rearranged to make it better. Don't be afraid to experiment.

- If it conforms to the design of the page, go into the article and add a few subheads. Each one will take up a line, so if the article is an inch short, adding three or four subheads will fill the blank space, while providing readers with additional information to help them through the article.

- If the story already contains subheads, or if you don't want to use them, find a passage that will grab the reader's attention and make it into a readout. This can be a few words or an entire paragraph—whatever you need for the article to fill the space.

- If the page composition will accommodate it, you can set the entire article two or three picas narrower and box the article with a 1-point rule (or thicker if so desire). This is one way in which to add emphasis to an article.

Here is an example of how a poorly designed newsletter can be transformed by following the design principles and pre-publication planning (spell checking, editing) outlined in this book.

❖ *Before - The bad example*

This is an example of what not to do with the first page of a newsletter: it has too much material crammed onto the page, and in all the wrong proportions. Beginning at the top, the name of the newsletter, "Numismatics Remuneration," tries to be arty by capitalizing the "T," and centering "Numismatics" between the two capital letters. This arbitrary capitalization only succeeds in making readers ask "Why is the T capitalized?" Also, the motto and date line are too large and bold, giving the headlines too much competition and making the top of the page much too busy.

The rest of the page is divided into three columns, with white space trapped between the first and second columns, adding nothing to the overall design. In the first column, blurbs referring to material on the inside pages are overpowered by enormous numbers inside gray screens, and there is no consistency of spacing. Some of the blurbs are directly under the boxes, but the blurb for page 6 is sitting atop the number 8.

The headlines in the first and second columns are the same size, the same typeface (Helvetica), and since they are positioned next to each other, difficult to read. These are "bumping heads." The kicker over the middle headline is too near the nameplate of the newsletter, and should be closer to the top of the headline. There is not enough white space under the headline, and so some of the descenders run into the first line of the article. The article flows, newspaper style, into the next column; however, it's also too close to the nameplate, and an article should not appear in a column next to its headline. The headline should have been one line, extending across both columns under the nameplate, instead of two lines in the middle column. The article in the third column has a headline that is too large, and the byline has too much space underneath it.

All of the body copy is set block style, with no indentation at the beginning of a paragraph. This is not recommended for newsletters. As you can see, it is extremely difficult to tell where the paragraphs begin. Also, the body text is Helvetica, the same font used for many of the headlines and for the nameplate. This excessive use of the same font gives the page a monotone, dull appearance.

Photos and artwork are supposed to enliven and enrich the material around them, but because of the size and poor positioning of this illustration, it doesn't enhance the page at all. Probably the worst feature of this design is how the very narrow boxed text is squeezed in the lower right corner of the page, causing the bottom of the third column to also be too narrow. This is a good example of bad

NUMISMATICS

RemuneraTion

A journal of know-nothing design and money-grubing slime **December 6, 1989**

Inside This Issue

Kicker over head

This Headline should be bigger

What is desktop publishing? It means different things to different people. To some it simply means setting type with a computer, on any of a variety of printers. To others it means creating the entire finished page on computer: writing the text, laying out the page, merging in the graphics, and finally printing a finished page on a laser printer or digital typesetter.

According to the ABC program "Business Week," by 1991, desktop publishing will be a three billion dollar industry.

Who will Benefit from Desktop Publishing? You will. Yes, you. The one flipping through the pages looking for the funny drawings. You may already be a publisher. Yes, you!

Publishing doesn't mean just books and magazines. If you're part of an office, school, any kind of organization or club, you're probably already creating a newsletter or flyer of events. If you work in any business, such as a real estate office or travel agency, you need to send out promotional flyers about your hottest listings, or bargain travel packages.

In the past, you've either had to type everything up and stick it on a page, or send it out to a typesetter and have a graphic artist paste up for you, which, before I arrived, cost about $1,000 per issue to produce. After I arrived, the costs dropped to almost nothing (although I must admit the Oreo budget rose dramatically).

The first major expense is typesetting. On a twenty-four page newsletter, if you sent typed pages to a typesetter, you should expect to pay about $500. If you prepared the copy on computer and sent it to the typesetter via modem (over the phone lines), that cost would be lowered to about $300 because the copy would the copy would not have to be retyped by the typesetter.

(These typesetting charges included corrections, inevitable, because some

cont'd p. 4

Headline is Too Big

By Author's name

Either way, an unpretentious little newsletter can quickly become so tedious and time consuming that you'd like to trick someone else into doing it for you.

So, if you're already a publisher, desktop publishing may be for you. It can even be fun, depending on how easily you are entertained.

Where was I?

On the following pages you will find examples of what you can do if you are: a small business, quick-print shop, ad agency, school, theater, fund raiser, restaurant, real estate office, fake estate office, travel agency, mail order catalog, writer, or an unpublished writer

A Word From Our Sponsors

Now you have to measure the type and make a dummy. A dummy is a simple mock-up of a page showing the basic format and where each story, picture, or piece of artwork is going to be placed on the page.

con'd p. 5

typography—see the river of white space running through this column? Also, notice how none of the bottoms of the columns line up, resulting in an uneven page that lacks definition.

❖ *After - The good example*

This design manages to get practically the same amount of material on the page, but does so in a balanced, inviting way. The nameplate, set in Times Roman, uses two solid black squares to define the corners; the centered motto and dateline are a good size, and surrounded by ample white space.

The large one line headline extending over two columns is aligned flush left, as is the kicker, "From the President." There is a proper amount of white space above and below the headline. The author's byline is aligned flush right because of the raised capital letter of the first paragraph. If the big initial letter had been dropped into the paragraph instead of raised, the byline could have been centered above the paragraph.

The font for the body text is Times Roman, and the paragraphs are indented, and easy to follow. The body copy is set ragged right to achieve an informal and friendly feeling. A thin rule appears in the gutters between the columns, helping to define the unjustified text. The "News Briefs" headline is the proper size, with the right amount of spacing above and below it. Notice the white space in the far right column next to the "News" headline.

The illustration of the "President" comes from *DeskTop Art,* electronic clip art on disk by Dynamic Graphics, touched up with PC Paintbrush. It's in correct proportion to the other elements on the page, and draws the reader's eye to the pull quote beneath it. Notice the ample leading between the lines of the pull quote. This example effectively points out how type can be used as a graphic element to attract the reader's attention.

The "Inside" listings under the pull quote are also large enough to be highly visible, but are still not overwhelming. Note the even, consistent spacing between the listings, and between all the elements on the page. A box containing calendar information anchors the lower left corner, and balances the strong visual interest created by the "Inside" listings. And, all three columns align evenly at the bottom.

The contrast between the bold sans serif headlines, and the casual, free-flowing body text build an interesting texture on the page, combining many diverse elements without becoming cluttered or crowded.

Numismatics REMUNERATION

Good design for fun and profit *May 1989*

From the President

Publishing Profits Up

By P. Tanner

What is desktop publishing? It means different things to different people. To some it simply means setting type with a computer, on any of a variety of printers. To others it means creating the entire finished page on a computer.

Writing the text, laying out the page, merging in the graphics, and finally printing a finished page on a laser printer or digital typesetter. According to the ABC program "Business Week," by 1991, desktop publishing will be a three billion dollar industry.

Who will benefit from Desktop Publishing? You will. Yes, you. The one flipping through the pages looking for the funny pictures. You may already be a publisher. Yes, you!

Publishing doesn't mean just books and magazines. If you're part of an office, school, any kind of organization or club, you're probably already creating a newsletter or flyer of events.

If you work in any business, such as a real estate office or travel agency, you need to send out promotional flyers about your hottest listings, or bargain travel packages. In the past, you've either had to type everything up and stick it on a page, or send it out to a typesetter and have a graphic artist paste up for you. Either way, an unpretentious little newsletter can quickly become so tedious and time consuming that you'd like to trick someone else into doing it for you. Doesn't that sound nice?

Continued on page 3

May Events

News Briefs

So, if you're already publishing something, desktop publishing may be for you. Here's more news for desktop publishers--it can even be fun, depending on how easily you are entertained and amused.

On the following pages you will find examples of what you can do if you are: a small business, quick-print shop, ad agency, school, theater, fund raiser, restaurant, real estate office, fake estate office, travel agency, mail order catalog, writer, unpublished writer looking for a way to do it yourself, home business, teacher, student, or any generally self-employed type.

Do you want to cut costs? Consider the production expenses.

President Tanner

"Who will benefit from desktop publishing? You will. Yes, you - the one flipping through these pages looking for the funny pictures."

Inside

❖ *Steps to success*

Before starting to format there are certain steps you need to take. Write your material, always remaining aware of your audience. If you have the text, then edit it, bearing the same considerations in mind. Write the headlines—more difficult than it would seem, but it's easier and quicker to modify existing text than it is to create something from scratch when you're trying to format. Place subheads in long articles while word processing (you can always remove them if the article runs too long, and it's more efficient than writing them while trying to design the page). Write all the captions, and run the spell check, too. Verify that names, addresses, phone numbers, and prices are all correct. These are steps that you have some control over, and it's not the fault of desktop publishing if delays caused by spelling and grammatical errors delay the layout and production.

It's tempting at first to head right for the computer and ignore design completely. But try some paper and pencil sketches first. They don't have to be beautiful, just give you some idea of what is going to go where. Sketches will help you determine how many columns to have, and what size the photos and illustrations will be (if you have any).

Does your company or group already have a recognizable style? Look at your letterhead and other printed material to see if there are elements in your previous publication that relate to this one. Only when you have completed all these steps should you begin working with the composition of the pages.

❖ *Training by design*

Many tools are available for novice desktop publishers. The latest twist in desktop publishing training involves lessons on videotape. Video instruction allow users to observe demonstrations of various techniques, duplicate the designs themselves, compare their work to the tape, and then review the steps again.

◆ Dynamic Graphics

➔ Dynamic Graphics, 6000 N. Forest Park Dr., Peoria, IL 61656
800-255-8800

A maker of electronic clip art, Dynamic Graphics, offers a *Step-By-Step Video Series* that includes a tape detailing design strategies and typesetting principles. The VHS tape is entitled "Desktop Design: Basic Electronic Graphic Techniques," runs 30 minutes, and costs $49.95. It shows the desktop publishing procedures necessary to create three graphics projects, plus an overview of hardware and software.

Dynamic Graphics also offers a series of two or three day "Visual Communication Workshops" that cover the basics of graphic design, newsletter design, and design for desktop publishing. Workshops cost between $225 and $725, and locations include Anaheim, Atlanta, Boston, Chicago, Denver, Orlando, and Washington D.C. They also offer a useful catalog of related graphics and design products; give them a call and request one.

You might also want to consult local community colleges, universities, and computer training schools for information regarding desktop publishing and design classes.

◆ Style sheets on disk

Many useful utility programs have sprung up around desktop publishing programs. For novice desktop publishers, predesigned style sheets can be a big help. They contain many practical tips about the basics of graphic design, and teach the user how to quickly modify a style sheet. Users load in their own text and graphic files, and can instantly tailor any element of the page layout to fit their individual document. See the Appendix for specific products.

❖ *Dive in*

Now you are ready. WordPerfect's desktop publishing capabilities are fun, no doubt about it. The only problem is that they can be so much fun that it's easy to neglect other trivial details, like composing understandable and well-organized text.

Experimentation is crucial, but you should always master the basics of good graphic design before trying anything too complicated. Graphic design is one field where the phrase "if a little is good, more would be better," does *not* apply. Try adding elements one at a time, rather than all at once on the same page. You can't go wrong if you plan in advance and keep it simple.

So be good, eat your vegetables, do your homework, and for dessert you'll get to play with WordPerfect's desktop publishing features, make friends, influence people, and be the life of the party.

6

Measure for measure

or Give 'em an inch

In the wacky world of desktop publishing, WordPerfect takes you one step away from the typewriter and one step closer to the typesetter. While this is wonderful, it means you are no longer just sitting there typing—you are now sitting there typesetting. And as every good typesetter knows, precision is important.

Luckily, WordPerfect is pretty smart when it comes to distances. You can measure in *inches* (who's foot was the original foot?) or *centimeters*. As much as you want to ignore them, they are far more logical and easy to use than inches. There are 10 millimeters in a centimeter, 100 centimeters in a meter, 10 centimeters in a decimeter ("cent" means 100 as in "century" and "dec" means 10 as in "decade"; think of them as pennies and dollars). You can also use *points* (there are 12 points in a *pica* and six picas in an inch)—are centimeters starting to look more attractive? WordPerfect also lets you use the "WordPerfect 4.2" measurement system, based on spaces and lines. This is relatively useless for desktop publishing because it ignores different sizes of type.

❖ *Where are you, really?*

Because of WordPerfect's measurement system, you can see exactly where you are on a page without having to enter View Document mode. At the bottom right-hand corner of the screen, WordPerfect displays cursor location information. Depending on what measurement format you made the default (Shift-F1 U), WordPerfect will display your location in inches, centimeters, or points.

The **Ln** marker shows you how far down the page the cursor is, and the **Pos** marker shows you how far across the page it is. These measurements include the header and footer, and offer a very accurate position reading. They are also invaluable when you want to calculate distances for advanced formatting.

◆ Get to the point...

Luckily, WordPerfect lets you use any of the forms of measurement at any time. Americans will probably find it easiest to set WordPerfect's default to inches, while Europeans will probably use centimeters as the default. As you will see, you can still enter line height in points, or enter any other measurement in any format.

If you enter a number by itself, WordPerfect will use whatever format the default is in. If the default is inches, and you enter 11 for height, you're going to end up with 11 inches between each line (and wonder why you ever got into desktop publishing).

But if you enter 11P in the Line Height field, WordPerfect will know you mean points and translate it into whatever the default is, in this case .15". If you change the default, WordPerfect will translate all the measurements in the document to the new default, and display them in the format you've chosen.

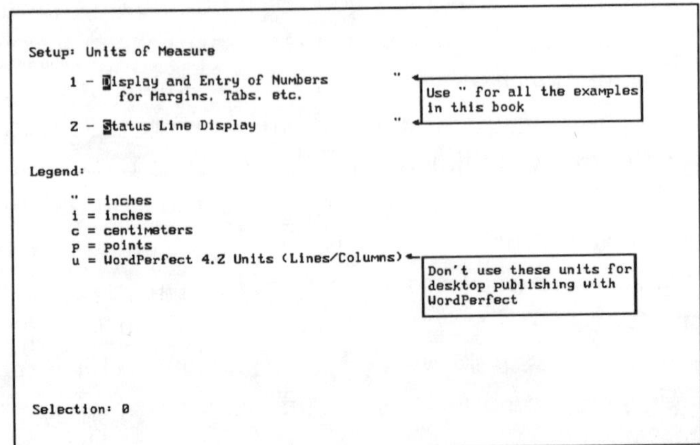

Units of measure.

This means you can use whatever format you're most comfortable with. However, WordPerfect *insists* you use points when selecting a font, and you should always use points for measuring line heights.

While points might seem foreign to you right now, they are essential because type is always measured in points. Body type is normally from 9 to 12 point. Subheads range between 12 and 18 point. Headlines generally run from 18 to 48 point, with 72 point and above reserved for declarations of war or advertisements for really good sales.

❖ *Turning leading into gold*

In typesetting, leading (line height) is all-important. It's called leading because in the olden days, typesetters used to insert thin strips of lead between the lines of type. Proper leading keeps the descenders (the parts of letters that stick *down* below the base of most characters, such as a "y"), and ascenders (the parts of letters that stick *up* above the top of most other letters, such as a "t") from running into each other.

Because type is measured in points, it is customary (and logical) to measure the space between lines (leading) in points. The general rule in deciding on line spacing is to add at least 1 point to the size of the type. (For example, 10-point type would have at least 11-point leading, and would be referred to as 10/11 or "10 on 11"). This is a good rule of thumb, but it's not the gospel. Use of less leading is rarely effective, while more leading can be used to fill otherwise blank pages. You can add as much as two or three points leading, depending on the typestyle and specific application you are working with.

- It's never a good idea to skimp on leading just to pack in more text. Here's an example of not enough leading:

- When you don't have enough leading, the letters can run into each other and the reader has difficulty distinguishing the letters on each line. The eye becomes confused, and forgets which line it was reading. It's also ugly.

- While double and triple spacing can be used for draft copies of text, it's not suitable for general typesetting. Here's an example of too much leading:

- When you have too much leading, lines of text are so far apart that they almost don't seem to form paragraphs, and this can make them difficult to read.

- If you put a line height change at the end of the line, it will take effect immediately, and affect the space after the current line. Always put line height changes on the line after a font change, the last line of your headline, or readout, otherwise the line spacing will appear uneven.

◆ Automatic line height

Because this is WordPerfect's default mode, you don't need to do anything special in order for WordPerfect to automatically set leading for you. If you've turned the feature off, to turn on automatic line height, press

SHIFT-F8 L H A [RET][RET]

Unfortunately, WordPerfect is sometimes a bit skimpy when it comes to leading. And while the leading that WP sets is never actually bad looking, it could look better.

WordPerfect's automatic leading can be as small as 1 point for body text, when 2 points would be better. When you use fonts created with Fontware, the automatic leading is much better, usually at least 2 points for body text. When using Fontware font, automatic leading is usually sufficient.

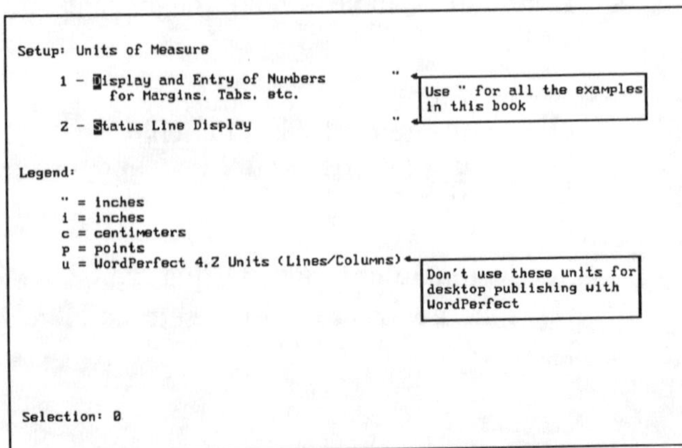

Always set line height in points. Make the leading at least one point greater than the point size of the font.

◆ Fixed line spacing

To set "fixed" line spacing, press

SHIFT-F8 L H F

and then enter a number followed by a **P** for points. Remember that the number should be 1 or 2 points larger than the size of the type. If you use 10 point type, enter either **11p** or **12p** and press **[ENTER]** twice.

The only problem with setting leading manually in WordPerfect is that the leading will be wrong if you change the size of the body text. The easiest way to get around this is to create an open style containing the type you want to use for body text, and the corresponding line height. Then, by changing the style, all the leading will change as well. For more information, see Chapter 10, *Styles.*

◆ Manual leading

Setting leading manually is essential in some circumstances. While mixing typesizes on a line should always be performed with caution, there are times when it's appropriate (such as in a "raised cap," a single large character at the start of a paragraph). When creating an outline, using larger type for the numbers causes them to stand out. However, when using automatic line height, WordPerfect will put more space below a line which has even as much as a single character in larger type. This makes leading uneven and unattractive. See Chapter 8, *Paragraphs,* for more information about raised and drop caps.

Here are some examples of the difference a little leading can make. The first number is the size of the type, the second is the amount of leading. WordPerfect's automatic leading corresponds to the 10/11 example. While there is nothing terribly wrong with it, it's a little on the tight side.

➻ 10/10

Oh I wanna be a cowboy, but I've never seen a cow. I'd like to punch them doggies, but I don't know how. I've never been in a saddle while following cattle, or had a home on the range...

➻ 10/11

Still I'd gladly exchange all my three piece suits for a ten gallon hat and a nice pair of boots, oh I wanna be a cowboy, but I don't know how.

- 10/12

  C-O-W B-O-Y. That's for me, though I don't know why. But a C-O-W A-R-D, a coward's all I'll ever be. Oh I wanna be an outlaw, but my in-laws say "no."

- 10/13

  They think it's just a phase that I'll soon outgrow. But some mysterious force tells me "go steal a horse" and of course something's got to give.

- 10/14

  Because when you live on the 11th floor, it's hard to get a horse through your elevator door. Oh I wanna be an outlaw, but I don't have the brains.

Leading can make a huge difference in a publication. Not enough leading makes lines of text difficult to read and "gray." Too much makes it hard to read and lacks contrast. Some art directors use an abundance of leading to achieve an avant garde, arty look, but leading that is smaller than the typesize is never acceptable, no matter what look you're going for.

❖ *When rulers collide*

Unfortunately, WordPerfect has a few idiosyncrasies when it comes to measurements. The most important is that it allows you to enter smaller numbers by using centimeters. The smallest number you can enter in inches is 72/100ths of a point, or 2/100ths of a centimeter, while if you enter the number in centimeters (with a "C" after it), you can enter 3/100ths of a point, or 1/100th of a centimeter, or 1/10th of a millimeter.

- .01 inches = .72p = .02c
- .06 points = .06p = .0c
- .01 centimeters = .03p = .01c

In this case, the smallest line width you can enter in inches is twice as thick as the smallest you can enter in points or centimeters. The smallest line width you can enter in points is twice as thick as the smallest you can enter in centimeters.

Most laser printers have a resolution of 300 dots per inch (considered rough by typesetting standard, but high enough so that few people notice the difference between lasersetting and typesetting). Still, the difference between .01" and .01c is noticeable, even at this resolution. And if you are going to have the final pages printed on a typesetting machine, these measurements will result in even more of a difference (the difference between a hairline (the thinnest line) and a much heavier line).

These idiosyncrasies come into play because WordPerfect may display a measurement of 0", even when there is a real measurement. In writing this chapter, WordPerfect displayed a measurement of 0" for both .06 points and .01 centimeters. The real measurements are still there, but they display as 0" unless I change measurement formats.

❖ *Secret System "W"*

WordPerfect has yet another secret up its little sleeve (a secret not even those clever folks at tech support were aware of for several months). You know about inches, points and centimeters, but did you know about "W's?" No, no, not the fashion tabloid, the measurement system. Well, neither did I, until I stumbled upon it one dark and stormy (actually, hot and sticky) night.

Could it be they named them for me—could these be Wills? (Stop that snickering or I'm going to send a note home to your mother.)

W's are some undocumented form of measurement that WordPerfect uses. **1W = 1/1200th of an inch,** and this makes a W the smallest form of measurement in WordPerfect.

If you enter W in units of measure, you get something akin to1200 units per inch (about four times the resolution of current laser printers). Could it be that WP expects to see 1200 DPI laser printers soon, and wants to be ready for them?

This means you can enter *any* measurement in W's. If you create lines that are 1W wide, they will print as hairlines, a single dot wide, even on 1200 dpi typesetting machines.

I don't recommend using this unit of measure for everything (it's too alien), but it's nice to know it's there when you want extremely thin lines or really infinitesimal control.

❖ Margins

If you're used to setting left and right margins such as 10 and 70, get ready for a shock. These same margins would now be 1" and 1". Why? Because now instead of measuring across the page, you have to measure in from the edges of the paper. Margin settings of 1" and 1" mean that your text will begin 1" from the right edge of the paper, and end 1" from the left edge of the paper.

The same applies to top and bottom margins. It really makes sense once you get used to it. Let's try it together by setting left and right margins at three-quarters of an inch. Press

SHIFT-F8 L M .75 [ENTER] .75 [ENTER] F7

Now let's create top and bottom margins of a half inch. Press

SHIFT-F8 P M .5 [ENTER] .5 [ENTER] F7

Here's a way to set left/right and top/bottom margins and save a few keystrokes in the process. We'll set left/right to a half-inch and top bottom to three-quarters of an inch.

SHIFT-F8 L M .5 [ENTER] .5 [ENTER][ENTER] P M .75 [ENTER] .75 [ENTER] F7

Notice how you can combine your formatting foray into one trip for both kinds of margins.

WordPerfect's default is 1" all around the page. When you are using laser printers, WordPerfect automatically sets a minimum margin of .25". If you try to set anything smaller, it will automatically return to .25".

Before you complain about this fascist measurement system, remember that WordPerfect's doing this for your own good. Because of the mechanics of paper handling, laser printers can rarely print any closer to the edge of the paper than a quarter of an inch.

And besides, it's very rare that you'd want to set margins less than .4" anyway. Otherwise the type gets so close to the edge of the page readers can't hold the page without putting their fingers over the type, and with some printing methods, this means getting ink on their delicate little fingers. If you want an illustration to "bleed" off the edge of the page, consider trimming the paper.

❖ WYSMBWYG

One of the big buzz-words in desktop publishing is called WYSIWYG, or Wizzy-Wig. This stands for "What you see is what you get," meaning that what you get on-screen should be an accurate representation of what you get on the page.

WordPerfect is only near-WYSIWYG in View document mode, but it's accurate in the ways that really count. It's not totally WYSIWYG because it doesn't display the exact fonts you're using, just generic serif or sans-serif fonts. This isn't terribly important because you only use the View document mode to be sure that everything is in the right place. Words, and even individual letters, are where they will be on the page.

But when you write and edit in text mode, WordPerfect could best be described as "What You See Might Be What You Get." Text screens have monospaced fonts (like typewriters), but desktop publishing uses proportionally spaced fonts. If the fonts on-screen aren't the same width as those in the printer, you're going to see only the vaguest approximation of the page when in text mode (you'll see what words are on which lines; lines on-screen will begin and end with the same words on-paper).

Some graphics cards, such as the Hercules RAM-font, will display italics and different sizes of type on-screen, but even these are only approximations of the finished product.

❖ Tab happy

You probably think you know what the tab key does. It adds a few spaces, usually five, and moves everything over, right? Wrong, hamster breath. The tab key actually inserts a tab code, and this code moves to an exact horizontal location on a line, determined by where you set the tab.

Tabs are essential when using WordPerfect as a desktop publishing program so we're going to spend some time with them. You can use tabs to indent the first line of a paragraph, or to indent entire paragraphs.

Like almost everything else in WordPerfect, you can set tabs in inches, centimeters, or points. You can place tabs on the tabline by moving to the point you want and pressing **L** (for a left tab), **R** (for a right tab), **D** (for a decimal tab) or "period" for a right dot leader tab.

Another method is to enter the exact location you desire. Just type the number (followed by the measurement unit if it's other than the default). If you want to set a whole slew of tabs, each separated by an even amount of space, you type **HOME HOME RIGHT-ARROW CONTROL-END.** This will remove all tabs currently set. Type **0,** and whatever increment you want the evenly set tabs to occur in, such as **0,.25"**

Any tab can be used as a dot leader tab by moving to the tab setting and pressing a "period". This causes the tab setting to reverse, so that it appears white on black.

◆ Tabs 'R Us

The biggest on-screen deception comes when you use the space bar. As I've said repeatedly, you simply cannot align text by using the space bar as you would with a typewriter. Here's an example.

A) This line appears on-screen to be indented the same amount as

B) This line

While they are only 1/100 of an inch off, it can really stick out. The problem becomes increasingly worse as you work with more text.

"Presidents and their Dwarf/Reindeer/Substance Equivalents"

PRESIDENT DWARF REINDEER SUBSTANCE

Abe Lincoln Doc Rudolph Copper

Dick Nixon Grumpy Blitzen Polyester

Jimmy Carter Happy Comet Legume

Ronnie Reagan Sleepy Prancer Teflon

Those four lines appear to line up on-screen, but they obviously don't print out that way. This is because each letter uses a different amount of space, and so each word ends in a different place. Bold and italic fonts take up different amounts of space than do medium ones. Even the width of a space is variable, depending on the typeface and size you use.

Here's the same example using tabs:

"Presidents and their Dwarf/Reindeer/Substance Equivalents"

PRESIDENT	*DWARF*	*REINDEER*	*SUBSTANCE*
Abe Lincoln	Doc	Rudolph	Copper
Dick Nixon	Grumpy	Blitzen	Polyester
Jimmy Carter	Happy	Comet	Legume
Ronnie Reagan	Sleepy	Prancer	Teflon

When you use tabs, text will line up on-screen and on paper. You won't always need the same number of tabs for each line. In this example, all the presidents have two tabs after their name, except for Reagan. His name is longer and if two tabs were used, his dwarf would be .2" farther to the right.

➾ Tip: An easy way to set tabs

To create this table quickly, without the need for tedious measuring, I set my tabs an even .2" apart. I used this small setting so I could add another tab between entries when I needed a little more space. The default setting of .5" is too large, and adding another tab would result in large gaping spaces.

Here's an example: I typed two tabs following all the president's names and it looked fine. But when I went into View Document, I noticed that Sleepy was too close to Ronnie, and so I added another tab before **all** the dwarves to make it even. If one entry is so long that the tab takes you one tab further then the rest, simply go back and add an additional tab to the lines above.

The horizontal ruling lines for the above chart are not WordPerfect graphics lines, but simply underlined tabs. WordPerfect's horizontal ruling lines do not print far enough down on a line, and overprint the bottom of characters. These horizontal lines are easy to create because you simply press **F8** at the start of each line, and the underline continues under the text and tabs. To make sure WordPerfect will underline tabs, type **SHIFT-F8 O U Y Y [RET] [RET]**. Vertical rules between columns are not quite as easy, but we'll get into that in Chapter 13, *Rules*.

Another tip for making evenly spaced tables can be found in Chapter 9, *Columns*.

◆ Musical tabs

All the tabs change places when you change the tab line. Because of this, you should always set tabs immediately proceeding an important table. If you want to keep the current settings, go to the start of the table and type:

SHIFT-F8 L T F7 F7

This will insert a code containing the current tab settings and keep them from being accidentally changed with a new tab setting from above.

If you change tables frequently and have more than one table with the same format, you might consider creating a style that contains nothing more than a tab setting. Then, when you change the style, the tables will all change consistently. For more information, see Chapter 10, *Styles*.

❖ *Moving anywhere with precision*

➻ If you want utmost control over the printed page, WordPerfect's Advance command is vital. Read on.

When you begin working with desktop publishing, you start to think in terms of fractional inches—tiny little increments.

Sometimes you want to move precisely a tenth of an inch down, but a return is too big. Or you want to move exactly a tenth of an inch to the right, but a space is too small and two spaces are too big.

This is when WordPerfect's little-known **Advance** feature rides to the rescue. Advance lets you move precisely up or down, to the left and right, or even a specific distance from the top of a page.

In this case, advance doesn't have to mean advanced. While it's terribly precise, it's not terribly difficult.

◆ Advance to go

To use Advance, press

SHIFT-F8 O A

You are now presented with 6 options: **U**p **D**own **L**ine **L**eft **R**ight **C**olumn.

When you select one of these options, you won't see any change on the editing screen. If you have reveal codes on, you'll see the code and the measurement status line at the bottom, which reflects the change. The difference will be apparent when you go into View Document. All text following the code is affected,

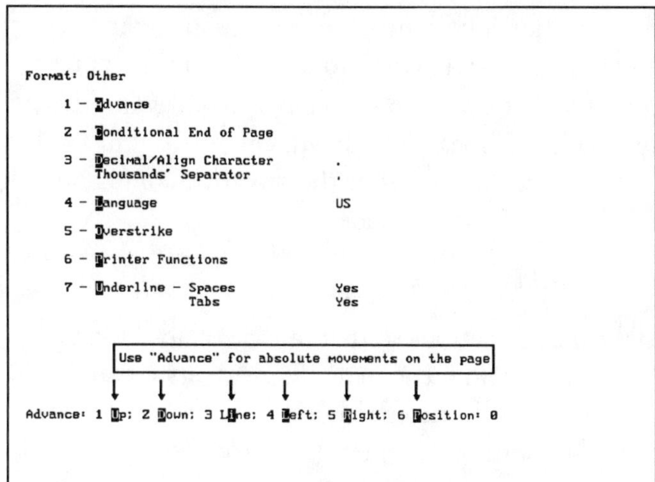

Advance command.

so if you choose Down 1", everything will be moved down one inch, starting at the code.

Up: Moves the text up from its current position. If you are on line 4.48" and advance up .1", the line will print at 4.38". If you edit the text and the line moves to 7.12", it will then print up .01" from that, or 7.11".

Down: Same as up, only down.

Line: While up and down are relative, based on the location of the code, Line is absolute. If you're on line 4.48" and select Line 5.58", the line will print at 5.58". If you edit the text and the line moves to 7.12", it will still print at 5.58" because of the advance code.

Left: As in up and down, only to the left.

Right: As in up and down, only to the right.

Column: As in line, absolute from the margins of the page, only horizontally.

I've used the advance command frequently because it allowed me to move text with great precision and to line everything up perfectly.

◆ Tip - Locking things in place

You'll often run into a situation where the body text is in the correct location, but headline or graphics above them are not.

Once I have material exactly where I want it, I lock it there with the advance command. I press

SHIFT-F8 O A I [ENTER]

This places the exact, current horizontal measurement in an advance code, and ensures that the text (or graphics) aren't going to move from this spot.

I can then move the cursor higher up on the page and, once again, use the advance command to subtly move headlines up or down, change leading, add or close up space. No matter what I do, I'm sure that the advance command will keep the rest of my page (or pages) perfectly in place.

◆ Tip - Safety first

➾ I also save before any major alterations so that in case of an error, all I have to do is clear the screen and retrieve my file. Advance can also be used to place evenly spaced horizontal lines on a page to create forms. An example may be found in Chapter 4, *Show & Tell.*

◆ Old math

I had my 4.0 average destroyed by a C in math class. When they started discussing real vs. imaginary numbers, I figured I might as well make up my own numbers; the teacher didn't agree. So when I say I hate "New" math, I mean it.

"Old" Math, however, doesn't bother me, especially with a $4 calculator in my hand. (I can remember when those things cost and weighed more than a computer—and I'm not even that old). The point of all this is that "old" math is often useful in desktop publishing. After using WordPerfect for a while, I realized that I could make my life easier if I stopped guessing at measurements and started using the WordPerfect ruler line instead. Don't bother trying to hold a ruler up to the screen, it won't work. But the numbers in the lower right-hand corner of the WordPerfect screen will tell you all you need to know.

Say, for example, you want to create a vertical line between the columns of the table we created with tabs. You'd have to know how tall the table was.

Here's an easy method: move the cursor to the last line of the table, and write down the number that appears after **Ln** in the lower right of the screen. Now move to the first line of the table, write down the number after **Ln,** and subtract it from the first number. You now know the height of the table. Simple, huh?

7

About faces

The technical side of fonts

You have IBM to thank for Courier. They designed it for their typewriters and it's probably what you've always used. Pica and Elite are popular, too, and are examples of fonts. Times Roman, Helvetica, Avant Garde, Bookman, New Century Schoolbook, Palatino, and Zapf Chancery are the kinds of fonts you'll be using for desktop publishing. These fonts are built into PostScript laser printers, such as the QMS PS 810 or the Apple LaserWriter. They're also available from Bitstream for use with the WordPerfect Fontware system.

The fonts built into PostScript printers can be printed in every size from 3 to 1199 point. These fonts can also be printed as *outlines*, with *shadows*, or in shades of *gray* instead of just *black*. PostScript also allows you to print fonts at any angle (see Chapter 11, *Graphics*), although WordPerfect supports only 90, 180, and 270 degree rotations.

PostScript printers can also use downloadable fonts. Fontware can install Bitstream fonts for PostScript printers, but WordPerfect does not yet support all of the fonts available from Adobe (the makers of PostScript). WordPerfect updates their printer drivers regularly, so call them for the latest information about which Adobe fonts are supported. But wait, there's more...

LaserJet printers use two types of fonts: cartridge and downloadable (also called "soft"). The fonts most useful in desktop publishing are called "downloadable" fonts, because you download them from the hard disk of the computer to the printer's memory. Cartridge fonts are limited to sizes up to 16 point, while downloadable fonts can be as large as 72 point.

The size you can use is contingent on how much memory the LaserJet has. The standard LaserJet II has 512K, and will print fonts up to 30 point. Adding more memory will theoretically allow the printer to print fonts up to 690 point. Realistically, however, a 72 point font takes up anywhere from 400 to 800K of disk space (depending on the font and symbol set chosen). A larger font would take megabytes of disk space, and take several minutes to send from the computer to the printer. *A complete set of bitmapped fonts for a single family can easily take up two megabytes of disk space.*

❖ *Waddya print?*

The type of printer you use will determine what fonts you can use. A PostScript printer has all the fonts mentioned earlier built-in. This is what they look like:

ITC Avant Garde — ITC Bookman

Helvetica — Helvetica Narrow

ITC Zapf Chancery — Times Roman

New Century Schoolbook — Palatino

If you have a LaserJet, you have Courier and a tiny print called "Line Printer." That's it. Of course, if you have a LaserJet Plus or Series II, you also have Times Roman (Dutch) and Helvetica (Swiss) with WordPerfect's Fontware.

But now it gets confusing. Times Roman is a typestyle, Times Roman Medium is a typeface. Times Roman Medium, bold, italic, and bold italic are also typefaces, and the four of them together are a typeface family (not unlike the Partridge Family).

Times Roman Bold is a totally different font than Times Roman Medium. *Times Roman Italic* is even more different, and Times Roman Bold Italic is yet another different font. So for each typestyle, there are generally four fonts: a medium, bold, italic, and bold italic. And it doesn't stop there; the LaserJet requires separate downloadable fonts for portrait (vertical) and landscape (horizontal) pages.

LaserJet: *POP QUIZ!* How many fonts does a LaserJet need to print 10-point Dutch medium, 10-point Dutch bold, 10-point Dutch Italic, and 10-point Dutch bold-italic? If you answered four, you can count. The LaserJet requires four separate font files to print the regular variations on 10 point Dutch. Each of these files must be created by Fontware, and reside on a hard disk. The four will take up about 20K each for a total of about 80K.

◆ Memory for faces

A note about printer memory. Most new laser printers come with at least 512K of memory. That's enough to do most tasks, but not enough to do a full page of 300 dots-per-inch graphics, or to combine a lot of downloadable fonts and graphics. New PostScript printers seldom run out of memory. They have at least 2 or 3 megabytes of memory, and this is enough to print a full page of 300 dots-per-inch (dpi) graphics, along with graphics. The following section applies mostly to LaserJet and compatible printers.

Everything takes memory: downloadable fonts, graphics, and even an area of the printer that handles formatting commands. You can't use 350K of downloadable fonts and expect to have much room for graphics.

If the LaserJet II flashes "20" or "21," this is an indication that the page is too complex to be printed with the amount of memory it has. What do you do about it? If you need to print a full page of graphics and only have 512K of memory, you have a couple of choices. You can print the pages using Medium or Draft quality. Medium resolution is 150 dots per inch. While this is only half as good as the laser printer best output, it also requires only half the memory. With 512K you can print an entire page of graphics, but only at 150 dpi resolution. At this resolution the graphics will have noticeably jagged edges. *Type will always print at 300 dpi.*

If you really need high-resolution graphics, try using less of them on each page, or make them smaller. The bigger they are, the more memory they take. Remember the "creative use of white space" graphic design rule: don't cram so much on the page and you'll use up less memory.

You can also consider using fewer typefaces (remember that every typeface, even bold and italic, takes up memory). Often simply reducing the number of typesizes you have can help. If you have only one line in 14 point, make it 10, 12, or some other size you use often. Make sure you remove the font from the Base Font list by pressing

SHIFT F7 S E C

and removing the + or * next to the font name.

Memory upgrades are getting cheaper. HP sells their own upgrade for the LaserJet; it costs less than $500 for an additional megabyte of memory, enough to print a full page of graphics. Other companies are selling similar upgrades for less. If an upgrade is not feasible (or you have a LaserJet Plus whose upgrades are violently expensive), you should consider a program like LaserTORQ that compresses the graphics so they take up less space. LaserTORQ is reviewed in Chapter 17, *Software.*

One more tip: memory isn't everything. Occasionally you will receive an error message on a LaserJet that has nothing to do with memory. If "21" appears on the LaserJet, the formatting of the page is simply too complex for the printer to follow. It's not the fonts, but the formatting itself: the rules, sometimes the graphics, and the justification and letterspacing. When WordPerfect justifies text, it not only sends text to the printer, but intricate and memory-consuming codes that tell the printer exactly where each letter needs to be placed. If you are confronted with the dreaded "21," follow the same steps as you would for "20:" place fewer elements on a page, smaller graphics, lower resolution graphics, or maybe even ragged text.

◆ PS

The fonts built into PostScript printers supply some of the typefaces used most commonly in typesetting. They provide you with an abundance of typographic choices, but they also cost at least twice (and sometimes three times) as much as a LaserJet or compatible printer.

◆ Additional fonts

Don't be disappointed if the fonts from your laser printer aren't quite as sharp and perfect as those you see in the Bitstream promotional material included with WordPerfect. They're the same font, but Bitstream prints their material on Linotronic typesetters with a resolution of 2450 dpi, as opposed to a 300 dpi laser printer. Their fonts are specially designed for the resolution of the printer, so they do look excellent on all printers. For a complete list of currently available Fontware fonts, call Bitstream at 800-552-3688.

See Chapter 17, *Software,* for programs that allow WordPerfect access to fonts other than Bitstream's.

◆ Cartridge

LaserJet: How much is that cartridge in the window? Pretty dear. Font cartridges cost anywhere from $150 to $600, and generally contain fonts no larger than 16 point.

That 16 point limit is a big one (or a little one), and serious desktop publishers are going to need larger type than that. So who needs cartridges? Owners of the original LaserJet that can't use downloadable fonts depend on them for attractive type. People who share printers or use them on networks will find that downloading fonts takes years, or at least it seems that way. Networks and most printer sharing boxes work at slow speeds, and make downloading tedious and inefficient.

If the printer has enough memory, you'll be able to use Fontware for all fonts, large and small. But using font cartridges allows you to access more than the limit of 32 downloadable fonts, and more importantly, to save precious memory for

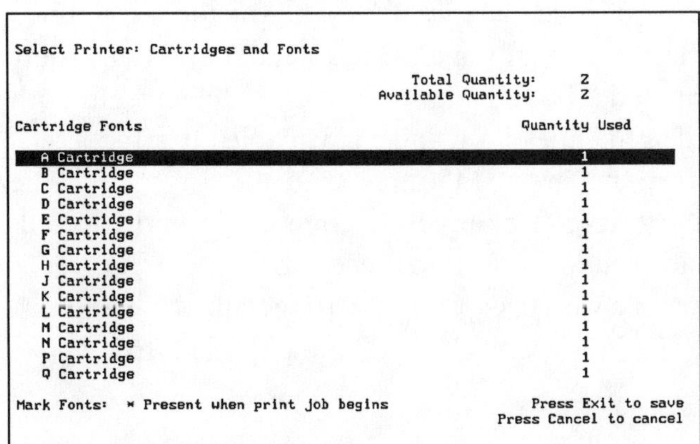

The LaserJet II can use two cartridges at a time. The original LaserJet can use one at a time. WordPerfect supports all Hewlett-Packard font cartridges. (SHIFT-F7 S E C F)

graphics and headline type. Cartridge fonts require no printer memory.

The most popular is the "B" cartridge, which contains TmsRmn (Times Roman) in 8 medium and 10 point medium, bold and italic, and Helv (Helvetica) in 14.4 point bold, portrait only. This is an early design, and type is not of the best quality.

◆ Tip: Font cartridge spacing

The "B" cartridge has very "loose" type; the letters are so far apart that they are difficult to read, and don't produce the best typesetting. When using this cartridge, the spacing can be vastly improved by adding this WordPerfect command

SHIFT-F8 O P W [ENTER] P90 [ENTER]

This command moves each letter closer together by 10 per cent, clearly enhancing the printed output from this cartridge.

The "F" cartridge is preferable to the "B" in several ways. First, the quality and spacing of the fonts is superior.

An excellent HP cartridge for desktop publishing is the Microsoft "Z" cartridge. This includes both TmsRmn and Helv in 8 medium, and 10,12, and 14 medium, bold, and italic. WordPerfect can simulate a bold-italic by overprinting each character twice, and while this is not as desirable as a real bold italic, it's more than acceptable.

◆ Super Cartridge

IQ Engineering has introduced a cartridge called the *Super Cartridge,* which just about says it all. This $499 cartridge includes 97% of all the fonts contained in all 25 HP font cartridges. The quality of the fonts is excellent and the variety can't be beat. The cartridge includes both Times Roman and Helvetica in both portrait and landscape, as well as full line-draw, and all available HP symbol sets. While the price may seem steep, it's only $145 more than the list price of the Microsoft "Z" cartridge. The fonts are completely compatible with the HP cartridges, and so spacing and justification are perfect. The *Super Cartridge* is truly a super investment for people who need to use cartridge fonts.

IQ Engineering, Box 60955, Sunnyvale, CA 94086; (408) 733-1161.

```
Select Printer: Cartridges and Fonts

                                    Total Quantity:  1000 K
                                Available Quantity:   672 K

Soft Fonts                                       Quantity Used

   (FW) Bitstrm Amerigo Roman 14pt (ASCII) (Port)          15 K
   (FW) Bitstrm Amerigo Roman 18pt (ASCII) (Port)          22 K
 * (FW) Bodoni Bold 11pt (ASCII) (Port)                    11 K
 * (FW) Bodoni Bold 12pt (ASCII) (Port)                    13 K
 * (FW) Bodoni Bold 14pt (ASCII) (Port)                    16 K
 * (FW) Bodoni Bold 18pt (ASCII) (Port)                    24 K
 * (FW) Bodoni Bold 40pt (ASCII) (Port)                   142 K
 * (FW) Bodoni Book 11pt (ASCII) (Port)                    11 K
 * (FW) Bodoni Book 12pt (ASCII) (Port)                    12 K
 * (FW) Bodoni Book 14pt (ASCII) (Port)                    15 K
 * (FW) Bodoni Book 18pt (ASCII) (Port)                    21 K
 * (FW) Bodoni Book Italic 11pt (ASCII) (Port)             11 K
 * (FW) Bodoni Book Italic 12pt (ASCII) (Port)             13 K
 * (FW) Bodoni Book Italic 14pt (ASCII) (Port)             16 K
 * (FW) Bodoni Book Italic 18pt (ASCII) (Port)             23 K

Mark Fonts:  * Present when print job begins        Press Exit to save
             + Can be loaded during print job     Press Cancel to cancel
```

Once you've created fonts with Fontware, they will appear in the list of soft fonts (SHIFT-F7 S E C F).

➻ Attention: Original LaserJet users

Font cartridges from GNU are the first that I know of to offer proportionally spaced fonts other than Times Roman or Helvetica for the original LaserJet. The "Writer's Series" provides Bitstreams' versions of Century Schoolbook, Garamond, Galliard, and Optima in 6 medium, 8 medium, 10 medium/bold/italic, 12 medium/bold/italic and 14 point bold.

They can also put any Bitstream font into a font cartridge, provided it takes less than 128K of memory. The first four fonts cost $199, and each additional font is $45. If you don't need that many fonts, and just want a good set of Times Roman and Helvetica-like fonts, Pacific Data Products also sells a Z cartridge for $99. It's fully compatible with the Microsoft Z cartridge, and costs $150 less. See Chapter 18, *Hardware*, for more information about Pacific Data and GNU.

◆ Fontware

The original LaserJet only used cartridges, but the LaserJet II can use both cartridge and downloadable fonts.

While the LaserJet II doesn't have the built-in versatility of PostScript printers, it's low-priced and still quite powerful. The Fontware system included with WordPerfect allows for useful downloadable fonts in many sizes (the more memory in the printer, the larger the fonts it can print), but few special effects.

Because there are about four times as many LaserJets as there are PostScript printers, most WordPerfect users are going to be using Fontware.

Fontware is a software package that takes outlines of fonts and produces bitmapped downloadable fonts. When a font is bitmapped, it means that each dot of the font (300 per inch, 90,000 per square inch) is written in a specially formatted file. The printer uses this file to print fonts, and requires one bitmapped file for each font it prints.

Fontware can create fonts from 3 point (extremely tiny and hard to read) to 72 point for LaserJet II's and compatibles.

While Swiss and Dutch are included with WordPerfect, Bitstream has a huge library of Fontware that WordPerfect can also use. About ten new typeface families are introduced every quarter; see Chapter 4, *Show & Tell* for examples of most of the fonts that are currently available (Amerigo, Serifa, Cooper, etc.).

◆ Tip: Lots-o-Fontware

If you are going to use lots of Fontware fonts, you may need to go into the PTR program included with WordPerfect, and remove any other printers that you won't be using (along with unwanted fonts and PS tables). The PTR program is less scary than you might think; it's logically designed and uses many WordPerfect function key commands. For complete documentation on the PTR program, call WordPerfect's 800 number. Or, if you're ready to dive in without documentation, you can follow my instructions that appear later in this chapter.

◆ Tip: Lots-o-fonts

If you are going to use lots of fonts, you may want to copy the printer definition file and give it a different name, such as PALATINO.PRS, and have one file for each major group of fonts. Otherwise, WP will download all the fonts when you initialize (or print), and your printer may not have enough memory to handle them all at once.

◆ Tip: Not Lots-o-disk space

If you are always low on disk space, you can download fonts from floppies. Yes, it's true, take it from a hard disk space miser like myself. However, they must all fit on a single floppy disk; otherwise, WordPerfect will have a temper tantrum and confront you with two choices. You can cancel the initialization (or print job), or you can start over (which isn't much help if the fonts aren't there). If you have 1.2-megabyte floppies, or the new 1.44-megabyte baby floppies, you should be able to cram quite a few fonts onto a single floppy. If you have 360K floppies, you can only store smaller sizes.

❖ Installing fonts

➺ POSTSCRIPT - If you use a PostScript printer, especially a "plus" version with the 35 built in fonts, chances are you may never need to actually install a font. You will simply install the Apple LaserWriter driver and have instant access to all the fonts built into the printer. A list longer than the screen will appear, displaying all the fonts available in the LaserWriter Plus and most other PostScript printers.

The PostScript printer driver works differently from the LaserJet in that it lists only font names, not sizes. Once you move the cursor to a font and press return to select it, WordPerfect asks what size font you want. You may select any size from 1 point (which would be unreadable) to 1199 point (where one letter will not even fit on a page).

Fonts can be selected in 1/10th of a point increments, so choosing 11.2 point type is possible. Fractional point increments are rarely necessary, much less noticeable, but they can be useful if the material has to fit with absolute precision (or if people constantly check up on you and you want to drive them nuts trying to measure the type).

If you want to use downloadable fonts, you have to remember that WordPerfect doesn't support all the Adobe downloadable PostScript fonts available. Before you dash out and buy a font, make sure that it's supported. At press time, WordPerfect supported a small selection of Adobe downloadable fonts. Call WordPerfect for the latest information about supported fonts.

To see which fonts your copy of WordPerfect supports, press

SHIFT-F7 S

Move the cursor to the PostScript driver (often called the Apple LaserWriter Plus). Press

E C

If WordPerfect can't locate the file called WPRINT2.ALL, it will ask you what drive it's on. Place the printer disk in drive A, and type

A:[ENTER]

"Downloadable Fonts" will appear on-screen.

Verify that WordPerfect has the correct settings for the amount of memory you have available. Most PostScript printers have at least 1.5 megabytes of memory, often 2 or 3 megabytes. Still, not all that memory is available for downloadable fonts. WordPerfect's default setting is 300K, which is large enough for about two complete families of downloadable fonts. If you have 2 megabytes of memory or more, you can safely use up to 500K of memory for downloadable fonts, and still have enough room to print a full page of graphics. If you want to change the amount of memory available for downloadable fonts, Press

Q

and enter the amount of memory you want for downloadable fonts.

Now press

F

and WordPerfect will present you with a list of the downloadable fonts it currently supports. Move the cursor over to the fonts you want to use. If you want WordPerfect to download the font each time you print (which can take several minutes using a parallel cable, longer with serial), press + next to the font name. If you share the printer with others and everyone uses different fonts, selecting the font with + will ensure that the fonts you need will be downloaded every time you print (it also ensures that you will be waiting around a while). I normally download about 800K of fonts, and it takes a good five minutes. I would have to be put in a strait-jacket if I had to wait five minutes every time I wanted to print something, so I mark fonts with a

*

as described later in this chapter.

If you are the only one using the printer, or if everyone uses the same fonts, mark the font with *. Fonts marked with * are only downloaded when you choose the initialize command:

SHIFT-F7 I

Marking the fonts with a * saves a lot of time because they don't have to be reloaded each time you print something; they will stay in the printer memory until you either initialize it again, or turn it off. When you initialize the printer, all fonts that were previously downloaded are erased.

However, if you forget to use the initialize command, the printer will either substitute another font that is close, or print the page using Courier. Either way, the page will have a different appearance than what you intended.

If you accidentally choose the wrong font, simply press the * or + again on that font to cancel it. You can install any or all of the fonts listed, provided you have enough memory. WordPerfect deducts the size of each selected font from the amount of available memory (this keeps you from trying to load more fonts than you have memory for). Once the fonts you have chosen fill the amount of memory you selected, WordPerfect will no longer allow you to mark new fonts without unmarking a previously marked font. When you are done, press:

F7

The next time you go to Base Font, WordPerfect will list the new fonts that you added.

FONTWARE - Fontware is an extremely self-explanatory piece of software. All you have to do is install the Fontware software. This involves putting in Disk #1, typing:

Fontware [ENTER]

Follow the on-screen prompts to create fonts. Remember, creating fonts takes ages, so try to do it on your lunch hours (why limit it to just one?), or overnight.

The program may come with a special LaserJet driver. If it does, copy this to the WordPerfect program directory, usually \WP50.

Portrait/landscape

The program will ask you a lot of questions about the type of printer you are using, and where you want the program copied. The only questions you might need help with are when the program asks if you want Portrait, Landscape, or both. If you only print portrait pages (tall, i.e. 8 1/2 x 11), choose "Portrait Only" in the installation. This will save you time and tremendous amounts of disk space. If you need both Portrait and Landscape (wide, i.e. 11 x 8 1/2) then select both.

Symbol Sets

LaserJet users have two choices for fonts, while PostScript users have one. If you have a LaserJet, you can choose between ASCII (the basic letters, numbers, and punctuation) or HP Roman 8. Unless you are going to use foreign characters, the only advantage the Roman 8 offers is a quasi-em-dash and two small bullets. In exchange, it takes twice as long to create, about twice as much disk space, and twice as long to download. Don't try to use the PostScript character set; it not only won't work, it will render the printer file unusable as well. If you use a PostScript printer, choose the PostScript character set.

Once you've installed Fontware, you will need to copy the fonts from the floppy to the hard disk. WordPerfect's installation program comes with Dutch (Times Roman) and Swiss (Helvetica). Go to the main menu, and press return on Add/Delete Fonts. Follow the on-screen prompts and within two minutes max, the fonts will be installed on-disk.

These fonts are special Fontware Outlines, and they cannot be used directly with just any printer. These are the outlines that will create the fonts you use with a LaserJet or compatible printer.

If you have at least 512K of memory (as all LaserJet Plus and Series II printers do), create Dutch and Swiss fonts in Medium, Bold, Italic, and Bold-Italic in the following sizes: 8,10,11,12,14,18,24,30 point. If you have more than 512K, you may also want to install fonts in 36, 48, and 72 point.

Fontware will check to make sure you have enough disk space, and tell you approximately how long it will take to build the fonts. If you don't have enough disk space, either copy files off the hard disk, or reduce the number of fonts or sizes you are trying to produce.

If you are creating ASCII fonts, this will seem like a short eternity. If you are creating Roman 8 fonts, it *will* take an eternity. PostScript fonts are created quickly. You may want to turn down the screen (so it won't "burn in"), and let the program run overnight.

Once you've created the Laserjet fonts, follow the directions for installing *downloadable* LaserJet fonts. If you've created PostScript fonts, follow the directions for PostScript printers.

➾ **LASERJET** - If you choose Base Font and all you see is Courier and Line Printer, chances are you haven't told WordPerfect which font cartridges and downloadable fonts you have. To do this, press

SHIFT-F7 S E C

(A note to yuppies, or anyone who habitually wears suspenders: this does not stand for the Securities and Exchange Commission, it stands for Select, Edit, Cartridges, and Fonts.) If the file WPRINT1.ALL (sometimes WPRINT2.ALL or WPRINT3.ALL, depending on your type of printer) is not on your current drive and directory, WordPerfect will ask where it can find it. Enter the drive and directory of the file. If you are going to use the original WordPerfect diskette (and you really should have made a backup), then put it in drive A: and type

A:\ [ENTER]

Note: If you're like me, you're having a good day when you can find 400K on the hard disk. WordPerfect's main printer files are very large, several hundred K each, and WordPerfect does not require that they be on the hard disk in order to print. I keep mine on backup floppies, and only use them when I'm adding fonts or changing my printer configuration.

WordPerfect will now give you a choice between cartridge or downloadable fonts. Be sure that WordPerfect has the correct settings for the number of cartridge fonts and amount of available memory. The standard LaserJet has one cartridge slot, and no memory for downloadable fonts. The LaserJet Plus has one cartridge slot, and 350K of memory for downloadable fonts. The LaserJet II has two cartridge font slots, and at least 350K of memory available for downloadable fonts (the other 162K of memory is reserved for other LaserJet functions). If your printer has more than the standard amount of memory, press

Q

and add the additional memory to the 350K so WordPerfect will know that there's enough memory to support more and/or larger fonts.

➻ Cartridge

If you have font cartridges, move the cursor to Cartridges and press return. You will see a list of the available HP font cartridges, listed by letters A - Z (1a). You can tell what letter the cartridge is by finding the number at the top of it (92286Z, or whatever letter the cartridge is). Use the cursor to move to the letter of the font cartridge and press

*

Repeat this for any additional cartridges you have available and press

F7

WordPerfect will add the fonts contained in the cartridge to its list of available Base Fonts.

➻ Downloadable

Besides Fontware, the only other downloadable fonts WordPerfect will use right out of the box are from Hewlett-Packard. If you want to use fonts by other manufacturers, see Chapter 17, *Software*, for information about programs that can install any soft font for use with WordPerfect.

Most of Hewlett-Packard's fonts were designed by Bitstream. However, because WordPerfect includes a Fontware installation program, Fontware is a better value. You need to tell WordPerfect which soft fonts you have, including those you've created using the Fontware installation program.

To do this, move the cursor to soft fonts and press

F

WordPerfect presents a list of all available HP soft fonts, grouped by set. The letters in parentheses are the designation for the set. If the word (LAND) appears after the font, it means that this is a landscape version of the font. The LaserJet cannot print portrait and landscape fonts on the same page, and will eject the paper before printing the font with a different orientation.

Move the cursor to the fonts you want to use. If you want WordPerfect to download the font every time you print (which may take several minutes with a parallel cable, longer with serial), press + next to the font name. If you share the printer with others who are using different fonts, selecting the font with + will ensure that the fonts you need will be downloaded every time you print (it also means that you will have some more time to kill).

If you are the only one using the printer, or if everyone uses the same fonts, mark the font with

*

Fonts marked with * are only downloaded when you choose the initialize command:

SHIFT-F7 I

Marking the fonts with a * saves a lot of time because they don't have to be reloaded every time you print. They will stay in the printer memory until you initialize it again, or turn it off. When you initialize the printer, all fonts previously downloaded are erased.

However, if you forget to use the initialize command, the printer will print the page with Courier, and you will either want to kick it or cry. But it's not the printer's fault, it's yours (or whoever was supposed to initialize the printer at the start of the day).

If you accidentally choose the wrong font, simply press the * or + again to cancel it. You can install any or all of the fonts listed, if you have enough memory. Remember that WordPerfect deducts the size of each font selected from the amount of available memory. When you are finished, press

F7

The next time you go to Base Font, WordPerfect will list the new fonts.

◆ Downloading

This is so simple it's almost funny. If you marked the downloadable font with a +, WordPerfect automatically downloads the file each time you print anything from a page to the entire file. If you marked the font with an *, Press

SHIFT-F7 I

That's it.

Downloading fonts can take anywhere from a few seconds to a few minutes, depending on how many fonts you're downloading, their size, how fast the computer is, and what type of printer cable you're using (parallel being many times faster than serial).

All downloadable fonts remain in the printer only as long as the power is on. Turn off the power and, zap, they're deleted and must be reloaded with the Initialize command before you can print with them. If you forget to initialize, most printers substitute Courier; the text will be there, but it will often be unreadable.

Now, there is one catch (oh, you just knew there would be, didn't you?), but it's relatively minor. The fonts you want to download must reside in a single directory (any one you'd like). Copy them from the floppy you purchased, or use the directory that Fontware creates called FONTS.

➾ If you also use Ventura Publisher, don't keep the same fonts in the same directory. Also keep your copy of Fontware's Ventura program in a different directory.

To check that WordPerfect knows which directory contains the WordPerfect downloadable fonts, press

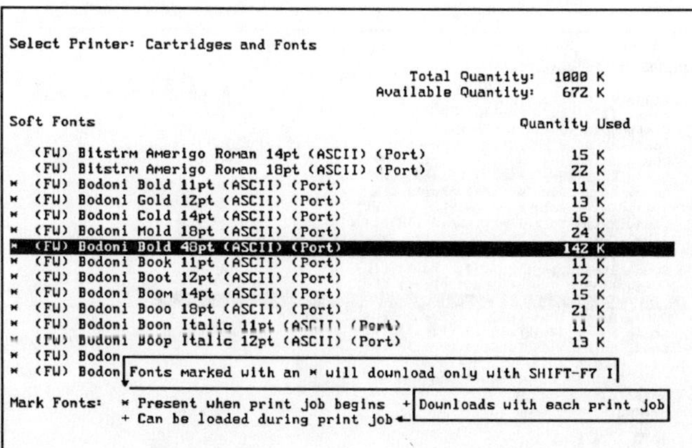

Select Printer: Cartridges and Fonts
Total Quantity: 1000 K
Available Quantity: 672 K
Soft Fonts
Quantity Used
(FW) Bitstrm Amerigo Roman 14pt (ASCII) (Port) 15 K
(FW) Bitstrm Amerigo Roman 18pt (ASCII) (Port) 22 K
* (FW) Bodoni Bold 11pt (ASCII) (Port) 11 K
* (FW) Bodoni Gold 12pt (ASCII) (Port) 13 K
* (FW) Bodoni Cold 14pt (ASCII) (Port) 16 K
* (FW) Bodoni Mold 18pt (ASCII) (Port) 24 K
* (FW) Bodoni Bold 48pt (ASCII) (Port) 142 K
* (FW) Bodoni Book 11pt (ASCII) (Port) 11 K
* (FW) Bodoni Boot 12pt (ASCII) (Port) 12 K
* (FW) Bodoni Boom 14pt (ASCII) (Port) 15 K
* (FW) Bodoni Booo 18pt (ASCII) (Port) 21 K
* (FW) Bodoni Boon Italic 11pt (ASCII) (Port) 11 K
* (FW) Bodoni Boop Italic 12pt (ASCII) (Port) 13 K
* (FW) Bodon
* (FW) Bodon
Fonts marked with an * will download only with SHIFT-F7 I
Mark Fonts: * Present when print job begins
+ Can be loaded during print job
Downloads with each print job

*Mark fonts with an asterisk * if you want to download them only once a day when you Initialize the printer (SHIFT-F7 I). Mark fonts with a + (plus sign) if you want them downloaded each time you print.*

SHIFT-F7 S E D

and enter the directory where the downloadable fonts are located, then press

F7 F7 F7 F7

◆ Downloading horrors

One annoying problem with downloadable fonts rears its ugly head when several people using different fonts share the same printer. One person will load their fonts, print away merrily, and then leave the printer filled with those fonts. The next unsuspecting person starts printing and - Gadzooks!, are they going nuts, or is there a gremlin in the printer?

There are several ways to alleviate this problem. If you have enough printer memory, you can simply load all the fonts anyone will ever need. Printer memory, however, doesn't come cheap, and so the next alternative is for everyone to always use the same fonts. If you think "Corporate Image," then this practice makes sense anyway. You don't want someone using Helvetica on promotional literature, when your stationery and business cards are printed with Times Roman.

You can also avoid this by marking the font files in the printer driver with a + instead of a *. Fonts marked with a + are sent to the printer every time you print. The down side of this method is that it can take a lot of extra time whenever you print.

Another way around this problem is by using common courtesy, a custom that is becoming far too uncommon. If most people who use the printer use a standard set of fonts, a copy of their printer driver (it will end in .PRS) should be handy. When you've finished printing with your fonts, clear the screen and select their printer driver. If their fonts are marked with an *, press **SHIFT-F7 I**. Their

The Initial Font is the default font for a document. Unless another font is specified, this font will be used for text, headers, footers, captions and everything under the sun.

```
Document: Initial Font

  Glucose 10 pitch (PC-8)
  Pokey 10 pitch (Roman-8)
  Gumby Bold 10 pitch (PC-8)
  Meatloaf Bold 10 pitch (Roman-8)
  Goudy Bold 11pt (ASPIC) (Port) (FW)
  Goudy Bold 14pt (ASCII) (Port) (FW)
  Goudy Bold 18pt (ASTHMA) (Port) (FW)
  Goudy Extra Bold 14pt (ASYLUM) (Port) (FW)
  Goudy Extra Bold 18pt (ASCII) (Port) (FW)
  Goudy Extra Bold 36pt (ASTRAL) (Port) (FW)
  Goudy Italic 11pt (ASCII) (Port) (FW)
  Goudy Italic 14pt (ASCII) (Port) (FW)
  Goudy Italic 18pt (ASCII) (Port) (FW)
* Goudy Roman 11pt (ASCII) (Port) (FW)
  Goudy Roman 14pt (ASCII) (Port) (FW)
  Goudy Roman 18pt (ASCII) (Port) (FW)
  Goudy Roman 36pt (ASCII) (Port) (FW)
  Line Umpire 16.66 pitch (PC-8)
  Line Draw 16.66 pitch (Roman-8)
  Solid Line Draw 10 pitch
  Silver Lining Draw 12 pitch

1 Select; N Name search: 1
```

fonts will be sent to the printer, and they might even drop all their plans for tarring and feathering you.

◆ Initial font

Every WordPerfect file contains an "Initial" font. Unless you insert codes to change it, the Initial font will be the default font that is used for everything from the text to headers, footers, footnotes, captions, footnotes, you name it. This font does not appear in the file (even if you press ALT-F3 for Reveal Codes). The only way to see or change it is to press

SHIFT-F8 D F

WordPerfect then presents you with a list of fonts available on the printer.

If you don't set it specifically, WordPerfect will examine the printer driver to see which font you've set at the initial font. To change this, press

SHIFT-F8 S E I

and move the cursor to the font you want. This will automatically be entered as the Initial font for every file using that printer driver.

◆ Tip: Getting drafted

I normally set my initial font to Courier 10 point for a number of reasons. First, since Courier is monospaced, all the text will fit on-screen, rather than extending off the right side of the screen. Second, Courier is the standard font for drafts; it's relatively big, easy to read, and easy to make editing marks on. Third, it's scannable, which means that all Optical Character Recognition (OCR) software can read it. Why is that important? Call me paranoid (you won't be the first), but I hate losing data. I make backups every day (sometimes several times a day), and also print out my work daily. Should some heinous mishap occur that prevents me from using my original or my backup, I can still use a scanner and OCR software to read my printed pages and enter everything back into the computer without having to retype it.

Courier is also an efficient base font because it keeps you from formatting when you should be writing. One of the great temptations (the vice, not the singing group) of desktop publishing is that you want to experiment with formatting rather than write and edit.

When you are ready to start formatting, press

SHIFT-F8 D F

and select the font you want to be the default for headers, footers, captions, footnotes, endnotes, etc. Once you've set an initial font, you can still override it (in the text, headers, footers, footnotes, captions, anywhere) by inserting a new base font with

CONTROL-F8 F

◆ That's a base font

Because WordPerfect can support so many fonts, how you choose them is important. And as with other WordPerfect features, there are several approaches you can use.

The first and most basic is Base Font. Base Font means that all of WordPerfect's other attributes, such as size and appearance, are "based" on this font you've selected. It becomes the default, the standard font. When you enter a Base Font code, it affects all text following it, until WordPerfect sees another Base Font code. If you want to switch from one typeface to another, you will always need to use Base Font by pressing

CONTROL-F8 F

A list of the fonts available for your printer will appear, sorted by the name of the font. Most printers will display a single listing for each size and weight of font. The letters following the typeface show the name of the font cartridge they are on.

This list is sensitive to your page orientation. If you are working on a landscape page, you will see only the fonts on your system that are available in landscape mode.

Base Font uses the same name-search feature as List Files. You can either scroll down the list with the cursor keys, or press **N** for **N**ame Search. Now press the first letter of the font you want, and WordPerfect will jump to the first font it finds beginning with that letter. Each additional letter you type will narrow the search until you are finally at the font you want.

Base Font is also useful when you want to specify an exact font (such as Times Roman 12 italic), rather than use WordPerfect's appearance attributes.

Because Base Font shows you a list of all the fonts available on your printer, it's also an effective way to determine that the font you're requesting is available. The Base Font list also contains important information regarding what font cartridge or downloadable fonts WordPerfect expects to be installed in the printer.

◆ Larger than Life

Another way to select fonts is by size and appearance. Size is obvious, in that it lets you make fonts bigger and smaller. But rather than use discrete font sizes, WordPerfect lets you choose fonts that are **F**ine, **S**mall, **L**arge, **V**ery Large, and **E**xtra Large. These sizes are relative, and depend on the size of the base font.

They also depend on the fonts you have available in the printer. If you're using a LaserJet with a Z cartridge and a 10-point base font, Fine will be Line Printer, Small will be 8 point, Large will be 12 point, and both Very Large and Extra large will be 14 point.

If you're using a PostScript printer (or have a wide variety of sizes available from Fontware and are using a 10 point base font), Fine is 6 point, Small is 8 point, Large is 12 point, Very Large is 18 point, and Extra Large is a rather strange 26 point.

The advantage of using size attributes over base font is that it is relative. If you change the size of the base font from 10 to 12 point, all the other sizes increase accordingly. Another advantage is that if you decide to change the body copy typeface, the size changes will still apply to whatever font you choose. On the other hand, if you had entered the sizes individually, you would have to go back and change them all manually (unless you used a style sheet, as covered in Chapter 10, *Styles*). This is also easier to use if point sizes confuse you.

Size is applied like underline and bold. You can either enter it as you go, or block the text you want to make larger or smaller, and then press

CONTROL-F8 S and the letter of the size you want (such as L for Large)

Fine 60%

Small 80%

Large 120%

Very Large 180%

Extra Large 250%

◆ Techno-nugget: "The Mysterious PTR Program"

For those not afraid to delve into their printer files with WordPerfect's PTR program, here's a way to see exactly what font WordPerfect will give you for each size, or to tell WordPerfect exactly which font *you* want it to use for each size. You can also tell WordPerfect not to show you italic and bold fonts as Base Fonts, just to use them when you select the attribute. This is useful when you have many fonts and don't want to have to search down the screen for the right one, or accidentally make the choice of turning all the text into italic or bold.

Before attempting this, ask yourself this question: Do I Feel Lucky? These instructions are meant for advanced or adventurous users. If you are the type of person who tends to make a mess of complex technical things, do this at your own risk. You can change things in this program that will make WordPerfect print strangely (or not at all). If this happens, you can reinstall the printer from scratch, but this is purely optional—you can live a long and happy life without the PTR program. So one more time, ask yourself this, "Do I really want to get into all this?" If the answer is "Yes," dive in. If the answer is "No, not the longest day I live, I'm sorry I even read this far," jump right down to the next subheading. If the answer is yes, go to DOS and type

PTR [ENTER]

(If you have a good imagination, you will hear wispy strains of the "Twilight Zone" theme song emanating from a location not far from your computer. If you don't, you'll hear disk drive noises.) If you haven't copied this program to your hard disk, put the disk labeled "PTR Program" in drive A: and type

A:PTR [ENTER]

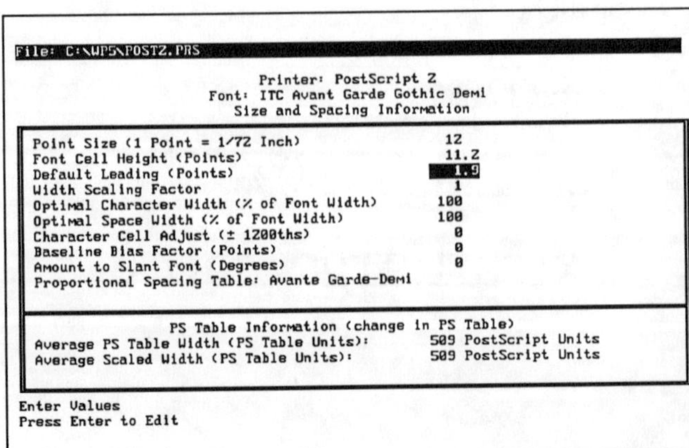

WordPerfect's PTR program allows you to change the default leading for each font. (But don't try it unless you are technically inclined.)

PTR uses the same major function keys as WordPerfect, so to retrieve a .PRS (single printer) file or an .ALL (many printers) press

SHIFT-F10

And enter the name of the file. One or more printers will appear on-screen. Move the cursor to the one you want and press

[ENTER]

Move the cursor to "Fonts" and press **[ENTER]**. A list of all the fonts in that printer driver will appear. Move the cursor to the font you are interested in and press

[ENTER]

Move the cursor to "Automatic Font Changes" and press

[ENTER]

This will show you the font WordPerfect will use when you select an attribute or size. If you want a printed copy of this, press **SHIFT-PrtSc** (if you are using a LaserJet the page will not eject automatically, and you will need to go to the printer and press the on-line key, then the form feed key, then the on-line key again).

You can change these selections by moving to the attribute or size you want to change and pressing **[ENTER]**. You will now be presented with yet another list of fonts. First un-mark the font WordPerfect has chosen by pressing the **[BACKSPACE]** key, then move to the font you want WordPerfect to use for this attribute and press *

File: C:\WP5\BODONI.PRS

Printer: HP LaserJet Series II
Font: (FW) Bodoni Book 11pt (ASCII) (Port)
Automatic Font Changes For
(FW) Bodoni Book 11pt (ASCII) (Port)

Feature	Font Name
Extra Large Print	(FW) Bodoni Bold 48pt (ASCII) (Port)
Very Large Print	(FW) Bodoni Book 18pt (ASCII) (Port)
Large Print	(FW) Bodoni Book 14pt (ASCII) (Port)
Small Print	(FW) Bodoni Book Italic 11pt (ASCII) (Port)
Fine Print	(FW) Bodoni Book Italic 11pt (ASCII) (Port)
Superscript	(FW) Bodoni Book Italic 11pt (ASCII) (Port)
Subscript	(FW) Bodoni Book Italic 11pt (ASCII) (Port)
Outline	
Italics	(FW) Bodoni Book Italic 11pt (ASCII) (Port)
Shadow	
Redline	
Double Underline	
Bold	

Enter Select Automatic Font Change:
Switch Cross Reference List:

WordPerfect's PTR program allows you to change WordPerfect's defaults for automatic font control, but should only be used by the young and the restless, or the brave.

To leave the font control for that single font, press

F7

Repeat this for each font you want to view or change.

If you want to remove a font from the list of base fonts, but still use it when you want bold or italic attributes, move down to "Miscellaneous Font Features" and press

[ENTER]

Move down to "Use Font Only For Automatic Font Changes" and press

*

Remember, once you do this, the font will not appear on the list of base fonts, and you will only be able to access it through attributes such as bold or italic.

If you want to do this for all your bold and italic fonts, you will have to repeat this process for each font individually. (Of course, if you accidentally delete something, you can bring it back immediately by using WordPerfect's Cancel command [the F1 key] to undelete.)

To leave the PTR program, press **F7** over and over until the program asks you "Save File?" If you are secure in the changes you made, press **Y** to save the file. If you are not, press **N**.

◆ All appearances

➾ WordPerfect has nine standard appearance attributes, illustrated at right.

These are the attributes of a PostScript printer: Bold Underline, Double underline, Italic, Outline, Shadow, Small Cap, Redline, and ~~Strikeout.~~ Notice how bold and italic affect underlines. Appearances can be combined in any and all combinations, depending on what the printer will support.

Bold

Italic

Bold Italic

Normal

Outline

Redline

Shadow

SMALL CAP

~~Strikeout~~

PostScript printers have special effects built in.

The true bold version of most fonts is more than just a double strike—it's a completely different design. While a true bold font looks better, if you don't have one or lack the memory for one, WordPerfect will make one for you by double striking the character and shifting it slightly. This pseudo-bolding looks okay, but not as authentic as a real bold version of a font. Sometimes it won't even be discernable. If you're using a light font (i.e., Futura Light), WordPerfect's bolding will show; but if you're using a font that is already fairly heavy, you won't notice the difference.

◆ LaserJet

Bold
Italic
Bold Italic
Normal
Outline
Redline
Shadow
SMALL CAP
~~Strikeout~~

Special effects on a LaserJet aren't so special, but PostScript-like effects can be made with Font Effects and LaserFonts, both from SoftCraft.

What happens when you have 30-point Times Roman available, and you choose an italic attribute? You will get italic in the size closest to your current font. If the closest size you have is 24-point, you get 24-point italic.

What if you didn't have Times Roman 30-point italic, but did have a 30-point Helvetica italic font? WordPerfect wouldn't even consider using the 30-point Helvetica italic, because your base font is Times Roman. It will insist on the next size of Times Roman it can find.

If no italic version of the base font exists, as in Bitstream's version of Avant Garde, WordPerfect will *underline* the text, as this is the traditional way to signify italics when none are available. Now SHIFT-F7 V comes in real handy because it lets you know what you're going to get before you print.

If you use any of these attributes frequently, you may want to create a macro to speed formatting and eliminate keystrokes, or change the underline key to italics using the soft keyboard feature. You may also want to use style sheets. See Chapter 10, *Styles*, and Chapter 15, *Macros*, for more tips on speed formatting and changing appearances.

Appearance is applied like underline and bold: you can either enter it as you go, or block the text you want to change the appearance of and press

CONTROL F8 A

and the letter or number of the attribute you want.

◆ Tip: Turn it off already.

When applying an appearance attribute such as italic, the WordPerfect manual tells you to repeat the process used to turn it on. In the case of italics, this means typing

CONTROL F8 A I

to turn the appearance on and off. But there's a short cut for turning the attribute off that requires only one keystroke rather than four. Instead of typing **CONTROL F8 A I**, press the **[RIGHT ARROW]** key once.

When you turn italics (or any appearance) on, WordPerfect inserts a matched pair of codes, one to start and one to stop the attribute. This prevents you from accidentally having bold, italic, or underlining on for an entire page (like I always used to have with WordStar).

Pressing the right arrow will move the cursor outside the stop code for italics (or any appearance), thereby turning it off. If you're a skeptic, turn REVEAL CODES on with **ALT F3** and see how it operates for yourself.

◆ Tip: Underlines mean italics

Always replace underlines with italics when using a proportional font. (The underline is a typesetters code; before desktop publishing, few typewriters had italic fonts.)

◆ Tip: Underlines are italics

Here's an easy way to change attributes globally (throughout the entire document) using styles. Most draft copies are printed in monospaced fonts, such as Courier, and use underlines to signify italics. Since the LaserJet doesn't come with an italic version of Courier, text marked as italic will print with an underline. When you select a proportional font, the italics will print as italic. But if you use a PostScript printer, or an other laser printer that includes an italic version of Courier, use the style trick.

◆ Tip: Underlines become italics

If you want to create a style that allows you to instantly change underlines to italics (and back), see Chapter 10, *Styles*.

◆ Color me puce

While there are currently few color printers with high resolution, functional color laser printers are on the horizon, and WordPerfect is ready for them. WordPerfect not only lets you select 11 standard colors, but it allows you to mix your own.

Appearance is applied as in underline and bold: you can either enter it as you go, or block the text you want to make larger or smaller, and press

CONTROL-F8 C and the letter or number of the color you want.

You mix colors by telling WordPerfect what percentage of each primary color you want. Black type is 0% red, 0% blue and 0% yellow, while white is 100% of each.

If you have a black and white printer, what good is the color setting? Not much if you have a LaserJet, but you can use the color setting to prepare separations for offset printing, as detailed in Chapter 14, *Printing*. For special effects on a LaserJet, see Font Effects in Chapter 17. If you have a PostScript printer, read the "PostScript extras" later on in this chapter.

◆ Blue feeling gray over you

If you have a PostScript printer, the colors menu opens up a Pandora's box in shades of gray. Gray type can be attractive and effective when used for emphasis or to lighten the impact of very large type.

While it seems logical that selecting "Other" and choosing 10% would result in 10% gray type, it's just the opposite: 10% gives you 90% gray (almost black).

If you select 90% for **all three** of the colors, you will get light gray characters. WordPerfect allows you to enter numbers in 1 percent increments and, while subtle, each percentage makes a difference. If you are printing the final pages on a Linotronic typesetter, the 1% increments will be more pronounced.

Remember to enter the gray screen you want in **all three** of the color categories, or you won't wind up with the exact shade you requested. Refer to the chart on the next page.

99 99 99

95 95 95

90 90 90

80 80 80

70 70 70

60 60 60

50 50 50

40 40 40

30 30 30

20 20 20

10 10 10

BLACK

OUTLINE

50 50 50

SHADOW

50 50 50

BOLD

50 50 50

While you may not have a color laser printer yet, if you have a PostScript printer you can use WordPerfect's color feature to create gray type.

If you select 90% for **all three** *of the colors, you will get light gray characters. WordPerfect allows you to enter numbers in 1 percent increments and, while subtle, each percentage makes a difference, as you can see.*

Remember to enter the gray screen you want in **all three** *of the color categories, or you won't wind up with the exact shade you requested.*

◆ Normalcy

The one function I haven't covered from the Font function key is #3, Normal. While it's fairly self-explanatory, it doesn't insert any code of its own. Selecting

CONTROL F8 N

tells WordPerfect to turn off any attributes you've selected from the Appearance, Size, and Menus, and bring everything back to the Base Font. Normal lets you turn off all attributes in a single command, and saves you the bother of having to turn them off individually. Normal does not affect color.

The command is also very effective when creating styles, as only opening appearance and size codes are entered automatically.

◆ Put on a happy space

One WordPerfect feature you may never use is word and letter spacing control. The name of this feature is a bit misleading for people who know about type. The letterspacing control is actually tracking. Rather than controlling the amount of space between letters for justification, it controls the amount of space between letters at all times. The wordspacing command really controls the space between words.

You would normally use the letterspacing command if your font appears to have too much space between each letter. When letters aren't close enough to each other, it's hard to differentiate between the spaces between letters and the spaces between words. The LaserJet "B" cartridge has a real problem in this department. Sometimes you just want to add more space between each letter (to strengthen the impact of a headline, for example). Press

SHIFT-F8 O P W [ENTER] P

and then a number less than 100% to make the letters print closer together, or a number greater than 100% to make them print farther apart. In general, setting the number at less than 90% will make each letter touch the next, and make text hard to read. A setting of more than 110% will create a noticeable gap between each letter and, while this is fine for headlines, subheads, kickers, or other larger type, it's impossible for body text.

If the space between each word seems too large or too small, you can alter it as well. Press

SHIFT-F8 O P W P

and then a number larger than 100% to make the spaces larger, or a number less than 100% to make them smaller. Whether it's for special effect, or just to improve the appearance of type, you may use WordPerfect's letter spacing (or tracking) frequently.

❖ *Jerome Kern, a man and his music...*

Oops, sorry, wrong Kern. Kerning is a process that moves specific pairs of letter closer together in order to create a more attractive, easier to read word.

Here's an example:

AWARE (unkerned)

AWARE (kerned)

Notice how there's less space between the letters of the second word. While kerning is more obvious with headlines and other large type, it can make a subtle improvement in smaller sizes. To turn kerning on press

SHIFT-F8 O P K Y F7

To turn it off, press

SHIFT-F8 O P K N F7

I've yet to have any occasion to turn kerning off. In fact, I entered it in my initial codes through the setup menu, so that the kerning on code is placed in all of my files as I create them. To do this, type

SHIFT-F1 I I SHIFT-F8 O P K Y F7

❖ *Making do with less*

What, you don't have a PostScript printer? You don't have 1.5 megabytes of LaserJet memory? Money *doesn't* grow on trees? Gee, then you can't possibly produce anything that looks attractive and professional, right?

Wrong. While PostScript printers or large quantities of LaserJet memory offer you power with a lot of options, you can easily do without them if you just use a little imagination.

Some noted designers avoid large type, believing that smaller sizes force the reader to pay attention. (Just as many designers think that you can't grab a reader's attention without using large type, but quoting them would only negate the intention of this section, so I'll simply pretend they don't exist.)

If you have a plain LaserJet with font cartridges, or even a LaserJet II with only 512K, your options are limited. The largest font in a cartridge is 16 point (normally only large enough for a subhead, not a headline), while a 512K LaserJet II is limited to about 30 point (adequate, but not really big enough for a commanding headline).

While size is a quick way to garner attention, it's not the *only* way. You can spruce up pages with small type by simply using ruling lines and white space. Ruling lines take up memory, however, and if your laser printer doesn't have much, you'll hate to use it sparingly. But white space takes up no memory, just imagination.

Rule This: Heavy ruling lines above headlines attract the readers eye and make the type seem larger and more commanding. When designing documents with related material, such as newsletters and newspapers, remember to use ruling lines above but not below headlines. This is because lines are a form of separation and a line under a headline breaks the connection between the headline and the material beneath it. In WordPerfect, .01" will give you a thin line, while .1" gives you a thick one. Also, make sure there's enough space under the line and above the headline.

Spaced Out: White space is, if not free, then at least reasonable. If the largest type you have is 14 point (as it is with the HP Z cartridge), one way to make it appear larger is to simply put a space between each letter. Make sure to add a couple of spaces between each word, and to be consistent with the amount of space you've added. The more complicated WordPerfect procedure is to press

SHIFT-F8 O P W [ENTER] P

and then enter any number above 100 (the normal letter spacing). Entering 200 gives each letter twice as much space as it would normally have, and you can enter any number up to 250. This also automatically makes the space between words larger. Be sure to set this back to 100 after the headline (or any expanded text) so that the regular body text is spaced correctly.

Of course, the ultimate bit of trickery involves both ruling lines and white space. A thick black rule over widely spaced text is going to take up the most space and grab the greatest attention when using small typesizes.

Lest you think that all this work leads only to artificially filled pages, the results, you will be pleased to know, are extremely attractive. Even designers who feel that large type is de rigueur often find it useful/hip to use small type and some of the tricks I've just mentioned. See the resume example in Chapter 4, *Show & Tell.*

◆ It's all symbolic

ASCII (pronounced Ask-key) no questions and I'll tell you no lies—or so it seems. But even though ASCII is an internationally standardized system for assigning decimal equivalents to letters, numbers, and common punctuation, once you get past ASCII 126 (~) it's Cole Porter time—anything goes.

Basically, you will want real opening and closing quote marks, em and en dashes, foreign language characters, and bullets. The bad news is that you can't get real quote marks on the LaserJet with WordPerfect (unless you know a ridiculously simple trick that I'll clue you in on later; ah, the suspense).

The IBM PC (254 characters) has its own symbol set (those little happy faces, line draw characters, and some international letters vital to upscale ice-cream establishments such as Häagen Dazs and Stëve's). This entertaining set has many different symbols which are useful for bullets, but no real opening and closing quote marks. The ANSI standard has 255 characters, including the typographic necessities of opening and closing quote marks and bullets. Yet another entire character set, referred to as the Symbol Set, is included in PostScript printers. This set has Greek and mathematical symbols, but doesn't have the same A-Z characters as the others.

Many people are used to working with typewriters that lack even such common symbols as "{}[]<> ^ |~' and \," and they don't miss real quotes, dashes, and bullets. Still, when you are ready for serious desktop publishing, these differences are important.

Say you want real opening and closing quote marks (and don't feel badly if you don't). The IBM PC character set doesn't support them at all. For PostScript printers, WordPerfect forces you to enter them as

CONTROL-V 4,32 [ENTER]

(the two on the keyboard, not on the number pad) for an opening quote mark, and

CONTROL-V 4,31 [ENTER]

for a closing quote mark. Of course, you can create a macro to simplify this process, or a complex macro to turn all the regular quote marks into opening and closing quote marks automatically.

As if that weren't confusing enough, many fonts don't even contain extended characters—those above ASCII 126. Hewlett-Packard sells fonts in both US-ASCII and Roman (foreign) character sets. HP's US-ASCII fonts contain nothing above ASCII 126, so, unless you're willing to use a little trickery, you can forget about opening/closing quotes, real dashes, bullets, and other typographic goodies.

While you can survive without the fancy typographic characters, be aware that pressing **CONTROL-V 4,32 [ENTER]** in WordPerfect won't give you a real opening quote mark unless it's in your font. WordPerfect will still display the character on-screen, but all you'll get is either a blank space or an unexpected character when the file is printed.

Fontware

LaserJet users have two choices for fonts, while PostScript users have just one. If you have a LaserJet, you can choose between ASCII or HP Roman 8. As I mentioned before, unless you are going to use foreign characters, the only features the Roman 8 offers are an em-dash, 1/2 and 1/4 symbols, and two bullets. In exchange, it takes much longer to create and takes up about twice as much disk space. Again, don't try to use the PostScript character set; not only won't it work, but it will mess up the printer file and make it unusable. If you use a PostScript printer, select the PostScript character set.

Adobe's Times Roman includes all the typographic niceties and a foreign character set. Weaver "TR," Glyphix "RM," and Conographic "Times" have the regular ASCII characters only (although Conographic Times comes with a set of "pi" fonts that includes several styles of bullets, arrows, copyright, and registered marks).

◆ Retain your compose-ure

Because there are far more characters than there are keys on the keyboard, WordPerfect had to come up with a way to enter them. They call this **Compose.** It allows you to create characters that are not on the keyboard (foreign characters such as ñ), by using ones that are. You can also enter characters that have no keyboard equivalent at all, such as æ.

To see exactly what characters and symbols the printer has, print the file called CHARMAP.TST on WordPerfect's "Conversion" disk. This file contains all the characters in WordPerfect's 12 different character sets. By comparing the printout with the tables in the WordPerfect manual's appendix, you'll be able to see which characters you can and cannot print. Printing this file is also advisable, because it provides you with a quick-reference guide for the symbols and characters available on your printer.

If you are using a LaserJet II printer (not the standard LaserJet, or the LaserJet Plus), you can print any of the IBM symbols that appear on the screen (the heart, the happy face, bullets, etc). These can be entered by either holding down the ALT key and typing their decimal equivalent on the Numberpad, or by using compose.

I find it easier to use the ALT key method for the LaserJet, because it requires fewer keystrokes than WordPerfect's compose. Bear in mind, however, that many of these symbols are available only in the internal "line-draw" character set, so you can only print them in the one built-in size.

If the character you want is not in the particular LaserJet font your using (such as an ASCII Fontware soft font), the LaserJet will print the correct character from one of its internal fonts, instead of the correct font. This doesn't make much difference when you're using symbols, but if you are printing a file in a downloadable ASCII font and ask for a foreign character, the LaserJet will print the character in Courier and it will look out of place. Also, the LaserJet's internal fonts are all 10 point, so they will look out-of-place with anything other than 9 to 12 point type.

The next two pages show charts of the IBM Character Set, with all the special symbols it includes. All of these symbols will appear on-screen in text mode, whether they can be used with your printer or not. While the LaserJet II can print them all, the only way to ensure that the character you've chosen will print is to

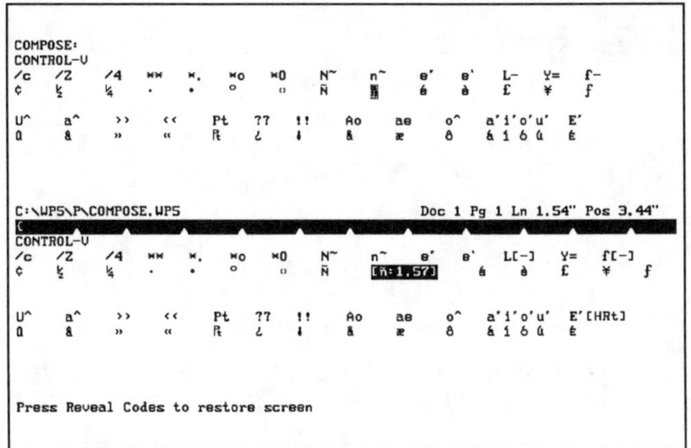

Compose is not a command for budding musicians. No, no, no. It's a way to combine two characters into one that isn't otherwise accessible from the keyboard.

use View Document, or to actually print it. On the PostScript version of the Character Set chart, note the symbols that are available using ALT-Key combinations.

If you're using a standard LaserJet or LaserJet Plus, HP sells a font cartridge that contains the "line draw" character set. This includes the entire IBM on-screen character set, and the foreign characters.

There are two ways to use WordPerfect's Compose feature. The first is to press **Control-V** (that's the two above the letters, not on the keypad), and enter the two characters that you want to merge into one. To create a ç, press

Control-V c ,

and WordPerfect will combine the two characters into one Cedilla. This is the easiest method if a keyboard equivalent is available for the each of the two characters you want to combine. Many of these characters will show on-screen; if they don't, WordPerfect will display either the first character you entered, or a small black square. If you turn Reveal Codes on (ALT-F3), and place the cursor on the character, WordPerfect will show the numerical representation for the character. Ü, for example, displays in Reveal Codes as [Ü:1,70].

If your printer has one half and one quarter characters, you can use Compose to access them. **CONTROL-V /2** gives you a one half character, **CONTROL-V /4** gives you a one quarter character.

If the two parts of the character are not available on the keyboard (such as a mathematical character), you must refer to a section of the WordPerfect manual's Appendix entitled "WordPerfect Characters." Find the character you

❖ LaserJet ASCII/ALT-Key symbols

									10										20									
1	2	3	4	5	6	7	8	9		1	2	3	4	5	6	7	8	9		1	2	3	4	5	6	7	8	9
☺	☻	♥	♦	♣	♠	•	◘	○	◙	♂	♀	♪	♫	☼	►	◄	↕	‼	¶	§	▬	↨	↑	↓	→	←	∟	↔

30										40										50									
	1	2	3	4	5	6	7	8	9		1	2	3	4	5	6	7	8	9		1	2	3	4	5	6	7	8	9
▲	▼		!	"	#	$	%	&	'	(	)	*	+	,	-	.	/	0	1	2	3	4	5	6	7	8	9	:	;

60										70										80									
	1	2	3	4	5	6	7	8	9		1	2	3	4	5	6	7	8	9		1	2	3	4	5	6	7	8	9
<	=	>	?	@	A	B	C	D	E	F	G	H	I	J	K	L	M	N	O	P	Q	R	S	T	U	V	W	X	Y

90										100										110									
	1	2	3	4	5	6	7	8	9		1	2	3	4	5	6	7	8	9		1	2	3	4	5	6	7	8	9
Z	[	\	]	^	_	`	a	b	c	d	e	f	g	h	i	j	k	l	m	n	o	p	q	r	s	t	u	v	w

120										130										140									
	1	2	3	4	5	6	7	8	9		1	2	3	4	5	6	7	8	9		1	2	3	4	5	6	7	8	9
x	y	z	{			}	˜		♀	ü	é	â	ä	à	å	ç	ê	ë	è	ï	î	ì	Ä	Å	É	æ	Æ	ô	ö	ò

150										160										170									
	1	2	3	4	5	6	7	8	9		1	2	3	4	5	6	7	8	9		1	2	3	4	5	6	7	8	9
û	ù		Ö	Ü	¢	£	¥	₧	ƒ	á	í	ó	ú	ñ	Ñ	ª	º	¿	⌐	¬	½	¼	¡	«	»	░	▒	▓	│

180										190										200									
	1	2	3	4	5	6	7	8	9		1	2	3	4	5	6	7	8	9		1	2	3	4	5	6	7	8	9
┤	╡	╢	╖	╕	╣	║	╗	╝	╜	╛	┐	└	┴	┬	├	─	┼	╞	╟	╚	╔	╩	╦	╠	═	╬	╧	╨	╤

210										220										230									
	1	2	3	4	5	6	7	8	9		1	2	3	4	5	6	7	8	9		1	2	3	4	5	6	7	8	9
╥	╙	╘	╒	╓	╫	╪	┘	┌	█	▄	▌	▐	▀	α	β	Γ	π	Σ	σ	µ	τ	Φ		Ω	δ	∞	φ	ε	∩

240										250				
	1	2	3	4	5	6	7	8	9		1	2	3	4
≡	±	≥	≤	⌠	⌡	÷	≈	°	•	·	√	η	²	■

❖ PostScript ASCII/ALT-Key symbols

```
                    10                  20
  1 2 3 4 5 6 7 8 9   1 2 3 4 5 6 7 8 9   1 2 3 4 5 6 7 8 9
              •                         ¶ §

30                  40                  50
  1 2 3 4 5 6 7 8 9   1 2 3 4 5 6 7 8 9   1 2 3 4 5 6 7 8 9
      ! " # $ % & ' ( ) * + , - . / 0 1 2 3 4 5 6 7 8 9 : ;

60                  70                  80
  1 2 3 4 5 6 7 8 9   1 2 3 4 5 6 7 8 9   1 2 3 4 5 6 7 8 9
< = > ? @ A B C D E F G H I J K L M N O P Q R S T U V W X Y

90                  100                 110
  1 2 3 4 5 6 7 8 9   1 2 3 4 5 6 7 8 9   1 2 3 4 5 6 7 8 9
Z [ \ ] ^ _ ` a b c d e f g h i j k l m n o p q r s t u v w

120                 130                 140
  1 2 3 4 5 6 7 8 9   1 2 3 4 5 6 7 8 9   1 2 3 4 5 6 7 8 9
x y z { | } ~     ü é â ä à å ç ê ë è ï î ì Ä Å É æ Æ ô ö ò

150                 160                 170
  1 2 3 4 5 6 7 8 9   1 2 3 4 5 6 7 8 9   1 2 3 4 5 6 7 8 9
û ù   Ö Ü ¢ £ ¥   ƒ á í ó ú ñ Ñ ª º ¿         ¡ « »

180                 190                 200
  1 2 3 4 5 6 7 8 9   1 2 3 4 5 6 7 8 9   1 2 3 4 5 6 7 8 9

210                 220                 230
  1 2 3 4 5 6 7 8 9   1 2 3 4 5 6 7 8 9   1 2 3 4 5 6 7 8 9
                              ß

240                 250
  1 2 3 4 5 6 7 8 9   1 2 3 4
```

need among the 12 different WordPerfect character sets, and press **CONTROL-V**. Type the number of the character set, a comma, the number of the character, and press **[ENTER]**. A Sigma will be entered as **CONTROL-V 8,36 [ENTER]**. (Because the Sigma is also included in the PC character set, it can be entered as ALT-228).

Printing the CHARMAP.TST file (on the WordPerfect Convert disk) will show you which characters you can and can't print, and what their Compose numbers are.

◆ What a bunch of bullets

A quick way to make three different sizes of bullets.

Small bullets:

CONTROL-V *.

(That was "asterisk period")

Medium Bullets

CONTROL-V **

Small hollow bullets

*o

Large hollow bullets

*O

◆ Quotability

Typewriters use the same character for both opening and closing quote marks, but typesetting uses two different characters. While WordPerfect does support these characters using the compose feature, you should also consider using the following.

•◆ Incredibly simple LaserJet TRICK

Real quote marks are not supported by WordPerfect for the LaserJet because they are not part of the regular HP symbol set. That's the bad news. The good news is that it's ridiculously simple to create them yourself. Robert Fenchel, Ph.D., of SoftCraft told me about this trick and I could have kicked myself for not thinking of it earlier. All you do is use the grave accent ' (the backwards apostrophe located under the ~on most keyboards) twice before a word, and the normal apostrophe twice after a word. Here's an example: "Simple." The quotes will appear widely spaced on-screen, but will print perfectly. In View Document, the opening quotes will have the correct appearance, but the closing quotes will look straight. Don't worry about it; the spacing will still be accurate.

Wasn't that easy? You won't appreciate how easy it was until you try to obtain real opening and closing quote marks by using the complex, technical procedure. If you're the kind who must have the genuine article, rather than a 99.99% facsimile, you will have to buy SoftCraft's FontWare installation program, and SoftCraft's LaserFonts program (or their "Word Processor Font Solution Pack" that contains both of them).

Using these two programs, you can pick and choose what you want from all among 560 of Bitstream's characters, create your own symbol sets, and give them whatever WordPerfect character set number you want. The program also lets you install any downloadable font, and creates outline and shadow fonts for the LaserJet. Some people will prefer the strategy mentioned above because you can see the quote marks (rather than little black boxes) on-screen.

For more information about this and other third party utilities, see Chapter 17.

PostScript: The simplest way to produce real opening and closing quote marks is by using the same crafty maneuver I just described for LaserJet printers.

If you want the real McCoy, WordPerfect's Compose feature can insert real typographic quote marks into your publications. To get an opening quote mark, type

CONTROL-V 4,32 [ENTER]

To get a closing quote mark, type

CONTROL-V 4,31 [ENTER]

Because the PC doesn't have real opening and closing quote marks in its character set, you will see a small square box on-screen where the quote mark will print. You can see the real character in View Document.

Macro: If you are going to use these frequently, it is advisable to create a macro. Since they are used so often, you will probably want to use an ALT-key macro, as they require fewer keystrokes. To create a macro that inserts an opening quote mark when you press **ALT-O**, type

CONTROL F10 ALT-O OPEN QUOTE [ENTER] CONTROL-V 4,32 CONTROL F10

Once you've created this macro, you will only need to press **ALT-O** for WordPerfect to insert an opening quote mark. For a closing quote macro, type

CONTROL F10 ALT-C CLOSE QUOTE [ENTER] CONTROL-V 4,31 CONTROL F10

◆ PostScript extras

PostScript endows you with a wide range of great options and effects not available on other printers. They should, they cost enough.

With PostScript printers, the special effects are indeed special. Outline and shadow can be applied to any PostScript font, except for Courier. Unlike all other PostScript fonts, Courier is a "stroke" font rather than an "outline," and so special effects will not work.

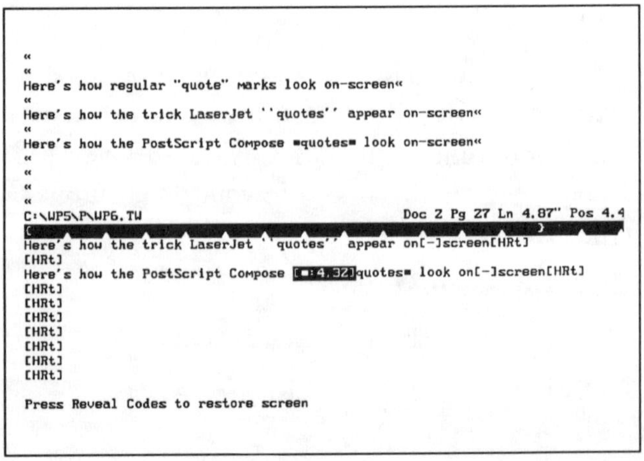

```
«
«
Here's how regular "quote" marks look on-screen«
«
Here's how the trick LaserJet ''quotes'' appear on-screen«
«
Here's how the PostScript Compose ▪quotes▪ look on-screen«
«
«
«
«
C:\WP5\P\WP6.TW                       Doc 2 Pg 27 Ln 4.87" Pos 4.4
Here's how the trick LaserJet ''quotes'' appear on[-]screen[HRt]
[HRt]
Here's how the PostScript Compose [▪:4,32]quotes▪ look on[-]screen[HRt]
[HRt]
[HRt]
[HRt]
[HRt]
[HRt]
[HRt]
[HRt]

Press Reveal Codes to restore screen
```

Since real typographic quotes aren't in the IBM character set, you have to kludge them. This is how they appear on-screen. (You'll get used to it.)

While outline is self-explanatory, the shadow effect has the additional bonus of being opaque; it will print solid white with a black outline, even when you place it on top of a graphic. (See the Abe Lincoln example.)

But as well as the obvious outlines and shadows, WordPerfect offers two additional undocumented PostScript type extras. The first is gray type, by pressing

CONTROL F8 C

Refer to the section about color earlier in this chapter.

The second extra is reverse type,or white type on a black background. While studies have shown (oh, another study, enough already) that white type is at least 18% harder to read than black type, there are times when it is effective, especially with larger sizes.

While "White" is an obvious choice in the color menu, you're probably wondering how to produce a black background. The answer? Graphics boxes. While I delve into excruciating detail about this in Chapter 11, *Graphics.* I know the suspense is killing you PostScript junkies out there, so here goes.

You should decide what type of graphics box you want to use. It can be a Figure, Table, Text, or User-defined box; it makes no difference (as you will find out if you can hack your way through the Chapter 11, *Graphics*). In this example, we'll use a figure.

Press

ALT-F9 F O

to set the Figure Options.

Press

G 100 [ENTER][ENTER]

Congratulations, you've just set the background of the box to black.

Now create a graphic Figure with

ALT-F9 F C

Make the box any size you want. If you want the background of the entire page to be black, create a page type box. Press

F

for... you guessed it, full. Now press

E

to edit the text inside the box. Set the type color to white with

CONTROL-F8 C W [ENTER]

and then type and format the text. Text inside a graphics box must not exceed one page. When you are done, press

F7 F7

You will be returned to the editing screen. If Reveal Codes is on, you will see the marker for the graphic; if it's off, you will see nothing.

If you preview the page with **SHIFT-F7 V,** you will get a great view of a black box. You won't see any type, however, because WordPerfect's View Document doesn't display white type on a black background. I guess they didn't think anyone would figure out how to use it. I guess they didn't know me...I guess they underestimated me.

You can examine the text only by printing the page. It will print perfectly, with white type on a black background. If you desire white type on a gray background, repeat the above steps, but when at Figure Options, enter a number lower than 100. The background setting works logically, with 100% being solid black and 0 being white. White type requires a background of at least 20% gray in order to be readable, and even that is not quite enough. On lower percentages of gray, the type may appear ragged because it is surrounded with dots placed far apart from each other. When printed on a typesetting machine, the grays will be much smoother, and the type easier to read.

❖ *Dingbats in style*

A good way to use Dingbats is with a paired Style. You must change to the Dingbat font, even if you want to print a single dingbat character. Talk about tedious. The paired style consists of nothing more than just a [Font:Dingbat 14pt] (or whatever size you want) code. Don't put anything in after the [Comment] code. When you want Dingbats, turn this style on, then use Control-V to choose the character. All dingbats are in Set 12 and are only in the special POST2.PRS driver on Disk 6.

➻ The chart on the next page shows where the Zapf Dingbat set has been mapped in the WordPerfect user-defined character set. You must select the Dingbat Font, then press **CONTROL-V** and the numbers which precede the dingbat you want to use (including the comma).

12,33	✁	12,74	✪	12,115	▲	12,190	❾	12,231	➧
12,34	✂	12,75	✫	12,116	▼	12,191	❿	12,232	➨
12,35	✃	12,76	✬	12,117	◆	12,192	➀	12,233	➩
12,36	✄	12,77	✭	12,118	❖	12,193	➁	12,234	➪
12,37	☎	12,78	✮	12,119	◗	12,194	➂	12,235	➫
12,38	✆	12,79	✯	12,120	❘	12,195	➃	12,236	➬
12,39	✇	12,80	✰	12,121	❙	12,196	➄	12,237	➭
12,40	✈	12,81	✱	12,122	❚	12,197	➅	12,238	➮
12,41	✉	12,82	✲	12,123	❛	12,198	➆	12,239	➯
12,42	☛	12,83	✳	12,124	❜	12,199	➇	12,241	➱
12,43	☞	12,84	✴	12,125	❝	12,200	➈	12,242	➲
12,44	✌	12,85	✵	12,126	❞	12,201	➉	12,243	➳
12,45	✍	12,86	✶	12,161	❡	12,202	➊	12,244	➴
12,46	✎	12,87	✷	12,162	❢	12,203	➋	12,245	➵
12,47	✏	12,88	✸	12,163	❣	12,204	➌	12,246	➶
12,48	✐	12,89	✹	12,164	❤	12,205	➍	12,247	➷
12,49	✑	12,90	✺	12,165	❥	12,206	➎	12,248	➸
12,50	✒	12,91	✻	12,166	❦	12,207	➏	12,249	➹
12,51	✓	12,92	✼	12,167	❧	12,208	➐	12,250	➺
12,52	✔	12,93	✽	12,168	♣	12,209	➑	12,251	➻
12,53	✕	12,94	✾	12,169	♦	12,210	➒	12,252	➼
12,54	✖	12,95	✿	12,170	♥	12,211	➓	12,253	➽
12,55	✗	12,96	❀	12,171	♠	12,212	➔	12,254	➾
12,56	✘	12,97	❁	12,172	①	12,213	→		
12,57	✙	12,98	❂	12,173	②	12,214	↔	Opening Quotes,	
12,58	✚	12,99	❃	12,174	③	12,215	↕	any font:	
12,59	✛	12,100	❄	12,175	④	12,216	➘	4,32 “	
12,60	✜	12,101	❅	12,176	⑤	12,217	➙	Closing Quotes,	
12,61	✝	12,102	❆	12,177	⑥	12,218	➚	any font:	
12,62	✞	12,103	❇	12,178	⑦	12,219	➛	4,31 ”	
12,63	✟	12,104	❈	12,179	⑧	12,220	➜		
12,64	✠	12,105	❉	12,180	⑨	12,221	➝	En Dash:	
12,65	✡	12,106	❊	12,181	⑩	12,222	➞	4,33 –	
12,66	✢	12,107	❋	12,182	❶	12,223	➟	Em Dash:	
12,67	✣	12,108	●	12,183	❷	12,224	➠	4,34 —	
12,68	✤	12,109	❍	12,184	❸	12,225	➡		
12,69	✥	12,110	■	12,185	❹	12,226	➢	4,22 ®	
12,70	✦	12,111	❏	12,186	❺	12,227	➣	4,23 ©	
12,71	✧	12,112	❐	12,187	❻	12,228	➤	4,41 ™	
12,72	★	12,113	❑	12,188	❼	12,229	➥	4,7 ¡	
12,73	☆	12,114	❒	12,189	❽	12,230	➦	4,8 ¿	

8

What's my alignment?

Paragraph technicalities

Before we explore paragraph alignment, justification, hyphenation, letterspacing, word spacing, and other universal themes, I'm going to try once more to show you how crazy it is to format while you write. Printing out drafts that look typeset is seductive, but dangerous. First, you can easily spend more time formatting than writing; but your written message is the one you are trying to get across, not the formatting.

Second, pages printed in just plain Courier look like just plain drafts. Ephemeral. Inconsequential. Easy to change. Pages printed in Times Roman or Helvetica, or even our old friend Upchuck #3, have a final, untouchable appearance.

There is an exception to this rule. If you are creating a document with the same format you've worked with before, and you know you're going to be using a headline, byline, subhead, whatever, it's okay to enter those codes. Just don't spend a lot of time checking back and forth between Edit and View Document mode. Don't worry about page breaks or line endings. Just worry about the text.

In Chapter 10, *Styles,* I'll cover ways to transform a standard Courier draft form into a completely formatted final form in as little as three keystrokes.

❖ *Alignment*

WordPerfect gives you a choice between only two basic forms of paragraph alignment: Justified and Ragged Right.

Justified: Many people consider ragged right easier to read, but justified type can fit far more copy onto a page. Justification is tricky because it requires careful hyphenation; you must also pay attention to letter and word spacing (covered later in this chapter) and to lines that aren't too short. Justified type looks more formal, appears more... typeset. Good justification is beautiful; bad justification is ugly and hard to read. Bad justification is easy; good justification is hard*er*.

◆ **TIP: Period space space**

Never ever use a double space after a period when setting justified type. Yes, I know what you learned in school, but that was for typing, and this is the glamorous world of typesetting. Because justification adds extra space between words, a space could be added after the period, resulting in three spaces that produce a huge gap. Ask any typesetter, and they'll tell you single spaces belong after punctuation.

Ragged: Ragged type is easier to set, and very much in style with many applications (*excluding* books and most magazines). It's less formal, takes up more space, and is less intimidating because it requires less attention to hyphenation and letter and word spacing.

Centered/Flush Right: WordPerfect also allows for text to be aligned centered or flush right (but these are not automatic). Once you've formatted a paragraph with centered or flush right alignment, WordPerfect puts a hard return at the end of each line; this makes further editing difficult.

Selecting either justified or ragged is simple. Press

SHIFT F8 L J N F7

to turn justification off and set the copy as ragged. Press

SHIFT F8 L J Y F7

to turn justification on and set the type with justified. You can turn justification on and off at will ("Fire at will" was never a favorite expression of mine), and use the code within styles.

STYLE WARNING: (You just know it's going to be something bad, don't you?) The justification code sometimes performs unexpectedly in styles. That's a polite way of saying that it doesn't work the way it should, or the way I think it should. If you want to use this code in a style, review Chapter 10, "Styles" for an agonizing and thorough trek through this earth-shattering ordeal.

CENTERING as you type: WordPerfect can center text as you write. Press return so that you are on a new line and press

SHIFT-F6

The cursor will jump to the middle of the line and, as you type, the words will appear to move to the left. WordPerfect can achieve spacing in much smaller amounts than the screen can, and so lines with an even number of characters will center more accurately on the printer (or in View Document) than they do on-screen.

CENTERING after you've typed, *or centering entire paragraphs.* Another way to center text is by blocking the area to be centered, using

ALT F4

(to block the text you want centered) then press

SHIFT F6

WordPerfect will ask you if you're sure you want to center the text, and you press

Y

to center it, or **N** to forget it. If you block a paragraph and center it, WordPerfect places hard returns at the end of each line, and the paragraph becomes a series of lines, rather than a single paragraph. If you want to edit the text later, it will not wrap as it did before you centered it.

TO MAKE TEXT FLUSH RIGHT as you type: Press

ALT F6

The cursor will jump to the right side of the screen, and everything that you type will move to the left from the right margin.

TO MAKE TEXT FLUSH RIGHT after you've typed *or to make an entire paragraph flush right:* mark the paragraph (or any amount of text) with **ALT F4** (to block the text that you want to move flush right), then press

ALT F6

WordPerfect will want to know if you're certain about this. Press

Y

to make the text flush right. Press **N** to cancel. As in centering, if you block a paragraph and flush right, WordPerfect puts hard returns at the end of each line, and the paragraph becomes a series of lines. Once again, if you want to edit the text later on, it will not wrap as it did before you made it flush right.

REMOVING: If you want to remove either centered or flush right codes, turn REVEAL CODES on with **ALT F3**. Put the cursor on top of the [Cntr] or [Flush Rt] codes, and press the **DELETE** key.

◆ Indents ahoy!

What's the difference between a tab and an indent? About a dollar fifty (just kidding). A tab indents a single line, while an indent (F4) indents an entire paragraph. Indents are indispensable for outlines.

- Using indents allows you to create perfect outlines without hitting returns at the end of each line. You can't justify outlines without using indents.
- For some hints on creating outlines that show on-screen but don't print, see Chapter 15, *Macros.*

There are actually two different types of indents. The first is good old reliable

F4

which indents an entire paragraph to the first tab stop. If you change the tabs, the entire paragraph will reform and indent to the new tab stop.

The second type of tab is called (in Wordperfect-ese) a Left/Right indent. If you press

SHIFT F4

WordPerfect will indent both the left and right margins of the paragraph by the amount of the first tab on the left. If that doesn't make any sense, try this explanation on for size: if margins are set at 1" from left and 1" from right, and tabs are set every .5", pressing **SHIFT F4** will indent both the left and right margins by .5". If you change tab stops so that you have only one, and it's set at 1.5", both the left and right margins of the paragraph will be indented by 1.5." Here's how it looks:

> This is a Left/Right indent because both sides of the paragraph have been indented by the amount of the first tab stop. This is useful for quotes and, if you're so inclined, screenplays.

◆ Playing hangman

They're called hanging indents because the first line of the paragraph seems to protrude, or hang out from the body of the paragraph. Hanging paragraphs are useful for numbered lists, outlines and, in rare cases, regular paragraphs of body text.

There are two ways to create hanging indents with WordPerfect. The first is the simplest, but works only when you have a numbered or lettered paragraph, as in an outline.

1. Type the number or letter of the paragraph (or use WordPerfect's automatic numbering with SHIFT-F5 P [ENTER]). Press **F4** for indent. The cursor will move as if you pressed the tab key; however, the entire paragraph, not just the first line, will be indented:Easy.

The second procedure is more complicated, but is still the only way to achieve a hanging indent in a normal paragraph.

This hanging indent was created by first pressing **F4** to insert a WordPerfect indent, and then pressing **SHIFT-TAB** to create a margin release. Unlike the margin release on a typewriter (which totally releases the margin), WordPerfect's margin release code moves backwards by one tab stop.

A) Margin release can also be used on numbered or lettered outlines (where you want the first line to jut out from the body of the paragraph). A hanging first line makes it easier to see where each point begins.

◆ It's only marginal

An important detail to remember about margins is *where* you set them. Because all WordPerfect codes affect everything that *follows*, you have to put the margin codes at either the very beginning of a file (use **HOME HOME HOME [UP ARROW]** to get to the very top), or preceding the part of the file that you want to change (including graphics). This is both good and bad. It's good because it allows you to place graphics, headers/footers, etc., outside the normal working area of the page; it's bad because it can be confusing.

Margins are *absolute*: everything will print within the margins, nothing will print outside of them. If you set a top margin of one inch, and a bottom margin of one inch, the headers and footers will print at least one inch from the top and bottom, and the text will print even farther from the edge of the paper. You can however, change margins anywhere on a page. If you place a new top and bottom margin code halfway down the page, WordPerfect will be able to change the bottom margin, but not the top (it's already finished with that part of the page). Left and right margins take effect immediately.

Here's another example: let's say you've set left and right margins of one inch and want the same margins for headers and footers. You must place the margin code *before* the header or footer code.

You'll only put headers/footers and graphics outside the normal margins of the page when you're going for a special effect. Let's say you wanted a margin of one inch from the left and right sides of the text, but only a half inch for the headers or footers. If you place a Left/Right margin code of .5", then the header or footer, followed by another margin code of 1", the headers or footers will have a wider margin than the text.

This isn't as obvious as it seems. It's all too easy to move to what you think is the top of the file using **HOME HOME [UP ARROW]**; you will not be at the top, however, but at the top after the codes. If you change the margins there, whatever codes are above the margin (headers, footer, graphics) will not be aware of these new settings.

For desktop publishing, margins are measured *in* from the edge of the paper. If you're used to working with old WordPerfect or a typewriter, this will take some getting used to. You might be tempted to set margins in familiar old WordPerfect units, namely lines and columns. These units are basically "decimal" inches, ten to the inch. But beware; while you can enter the left margin at 10u (the u tells WordPerfect that you're using the old WordPerfect units), you can't enter it at

70u (because this measurement measures *in* from the right side of the page). If you did enter the margin at 70u, you would end up with a printed area only half an inch wide, with one inch of white space on the left, and 7 inches of white space on the right.

Most laser printers cannot print closer than a quarter of an inch (.25) from the edge of the paper, because they have handling mechanisms that must be able to grasp the paper. Since printing can be very light at the extremities of the page, I never set margins less than .3" inches from the edge of the paper.

◆ How long, oh Lord, how long?

The question of how long a line should be has been asked repeatedly throughout the ages. According to typography and design expert Jan White, a centuries-old formula for line lengths is one-and-a-half alphabets, or approximately 39 characters long. Obviously, this will vary depending on the size and width of type. You can go longer or shorter, but very long lines are confusing while very short lines are choppy. Of course, in the very book where he states this, he uses 65-75 characters per 5 inch line.

Another formula uses 9-10 words per line with serif type, and only 7-9 words per line with sans serif type. Longer lines often require more leading (line height in WordPerfect lingo), as do heavier typefaces.

It all comes down to what the publication is going to be used for. Books and newsletters can have longer lines, because readers are expected to read them thoroughly at arm's length. Advertising copy should have shorter lines, in that you don't expect to have the reader's undivided attention. You have to make your point quickly, and short lines do just that. However, you need to be aware of how each line ends, so that each line is understandable by itself.

❖ *Hyphenate this*

Before I say anything else, let me say that hyphenation can be annoying. I never turn hyphenation on until I start formatting; it drives me mad to have WordPerfect ask me if I want to hyphenate something while I'm trying to write. I don't care about hyphens while I'm writing and neither should you since every little edit will change hyphenation.

I find it obnoxious to have WordPerfect stop me over and over and repeatedly ask my opinion about hyphenation (as if *I* would know). I always feel compelled to check the dictionary and it's really a bother. But you must pay attention to hyphenation when you're formatting.

Hyphenation is also essential in producing attractive, justified text. Hyphenation causes justified lines to appear more even, so large gaps aren't apparent between words and letters (these gaps are called "rivers."). Hyphenation also makes text both easier and harder to read. Easier, because the words and characters are set more consistently, and more difficult, because readers are sometimes thrown by hyphenated words.

◆ Short takes

You can only hyphenate words of more than one syllable. This isn't a WordPerfect rule, but a rule of English. Words like "the," "mess," "gross," and "quite," can't be hyphenated because they are monosyllabic. WordPerfect, however, often pops up monosyllabic words for hyphenation. Press the **F1** key when such words come up; F1 cancels the hyphenation on single words.

Hyphenation can also be dangerous and/or libelous. Witness this famous example: "Throughout his long career he was known as the-rapist to the stars..." Uh oh.

Hyphenation requires a lot of attention. When you print the next-to-final copy, take a moment to sit down and check the hyphenation. Is there enough of it, or are there gaps in the text? Is there too much of it? Are they in the right place?

One of the more fussy canons about hyphenation is: "Don't have more than two lines in a row hyphenated." It won't stand out like a sore thumb if three lines in a row are hyphenated, but the text will be harder to read. WordPerfect cannot prevent this automatically, so it's one more item you'll want to keep an eye out for.

While WordPerfect's built-in hyphenation is fine, it can be dramatically improved with an optional hyphenation dictionary. These dictionaries typically take up about 360K of disk space, and provide you with comprehensive, accurate hyphenation.

Even with these special dictionaries, however, WordPerfect will frequently ask you how to hyphenate a word (as if *you* should know).

◆ Turning hyphenation on

You have two choices when you turn hyphenation on: manual or automatic. Manual hyphenation allows you the most control, but is the most demanding since it asks you about every single word. Automatic hyphenation is the most practical because there are many words WordPerfect doesn't need help with; it only questions you when it's not sure about hyphenating a word.

When WordPerfect asks you to help it hyphenate, you are faced with four choices:

1) Press the **ESC** key to hyphenate where WordPerfect suggests.

2) Use the left and right cursor keys to mark where you want the hyphen to go.

3) Press **F1** to Cancel that particular hyphen. This causes WordPerfect to insert a [/] command that means "Don't hyphenate this word."

4) Press **F7** to have WordPerfect temporarily forget about hyphenation and stop its insistent beeping at you. The temporary aspect is important. WordPerfect typically hyphenates as you move through a file; if you were to go to the bottom of the file, WordPerfect would try to hyphenate the entire file. Pressing **F7** forces WordPerfect to stop hyphenating, at least for the next function. It also works in View Document. But once the function is complete, hyphenation rears its ugly little head again.

◆ Hand tuning

Once you print a publication, you'll notice that certain lines may contain space between the words. Often you can supplement WordPerfect's hyphenation with your own to alleviate these problem lines. If the last word on the previous or problem line, or the first word on the next line, appear as if they could be hyphenated, move the cursor to where you want the hyphen to be and press **CONTROL -** . This will insert a "soft" hyphen that only appears when used at the end of a line. WordPerfect only reformats the line when you move the cursor back up, above, and back down again, so move the cursor to the problem line, and then press the **[DOWN ARROW]**.

If there is room to add the newly hyphenated word, WordPerfect will break the word. But if there isn't enough room, WordPerfect will ignore the soft hyphen you've inserted. Sometimes it looks as if there should be enough room, but WordPerfect is calculating in very small increments; if it determines that there isn't enough room, it won't use your hyphen.

◆ Tuning out

There are times when you'll want to remove all traces of WordPerfect's hyphenation and start from scratch. I do this when I drastically change the format of a publication (from two to three columns), or make changes in type size. This requires WordPerfect to re-hyphenate everything, and then I can make sure I approve of what it's done. To remove all traces of old hyphenation, use search and replace. Search for **CONTROL -** and replace it with nothing (not even a space). This will remove all old soft hyphens. Next, move back to the top of the file (HOME HOME [UP ARROW]), search for **SHIFT F8 L** /, and replace it with nothing. This will eliminate all the cancel hyphenation codes.

◆ Regular hyphens

When you press the **- key** (underneath the underline character), you insert what WordPerfect calls a hard hyphen. This is the normal hyphen that you'll use for most words. It will print anywhere; in the middle, or at the end of a line. WordPerfect will also use this hyphen to break words that are located at the end of a line.

◆ Non-breaking (or "Hard") hyphens

If you want to use a hyphen in a word or group of words, but don't want WordPerfect to use the hyphen to break the words at the end of the line, you should enter a "hyphen character." You do this by pressing **HOME -**.

◆ Hyphenation zone

Changing the hyphenation zone allows you to specify when you want WordPerfect to hyphenate a word. The default is 10% on the left, 4% on the right. If more hyphenation, is desired, make these numbers bigger. If you do, however, be prepared for WordPerfect to ask you about lots of small words that can't be hyphenated. If you don't want to hyphenate them, press **F1**. If you want less hyphenation, make these numbers larger. I find that a setting of 10% and 10% works well. If you want WordPerfect to hyphenate fewer words, make the numbers smaller. A setting of 0 is equivalent to turning hyphenation off.

◆ Dash it all!

There's a big difference between a hyphen and a dash. While you may routinely use two hyphens instead of a dash, most laser printers have an "endash" or "emdash" character. The endash is the same width as the letter "n" and an emdash is (you're way ahead of me here) the same width as the letter "m."

LaserJet/PostScript: Both these printers can print genuine emdashes and endashes with one difference. PostScript printers can print them in any size, while the LaserJet II can usually only print them in the built-in 10-point Courier. Fontware's downloadable fonts do include em and endashs in all sizes.

Endash: Use the compose feature to create an endash. Type **Control 2 4,33 [ENTER] HOME [ENTER]**. The **HOME [ENTER]** at the end inserts an "invisible soft return," which, if necessary, causes WordPerfect to break the line rather than hyphenate.

Emdash: To create an emdash, you will also use the Compose feature by typing **CONTROL 2 4,34 [ENTER] HOME [ENTER]**. As with the endash, the **HOME [ENTER]** at the end will insert an "invisible soft return."

◆ Incredible simulation LaserJet

If you are using 9-, 10-, or 11-point type, the easiest way to simulate a hyphen is to press **ALT-196** (on the keypad) twice. This dash belongs to the IBM line drawing set and works just fine, while two in a row align perfectly so that there's no blank space between them.

Complicated LaserJet: If you are using larger type, and want or need to simulate an en-or-emdash with type hyphens, type **HOME —**. WordPerfect will keep the two dashes together at the end of a line. If you are using ASCII symbol fonts, you won't have a real emdash. Still, you can create a close facsimile. Type **HOME-HOME-HOME-HOME-** and then press the **[LEFT ARROW]** key so that the cursor is between the first two hyphens. If you are using 10-point type, enter **SHIFT-F8 O A L .01**. Put the cursor between the second and third hyphen and repeat this procedure. Now put it before the third and fourth hyphen and do it again (you probably haven't had this much fun since high school). You won't see any difference on-screen (it will just look like you've got four hyphens in a row). But you will see what appears to be a real emdash in View Document and when you print.

If spaces are still visible between the hyphens, make the .01 number larger. This command tells WordPerfect to move to the left 1/100th of an inch before it prints the next hyphen. Sometimes that's enough, sometimes it isn't. Making the number .02 should work for any 10 point font, but the dash will be shorter.

If you want to repeat this trick with larger headline fonts, you'll have to experiment with the correct number to use. A large font can use .1" or more to eliminate the space between the hyphens. If you type a hyphen at the left margin, then check the ruler line at the bottom of the screen to see just how long your hyphen is. (This is starting to sound like a Mr. America contest: "Just how long *is* your hyphen?") If the number is bigger than the length of the hyphen, the second hyphen will simply print over the first (or even to the left of it).

Since you obviously don't want to press almost 40 keystrokes every time you want a dash, you can turn the whole dreary procedure into a macro simply by "recording" your keystrokes. Press **CONTROL-F10** to start the macro. When WordPerfect says "Define Macro," type a name; go for something clever like **DASH [ENTER]**. When "Macro Definition" appears, type a description of the macro. Let's try making a dash out of four hyphens **[ENTER]**. Now you get to experience the thrills and chills of the entire spine-tingling process, starting with **HOME-HOME-HOME-HOME-** and **SHIFT-F8 O A L .01 [ENTER]** between each of the hyphens.

When you are finished, press **CONTROL-F10** again. The next time you want a dash, press **ALT-F10 [ENTER]**. WordPerfect will play back your keystrokes and create another dash.

If none of that makes any sense, try it for yourself, or see Chapter 15, *Macros* (my fingers are getting tired).

❖ *Limiting yourself*

I told you that justification was more complicated than you imagined. And probably more boring. But before you doze off, this next section will unravel the mystery behind justification limits.

These limits control the amount of space that WordPerfect can add between words when it justifies. You can instruct WordPerfect to add lots of space between each word (which looks terrible) or split the extra space between words *and* letters.

With WordPerfect's default, spaces between words can be compressed down to 60% and enlarged to 400% of their normal size. The 60% figure is acceptable, but would you really want the equivalent of *four* spaces between words? I don't think so—it looks unprofessional.

You should aim for a decent mix of space between words and letters. I use a setting of 60% for compression, and 150% (a space and a half) for expansion. To enter that setting, type **SHIFT-F8 O P J 60 [ENTER] 150 [ENTER] F7**. If you want to use that as the default, type **SHIFT-F1 I I SHIFT-F8 O P J 60 [ENTER] 150 [ENTER] F7**.

Warning: Some people *hate* letterspacing; they claim it makes text difficult to read and ugly. Personally, I like letterspacing, and I find type with gaping spaces between words hard to read and ugly (so there). Most publications utilize a mix of space between words and space between letters, as I've suggested.

◆ Widows and orphans - a Dickensian touch

Widows and orphans, a staple of 19th century literature. And now, these two pathetic characters hit you right where you live, or at least where you desktop publish.

Orphans are desolate little words or lines all by themselves at the bottom of a page or column. Their mothers are widows, lonely lines all by themselves at the top of a page.

But WordPerfect has a feature that prevents single lines from being stranded all by their lonesome. This feature is not a default; to turn it on you need to type

SHIFT-F8 L W Y

If you want to use it as a permanent default that will be applied to all new files you create, type

SHIFT-F1 I I SHIFT-F8 L W Y F7

When W/O is turned on, WordPerfect will pause briefly at any page break where a widow or orphan might be occurring. If you have a four line paragraph, WordPerfect may break it after the second line (so that one page ends with two lines and another begins with two lines). If you have a three line paragraph, WordPerfect will not be able to break it correctly; it will simply move the entire paragraph to the next page.

Be aware, however, that pages and columns won't end on exactly the same line. WordPerfect has no magic method of spacing (also called feathering) a column so that it ends up equal in length to another column. This is more of an inconvenience than a gaffe; it's perfectly acceptable for columns to end unevenly, and this can actually be an artistic virtue if they end unevenly enough.

While this feature is useful, it's not foolproof. As a matter of fact, it's extremely easy to fool, so be sage enough to keep an eye out for it. While the W/O feature always functions correctly when splitting a paragraph, it doesn't work the way you might expect with single line paragraphs, such as subheads; it completely ignores them, forcing them to become orphans. (Maybe WordPerfect should open an adoption agency).

In essence, the only sure way to avoid Widows and Orphans is to watch out for them yourself.

◆ Raising initial caps from the dead

Or at least from the lifeless. "Raised Initial Caps" allow you to easily add visual interest to a page without the use of graphics. You've seen them used hundreds of times in magazines and newspapers; they're the big letter at the start of a paragraph.

Most initial caps are "drop caps" set into the body of the paragraph, and can be difficult to use with WordPerfect. Raised Caps are easy and provide as much visual interest. Their only drawback is that they take up more space.

Raised caps are normally done in the same font as the body copy or headline. It can also be effective to use a contrasting typeface for drop caps. If you're using Times Roman for the body copy, try Helvetica (or better yet, something interesting like Avant Garde) for the raised cap.

Here's how to do it:

1. Set line spacing to fixed with **SHIFT-F8 L H F**, and a number that is a point or two larger than the body text (otherwise WordPerfect would leave extra space *under* the line for the descenders of the large letter).

2. Press an extra return or two, depending on how large the first letter is. If the normal type is 10-point on 11-point leading, and you want to use a 36-point raised cap, you need at least two blank lines before the paragraph with the raised cap. If you are using the Extra Large appearance, leave at least 1 blank line before the paragraph.

3. The easiest way to create the big cap is to block the first letter with **ALT-F4**, then press **CONTROL-F8 S E** for an extra large raised cap. If you have a 10-point base font, Extra Large will give you type approximately 25 points tall, or the nearest size available on the printer. (For the LaserJet, this will probably be 24 point.)

If you want to set a specific font size, put the cursor on the second letter of the paragraph (right after the raised cap). Type **CONTROL-F8 F [ENTER]** (if you have a PostScript printer you'll need **2 [ENTER]**'s). This inserts a code with the current font size. Now place the cursor on the first letter. Type **CONTROL-F8 F**, move the cursor to the font you want, press return (for PostScript printers, enter one return, the point size you want, then another return).

4. Print as usual, and enjoy the delicious aroma of freshly brewed coffee... oh, wrong hype, sorry.

◆ Drop that cap, puppy... spit it out...

Drop Initial Caps are the opposite of raised initial caps. Instead of sticking out above the paragraph, they are set into the paragraph. While drop caps can be especially attractive, they are also especially difficult with WordPerfect (at least initially). To set them into the paragraph, they must be placed in a graphics box. It's the sizing of the box that is important, but can sometimes be terribly frustrating.

If you have a weak stomach for computers, or high blood pressure, don't try this. Granted, it's great when you get it to work—very flashy and elegant; but it's also one giant pain in the...wherever it is you get pains in.

If you're sure of your sanity, let's try it together, shall we? While this procedure may seem exceedingly tedious, in actuality it's just monotonous. But once you've done it for one letter of a particular font and size, you can use the same basic settings for other drop caps of the same font and size (unless they're an "M" or "W," which are wider, and might require some manual recalculation).

1. Set Text Box options so that there is no line around the box by typing **ALT-F9 B O B NNNN G 0 [ENTER]**. To make sure that there is no extra space inside or outside of the box, type **O 0 [ENTER] 0 [ENTER] 0 [ENTER] 0 [ENTER] 1 0 [ENTER] 0 [ENTER] 0 [ENTER] 0 [ENTER]**. A common mistake is to forget this step, and if you do, none of the measurements will function correctly. There will be big gaps both inside and outside of the text box, resulting in tons of blank space around the drop cap and a terribly shabby appearance.

```
                                                              Vol 1. No
                                              Any way you slice it, we'r

TXT lis last year has been one of
    great change for Mama Rowby
and her family of fine foods. Corporate
Raider/Pond Scum Walter Scanlan
tried to wrest the company away from
the family that has owned and opera-
ted it with such great care for lo these
past five years, and if it hadn't been
for the great spirit of loyalty among
management and employees. Mama
Rowby's Pies would have become just
another corporate conglomerate, in-
stead of the caring, loving, gold mine
it is.«
      Last year pie consumption sky-
rocketed the world over, partly due to
our massive advertising campaign, and
the ''Miss Cutie Pie'' competition, co-
hosted by Morgan Fairchilde (desper-
C:\WP5\PIC\ROWBY3.WP5

      Another hot new line will be
retailed under the Cajun Queen moni-
ker, and will include ''Blackened Re
Cherry,'' and ''Fruit-Slaw Jumbalya.
The sleeper of the new trio will be
''Dr. Ruth's Good Pies,'' packaged w
illustrated instructions for unortho
uses. These flavors will be offered
only soft and safe fruits, such as B
ana and Cherry.«
      This fall, Mama will be starri
in her own syndicated cooking show
where she and her guests (Dr. Ruth i
at the top of the list) will help so
world problems and promote ''Peace
Through Pies.'' The show is pre-sold
175 of the largest markets, and will
a perfect platform for increasing cu
tomer awareness of ''Pie Possibiliti
Col 2 Doc 2 Pg 1 Ln 2.04" Pos 3.38"
```

A dropcap appears on-screen as a small graphics box.

2. Create a Text Box by typing **ALT-F9 B C**. While it seems logical to make this single character a "character" type box, this will only cause the rest of the paragraph to be spaced unevenly. Make sure the type of the box is PARAGRAPH, the horizontal position set to LEFT, and the size - ah, the size, we'll get to that.

3. Press **E** for edit. (Don't press C for caption, because this letter is not a caption, but contains the contents of the graphics box).

4. Type **CONTROL-F8 F**, and select the font for the drop cap. In most cases, it should be smaller than the headline, and at least twice the size of the body text. If you want a drop cap to be exactly three lines tall, you need to calculate point size by multiplying leading or line height by the number of lines you want. If you are using a 10-point body font with 12-point leading and want a 3-line drop cap, you want a 36-point font. Select font and size: **CF8 F**. In our example, we'll choose 30-point Times Roman (Dutch) or 24 point, which would be two lines tall. (I'm using this size because anyone with a LaserJet Plus or II can easily use a 24 point font). Then type the letter you want capped.

5. (Now comes the tricky part). Calculate how wide the box needs to be by placing the cursor on the letter and reading the measurement in the lower right-hand corner. Move the cursor to the right of the letter, and note that number. Subtract the first number from the second, and you have the width of the character (in this case, using a 24 point Times Roman "D," the width is .21"). Even when you set all inside margins to 0 with the graphics option, WordPerfect still requires a little breathing room inside the box, and so we're going to make the box .25" wide.

While you're at it, check the vertical position. The vertical measurement is shown on-screen with Ln in front of it. Press **[ENTER]**, note this new number, and subtract the Ln location of the first line from the Ln location of this line. In this example, the height was .35". Once you have the measurement, backspace to remove the hard return.

WordPerfect tends to be generous when it figures out the height of a character, because it includes the automatic leading. Measuring the height of the character manually is preferable because it keeps WordPerfect from trying to leave extra space (which is unnecessary and unattractive) under the character. In this case, let's make the box .30" high.

Press F7 S B .25" [ENTER] .30" [ENTER] F7

6. If your stars were in the right location, you will see a tiny box on-screen, two lines high. The words "TXT 1" (or whatever number the box is) will probably appear over the first word of text, making it invisible in text mode. To make sure all is in order, go into View Document with **SHIFT F7 V**

7. If the letter *does not appear,* the text box will have to be wider, taller, or both. If you are experiencing real problems with sizing the box (and don't be surprised if you do), your best friends will be "trial and error."

Same Size, Same Channel: If you want to create more drop caps in the same size and font, simply copy the first one you made. You can search for it with

F2 ALT-F9 F F

or press

ALT-F9 B E

and the number of the box. (WordPerfect will automatically search for the box. Press F7 to leave graphic edit.)

To ensure you're getting only what you want (and not what you deserve), turn Reveal Codes on with **ALT-F3**. Put the cursor on top of the [TEXT BOX] code, and press **ALT-F4** to turn block on. Press the **[RIGHT ARROW]** key to include the [TEXT BOX] code inside the block, and press **CONTROL-F4 B C**. Move to where you want this new drop cap to appear, and press return. If the new paragraph doesn't start with the same letter, you can edit this box to change the letter inside to whatever you need. Just remember, an "M" or "W" will take up more space than other characters, so you may have to adjust the size of the box using step 5 above.

◆ Other effects

Drop caps are created using the Graphics features, and so you can incorporate more than just big letters. You can use the Option command to print a box around the cap. This becomes tricky, however, as the letter has to be placed perfectly and evenly within the box. The same warning applies to using a shade of gray for the graphics box's background. If you have a PostScript printer, you might apply a shadow attribute to the letter so that it will print white over the gray background, or choose a black background and white type.

Every time you add another effect, you call more attention to the drop cap. The sheer size of a drop cap is usually adequate, and too much fancy footwork can quickly work against you by giving the page a "busy" appearance.

◆ Block party

Search and replace can be a valuable tool for quickly changing paragraph formatting. While styles can be a more efficient way of changing complex formatting, there are times when you haven't planned ahead and created a style. This is when search and replace comes in handy.

WordPerfect doesn't permit you to use all codes for replacing, but it does let you use returns, tabs, indents, center, flush right, and column on/off as replacement text.

If you sometimes format paragraphs with the first line indented, and sometimes format them in the block style with a line of space in-between, here's an example of how quick and useful replacing formatting codes can be.

The two styles may be cousins, but they're still worlds apart (not unlike the Patty Duke show... "*While Cathy adores the minuet, the ballet Russe and Crepe Suzette, Patty loves to rock and roll, a sox hop makes her lose control, what a wild duet! But they're cousins...*" My, the natives *are* getting restless, aren't they? Settle down, class. Back to work).

To change from block to indent, or from indent to block is a simple matter of search and replace. While this system is easy, it depends on the kindness of strangers... or at least on your consistency. It will only work on paragraphs indented with tabs; paragraphs indented with spaces are a no-no. Likewise, this will not work in a consistent fashion if at times you use one blank line between blocked paragraphs and at other times use two. You know, "Garbage in, garbage out."

INDENT TO BLOCK: Let's say your file is in indent format, with a tab indenting the first line of each paragraph. To turn this little baby into block format, press

ALT-F2 N [ENTER][TAB] F2 [ENTER][ENTER] F2

That tells WordPerfect to perform a search and replace to find all returns followed by tabs (the indent of the first line), and to replace them with two returns. Depending on the length of the file, this can take seconds or minutes.

BLOCK TO INDENT: Now we're going to do the opposite: take a file in block format and turn it into indent format. Press

ALT-F2 N [ENTER][ENTER] F2 [ENTER][TAB] F2

Uh badee, badee, badee, that's all folks!

9

Columns as I see 'em

Columns & tables

WordPerfect has always had excellent control over columns, and now it's even better. But before you use columns, try to answer this seemingly simple question: why use columns?

- Because they're there
- Because it's hip
- Because they make a personal statement
- Because they are low calorie
- All of the above
- None of the above

Give up? The answer is "none of the above." Turn the page for the real reasons.

- Most importantly, columns can make type easier to read by keeping the line from getting too long.
- Columns give you the ability to put several different stories on a page and have them look like several different stories.
- Columns allow you to get more type on a page. It's true—a two column format can contain more words than a one column format.
- All of the above.

You won't need columns all the time, and like everything else in design and typography, you should only use them when they are appropriate.

◆ How many is enough?

The next logical question is, "How many columns do I need?" The answer is not unlike Abe Lincoln's response to the question, "How long should a man's legs be? Long enough to reach the ground." You need as many as will do the job.

Since almost all laser printers are limited to 8 1/2 by 11 inch paper, you generally won't use more than three columns, lest they get too narrow and become difficult to read and follow. Even large tabloid size newspapers use five or six columns at most.

Newsletters and magazines are fine in either two or three columns. Three columns offer you more design flexibility, but are also more complicated to work with. The only time you'll use anywhere near WordPerfect's limit of 24 columns is when you are using parallel columns to create complex tables of information.

◆ In the gutter

When you create columns in WordPerfect, the default places a half inch space between them. While that doesn't seem like much, it's about two times more than you would normally choose. Columns generally have between .2" and .3" between them. This area is known as the gutter.

Don't think that just because WordPerfect automatically wants gutters to be a half inch that it somehow knows better than you do. It doesn't. Whenever you create columns, make sure you set the "Distance between columns" at around .2".

◆ It takes two

There are two different types of columns in WordPerfect: Newspaper and Parallel. Newspaper columns "snake" text from the bottom of one column to the top of the next. Parallel columns are designed for several paragraphs of text that must remain side by side. Parallel offers an additional option called "block protect;" this ensures that the columns are not split by page breaks. Because WordPerfect permits you to turn columns off and on at any time, and set uneven column widths, you have tremendous possibilities at your beck and call.

❖ *All the news*

First we're going to set up two newspaper type columns. To set up a column, press

ALT-F7 D

WordPerfect then gives you four choices: Type, Number, Distance between Columns, and Margins. Newspaper column is the default, so you don't have to change it. Two columns is also the default, so you don't have to change that either.

◆ Setting distance between columns

However, you do have to change the distance between the two columns. Press **D** and enter .25" **[ENTER]**. Once you've set the distance, WordPerfect automatically calculates the margins so as to create columns of equal widths. If you want one column to be wider than the other, press **M** and change the margin measurements that WordPerfect is displaying. These margin settings are initially within the margins you've set for the document using **SHIFT-F8 L M**, but you can set these numbers outside the main margins if you so desire.

```
Chapter 9«                          question ''How long should a
Columnation that's the name of      man's legs be? Long enough to
the game«                           reach the ground.'' You need as
«                                   many as will do the job.«
WordPerfect has always had            Since almost all laser
excellent control over columns,     printers are limited to 8 1/2"
and now it's even better. But       by 11" paper, you generally
before you use columns, try to      won't use more than three
answer this seemingly simple        columns, lest they get too
question: why use columns?«         narrow and become difficult to
«                                   read and follow. Even large
A)   Because they're there«         tabloid size newspapers use
B)   Because it's hip«              five or six columns at most.«
C)   Because they make a              Newsletters and magazines are
personal statement«                 fine in either two or three
D)   Because they are low           columns. Three columns offer
calorie«                            you more design flexibility,
E)   All of the above«              but are also more complicated
F)   None of the above«             to work with.«
«                                     The only time you'll use
Give up? The answer is F, none      anywhere near WordPerfect's
of the above. Now, here are the     limit of 24 columns is when you
real reasons: «                     are using parallel columns to
«                                   create complex tables of
C:\WP5\P\WP9.TW                                 Doc 2 Pg 1 Ln 1" Pos 1"
```

When you create columns, WordPerfect shows the columns side-by-side, even in text mode. (Consider yourself lucky you're not using Microsoft Word.)

WordPerfect displays the left and right margins for each column. You enter a measurement, and then press return. When you are in the left column, the up and down cursor can be used to move between the measurements for the left side of all columns. But to set measurements for the right column, you must first press **[ENTER]**. When in the right column, you can use the up and down cursor to set the right margin for all columns.

If you set the wrong number, don't worry. If you press **F7 M** WordPerfect returns you to the top of the measurements, and you can enter them again. The measurements are only set when you press **[ENTER]** for the last time and are returned to the one line math/column menu at the bottom of the screen.

While the column margins are now set, they don't take effect until you press **C** for Column On/Off. Once you do, the text will begin to format on-screen.

At first the text will have an odd appearance; one column may overlap with another and there won't seem to be any space between them. The quickest way to format all the text is to press **HOME HOME [DOWN ARROW]**. This moves you to the bottom of the WordPerfect file, and forces WordPerfect to format the text and display it correctly on-screen.

In addition to formatting the text, WordPerfect is also calculating the "Display Pitch,"(the amount of space required between columns on-screen). You can set the display pitch manually by pressing

SHIFT-F8 D D

While it's best to leave the setting on automatic, you can set it to manual when WordPerfect has too much or too little space between columns. This feature only affects how text looks on-screen, not on paper.

```
time. and like everything else
in design and typography. you
should only use them when they
are appropriate.«
«
How Many is Enough?«
The next logical question is
''how many columns do I need?''
The  answer is not unlike Abe
Lincoln's response to the
--------------------------------------------------------------------------
                                  question ''How long should a
                                  man's legs be? Long enough to
                                  reach the ground.'' You need as
                                  many as will do the job.«
                                    Since almost all laser
                                  printers are limited to 8 1/2"
                                  by 11" paper. you generally
                                  won't use more than three
                                  columns. lest they get too
                                  narrow and become difficult to
                                  read and follow. Even large
                                  tabloid size newspapers use
                                  five or six columns at most.«
C:\WP5\P\WP9.TW                             Col 2 Doc 2 Pg 1 Ln 3.5" Pos 4.37"
```

Sometimes it can be difficult to write and edit with columns side by side. You can force columns to appear sequentially, rather than side-by-side, using setup. (SHIFT-F1 D S N).

The standard display pitch setting is .1" (10 characters per inch), and this gives a fairly realistic view of the page. If you use a larger number (such as .02"), the space between columns (or the length of tabs) will appear smaller. If you make the number smaller, the space between columns and the length of tabs will appear larger. No code is inserted in the file when you change the display pitch, but it is saved with the file you are editing.

If you don't want columns to appear side-by-side while you are editing, press

SHIFT-F1 D S N F7

and columns will appear offset. They will print side-by-side, however.

◆ Getting around

While it's convenient to have columns displayed side-by-side on-screen, moving around can be very confusing. If you are pressing the **[DOWN ARROW]** key and reach the end of a column, you won't move to the top of the next column, but to the next page. And you can't get from the left column to the right one simply by pressing the **[RIGHT ARROW]**.

To move between columns, you must use what WordPerfect calls the GOTO key: **CONTROL-HOME** (most often the 7 on the number-pad, although some keyboards have a separate HOME key).

GOTO [RIGHT ARROW] moves to the next column on the right.

GOTO [LEFT ARROW] moves to the next column on the left.

GOTO HOME [RIGHT ARROW] moves to the *last* column.

GOTO HOME [LEFT ARROW] moves to the *first* column.

GOTO [UP ARROW] goes to the top of a column.

GOTO [DOWN ARROW] goes to the bottom of a column.

If you are at the bottom of one column and press the **[RIGHT ARROW]**, or **CONTROL [RIGHT ARROW]** key, you will move to the next word at the top of the next column.

If you are at the top of one column and press the **[LEFT ARROW]** or **CONTROL [LEFT ARROW]**, you will move to the previous word at the bottom of the previous column.

All this moving around can be very bothersome, so I don't suggest you write in column mode unless you need to fit material into a very specific area.

```
     The second and more advanced method is to use Advance Right.
Advance is an absolute fixed value, no matter what column it
appears in. The advantage of this method is that you can set the
tab for other items, change the column layout, and still retain
an exact, uniform indent. The disadvantage is that it requires
more effort than pressing the tab key. And it doesn't change
automatically when you change the tabs.«
To set an indent of .3" with Advance, you'd type «
SHIFT-F8 O A R .3" [ENTER] F7«
Since this is a lot to go through whenever you begin a new
paragraph, you'll want to create a macro if you plan to use this
C:\WP5\P\WP9.TW                                Doc 2 Pg 4 Ln 7.5" Pos 1"
more effort than pressing the tab key. And it doesn't change[SRt]
automatically when you change the tabs.[HRt]
[AdvRgt:0.3"]To set an indent of .3" with Advance, you'd type [HRt]
[BOLD]SHIFT[-]F8 O A R .3" [ENTER] F7[bold][HRt]
Since this is a lot to go through whenever you begin a new[SRt]
paragraph, you'll want to create a macro if you plan to use this[SRt]
system. See Chapter ???, Macros.[HRt]
[Tab]As you've hopefully learned by now, you should never ever,[SRt]
under the penalty of seeming really stupid, indent anything using[SRt]
spaces. [HRt]

Press Reveal Codes to restore screen
```

Advance Right (SHIFT-F8 O A R) can be used instead of tabs to indent the first line of a paragraph.

◆ Indenting tricks or making advances

Because many people indent the first line of a paragraph using the tab key (and rightly so), they continue to do this when in columns. Sometimes they're lucky and it works, but more often, the indent on one column doesn't match the indent on the other columns.

Unless you change them, tabs are set every half inch, and yet columns are rarely set so to match this figure. The two ways to ensure that the first line indents are correct are to set new tabs, based on the measurements of the columns, and to use advance.

When you set columns, you create a code that contains all the margins of the columns. A two-column margin code might look like this: [Col Def; 2,1",4.12",4.37",7.5"]. The first number indicates how many columns you are using, the next number is the left margin of the first column, then the right margin of the first column, the left margin of the second column, the right margin of the second column, etc.

Just by turning Reveal Codes on with **ALT-F3** you can see what the column measurements are. Using this example, if we wanted a first line indent of .3", we would look at our code and find that the left margin of the first column is 1", while the second column is 4.37". In this case, we'd set two tabs: 1.3" and 4.67", then when we press a tab at the beginning of each line, the indents would match.

The second and more advanced method is to use Advance Right. Advance is an absolute fixed value, no matter what column it appears in. The advantage of this method is that you can set the tab for other items, change the column layout, and still retain an exact, uniform indent. The disadvantage is that it requires more effort than pressing the tab key. And it doesn't change automatically when you change the tabs.

To set an indent of .3" with Advance, you'd type

SHIFT-F8 O A R .3" [ENTER] F7

Since this is a lot to go through whenever you begin a new paragraph, you'll want to create a macro if you plan to use this system (see Chapter 15, *Macros*).

As you've hopefully learned by now, you should never ever, under the penalty of seeming really stupid, indent anything using spaces. (Although I'll let you in on a secret. I "indented" this paragraph using spaces, just to be a troublemaker.)

◆ Parallel columns

Parallel columns are an excellent way to make tables, especially when one or more of the entries is longer than a single line. If all the entries are only one line long, tabs will work just as well. Another logical reason to use parallel columns for tables is that you don't have to figure out where to set tabs when you just want WordPerfect to give you equally spaced tables.

The key to using parallel columns is understanding that a Hard Page [Hpg] (created by pressing CONTROL-ENTER) code doesn't start a new page, but a new column. When placed in the last column, it turns columns off, adds a black line, and then turns them back on.

◆ Table with block protect

The only difference between ordinary parallel columns and those with block protect is that the information in protected columns won't be split by page breaks.

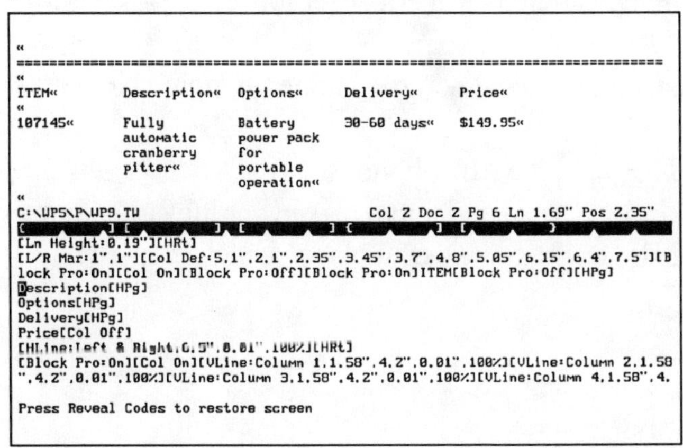

This is how the codes for parallel columns appear. Notice how the text appears side-by-side on the top half of the screen, but not in the lower Reveal Codes (ALT-F3) half.

If necessary, WordPerfect will move the entire set of columns to a new page. When you press **CONTROL-ENTER** at the last column, the block protect is turned off, then turned back on with the next set of columns.

To create a table with block protect, type

ALT-F7 D T B

You can now set the gutter and margin as you did with newspaper type columns. In this example, we'll create a 5 column table—join me, won't you? (That wasn't really a question—you'd better join me or else.)

◆ Set margins

To ensure we're working with the same margins (not unlike playing with a full deck), set the margins to 1" left, 1" right by pressing

SHIFT-F8 L M **1** [ENTER] **1** [ENTER] F7

◆ Set base font

Set the base font to Times Roman (or Dutch) 10 point.

SHIFT-F8 D F

◆ Create a block protected table

To create a block protected table, press

ALT-F7 D T B N5 [ENTER] D .25" [ENTER]

We're going to use the margins that WordPerfect set for us. Press **C** to turn columns on.

Type the following table (soon to be seen on the Home Shopping Network).

Press **CONTROL-ENTER** to end each column.

Isn't that fun? Isn't that easy? Isn't that going to make your life easier and so much more productive? Isn't the world a wonderful place? Quick, slap me.

ITEM	Description	Options	Delivery	Price
107145	Fully automatic cranberry pitter	Battery power pack for portable operation	30-60 days	$149.95
5394875B (beige) 10234723 (red)	Hand carved bust of Marie Osmond, made of genuine imitation plastic. Every tooth a masterpiece.	Genuine Faux marble base. (Faux marble, that's the richest kind)	45 minutes, less on weekends	$1.29
555 (English) 777 (French) 999 (Esperanto)	Hardbound copy of the best selling *Generic Quick Weight Loss Diet,* 2nd Edition	Full Size cutout of Twiggy. Has everything going for it and nothing to lose.	After October 19.	$21.95US

◆ Horizontal rules

If you want a ruling line between each full set of columns, wait until you've pressed **CONTROL-ENTER** at the last column so that WordPerfect turns the columns off, and then on again. Then press **[UP ARROW] [ENTER] ALT-F9 L H [ENTER] [DOWN ARROW]**.

◆ Vertical rules

In the table we created above, horizontal rules lead the eye through all the elements of a single item. The table is easier to read because it is line-oriented; the horizontal rows are the focus, and the vertical columns are just subsections.

In this case, vertical rules would only be confusing, because they would break up the elements of an item, interrupting the rows.

But in column-oriented tables, where vertical columns of information are important, vertical rules can make a table easier to read.

To create vertical rules between the columns, you must be below the [Col Def:] and [Col On] codes. Press

ALT-F9 L V

to select a vertical line. Press

H B

to instruct WordPerfect to place the line between columns. Press **1** to put the line to the right of column 1.

If the table is full-page, and you want the line to run top to bottom, press return. If you want the top of the line to begin on the line where the cursor is, press **V S [ENTER]**. This inserts the current line location. It also calculates the distance between the cursor and the bottom of the page, and inserts this number under "Line Length." If you don't want the line to run to the end of the page, press **L** and type in the length you want for that line.

- Repeat this process for each intercolumn line

◆ Tip: Making vertical rules float with text

Unlike horizontal rules that float with text, vertical lines are anchored to an exact location on a page. If you set a vertical 4 inch line to start at 2.25" from the top of the page, it will always start at 2.25" from the top of the page, no matter where the text has moved.

This can be disastrous when you are working with tables and you want to, say, move the table from page 1 to page 3. The table will move, but the lines won't. The most basic solution is to put the table on a page by itself. Boring. Or you can wait until the last minute to place the vertical lines when you're sure that all editing is complete and the text is not going to move.

My few remaining brain cells ached as I tried in vain to come up with a way to get vertical rules to move with the text. I even tried using the vertical bar character | but this only produced a broken line and looked crummy.

I gave up. And true to the Zen (and Zulu) cliche, it was then, and only then, that I came up with the answer.

◆ Tip: Superduper tip—so clever it surprised even myself

Are you ready for this? It's no picnic in Holland, but it's not all that tough either. This is how it looks:

Events to look forward to:

Spring	Summer	Fall	Winter
East: Rain West: Clouds Hay Fever, runny nose, itchy eyes	E: Humidity W: Sunstroke Heat frustration, heat rash, insects	E: Leaves W: Sunstroke Weddings Anniversaries	E: Snow W: Sunstroke Colds, flu, family reunions

◆ Here's how the codes look

[Col Def:4,1",2.4",2.7",4.1",4.4",5.8",6.1",7.5"][Col On] [Usr Opt][Usr Box:1;;]Spring[HRt][HRt]West: Clouds[HRt]East: Rain[HRt]Hay Fever, runny[SRt]nose, itchy eyes[HPg] [Usr Box:2;;]Summer[HRt]

◆ The magic is all in those innocuous little [Usr Box] commands

- Create the table using parallel columns.
- When the table is finished, move the cursor to the last line of the table and write down the number after Ln in the lower right-hand corner of the screen.
- Move to the first line of the table, write down the number after Ln, and subtract it from the first number. You now have the height of the table.
- Go to the first column and line of the table. Type **ALT-F9 U O** to set user-defined box options. Press **B N S N N [ENTER]** to create a box with a ruling line on the right side.
- Press **ALT-F9 U C W N H R S B .1" [ENTER]** and the height of the table. Press **[ENTER][ENTER]**. You have just created a tall thin box that won't shove text out of the way. All that will appear of this box however, is the line on the left side; this will print .1" to the right of the right margin.

- Turn on reveal codes with **ALT-F3**, and press **[BACKSPACE]** over the [User Box:] code. Press **F1 R** to undelete it. Move to the next column and press **F1 R**. Repeat the **F1 R** step for each column. This creates a copy of the original box for each column. You will probably not want a ruling line to the right of the last box, so don't bother placing one in the last column.

Impress your friends and neighbors with your handiwork (tell them it was all your idea—what do I care?), and bask in their befuddled indifference. You can move the table wherever your little heart desires, and those lines will move right along with them. (This is great—I only have two more miracles to go.)

Note: This is brilliant but it's not foolproof, as that would be a contradiction in terms; some restrictions will apply (just pretend you're buying an airline ticket). The only item you have to pay attention to is the right margin of each column. Use preview to check that the text doesn't run into the lines. If it does, press a return before the offending word.

◆ Parallel universes

Now we explore the next major use for parallel columns. A drum-roll please. Parallel columns can be used for creating entire multi-column documents, especially when one column will contain only headlines, sideheads or pull-quotes.

For an example of what this may appear like when in the wrong hands, see the "Babies in Space" example in Chapter 4, *Show & Tell.*

In this example, the first column is used only for pull quotes and artwork. Using newspaper columns would require constant checking to make sure the first column was kept clear, and would make it difficult to ensure that pull quotes floated with their respective text.

But using parallel columns actually makes this genuinely easy. The margins here were set at .5" to 2.5" for the first column, and at 3" to 8" for the second column.

The cursor is in the first column when you turn the columns on. You can type an intro or pull quote here, or just press **CONTROL [ENTER]** to end the first column and begin the text column. Because parallel columns will span pages, the wide text column will continue until you press **CONTROL [ENTER]** again to create another side-head or pull-quote.

This format is blissfully simple to use, and the white space of the first column, combined with pull quotes, makes this format easy to read as well.

You could extend this design to a three column format, where the first two columns are used for staggered pull-quotes. To create a sense of order (in a somewhat random but not uninteresting design), the first column is always a certain type (in this case 14 point), and the second column is always italics.

The advantage of this system is that it gives you more room to play (why bother with all of this if you aren't going to at least pretend to have fun?). The first column could contain art and the second pull-quotes, or the first could be for editorializing, the next for pull-quotes; the possibilities are bound only by the amount of time you can play before someone starts screaming at you to do some real work.

◆ Play time — constructing a table

Okay, I've been talking about having fun, so now we're going to make a valiant attempt at it.

You've been working hard reading this book; (even thumbing through the pages while you dawdle in the bookstore has probably been an effort). It's time for a break. You have two choices; you can get out a bath towel, lie down on the floor and take a nap like you did in kindergarten, or you can play the following game with WordPerfect. The bath towel route will be nostalgic but not much else (floors having become so hard lately), but the WordPerfect game will be enlightening, and could possibly develop into this year's hot party item.

Set up two parallel columns. If your retention rate is such that you don't remember how, here's a clue: the codes you need are concealed somewhere in this chapter. (Was that too much of a clue?). Make sure you first define the columns, then turn them on.

This table is going to be full page, and so, let's put a vertical rule down the center (between the two columns). You can use a regular

ALT-F9 L V H B I [ENTER]

rule instead of the fancy-schmancy trick because this table is not in danger of moving.

Type the word "HAPPY" on the first line of the first column, then press **CONTROL-RETURN** and type the word "MISERABLE" on the first line of the second column.

Use your new-found knowledge of parallel columns and CONTROL ENTER to produce a list of all the items that make you happy and all the petty annoyances and such that make you miserable. Think of everything (and every*one*) you can, then print the file. Finally, cut or tear the paper down the middle, between the two columns. Throw away the miserable side in a symbolic act of defiance, and tape the HAPPY side at your workplace, or wherever it is you spend the most time.

If your life doesn't change overnight, trade your copy of WordPerfect for a package of Sara Lee frozen brownies. That should make you feel better.

10

Styles change

Style never does

Flexibility and consistency: the two major reasons for using style sheets. With them you can change the style of a document repeatedly in the least amount of time, and make sure that the elements remain uniform within that document, or a whole slew of documents.

While the idea of style sheets isn't new, the way WordPerfect implements it is. Even if you are familiar with style sheets in Ventura Publisher or Microsoft Word, it will not be of much value, since WordPerfect's style sheets are nothing like them. They're sometimes better, sometimes worse, and perhaps a little easier to comprehend.

WordPerfect's style sheets are really more like formatting macros than the style sheets used in other programs. You create a style by entering all the formatting commands you would otherwise have to enter manually. Style sheets can use

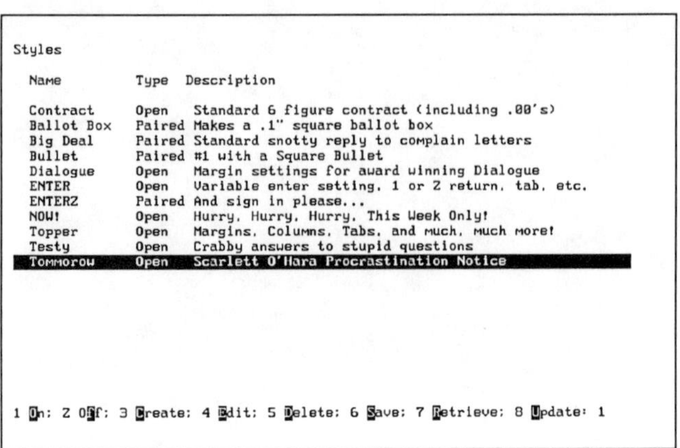

When you press ALT-F8, WordPerfect displays a list of the styles you have created. Not shown on the menu is **N** *for Name Search, a must when using styles with macros.*

any WordPerfect command, including ruling lines, fonts, line height, colors, leading, indents, and text.

There are two types of styles: "paired" (works like bold and underline codes—one at the beginning and one at the end of text to be affected), and "open" (applies to all text following the code). Paired styles can be used on any amount of text, from a single letter to an entire file.

When you create a style, you first give it a name, and then enter all the commands you want. Then, when you are writing (or better yet, formatting) the text, you can select from a list of styles to arrange the text to your liking. When you turn on a style, it creates a code that contains all the formatting you entered. You can use a style as many times as you like, and each time it will copy all of those formatting commands to your new document. This means that if you don't remember exactly what font, or line height, or indent you used previously, you can just select a style containing all the correct codes.

But the really "neato-keeno" part comes when you change something. You go into the style, change the codes, and voila: for every time you've used that style name, the codes for that text change as well, corresponding with the single change you made in the style. Change the font? Zap, it all changes. Change the size? Poof, it's done. No tedious manual search and replace, no fear of missing anything.

You can change the contents of styles to your little heart's content, secure in the knowledge that the text is going to be quickly, easily, consistently, and accurately updated.

◆ But first, a note about disk space

Using Styles takes up disk space. Sometimes an awful lot of it. Some people never notice how much disk space they have, while others are compulsive about it. (If I fit into the second category, it's only because I never have enough.)

One of my theories is that no matter how much disk space you have available, you'll fill it. It's always worked for me (or against me.) While WordPerfect 4.2 used very compact files, WordPerfect 5's files are much larger. It's not unusual for a file containing the same text to be twice as big. And all this wondrous formatting takes its toll in disk space.

Paired styles take up the most space; they have both opening and closing codes, and each code can contain an abundance of other formatting codes. The closing code always returns everything to status quo (as it was before the first code), and this can entail even more formatting.

While I would never advocate being stingy with disk space, you will notice the hard disk filling up much faster than it used to.

❖ *Just your type*

Recognizing the difference between the two types of styles is important because they are used for different applications.

➻ Paired

Paired styles function like bold or underline commands; one appears before the text you want to style, and the other appears after. When you type

ALT-F8

move the cursor to the style you want, then press

O

for "on." Two codes are placed in the file: the beginning and ending codes. Once you turn it on, you can type normally, then press

ALT-F8 F

to turn it off. Or you can simply press the **[RIGHT ARROW]** key once to turn it off (I find this to be easier and faster).

You can also block text with **ALT-F4**, then apply a style to the marked area with **ALT-F8**, move the cursor to the style you want, and press **O**.

The advantage of paired styles is that, unless you specify otherwise, the ending code returns everything to "normal,"(or at least to the way it was before the Style On code). This means that even if you make many changes (choose a different font, new line height, margins, whatever), they all return to normal after the ending code.

Paired styles can affect anything from a single character to an entire document. They're effective for font changes, line spacing, ruling lines, appearance attributes, anything that will apply to only a portion of text. I use paired styles for headlines, subheads, pull-quotes, even something as simple as italics (which I can instantly change to underlines).

The sample style sheet called LIBRARY.STY on the Conversion disk cleverly uses styles to create headlines and subheads, and simultaneously mark them for a table of contents. It also offers a helpful example on automatic paragraph numbering (with an extra tip on right aligning the numbers so that the periods all line up).

If you have the units set to inches, the Right Par style may mystify you. How can it right align a number, and still indent a paragraph to the same spot the number is aligned to? The style uses an advance left code of .01c, which moves the cursor to before the tab stop, thereby causing the indent to go to the same tab stop the number is aligned to. If that didn't make any sense, you'll probably never use it.

➾ Open

Open styles don't have a beginning and end as do paired styles; you turn them on and they affect all text that follows them. They're good for major formatting changes (margins, fonts, line spacing, headers, footers, bullets, etc).

❖ *WordPerfect with style*

But enough chit-chat. Let's make a style. Press

ALT-F8

the Style key. If you specified a style in Setup (Shift-F1 L), then you will see a list of styles. If not, the screen will display "Styles, Name, Type, Description" but nothing else (except for a menu line at the bottom of the screen).

After you create styles, this blank screen will be filled with a list of styles. You'll see the name, the type (paired or open), and a description that you can enter.

Press **C** to create a style. The first step in creating a style is to name it. The name can be up to 11 characters long, and it's best to choose something simple and short (like Dukakis). For this example, type

Subhead [ENTER]

Press

T

to tell WordPerfect the type of style you want, then type **P** for paired, or **O** for open. For this example press

P

Now press

D

if you want to type a detailed description. You can enter up to 54 characters in length. This procedure can be used to jog your memory when you have so many styles that you don't remember what they do. Humor me and type

A subhead with a ruling line above **[ENTER]**.

It's finally time to instruct WordPerfect about what you want this style to do. Press

C

```
Styles: Edit

     1 - Name            subhead
     2 - Type            Paired
     3 - Description     Help. I'm being held captive inside a style sheet...
     4 - Codes
     5 - Enter           HRt




Selection: 0
```

When you define a style (ALT-F8 C), you name it, specify whether it's an open or paired style, give it a description, designate what the Enter key will do, and then enter any formatting instructions.

If you are editing in open style, reveal codes will be on but the screen will be otherwise blank. If you are editing in a paired style, reveal codes will be on, and a comment will appear on-screen.

If we were creating an open style, you would enter all your codes, then press **F7**. We aren't.

◆ Creating a paired style

Instead we're going to create a paired style for our little example. In paired styles, everything preceding the **[Comment]** mark will be in the opening code of the style pair and will affect the text inside the code pair; everything following the comment will appear in the closing code. If nothing is placed after the comment, WordPerfect will automatically return your text to how it was before the opening style code. You can also put any codes you want after the comment; these will affect all text that follows the code, not just the text between the markers.

Now let's create a subhead style that has a horizontal ruling line above. Because we don't want a page or column break between the ruling line and the subhead, we're going to enter a conditional end of page (page break). This will start a new column or page if there isn't enough room for the entire subhead, along with several lines of text below it. We're going to set the conditional end of page to six lines. To do this, type

SHIFT-F8 O C 6 F7 F7

Press an additional

[ENTER]

to add an extra space above our (we've been through so much together I feel like it's ours to share) subhead.

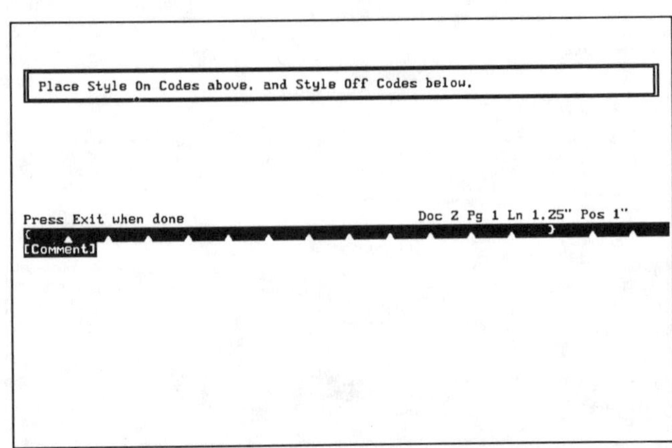

When creating a paired style, any codes placed before the comment appear in the "Style On" code, while comments placed after the comment take effect in the "Style Off" code.

We want to have the ruling line and subhead extend into the left margin. To do this, we're going to change the margins. Press

SHIFT-F8 L M .5 [ENTER] 1 [ENTER]

(If you don't have a ruling line and just want a subhead to stick out from the right margin, you could press SHIFT-TAB and insert a [Mar Rel] code, but an actual margin change is necessary for the horizontal line).

◆ Horizontal ruling lines

Now it's horizontal line time. Be a good sport and enter

ALT-F9 L H [ENTER][ENTER]

This will insert a horizontal ruling line the length of the margin, be it a column or an entire page. Even if you change margins, this line will still run from the left margin to the right margin (a nifty little feature).

◆ Adding white space

We need a little space between the ruling line and the subhead, so press

SHIFT-F8 O A D .01" [ENTER]

This enters an advance command that moves us down precisely 1/10th of an inch.

◆ Selecting a font

If you desire a contrasting typeface for the subhead, you can press **CONTROL-F8 F** and select a font (If you've just pressed CONTROL-F8, press F1 now to cancel it).

◆ Sizing a font

Because we want our subhead to be a bit larger, we're going to enter a size code using

CONTROL-F8 S L [ENTER]

Notice how only the opening [LARGE] code appears. There is no need to enter a closing code, because this is a paired style. WordPerfect will automatically switch off all codes entered before the [Comment] mark. Now let's really go for broke and press

F6

to add a [BOLD] code.

◆ Letterspacing

We're going to throw all caution to the wind and get downright artistic. Pretend you know what you're doing and follow me right down the garden path. Press

SHIFT-F8 O P W P 200 [ENTER] 200 [ENTER] F7

You have now unwittingly been a co-conspirator in increasing the space between letters and words by 200 percent; all the letters and words now have twice as much space between them. This is the type of element people pay big bucks for, but it's yours free, as my personal gift (it was either that or a cubic zirconium ring). If you hate the way the letterspacing looks, you can always come back into this style and delete it, but what the heck—it's good to experiment! (I feel like Auntie Mame.)

Move the cursor to the right of the [Comment] code so we can add codes to the closing half of the style. In this case, we want a little additional space below the subhead, so we're going to add yet another advance command. Follow the bouncing ball and press

SHIFT-F8 O A D .1" [ENTER] F7

You have now been returned to the list of styles. Press

O

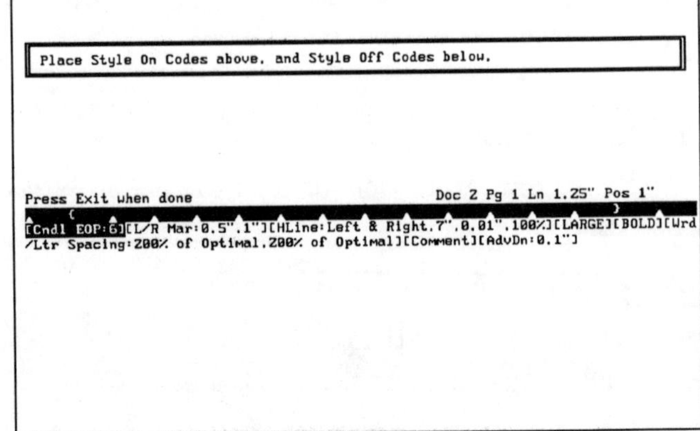

```
Place Style On Codes above, and Style Off Codes below.

Press Exit when done                          Doc 2 Pg 1 Ln 1.25" Pos 1"
[Cndl EOP:6][L/R Mar:0.5",1"][HLine:Left & Right,7",0.01",100%][LARGE][BOLD][Wrd
/Ltr Spacing:200% of Optimal,200% of Optimal][Comment][AdvDn:0.1"]
```

This paired style creates a conditional end of page, a horizontal ruling line above, large type, and additional spacing between each letter. The closing half returns everything to normal, then advances down one tenth of an inch.

to turn this style on so we can use it, and press **F7** to leave the list of styles.

That wasn't so awful now, was it? Ah, the tales you'll have to tell your wide-eyed grandchildren about working with stone-age computers that everyone thought were so futuristic at the time.

◆ Reveal codes on

To demonstrate exactly what you've been a party to, I ask only that you press **ALT-F3** and look at the bottom half of the screen.

You'll see two style codes. Move the cursor so it's on top of the [Style On:Subhead] code, and suddenly the code will explode (or at least pop open) and say:

[Style On:Subhead][HRt]

[L/R Mar:.05",1"][Cndl EOP:6][HRt]

[Hline:Left & Right,7",.01",100%][AdvDn:.01"][HRt]

[LARGE][BOLD][Wrd/Ltr Spacing:200% of Optimal,200% of Optimal]

See? You receive all the codes you entered into the style whenever you turn that style on. But wait, there's more. Press the **[RIGHT ARROW]** key so the cursor is right on top of the [Style Off:Subhead] code. As in the Style On command, the code will expand to reveal the contents of the style:

[Style Off:Subhead;[AdvDn:.01"][L/R Mar:1",1"]

[Font Dutch 11 pt][Wrd/Ltr Spacing:Optimal,Optimal][bold][large]

I've set the font designation in italic, because this may have a different appearance on your screen (depending on what font you were using before the Subhead style).

Place the cursor between the On and Off codes, and type some text for the subhead. It may appear highlighted on the screen, depending on how WordPerfect was set up with SHIFT-F1 D C. What you won't see, however, is the additional space between the letters; this will only show up in View Document (SHIFT-F7 V).

◆ The only certainty is uncertainty - changing a code

Okay, so you didn't go for all that space between the letters. You thought it looked like a mistake. Don't be glum, you're not alone—it's an acquired taste.

So take charge and change it. The real power of style sheets is that they allow you to change your mind, refine the style, without a lot of manual labor.

Press

ALT-F8

and move the cursor to the subhead style. Press

E

to edit it. Press

C

to reach that pesky little code. Move the cursor until it is on top of that accursed [Wrd/Ltr Spacing] code and press

DEL

There, all gone. Press

F7 F7 F7

If you were working in the middle of a long document, you might have had to wait a while after pressing the last F7. This is because WordPerfect reviews the entire document from the top, searching and changing the Subhead style whenever it finds it.

If the cursor is between two paired styles and you press ALT-F8 to edit the style, the cursor will immediately move to the name of the style you are in.

◆ That's a no no

Once you've created a style and used it in the text, the one element you shouldn't change is the type of style (paired or open).

While WordPerfect allows you to change the type of a style at any time, type changes are not reflected in the text, and this can make formatting confusing. You might think that when you change a style from paired to open, all the styles in the text change as well. Think again.

If you do need to change from one type to another, remove all the old style codes and put in new ones. You can remove style tags quickly using search and replace. If they are paired styles, search for Style On; if they are open, search for Open Style. Although you cannot replace them with another style, you can replace them with nothing (an expedient way of kicking them out of the file so you can replace them with new ones). This is why it's important to reflect about what type of styles you will be needing, before you start creating and placing them in the text.

◆ Renaming a style

A similar dilemma occurs when you rename styles. It's logical to assume (as I did) that when you rename a style, the style codes you've already placed in the text are also renamed. But this is not the case. Once you place a style in the text, the name in that style code never changes.

If you rename a style, it will no longer change the styles that you created with the original name. When you use this style, it will place codes with the new name in the text. So just by changing the name you can, in essence, create a new style, one that is unrelated to the style of the previous name.

If you change the style back to its original name, it will once again affect the styles you created with that name.

❖ *Hard facts about the Enter option*

There's one more option you should be aware of at this point. I didn't explain about the "Enter" option because you'll rarely ever want to change it. (Doesn't "The Enter Option," sound like a spy novel title—something about revolving doors?).

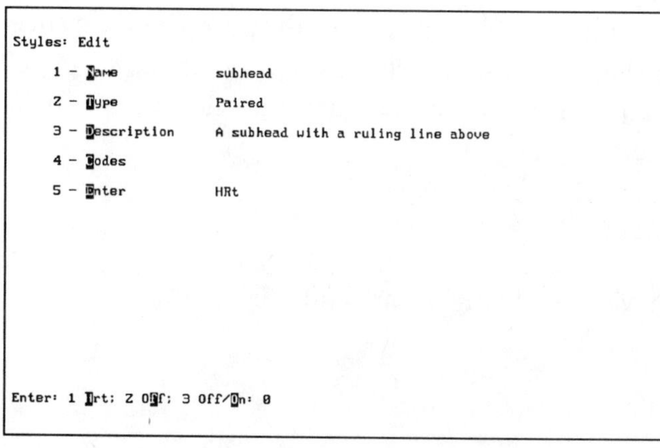

The often confusing "Enter" option can change the way the ENTER key works when in a Paired Style.

To go into styles, press

ALT-F8

Now, move the cursor to a style and press

E

Notice #5 "Enter"? This feature only appears on paired styles; it allows you to change how the enter key works when it is inside a style.

◆ Normal

Press **E** and three choices will appear. If you press **H**, the Return/Enter key will do just that, return or enter. The style will remain on. I find this to be the most practical and efficient method, since the code only turns off when I specifically turn it off. At times I may need to place hard returns in my text, and I wouldn't want them to turn off a style.

◆ Off

If you press **F** the style will turn off. Pressing an additional **[ENTER]** will begin a new line.

◆ Off/On

The most enigmatic of these choices is **O**. By pressing the **[ENTER]** key you can turn a code off, then back on. If you can discover a truly effective way to use this feature, write me, because I can't.

Yes, I know what it's supposed to do, and it does, but once you've used it, editing can become quite difficult. Here's an example. Retrieve the style sheet named "LIBRARY.STY" on the Conversion disk. I'm getting ahead of myself here, but it's important to elaborate upon this point (and it's not often you get this kind of unexpected excitement).

Put the Conversion disk in drive A: and type

ALT-F8 R A:LIBRARY.STY

Move the cursor to the style called "Right Par" and press

O

to turn it on.

Bingo! You'll notice that an automatic paragraph number has been created. When you press a single return, a double return appears on-screen, along with the paragraph number and indented paragraphs. Type a couple of paragraphs here so you have something to work with. C'mon, it's kind of fun (but little do you know what you're getting into.)

Now the mystery and intrigue begins. Why don't you try to combine two of those numbered lines? You can't simply backspace as you normally would to combine two paragraphs. If you do, WordPerfect will ask if you want to delete the Style On, and then ask about the Style Off. If you answer **N**, you can't combine the paragraphs. If you answer **Y**, the paragraphs combine, but they lose all their formatting in the bargain: the automatic number, the indent, the whole shebang.

Of course, you could have blocked the second paragraph, deleted it, and then undeleted it back in the first paragraph, but that's tedious (at least for someone with a limited frustration span such as myself).

The biggest drawback is that it just plain gets in the way. It makes editing slower and in the end you don't gain very much.

> ➺ Here's a hint for bringing back a style you've deleted by accident. Make sure the cursor is in the exact same place it was when you deleted the style, and then press **F1** (the Cancel Key).

◆ Make it easy on yourself

This whole situation can be alleviated by changing this style from a Paired to an Open style. Type

ALT-F8

and move the cursor to the style Right Par. Press

E

for edit. Type

T O

to change the type of style to open. You'll see that the "Enter" choice has disappeared entirely. If you press

C

you'll notice that the [Comment] is gone, as are the two returns that followed it. (You'll also notice that your entire office has been repainted and has new furniture in it. This is a powerful command.)

Press

F7 [ENTER] O

to exit, and turn the style on.

The paragraph number will appear, and when you type, the text is indented. The only difference is when you press return, that's all you get—a return. If you need another automatic number and an indent, you have to type **ALT-F8**, move the cursor to the style you want, and press **O**. If that's too much trouble, create a macro of it (see Chapter 15, *Macros*). Personally, I find this less of a nuisance than having to edit in a special way simply to accommodate my formatting (but that's just me).

❖ *It's not my default*

If you want WordPerfect to automatically load a style sheet whenever you create a new document, the "Library" can be that style. WordPerfect includes a library file on its Conversion disk but, unless you are writing a thesis, its most valuable use is as an example.

To automatically load a style sheet, press

SHIFT-F1 L L

and type in the full path name of the file containing the styles that you want to become defaults. The subdirectories must also be included in the full path name. Here's an example: \WP50\STYLES\IZZY.STY. While you can name the default style whatever you want (it doesn't have to be in a directory called STYLES, have the file name IZZY, or end in the letters .STY), the file name alone

The Setup menu (SHIFT-F1 L) allows you to specify which style sheet will be the "default." It will automatically be loaded with each new file you create.

```
Setup: Location of Auxiliary Files

     1 - Backup Directory                 C:\WP5
     2 - Hyphenation Module(s)            C:\WP5
     3 - Keyboard/Macro Files             C:\WP5
     4 - Main Dictionary(s)               C:\WP5
     5 - Printer Files                    C:\WP5
     6 - Style Library Filename           C:\WP5\SCHLOCK.STY  <--------
     7 - Supplementary Dictionary(s)      C:\WP5\WP{WP}EN.SUP
     8 - Thesaurus                        C:\WP5

Selection: 0
```

isn't enough. Use the whole path name so that if you change directories in WordPerfect, the program knows where to look for the file.

Once you do this, WordPerfect will automatically load the style sheet you've selected into each new file you open.

❖ *Save that thought*

If flexibility and consistency are the two major reasons for using style sheets, it's only natural that these benefits extend beyond one single file.

Any big project should be broken down into individual chunks, or chapters. This allows for improved comprehension and is easier and faster for WordPerfect to process. While WordPerfect can theoretically handle documents thousands of pages long, it's most efficient when files are kept well under 100 pages.

If you want to use a single style sheet for, say, 17 chapters, you don't have to recreate the style for each document. WordPerfect allows you to save a style sheet in a file, and then load it into another document. Even after you've created a style sheet, you can still load a different one into the file. You can overwrite styles with the same name, or load only the styles that don't currently exist.

If you're up to this pulse-pounding excitement, follow along with me in this next example:

◆ Saving a style sheet

Press **ALT-F8** to enter the style menu. Press **S** to save the styles to a separate file. WordPerfect will ask you for a file name. [It's advisable to end style sheets with .STY because it makes them easier to distinguish from files containing text. It's not, however, mandatory, so if you want to end all your style sheets with .POO (for your favorite bear), go right ahead.]

If the name you select already exists, WordPerfect asks you to press **Y** (to write over it) or (**N** to choose another name), just as it does when you save a file.

◆ Retrieving a style sheet

Press **ALT-F8** to retrieve the style menu. For this example, we'll be using a style sheet that came with WordPerfect. However, you can also retrieve style sheets you've made yourself, or styles from any WordPerfect file that contains styles.

Put the Conversion disk in Drive A: (the floppy drive), and press **R** to retrieve a style. WordPerfect requests a filename. Enter **A:LIBRARY.STY [ENTER]**.

If the name of any of the current styles matches the name of a style in the file you are retrieving, WordPerfect will say "Style(s) already exist. Replace? Y/N?" If you answer **Y**, WordPerfect loads the new style, replacing and deleting the old one. If you answer **N**, WordPerfect loads all the styles that don't have the same name, but leaves the ones with the matching names unchanged.

❖ *Tip: Sharsies, sharsies*

If you want to load the style sheet from a particular file, but forgot to save it to its own file, don't worry. You can extract the styles from a file, even if you haven't saved them separately.

Once you press **R** for retrieve, type the name of the file that contains the styles you want and press **[ENTER]**. WordPerfect will only retrieve the styles, not the entire file.

◆ Updating

If you've selected a default style sheet, WordPerfect provides you with an extra convenience. Let's say you're sharing a style sheet between several different files, as in the chapters of a book. You've created a style called "subhead," and now want to change all the subheads in all the book files.

You can change the styles from within any of the chapters. Press

ALT-F8 S

and save the style sheet, using the name of the default style sheet. WordPerfect will ask if you want to overwrite the file. Answer **Y** for yes. The changes will be saved to the default style sheet.

When you load another chapter, simply update the style sheet by pressing

ALT-F8 U

for Update. WordPerfect will copy all the styles from the default file into your current file.

Warning: This will **overwrite** all the styles with the same name in your current file, and the default style sheet. It will do this *without warning*, and will not even have the courtesy of asking you to confirm first. However, it will not delete any new styles you might have added to this chapter.

❖ *How high the line?*

If you read Chapter 7, *Fonts,* you know that WordPerfect's automatic line height does not always give you sufficient leading. (If you didn't read that chapter, it doesn't hurt me; it's *you* who will be sorry for it when you can't get into a good college or hold down a good job.) That's why I add the Line Height Fixed command to my styles.

If you are using specific point sizes, remember to add 1 point to the leading. All you have to do is include a Fixed Line Height command inside the style: **SHIFT-F8 L H F**. Now enter a number that is 1 point larger than the size of the font, followed by a **P** (so WordPerfect knows that the measurement is in points). If you were using 10 point type, you'd enter **11P**.

If you are using size attributes such as Large, Very Large and Extra Large, remember that these sizes are based on the size of the body text. Large is 20% bigger, Very Large is 80% bigger, and Extra Large is 250% bigger. Take that into consideration when you are setting the line height.

❖ *Graphics secrets*

Almost every WordPerfect command can be placed in a style. The most notable exception is graphics files. Graphics boxes can be placed in styles, but you cannot put graphics files into these boxes.

If you wanted to create a style for a newsletter that contained a logo, with an accompanying graphic, you could not place the entire logo into the style. You would need to use a paired style, and place the graphics box between the opening and closing style codes.

WordPerfect also has a quirk (it's not a bug or a feature) about creating graphics boxes between two paired style codes. If you put the cursor between the two style codes and create a graphics box, the box code will appear *following* the closing style code.

A more important problem (possibly a bug, clearly not a feature) is that sometimes the graphics box may not even be created, or may somehow place itself inside the style (as it did when I used the "Subheading" style from the

LIBRARY.STY file on the Conversion disk). The graphic completely disappeared the next time I changed a style and they were updated.

All of this could cause you a lot of grief, but in return for your loyal readership, I'm going to tell you how to get around this problem by letting you in on a hard-earned secret.

The first solution is to place any type of text, even a space, between the two codes, and then create the graphics box. That one tiny space will cause the graphics box code to appear between the paired style markers.

If you should forget this trick, and find that the graphics box appears outside of the styles, delete the graphics box code, move between the two codes and press **F1 R**.

◆ Intercolumn rules

WordPerfect will not automatically place vertical lines between columns on all pages (these lines are not surprisingly called "intercolumn rules"). You can remedy this by putting the intercolumn rules inside an open style that is placed on every page. For more information about using lines in styles, see Chapter 13, *Lines*.

❖ *Table-matic*

Because WordPerfect styles can contain column definition commands, you can reuse column definitions without having to recreate them.

This is especially useful when you create complicated uneven width columns, or tables. The advantage of using styles for tables (whether they are created with tabs or columns) is that styles guarantee the tabs, margins, and columns will be consistent, even if you change them for the rest of the document. Also, with a paired style, everything (tabs, margins, columns) reverts to normal after the closing code of the style.

To create a table style, create a paired style that contains specific column or tab settings. If you want to get fancy, with a horizontal line above and below the table, move the cursor to before the [Comment] code and press

ALT-F9 L H [ENTER]

then move the cursor after the [Comment] code and press

ALT-F9 L H [ENTER]

❖ *Headers, footers, and all that jazz*

While I don't recommend putting headers and footers into styles, I do recommend putting styles into headers and footers. This is not unlike taking the girl out of the country and yet being unable to take the country out of the girl.

Serious Warning: (Try to imagine submarine depth-charge alert noises here such as "Wooop Wooop") If you place a header into a style, WordPerfect will dupe you into thinking that you can edit it from within the text. You will see it, edit it, even View Document with the changes in place. But if you edit any style, WordPerfect will go back through the document and update the codes (including the header that you changed) with the current style codes. The changes you made will be lost, and you will be mightily confused, if not downright irate.

If you are using a standard header or footer, that you know you won't change, it's fine to include it in the "Topper" style (to be covered momentarily). You can edit the header or footer if you remember to go into the style editor and change it. My problem is that I tend to forget, edit it from the regular text, and then pull out little clumps of hair when my changes disappear. (I don't know about you, but I don't have enough hair or Minoxidil left to afford losing little clumps on a regular basis.)

Now that you've been duly warned, I'll tell you how to use styles inside headers or footers for consistency. Create an Open style that contains all the formatting for a header or footer, but not the header or footer itself.

Here's an example of a footer that has a ruling line above:

[Hline:Left & Right,6.5",.05",100%][HRt]

[AdvDn:.01"][Font:Helv 8pt][Flsh Rt]Page ^B

This code inserts a horizontal ruling line, advances text down an additional .1" (one return isn't enough, two is too much), changes the font, and even sets the page number flush right.

If the text in headers and footers varies from chapter to chapter, using a style in this manner will guarantee consistent formatting.

When you create a header or footer, simply press **ALT-F8**, move the cursor to the header or footer style and press O. The style code will appear.

❖ Where's Cosmo?

If you are creating a large project that has been split into many separate WordPerfect files, you can take style sheets one step farther by creating what I call "Topper" files. I call them that because they contain all the codes used repeatedly at the top of each file (and because I've always liked Cosmo).

There are disadvantages to placing all these codes into a single style, especially when you use headers and footers. To change a header or footer created in a style, you'd have to first go in and edit the style, and then edit the header and footer. If you accidentally edited the footer directly (not in the style editor), the next time you edited any style, WordPerfect would update all the styles. As a result, changes you made directly to the footer (not from within the style editor) would be lost.

Putting headers and footers in a style compromises your ability to share styles between files; if you updated the styles in a file, the header and footer specifics for that particular file or chapter would be lost.

Bearing all this in mind, I like to create a WordPerfect file that contains the styles I want (including header and footer styles), along with formatting, such as headers and footers, margins, even graphics boxes if they are used at the beginning of each chapter.

```
Chapter 10«
Style Sheets«
«
Flexibility and consistency: the two major reasons for using
style sheets. With them you can change the style of a document
repeatedly in the least amount of time, and make sure that the
elements remain uniform within that document, or a whole slew of
documents.«
    While the idea of style sheets isn't new, the way
WordPerfect implements it is. Even if you are familiar with style
sheets in Ventura Publisher or Microsoft Word, it will not be of
C:\WP5\P\WP10.TW                                Doc 2 Pg 1 Ln 1" Pos 1"
[Open Style:topper:[Paper Sz/Typ:11" x 8.5",Standard][T/B Mar:0.5",0.3"][L/R Mar
:0.5",0.5"][Font:Stalagtite Roman 36 pt (UKASCII) (Land)][Ln Height:0.5"][Tab Se
t:1.5",3",3.75",6.5",7",0.5"]][Footer A:Z; ... ]Chapter 10[HRt]
Style Sheets[HRt]
[HRt]
Flexibility and consistency: the two major reasons for using[SRt]
style sheets. With them you can change the style of a document[SRt]
repeatedly in the least amount of time, and make sure that the[SRt]
elements remain uniform within that document, or a whole slew of[SRt]
documents.[HRt]

Whack Reveal Codes to restore screen
```

A Topper style is placed at the top of a file, and contains global formatting commands for the entire document.

I also place a comment code at the end of my "Topper" file, consisting of information about what formatting is contained in the file.

When you produce a major change in your formatting, put the cursor to the right of the [Comment] code, press **ALT-F4** to turn Block on, then press **HOME HOME HOME [UP ARROW]** to include all the formatting in the block. Press the **[DEL]** key and then read in the latest "Topper" file. Only one more step: you must go into styles with **ALT-F8**, press **R** and retrieve the styles from the "Topper" file (they aren't brought in when you add a file to the current document).

◆ Library

Always consider going into Setup, **SHIFT-F1 L L** and entering the name of the "Topper" file. Then simply press **ALT-F8 U** to update the styles from the "Topper" file to the current file.

❖ *But baby, it's cold outside*

Brrrr. It's the software equivalent of a Dove Bar!

One of the most useful features of style sheets can also be one of the most dangerous. Because a change in a style affects *all* text within that style, it's possible to change a style to suit your current purpose, without remembering that those changes will also be made in the rest of the file.

However, there's a quick way to *freeze* the document so that all the style sheet formatting remains intact, but (at least temporarily) unchangeable.

Go into Styles with **ALT-F8** and save the style sheet to a separate file. I usually give that file the same first eight letters as my text file, but end it in .STY. to identify it as a style sheet.

Now, while still in the Styles menu, you delete each individual style in a document by pressing **D Y** repeatedly until the list of styles is empty. Press **F7** to return to the text.

You'll notice that the style codes are still there, and if you go into Reveal Codes, you'll see that the styles still contain all the formatting they did before you deleted the list of styles.

If you change your mind and want to change a style, simply go into styles and retrieve the style you saved (before deleting). You can now edit any of those styles, and the file will be unfrozen.

❖ *With six you get egg roll*

No, WordPerfect can't give you the ability to squeal like Doris Day. But can Doris give you the ability to use as many style sheet files as you want? WordPerfect can.

Normally one style sheet is quite sufficient, thank you. But there are times when you might want more than one. WordPerfect files can only use one style sheet at a time, but you can retrieve style sheets as often as your little heart desires.

Remember that when you retrieve a new style sheet, the style codes you've placed in the text still have the same name; only the formatting codes within them change. When you retrieve a new style sheet, only those styles with the same name as the ones in use will have any immediate impact. The others will be added to the list of files, but won't function until you turn them on.

Here's a prime example. Suppose you have several standard types of documents: a report, a newsletter, and a standard draft format. Your draft format is Courier, double spaced, 1.5" margins on both sides, 1" margin on the top and bottom. You use this format for printing drafts so that there's plenty of room to write notes. You have a style sheet called DRAFT.STY for this format.

As you write, you know what will be used as a headline or subhead, so you include those styles. The draft style sheet centers, emboldens and underlines headlines, and bolds subheads with two extra spaces above each one.

Once you've completed the text corrections, you should format the text into a standard two column report. Retrieve the REPORT.STY and zap: the text is set ragged right in two columns with hyphenation, the headline is Extra Large, the subheads are large and bold with ruling lines above. The document is complete with footers and ready to go. Total time for formatting: about 15 seconds. Finally, consider adding some snazzy and misleading charts and graphs (this will take 15 minutes on a good day).

You present the report, get a bonus, a raise, a company car, and a vacation in the Bahamas (remember, this is an ideal example—no one said that it had anything to do with reality).

Now it's time to take the revised report (everyone's a critic) and publish it for your customers. You retrieve the NEWSLET.STY sheet and bingo: you've got a three-column justified newsletter. The charts and graphs have re-sized themselves to fit into the new columns automatically. Total time for formatting: oh, say 15 seconds, give or take another half hour to futz around with details.

The moral of this story is that sometimes two (or three) style sheets are better than one. In this case, I've included footers in the Topper style because they are standard and won't have to be customized for a series of chapters. This is an example of a *nested* style: the Topper style includes a footer that contains the Footer style.

Here are the codes for the three style sheets. Remember, the [Comment] code is built-in to the paired style (so don't enter the comment, just the codes after it; comments meant just for you have been inserted between {} brackets and aren't to be typed into the style). Unless you see a [HRt] code, don't press return—the codes are on separate lines for clarity, but they may not appear that way on your screen. For PostScript users: Times Roman is identical to Dutch.

❖ *Draft.sty*

FOOTER (open):

[Font:Courier 10 pitch][HRt]

[Cntr]DRAFT [-] [Date:3 1, 4]

{This is a date code: the current date will be printed automatically on the bottom of each page}

[-]Page ^B

{The ^B is for a page number}

HEADLINE (paired):

[Cntr][UND][BOLD][Comment][C/A/Flrt]

{This code is inserted automatically when you press [ENTER] and create the [HRt] code}

[HRt]

[HRt]

SUBHEAD (paired):

[HRt]

[HRt]

[UND][BOLD][Comment]

TOPPER (open):

[L/R Mar:1.5",1.5"][T/B Mar:1",1"]

[Font:Courier 10 pitch][Ln Spacing:1.5]

❖ *Report.sty*

FOOTER (open):

[HLine:Left & Right,6.5",0.01",100%][HRt]

[AdvDn:0.1"][Font:Dutch 08pt][Flsh Rt]REPORT [-] [Date:3 1, 4]

[-] Page ^B[C/A/Flrt][HRt]

HEADLINE (paired):

[Cntr][EXT LARGE][Comment][C/A/Flrt][HRt]

SUBHEAD (paired):

[HLine:Left & Right,7.5",0.01",100%][HRt]

[AdvDn:0.1"][BOLD][LARGE][Comment]

TOPPER (open):

[HZone:10%,10%][Hyph On][Font:Dutch 10pt]

[L/R Mar:0.5",0.5"][T/B Mar:0.5",0.5"]

[Footer A:1;[Open Style:footer] ...]

[Col Def:2,0.5",4.1",4.4",8"][Col On]

{*Two columns. Use a distance between columns of .3"*}

❖ *Newslet.sty*

FOOTER (open):

[Font: Dutch 08pt][HLine:Left & Right,7.5",0.01",100%][HRt]

[AdvDn:0.1"][Cntr]

HEADLINE (paired):

[HLine:Left & Right,6.5",0.05",100%][HRt]

[AdvDn:0.1"][Cntr][EXT LARGE][Comment][C/A/Flrt][HRt]

SUBHEAD (paired):

[Cndl EOP:5]

{This conditional end of page serves to keep the ruling line, the subhead, and the text on the same page or column}

[HRt][HLine:Left & Right,7.5",0.01",100%][AdvDn:0.1"][HRt]

[BOLD][VRY LARGE][Comment]

TOPPER (open):

[HZone:10%,10%][Hyph On][Just On][Font:Dutch 10pt]

[L/R Mar:0.5",0.5"][T/B Mar:0.5",0.5"]

[Footer A:1;[Open Style:footer] ...]

[Col Def:3,0.5",2.83",3.08",5.41",5.66",8"]

{Three columns. Use a distance between columns of .3"}

[Col On]

◆ Tip: "Topper" too

While the Topper styles I've presented so far are all open styles, there are times when you might want to use a paired style for a topper. One such situation is when you have a multi-column page and want the headline to span all the columns (as most headlines do).

In this little scenario, we create the following styles:

TOPPER (paired):

[L/R Mar:0.5",0.5"][T/B Mar:0.5",0.5"]

[Comment]

[Col Def:3,0.5",2.83",3.08",5.41",5.66",8"][Col On]

{Three columns. Use a distance of .25" between columns}

HEADLINE (paired):

[Cntr][EXT LARGE][Comment]

Notice how the Col Def and Col On are *after* the [Comment]; this ensures that they won't go into effect until the Style Off code.

To use these styles, turn the Topper style on, be sure the cursor is highlighting the Style Off code, and turn on the HEADLINE style.

The codes will look like this:

[Style On:Topper] [Style On:Headline] [Style Off:Headline] [Style Off:Topper]

Type the headline between the Style On:Headline and Style Off:Headline codes. The headline will be extra large and centered across the entire page, but all text following the Style Off:Topper code will be in three columns.

◆ Tip: The name game

Vanna vanna bo banna, bananna fanna fo fanna, me my mo manna, Vanna! Yes, relive those stupid Sixties with this collection of your favorite hits! Hits like, "The Name Game!" (I only put this in so you'd remember how you used to joke around with your friends about what rhymed with "Chuck"). By the way, can you name the artist who recorded this monster hit?

Back to business. I always use Topper Styles, even if I'm not using columns and other fancy formatting. It's reassuring to know that no matter what style sheet I load, they will all work together because they have a Topper style.

It's advisable to be consistent about what you call your styles, so that you can change style sheets at any time without having to block text and apply styles again.

Okay, so you knew the singer was Shirley Ellis. Now, for the trip to Hawaii, who wrote the song? (Big hint: his name is in the game.)

❖ *Red letterhead day*

Tired of the high cost of stationery? Fed up with running out of letterhead just when you need it most? Fatigued, listless? You've got two choices: Vitametavegamin, or styles. A single style can contain an entire letterhead (if the letterhead doesn't contain a graphic).

One advantage of using a style for a letterhead is that it's instantly available. You turn on the style and voila! Here are two examples of letterheads one of my favorite baddies might have used (san the suspicious spots).

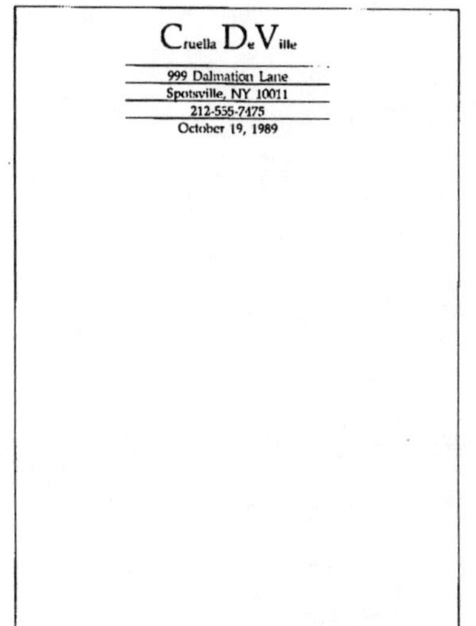

Cruella DeVille

999 Dalmation Lane
Spotsville, NY 10011
212-555-7475
October 19, 1989

The first one is for personal use, is rather on the loud side, and takes up a good portion of the page all by itself. The second is for business purposes and is far more tasteful. However, each has its use; sometimes you want to brag, other times you want to stun them with modesty. Because these are both styles, you can choose the one best suited for you right before you print.

(Remember. Don't press return unless there's a [HRt] code. Keystrokes are inside < >, and comments are inside {}.

◆ **Personal (open):**

```
[L/R Mar:0.4",0.4"][T/B Mar:0.4",0.6"][Figure:1;;]
[L/R Mar:1",1"][T/B Mar:0.3",0.3"][Footer A:1;[HRt]
[Font:Palatino 8 pt] ... ][HRt]
[HRt][Font:Palatino 12 pt]
[EXT LARGE][Cntr]C[ext large]ruella
```

[EXT LARGE]D[ext large]e[EXT LARGE]V[ext large]ille[C/A/Flrt][HRt]

[HLine:Center,3",0.01",100%][HRt]

[HRt]

[Cntr][Date:3 1, 4][C/A/Flrt][HRt]

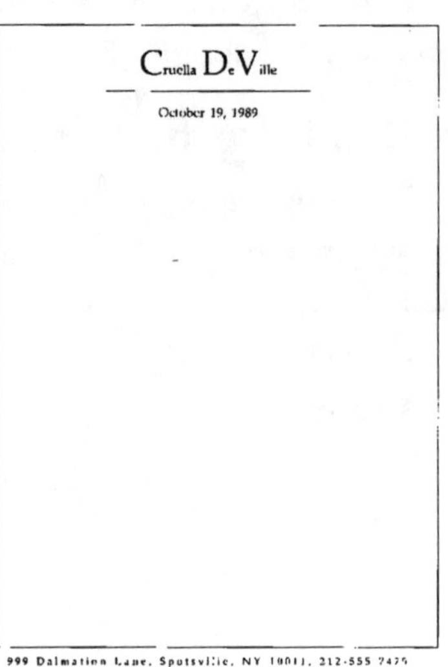

◆ **Business (open):**

[L/R Mar:0.4",0.4"]

[T/B Mar:0.3",0.5"][Figure:1;;]<TP VF WN>

{*I've set a wide margin before the figure because it actually is a full full page box with a ruling box around it, and I didn't want it to interfere with the text. Notice how I change the margin next so that the body of the letter is well within the full page box*}

[L/R Mar:1",1"][HRt]

[Font:Palatino 12 pt][EXT LARGE][Cntr]C[ext large]ruella

[EXT LARGE]D[ext large]e[EXT LARGE]V[ext large]ille[C/A/Flrt][HRt]

[HLine:Center,3",0.01",100%][Ln Height:0.12"][HRt]

[Cntr]999 Dalmatian Lane[C/A/Flrt][HRt]

[HLine:Center,3",0.01",100%][HRt]

[Cntr]Spotsville, NY 10011[C/A/Flrt][HRt]

[HLine:Center,3",0.01",100%][HRt]

[Cntr]212[-]555[-]1212[C/A/Flrt][HRt]

[Cntr][Date:3 1,4][C/A/Flrt]

If you want to create a letterhead with a graphic logo, you'll need to create a separate letterhead file containing the text and the graphic. I close mine with a comment, so it's easy to delete the letterhead graphics before saving the file, thus conserve disk space. Place the cursor under the comment and just backspace until all traces of the letterhead format have been deleted.

For an example of a letterhead with a graphic, see Chapter 4, *Show & Tell.* (You'll notice I haven't included a sample of my signature on my stationery, lest anyone start signing my checks as well as duplicating my letterhead.)

❖ *Changing your mind, changing your style.*

We've seen how styles can affect a paragraph, but they're also useful for text as small as a single character.

◆ Tip: Underlines become italics

Instead of pressing F8, or using CONTROL-F8 A U for underlines, create a paired style called UND/ITAL. Type

ALT-F8 C N UND/ITAL [ENTER] C F8 F7 F7 F7

Use this style every time you want an underline. When you are ready to print the final draft, edit this style by typing

ALT-F8

Move to the UND/ITAL style, press

E C [DEL] CONTROL-F8 A I F7 F7 F7

All previously underlined text will now appear in italics.

To hasten this even further, create a macro that will apply this style with a single keystroke. To create the macro, press

CONTROL-F10 ALT-U UND/ITAL [ENTER] ALT-F8 N UND/ITAL [ENTER] O CONTROL-F10

This will automatically summon the UND/ITAL style anytime you press ALT-U.

❖ *Searching and replacing styles*

What if you want to replace all the underlines with the UND/ITAL style? No can do. You can't search and replace styles because WordPerfect doesn't permit you to utilize styles as replacement text. But you can achieve identical results with a macro. No, don't start scouring through the macro chapter (you can put down that Brillo pad), I'm including it here.

In this example we're (is this like a nurse saying "Now we're going to have a shot?") going to create a macro that searches for [UND][und] codes and replaces them with the Und/Ital style you just created (if you've been following along like a good reader).

This may seem endless, but once you've created this macro you can use it over and over again. Be aware that you must follow the directions exactly—leaving out a single keystroke will mess everything up and could even make the macro destructive (kind of like a little Arnold Schwarzenegger running around inside the computer. Don't you love reading stuff like that? Doesn't it make you want to give up and find a job as a mud wrestler or something?). Don't try this unless you've already created a style called "UND/ITAL" that is currently available in the list of styles.

Make sure Reveal Codes is OFF, then type:

CONTROL-F10 UND2STY [ENTER] **Turn underlines to UND/ITAL style** [ENTER] F2 F8 F2 ALT-F4 F2 F8 F8 [LEFT ARROW] [BACKSPACE] F2 ALT-F8 N UND/ITAL [ENTER] O [LEFT ARROW] [BACKSPACE] CONTROL-F10

This will find only a single set of underline codes and replace them with the style. If you want this to automatically find and replace all the underlines with the UND/ITAL style, use the same keystrokes for the macro, but add the following before the last CONTROL-F10:

ALT-F10 UND2STY [ENTER]

This will repeat the macro until all the underlines have been found and replaced. In case you didn't notice, this style was a perfect segue to the next tip...

❖ *Tips, tricks & techniques*

When I first started using WordPerfect 5, I created macros that called up styles. Unfortunately, the macros would no longer work when I added or deleted styles because they were relying on cursor movements to select the correct style.

I have my own unique method for learning about software. I press every key on the keyboard, see what it does, and when it does it. I try out every feature in every conceivable way, and while this technique takes time, it works.

This method led to a solution for this macro problem. In the great tradition of American explorers, I stumbled onto a vital feature that WordPerfect's manual fails to mention.

◆ Undocumented boon—styles & macros

Okay, okay, enough breathless anticipation. The feature is none other than our friend "name search," found in almost every list WordPerfect presents. Name files, Base Font, all of these have **N** on the menu. You press it, type the name you are searching for, and WordPerfect jumps to that name.

Style offers this feature as well, although it's not on the menu (possibly because there's no room for it). Still, even if the programmers at WordPerfect didn't think it was important enough to acknowledge, I **know** that it's indispensable when you are devising macros.

Whenever you create a macro that uses a style, use the Name Search feature rather than moving the cursor to the style you want. Then, no matter how many styles you add or delete, the macro will still call up that particular style.

Call me silly, but I feel like I've discovered a planet somewhere. Maybe they'll name it after me. (Probably not.)

◆ Block protect in styles

Block protect is a useful WordPerfect feature that protects a block of text from being interrupted by column or page breaks. While the WordPerfect manual does not mention it in relation to paired styles, you can still use them together to great advantage.

To create a block protect, you turn block on with

ALT-F4

and highlight the text to be protected, then press

SHIFT-F8

To use it in a paired style (it wouldn't make any sense to use it in an open style), the area you've blocked should extend over the [Comment] marker. When you press **SHIFT-F8**, WordPerfect asks you to confirm. Press **Y**. [Block Pro:On] appears at the beginning of the area, and [Block Pro:Off] appears at the end of the area you blocked.

This maintains text between the Style On and Style Off in the same column or on the same page. This is especially helpful if you are including horizontal lines in styles; you don't want the line printing at the bottom of one page or column and the text at the top of another. Block protect keeps the lines with the text.

Of course, you can't block protect more than a page, or WordPerfect will be forced to put in a page break anyway.

◆ Conditional end of page

This feature is similar to Block Protect and permits you to keep an absolute number of lines together.

To create a [Cndl EOP], type

SHIFT-F8 O C

and then the number of lines you want to stay together. Example: **SHIFT-F8 O C 10** dictates that the next 10 lines will stay together. If there's not room on this page, a page break will appear and all the lines will be together on the next page or column.

❖ *[Just on] in time*

One of the petty complaints I have about WordPerfect's styles is how it handles justification. When you create a style, WordPerfect considers the default for the document as the default for the style. If you haven't changed Initial Codes using setup **SHIFT-F1 I I**, then the default is justification on.

This means that if you create a style where you turn justification off, WordPerfect will work just fine and will insert a [Just Off] code in the style. But if you want to include a [Just On] code in a style, and press **SHIFT-F8 L J Y,** WordPerfect won't enter any code in the style; it assumes it's already on, so you're not really changing anything.

The fix for this is simple. If the default is Just On, and you want to include a Just On code, you should first enter a Just Off code, and then another Just Off code, like this: **SHIFT-F8 L J N J Y**. Both codes will be in the style, but only the code that changes the state of justification applies.

◆ Taking it hard

If your chapters always begin a new page, consider creating a style called CHAPTER to include a hard page break at the beginning of the style. If you want the chapters to always start on a right hand page, include a Force Odd code with **SHIFT-F7 P O O**. Then the chapters will automatically start on a new right-hand page with an odd page number.

❖ *Ventura with love*

As wonderful as WordPerfect is for desktop publishing, there will be those among us (even myself at times) who yearn for more power. My choice for this is Ventura Publisher. It's a brilliant program, and its design has inspired many WordPerfect features. Did I hear somebody snicker, "What's Ventura got to do with WordPerfect?" Well here's the answer: This book *is* called *WordPerfect 5: Desktop Publishing In Style,* and Ventura is but one more way to desktop publish with WordPerfect.

If someone has sold you a copy of PageMaker, fear not (well, fear a little: PM is too slow for the likes of me). This trick works almost as well with the "P" word; the concept remains the same, only the codes have been changed to protect the innocent.

One annoying element with Ventura is that its codes can clutter a text file until it becomes unreadable. But WordPerfect's style sheets are a prodigious (don't you love that word?) way of keeping files readable right up until you plug them into the Big V. This is contingent on WordPerfect's ability to include text in a style, and so even Microsoft Word can't do this (ha, ha, ha).

The heroes of this little adventure are two style sheets: the first for easy to edit, double spaced draft printouts, and the second for fully formatted, code clogged Ventura-ready files. Both are simple.

The draft style allows headlines, subheads and readouts (or pull-quotes) to stand out from regular text by using extra hard returns, underlines, bold, centers, or indents. The final style removes all extra returns and replaces them with Ventura tag names. Even underlines become real Ventura italics codes. Woo-wee.

Here's the VPDRAFT.STY:

BYLINE (paired):

[Tab][BOLD][Comment]

HEADLINE (paired):

[HRt]

[HRt]

[Cntr][BOLD][UND][Comment][C/A/Flrt][HRt]

[HRt]

READOUT (paired):

[Indent][Indent][BOLD][Comment]

{You can use either left indent F4 or Left/Right indent SHIFT-F4}

SUBHEAD (paired):

[HRt]

[UND][Comment]

TOPPER (paired):

[L/R Mar:1.25",1.25"][Ln Spacing:1.5]

UND/ITAL (paired):

[UND][Comment]

Here's the VPFINAL.STY
BYLINE (paired):

@BYLINE =

[Comment]

HEADLINE

@HEADLINE =

[Comment]

READOUT

@READOUT =

[Comment]

SUBHEAD

@SUBHEAD =

[Comment]

TOPPER

[L/R Mar:1",1"]

UND/ITAL

<MI>

[Comment]

<D>

<MI> stands for Medium Italics, and <D> stands for Default, because it returns text to its normal attribute.

While Ventura will read the 5.0 format (or should very soon), you'll want to save the file to WordPerfect's 4.2 format when you use this tip. This locks the formatting and text tags in place, so that Ventura doesn't ignore it.

Once you've run the file through Ventura, those codes are going to be there forever and ever... unless you use a fancy- schmancy macro. For another Ventura tip, see Chapter 15, *Macros.*

◆ Hey, big number

One of the hallmarks of the Mac-ish style I normally deplore is giant sized numbers. I still decry how the Apple ads lead you to believe that serious business people sit around poring over cutesy pictures. However, these outlines with large numbers are lighthearted and quite effective at attention grabbers. The numbers are used in outlines in the same way raised caps would be used in paragraphs.

A few words of warning regarding graphic design, since we are treading on Machiavellian territory. These big numbers can easily overshadow the actual content of the outline. They're a good device for diverting attention if you don't want people reading too closely. But if careful and prolonged work with the outline is required, or the subject is formal or serious, these big numbers will probably be obtrusive. Also, this Mac-hination is best for small outlines; on long outlines they become tedious or just plain silly.

Now that you've been warned, go ahead, live the Mac fantasy, but at a fraction of the cost. Intimidate your business acquaintances. Sit in gray offices and say "We did that in-house, on our computer system, with just a word processing program." Sneer at them smugly when they snivel, whine, and beg to know what kind of computer you used. Don't give in too much—just say: "Not a Mac... something less expensive and more efficient..."

This style automatically numbers the paragraph by using WordPerfect's numbering feature (the #'s automatically update when you change the outline, saving you tons-o-time and aggravation), makes the number big and bold,and then indents the body of the outline to the next tab stop.

Create an open style called BIG NUM using the following codes.

➟ BIG NUM (open):

[VRY LARGE][BOLD][Align]

{*Pressing CONTROL-F6 commands WordPerfect to temporarily make the next tab a decimal tab, and align the number of the decimal. This allows for a neater presentation when the numbers go from 9 to 10, or from 99 to 100*}

[Par Num:Auto][vry large][bold][C/A/Flrt]

{*The C/A/Flrt code appears when you press F4 to create the next Indent code*}

[Indent]

For other outlining tips, see Chapter 8, *Paragraphs*, and Chapter 15, *Macros.*

❖ *Square bullets and ballot boxes*

"What a segue to Graphics," or "Pardon me Miss, is that the Pottsylvania Choo Choo?" (In case you didn't get it, that was for all our Rocky and Bullwinkle, or Moose und Squirrel fans.)

Square bullets and ballot boxes are de rigueur for anyone who is anyone, or at least for anyone who wants square bullets (so much more Vienna Secession/Josef Hoffman than round bullets), or is preparing a questionnaire.

Using a combination of styles and graphics, WordPerfect lets you produce bullets in any size (and I mean any size): from a hundredth of an inch (since this would bear an uncanny resemblance to a period, why bother) to full page (which would be more akin to a bomb or hand grenade than a bullet).

These two styles are almost identical. The only component that changes is the graphics option. For this example, I've used the User-defined Box, since it's unlikely that with three other types of graphics boxes to use, you'll need this for any other purpose.

While you might think these would be open styles, I've created them as paired styles for one simple reason. User-defined boxes normally have no shading or lines around them, but this little ruse changes all that. The square bullet is nothing more than a user box with a 100% background and no lines around it, while the ballot box is nothing but a 0% background and single lines all around it. If I should become delirious and create other graphics as User-defined, they will have the normal user defaults of 0% gray background and no lines around them.

If you are sure you won't lose control in the middle of a work day and start a user-defined frenzy, you can create these open styles. None of the codes will change. And the area after the comment is left blank anyway, so that the style will automatically return the text to how it was before the style.

◆ Ballot box (paired):

[Usr Opt]<BSSSS>[Usr Box:1;;]<TC SB 12p [ENTER] 12p>

[Comment]

[Indent]

You will need to vary the size of the box depending on the size type you are using. Remember that you can enter the size in points by following the number with a P and by making the box the exact size of the type.

The indent can be either F4 or SHIFT-F4.

◆ Square bullet (paired):

[Usr Opt]<G 100>[Usr Box:1;;]<TC SB 12p [ENTER] 12p>

[Comment]

[Indent]

Again, vary the size of the box in accordance with the size of your type. Enter the size in points by following the number with a P and make the box the exact size of the type. The indent can be either F4 or SHIFT-F4.

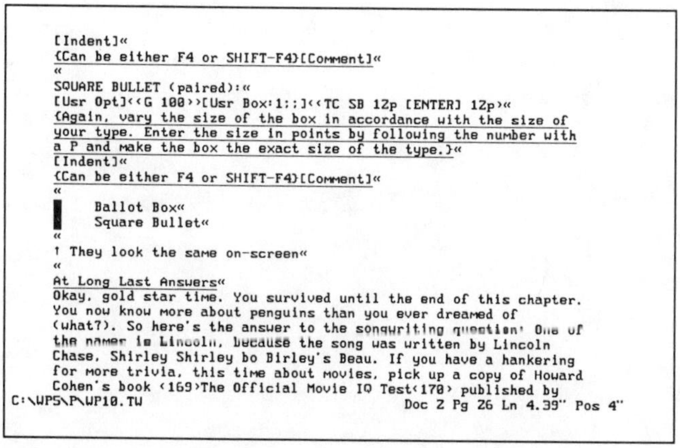

```
[Indent]«
{Can be either F4 or SHIFT-F4}[Comment]«
«
SQUARE BULLET (paired):«
[Usr Opt]<<G 100>>[Usr Box:1;;]<<TC SB 12p [ENTER] 12p>«
{Again, vary the size of the box in accordance with the size of
your type. Enter the size in points by following the number with
a P and make the box the exact size of the type.}«
[Indent]«
{Can be either F4 or SHIFT-F4}[Comment]«
«
█    Ballot Box«
█    Square Bullet«
«
↑ They look the same on-screen«
«
At Long Last Answers«
Okay, gold star time. You survived until the end of this chapter.
You now know more about penguins than you ever dreamed of
(what?). So here's the answer to the songwriting question: One of
the names is Lincoln, because the song was written by Lincoln
Chase, Shirley Shirley bo Birley's Beau. If you have a hankering
for more trivia, this time about movies, pick up a copy of Howard
Cohen's book <169>The Official Movie IQ Test<170> published by
C:\WP5\P\WP10.TW                                Doc 2 Pg 26 Ln 4.39" Pos 4"
```

❑ *Ballot Box*

■ *Square Bullet*

Ballot boxes and square bullets appear as solid blocks on-screen.

◆ At long last answers

Okay, gold star time. You survived until the end of this chapter. You now know more about penguins than you ever dreamed of (what?). So here's the answer to the songwriting question: One of the names is Lincoln, because the song was written by Lincoln Chase, Shirley Shirley bo Birley's Beau. If you have a hankering for more trivia, this time about movies, pick up a copy of Howard Cohen's book "The Official Movie IQ Test" published by Putnam. (Come on, there's more to life than WordPerfect and desktop publishing... well, just a little...)

In graphic detail

Graphics boxes for every occasion

A picture's worth a thousand words, or so the saying goes. Of course it took words to express this cliche. Graphics are the other half of desktop publishing but, to many people, graphics are the darker, more mysterious half. Few of us consider ourselves "artistic," and the mere mention of the word "graphic" can conjure up images of beatniks in black tunics with bongos and berets. "It's cool man, real graphic."

In true desktop publishing, text without graphics is like Lucy without Ricky, Fred without Ginger (or Ethel), Rocky without Bullwinkle...you get the picture (pun intended). Graphics don't have to be intimidating. They may be messy, confusing (especially file formats, which I'll cover later), often slow to print, but not intimidating.

Graphics don't have to be pictures (or charts, graphs or diagrams) either; and in WordPerfect, the graphics features includes both horizontal and vertical lines.

(Don't confuse this feature with Line Draw, which uses a font built into printers such as the LaserJet II.) In fact, lines are so important that I've decided to grant them a chapter of their very own. Lucky them.

WordPerfect's graphics can print on any printer capable of graphics, such as laser, and many dot matrix printers. Most daisy-wheel printers do not have the ability to print graphics.

WordPerfect's graphic feature is the most sophisticated available for any PC-based word processing program. That's not just hype. WordPerfect's graphic feature borrows considerably from some of Ventura Publisher's bag of tricks: WordPerfect automatically wraps text around graphics, attaches captions to pictures that always remain with their assigned graphic, and floats graphics so that they always stay with their associated text. You can even make graphics larger or smaller, flop (believe it or not, the industry jargon for "flip") them so they are facing in the opposite direction, crop them so you use only a portion of the graphic image, even invert them so that everything that was black prints as white, and vice versa.

As if that weren't enough, WordPerfect also lets you use Graphics Boxes for text. While this may seem like a contradiction in terms, text is often used as a graphic device, specifically in "readouts" or "pull-quotes" small chunks of text taken out of context and enlarged on a page as an attention grabber.

❖ *One for all and all for four*

There are four types of WordPerfect Graphics Boxes: Figure, Table, Text, and User-Defined. Before you put your hand to your forehead and sigh melodramatically at how complex this must be, here's the good news: all four types of graphics boxes work identically.

Why on earth are there four of them? As creative as WordPerfect is, its uses have still been dictated by the needs of academia and big business. Long technical documents, whether for documentation or theses, require "lists of figures," special appendices that list all the charts, pictures, or other graphic items in the document. WordPerfect offers four different types of graphics boxes so that you can compile four different lists. One list is for figures, another for tables, and while Text and user-Defined are not traditional categories, these too can be used for lists that may be specific to a particular field.

```
Options:    Figure

     1 - Border Style
              Left                              Single
              Right                             Single
              Top                               Single
              Bottom                            Single
     2 - Outside Border Space
              Left                              0.16"
              Right                             0.16"
              Top                               0.16"
              Bottom                            0.16"
     3 - Inside Border Space
              Left                              0"
              Right                             0"
              Top                               0"
              Bottom                            0"
     4 - First Level Numbering Method           Numbers
     5 - Second Level Numbering Method          Off
     6 - Caption Number Style                   [BOLD]One One Thousand, 1[bold]
     7 - Position of Caption                    Below box, Outside borders
     8 - Minimum Offset from Paragraph          0"
     9 - Gray Shading (% of black)              0%

Selection: 0
```

Graphics box options, in this case, Figure Options, (ALT-F9 F O) let you set the type of border to print around a box, as well as spacing inside and out, caption positioning and numbering style, and the percentage of gray for the background.

Remember that captions will automatically be included if you are creating lists. Figures are included in list 6, Tables in list 7, Text boxes in list 8, and User-Defined in list 9. So there you have it: an explanation for this apparent redundancy.

◆ These are the defaults

Each of the four box types have their own defaults for borders, numbering method, position of the caption, and gray shading (whether the box is filled with a gray pattern, and if so, how much).

- **Figure:** Arabic numerals, single line around the box, .16" border of white space outside the box. "Figure 1" as the caption number, with the caption below the box and outside the borders.
- **Table:** Roman numbers, a thick line at the top and bottom, none at the sides. .16" border of white space both inside and outside the box. "Table I" as the caption number style, with the caption above the box and outside the borders.
- **Text:** Arabic numerals, a thick line at the top and bottom, none at the sides. .16" border of white space both inside and outside the box. "1" as the caption number style, with the caption below and outside the borders, and a 10% gray shading.

- **User-Defined:** Arabic numerals, no border lines, .16" border of white space outside the box, "1" as the caption number style with the caption below the box and outside the borders.

These defaults can be changed at any time using the Options menu described later in this chapter. (Trivia: what star says this line, in what movie, and to whom? "Don't. Stop. Don't stop. Why are you stopping?" A hint: think white crepe and subway vents.)

◆ Class, suborder, genus, species

The folks at WordPerfect are great with programs, but not so great with words. Once they latch onto a word they like to employ it for as many functions as possible. That's economical, but confusing. *Styles* are both style sheets and the individual styles within them. There are seven *types* of graphics boxes, but four of them are one type, and three of them are another type.

Let's call the first *type* "type1" and the second "type2." While "type1" only makes a difference in what lists are generated, all three "type2" graphics boxes are worlds apart.

Any graphics box you create must be one of the type2 boxes: a "Page" box which is attached to a particular position on a page, and will not move with text; a "Paragraph" box which is attached to a particular paragraph, and moves with the text; and a "Character" box which replaces a single character in a paragraph, and moves with the very words of that paragraph. Each type of box has its own strengths and weaknesses; each has its own use.

◆ Page

Always prints in the exact position you select on a page. You can place Page boxes by margins, or by column. They are the only "type2" of graphic that can span several columns, and have the text from all columns wrap around correctly.

Uses: Full page graphics; boxes around an entire page; logos/banners/flags; letterheads; "inside this issue" box; pull-quotes to be placed on a particular part of the page or to span several columns. Any text that requires precise placement on a page, or that needs to span several columns.

◆ Paragraph

Always stays with the paragraph it is attached to. Will automatically re-size box and graphics inside when margins change. Can be placed to the left or right of a paragraph, or be set to fit within both margins. Graphic will resize itself automatically if you change margins or columns.

Uses: Illustrations that must be accompanied by their associated text, such as diagrams, charts and graphs; tables with complex formatting that you don't want to change; pull-quotes or readouts that float with text, or resize with changing margins or columns.

◆ Character

Replaces a single character, and moves with the letters of a paragraph. The only type of graphics box that will print in footnotes or endnotes. Text doesn't wrap around character boxes as in page and paragraph boxes; when the line containing the character box wraps around, the next line begins below the box. If you copy or move any other type of graphic into a footnote or endnote, it automatically becomes a character box.

Uses: Small graphics, bullets, ballot boxes, drop caps (see the Chapter 8, *Paragraphs*), company logos, special graphics such as "key caps," must move not only with paragraph but by letter by letter in paragraph. Also effective for headers, footers.

➻ Tip: Scan a fancy headline alphabet (public domain, please), letter by letter, and utilize character boxes for each letter of the headline.

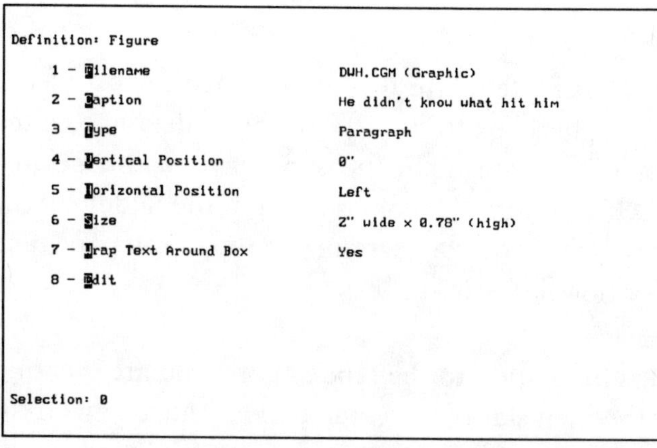

Figure Definition lets you choose the size and placement of the graphic box on the page, as well as its contents.

(ANSWER: The star who said "Don't stop..." was Marilyn Monroe, the movie was "Seven Year Itch," and the lucky guy was Tom Ewell. This is the movie with the classic scene where Marilyn's skirt is blown up in the air by the subway vent...who could ever forget?)

◆ Creating a graphics box

Let's stop talking about it and start doing it. Creating a graphics box is about as tough as opening up a box of cereal. Before you get the hang of it you rip the box top off, but a few boxes later you're keeping that little tab intact and closing the box top again like a pro. WordPerfect's graphics are similar, but 100% salt- and sugar-free (although possibly "high in roughage").

ALT-F9 is the graphics key. You will press this to access any graphics command, to create graphics, or to edit them. In this modest little example, we're going to create a paragraph type2 figure box, fill it with a graphic supplied on the Fonts/Graphics disk, edit the graphic, and change the type of graphics box (page, paragraph, character) as well as defaults (figure, table, text, user). We'll also experiment with the options feature.

Type **ALT-F9 F C** to create a figure box. You are now cheek to jowls with the graphics menu. This menu remains the same no matter what type1 of graphics box you choose.

Type allows you to choose between paragraph, page, and character type boxes. This is the option I set first. You would base this decision upon how you plan to use the box. Let's start out by creating a paragraph type2 box to move along with the paragraph. Since this is the default for all graphics boxes, we don't have to change it.

Vertical Position tells WordPerfect the distance from the top of the paragraph that you want this graphics box to start. With the 0" default, the top of the box will start at the top of the paragraph. You don't have to change anything if this is what you want. If you want the box to begin in the middle of the paragraph, type **V** and enter the correct distance from the top of the paragraph you want the box to begin. For now, leave it at 0".

Horizontal position differs in relation to the type2 of box you are creating. The default is "right" so that the right side of the graphics box is aligned with the right margin. Let's make this box align with the left margin. Press **H L**. The other choices are **C** (for centered), and **B** (so that the graphics box stretches from one margin to the other), The "B" setting can also resize itself automatically when the margins change. However,you cannot change the width of the box because it is dependant on the margins.

Editing may change the size of a graphics box automatically as the text inside it gets longer or shorter. However, WordPerfect has a tendency to ignore this, and will not change the size unless you force it to. You can have WordPerfect resize the box automatically (that sounds like a contradiction but it's not), by pressing **H B** again, WordPerfect will now resize the box to fit the new text.

Size allows you to change the ________ of a graphics box. Fill in the blank for yourself. If you guessed "Size," buy yourself a special treat. If you guessed "Potato," there'll be no dessert for you tonight.

You can set either the width, the height, or both the width and height. If you set only the width, WordPerfect calculates the correct size for the height so that the graphic is sized proportionally. If you choose the height only, WordPerfect calculates the correct size for the width. If you choose to size both, you can stretch the graphic and distort it. For this example, press **S W 2" [ENTER]**. Notice how the width changed to 2".

When you set just the width, WordPerfect will only automatically change the height if you retrieve a graphic that is not a perfect square. If you select the height only, WordPerfect will only change the width when you retrieve a graphic. If you select both, WordPerfect will not change either of them, and will place the graphic inside the space you've chosen. The graphic may have large uneven margins, but will always be sized proportionally, unless you specifically distort it using the scale command.

Wrap Text Around Box lets you specify whether WordPerfect should wrap text around the box, or print text underneath the box as if it weren't there. You would rarely choose **N** (so that WordPerfect would print the graphic right over the text). You could use this to create a box around the entire page (specifics on this a little later), to print a gray screen, or to print a very light graphic in the background. If you choose to use this with dark graphics, you will not be able to read the text underneath the gray screen.

Edit allows you to edit the contents of the box, be it graphics or text. Since we have nothing in the box right now, let's hold off on this option for just a sec.

Filename lets you enter the name of the graphic, or the WordPerfect file you want inside the box. If you are going to use a WordPerfect file, remember that graphics boxes cannot be longer than a single page. If you try to make them longer, WordPerfect will warn you, and won't let you leave the edit mode until you've shortened the file.

Put the WordPerfect disk labeled "Fonts/Graphics" in drive A:. (If you've already copied it to the hard disk, you will need to replace "A:" with the complete path name of the file's location on the hard disk).

Type **F A:pencil.wpg [ENTER]**. The file will take a couple of seconds to load, but then you will notice that while the width of the box is still 2" (as we set it), the height of the box is now 2.71".

Let's create a caption for our masterpiece. Press **C**. The screen says "Figure 1," and if that was sufficient, you could press **F7** right now. But we don't believe in compromise, so press [BACKSPACE] and type: **Pencil Pushing for Fun & Profit.** The text may wrap around as it does with normal editing. Press **F7** to leave the caption editor. Unless you specifically change it with CONTROL-F8 F, WordPerfect will use the default font (as set with SHIFT-F8 D F).

If you plan to use captions, I suggest you create a caption style, an open style that includes the font you want, and perhaps even an AdvDn code (SHIFT-F8 O A D) to add a little white space between the line around the graphic and the caption. Remember, a style will not only increase consistency between pages, but will enable you to change caption styles without having to edit each and every one by hand.

The excitement mounts. You're about to edit a graphic. If you have a weak heart, experience motion sickness, or have back problems, throw caution to the wind and follow along anyway.

❖ *Edit fever*

Press **E** to edit the graphic.

If the monitor and video card you are using has graphics capabilities, you will see the pencil on-screen in all its line-art glory. If you use a non-graphics screen,

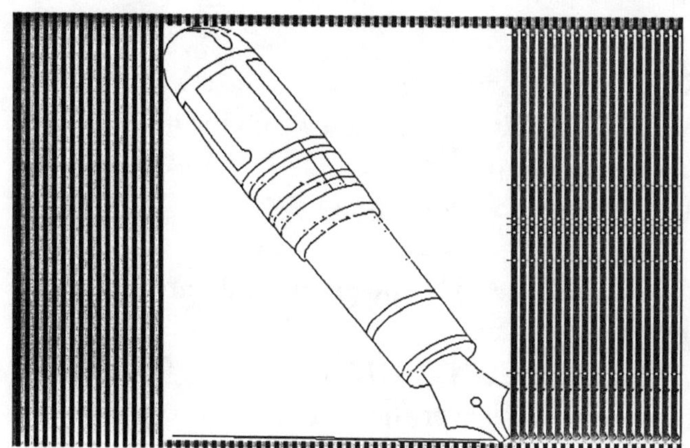

Graphics Edit (ALT-F9 F E E) gives you the power to alter the size and rotation of graphics, as well as mirror or invert them. The graphic has not been edited... yet.

such as those on basic IBM PC's, you should seriously consider buying either a Hercules graphics card, or an EGA card and a new monitor. (Or, you could always just use your imagination and send that money directly to me.) Although, while WordPerfect is incredibly clever in using periods to represent lines, it's only approximate, and doesn't work at all for bitmapped graphics.

Now you have a plethora of ways at your disposal to control the unsuspecting pencil on the screen.

Listed along the top of the screen are shortcuts for manipulating the graphic. Along the bottom of the screen are menus for more precise movement. Right now you'll see a single thin line around the graphic. This is the default for figures. If you changed to a thick, dashed, or other type of line with Options (explained sooner than you think), see these lines would appear on-screen, as you selected them.

You will see **(10%)** in the lower right hand corner of the screen. This is an important number, because it indicates the amount of movement, rotation, or sizing that WordPerfect will employ when you use the short-cut keys. You can change this number by pressing the **[INS]** key. Pressing it once will give you 5%, another press gives you 1%, and another gives you 25%. They are the only automatic increments you can choose from, although you can move in larger increments by using the menus along the bottom. Press the **[INS]** key until 10% is once again displayed at the bottom of the screen.

Now we're going to try out some of the quick keys. (I bet you didn't know a person could have this much fun in front of a computer, did you? You're not having fun yet? Just wait.)

◆ Quick move

Press the **[LEFT ARROW]** key a few times and notice how the picture moves to the left. Press the **[RIGHT ARROW]** key and watch the picture move to the right. **[UP ARROW]** moves the picture up, and **[DOWN ARROW]** moves the picture down. Am I moving too fast for you?

The distance by which the picture moves with each keystroke depends on the percentage displayed in the corner. At 25%, the picture will move 25 times more in a single keystroke then it will at 1%.

Since the picture has moved, press **CONTROL-HOME** (the GOTO key) to reset it to its original position. This can be very helpful should you accidentally mess up the picture.

◆ Quick size

Not let's play with another short-cut: sizing. When you press the **[PgUp]** key, the picture will enlarge by the percent specified in the corner. Pressing **[PgDn]** reduces the size of the picture by the same increment. If the picture is too large, it won't all fit into the box. This is useful if you only want to use a portion of the picture.

If you've set the options so that the box has an internal margin, the edges of the picture may disappear (even though they are still inside the box). When you're through experimenting, press **CONTROL-HOME** to restore the picture to its original form.

◆ Quick rotate

This picture can be rotated to any angle because it uses a format called "line art." This format includes Lotus .PIC files, and AutoCAD.DXF files. Bitmapped graphics, such as PC Paintbrush, TIF, and Halo, cannot be rotated, no matter how hard you try. You can find more information on file formats later in this chapter. Bor-ing!!

Press the + key on the keypad (not the one over the =), and the graphic will rotate counter-clockwise by the percent indicated in the corner. 25%=90 degrees, 10%=45 degrees, 5%=27.5 degrees. (If that's too complicated, just stand on your head.) Pressing the - key on the keypad will cause the graphic to rotate clockwise. When you start to feel nauseous from all this rotation, take a Dramamine or press **CONTROL-HOME** to restore the picture to normal.

◆ Quick invert

This feature only functions with bitmapped graphics, and won't have any effect on the pencil graphic, or any other line-art. If you were using a bitmapped graphic, pressing **SHIFT-F3** would turn everything white to black, and everything black to white, presenting you with a negative of the original image.

If you require precision over your editing, you can use the menus along the bottom of the screen. This allows for more accurate control than short-cut keys because these movements can be increments as small as 1w.

◆ Precise move

Press **M**. The first number you enter will move the graphic horizontally. If you enter a positive number, the graphic will move to the right; if you enter a negative number, the graphic will move to the left. Once you've entered the first number, press **[ENTER]** and the second number. This number controls vertical movement. A positive number moves the graphic up, a negative number moves the graphic down. Once you've entered the second number, press **[ENTER]**.

◆ Precise scale

Press S. WordPerfect will respond with "Scale X: 100." What the program wants to know is how *wide* you want the image to be. 100 is the normal size of the graphic. If you enter a larger number, WordPerfect will widen the picture; if you enter a smaller number, WordPerfect will narrow the picture. Once you've

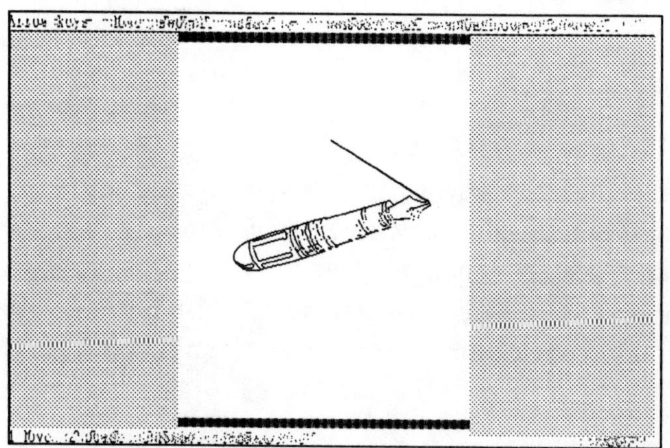

Here's the edited pencil. It has been rotated and sized. Line art can be sized, rotated and mirrored, bitmapped graphics can be sized and inverted.

entered a number, press **[ENTER]**. Now WordPerfect replies with "Scale Y: 100": how *tall* should the image be. A larger number makes it taller, a smaller number makes it shorter.

By entering different numbers for the width (X) and height (Y), you can distort the image. If you don't want the image to be distorted, enter the same number for both X and Y.

◆ Precise rotate

Press **R**. You can enter the rotation in 1 degree increments, but you must enter a positive number. The graphic will only rotate counter-clockwise with this method. Once you've entered the number, press **[ENTER]**.

◆ Mirror or flop

WordPerfect now asks if you want to mirror the image. If you press **Y**, WordPerfect will flop (flip horizontally) the graphic. If you press **N**, WordPerfect will leave it as it is. This feature is especially useful when you have a graphic that faces off the page. Professional graphic design generally calls for graphics that face //inwards; the reader's eye is led into the page, rather than off of it. Rotation and mirror image only work for line-art.

◆ Invert

This is no more precise than pressing **SHIFT-F3**, but it's easier to remember because it's listed on the menu. Again, this feature works on bitmapped graphics, but not with the pencil graphic, or any other line-art. If you were using a bitmapped graphic, pressing **4** would turn everything white to black, and everything black to white.

❖ *Save or abandon?*

To leave editing you press the EXIT key: **F7**. If you want to restore the picture to its original state, press **CONTROL-HOME F7**. If you want to cancel the changes you just made but keep previous changes, press **F1**.

To behold your masterwork, live and in-person, press **SHIFT-F7 V**. You should see the pencil, surrounded by a thin line; the text (if any) should flow around the graphic.

Unaltered Clip Art (MGI)

Mirrored (Flopped) (MGI)

75%, Rotated 15 degrees

Sized 200% X - 100% Y

200%, moved X 1.25 2.25 Y

999%, close up on "S"

Bitmapped .IMG file

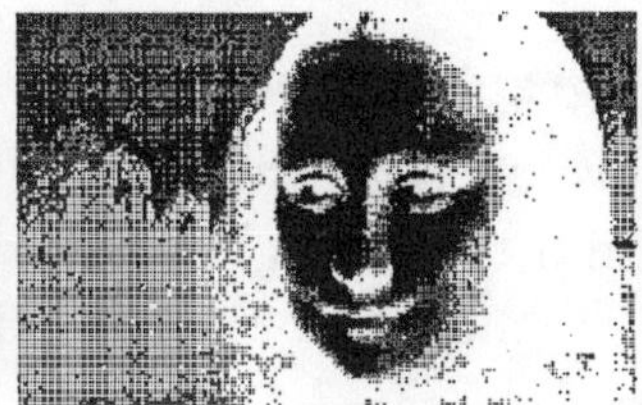

Bitmapped .IMG, Inverted

Bitmapped, 200% cropped

Bitmapped, 400% cropped
Moved -2.87 H 1.54 V

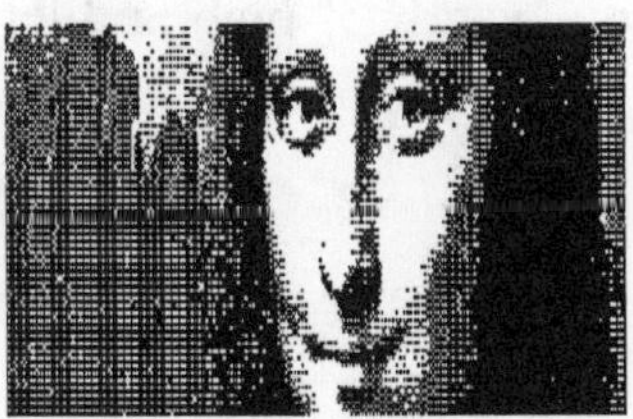

Sized non-proportionally
100% X 200% Y

100%, Inside Margin of .2"
(Dotted line shows box size)

Now you're back at the figure menu. Press **F7** to save the graphic as a code in the file.

Normally, if you were pleased with the changes you'd made or the graphic you'd created, you would press **F7** to exit. If you were unhappy with the outcome, you would press **F1**. (But since you never saved the graphics box with F7, *you will lose it if you press F1 now.*)

If you're ever dissatisfied with changes to a graphic, pressing **F1** will cancel the changes and restore the graphic to its previous state.

❖ *More changes*

You can change any part of a graphics box at any time, its type1, its type2, its location, its size, its caption, even its contents.

Let's say you're in a fickle state of mind and now want the box to print in the lower left hand corner of the page. We're going to change the box type2 to Page; it will now print in the lower left-hand corner of the page, no matter where the paragraph is.

(If the brass upstairs change their tiny feeble mind, tell them it's impossible and titter behind their back. Then barge back in a few minutes later, say you just made word processing history and figured out a way. Of course, they'll respond by giving you a large raise, a company car, and a long vacation. C'mon, you'll never know unless you try.)

◆ Changing type - paragraph/page/character

Press **T A** to change this to a page type2 box. With WordPerfect's default, is to make this box will print in the upper-right hand corner. To move it to the bottom of the page, press **V B**. To move it to the left-hand corner, press **H M L**.

◆ Changing size

Now let's make the box exactly 3" high and let WordPerfect calculate how wide it should be. Press **S W 3" [ENTER]**, and notice that the graphic is now 4.07" wide.

◆ Changing graphics files

If you want to place a new graphic in this box, type F and the name of the new graphic. WordPerfect will ask "Replace Contents with (your filename here) Y/N?" If you press **Y**, WordPerfect will remove the current file and replace it with the new file you've selected.

◆ Remove a graphic

If you want to remove the graphic file from the graphics box, press **F** and then the **[DEL]** key until the name has been erased. Press **[ENTER]**. WordPerfect will ask, "Clear Contents?" If you press **Y**, WordPerfect will remove the graphic (but keep the graphics box). If you press **N**, WordPerfect will leave the current graphic in place.

◆ Change partners and dance

You get the picture. You can re-edit the picture, change the caption, whatever your little heart or your employer's little mind desires.

◆ Changing type: Figure/table/text/user

If you want to transform a figure into a table (and you're not Doug Henning), or any type1 of graphic into any other type1, press **ALT-F9** now. A list of the types will appear at the bottom of the screen. Press **U** and you will have changed the graphic into a User-defined box. Press **ALT-F9 F** to turn the box back into a Figure.

◆ Let's all play "What was that filename?"

I don't know about you, but I've got a memory like a sieve. I can't remember names, dates, places, or sometimes even which vegetables I like.

Remembering file names is way down on the list of things that I remember. Thankfully, WordPerfect added a feature (at the last minute, in the 7/11/88 release), that allows you to use List Files to select files for graphics boxes.

Let's try it. Press

ALT-F9 F C

Now we're going to select a file. Press

F F5 [ENTER]

Voila! Our friend "List Files" appears, to jog our sometimes pre-senile memories. You can do everything you can do in normal List Files, including copying, renaming and deleting files.

◆ Sharing and caring without swearing

If you've got a graphic in one file and want to get it into another file, what do you do?

When you're in Edit mode, inside any graphics box, you can save a graphic as a .WPG graphic. Press **F10** and give the file a name. The editing changes are not included in the new file.

◆ Tip: Text editing

If you place text in graphics boxes, it can sometimes be tedious to remember which box contains which text. It can also take a slew of keystrokes just to get inside a box and work on the text.

To quickly edit text in a graphics box, use Extended Search: **HOME-F2.** This will find the text in the box and immediately put you in edit mode. Once you've finished editing, press **F7 F7** to get out. When using Extended Search, you can use the up and down arrow keys to search forwards or backwards, or go to the top of the file first (by pressing HOME HOME HOME [UP ARROW]), and then press **HOME-F2**. I find this much easier than using **ALT-F9 F E 1 [ENTER] E.**

For another tip, see *Text in a box* on page 299.

◆ Back to where you once belonged...

There's no place like CONTROL-HOME, there's no place like CONTROL-HOME, there's no place like CONTROL-HOME...

When you edit a graphic, WordPerfect moves to where the graphics box code is. It could be hundreds of pages away from your current position, and WordPerfect would automatically find it.

While this is helpful, once you've edited the box and press **F7** to leave, you are returned not to where you were when you decided to edit the box, but to the position of the graphics box code.

This is not unlike Dorothy's house being dropped into the Land of Oz. But you don't have to find a professor with a balloon to instantly get back home.

Simply press **CONTROL-HOME CONTROL-HOME** and WordPerfect will zip back to where you were before you edited the graphics box. Put that in your $165,000 Ruby slippers and smoke it.

❖ *Optional equipment*

There's only one more major function you need to be familiar with in graphics: how to control their options.

(LONG SENTENCE ALERT - this next sentence/paragraph is very, very long. Not as long as E.L. Doctrow's but getting there. Any readers who get woozy or confused reading really long sentences should avoid it.)

Graphic Options include the type of border around them, how much blank space is kept between the graphic and the text, how much blank space is kept between the contents of the box (graphics or text) and the line around the box, the numbering method, the position of the caption, and the background shade of the box. (Try to say that in one breath.)

As long as we still have that figure with the pencil graphic, why don't you join me in seeing how the options can affect the graphics box. (Afterwards you can take me out to dinner. Just remember, I'm a peanut butter and chocolate man, and I can't stand caviar.) Where were we?

In this example, we're going to change whatever we can, can, just for the sake of change. Press

ALT-F8 F O

to select options. You can set options separately for each of the four box types; these options will remain in effect until you create a new option code.

◆ Borders

WordPerfect provides you with seven different types of borders: None, Single, Double, dAshed, dOtted, Thick and Extra thick. All that's missing is Original Recipe and eXtra Crispy.

You can set the border independently for each of the four sides of a graphics box. For most graphics, you'll probably want either none or a single line on all four sides. But for special uses such as readouts and pull-quotes, you might consider an extra thick line on the top, a dotted line on the bottom, and none on the left and right sides. For coupons, you'd use dashed lines on all four sides.

Let's lose control and demonstrate our utter lack of good taste by choosing a different type of line for each side. Some call this look "new-wave," others call it "funky," those who still think that it's 1968 call it "cool," and eight to ten-year-olds call it "rad." I don't care what you call it as long as you call me for dinner. Actually, I recommend that you never use more than two different types of lines around a single box (but total disregard for decorum never hurt anyone too severely). Press

BAODE

to put a dashed line on the left, a dotted line on the right, a double line on top, and an extra-thick line on the bottom. (While I don't think this has a very "hip" appearance, the code sounds like something straight out of Michael Jackson: "Oh yes, I'm BAoDe, I'm BAoDe... Isn't it amazing that anyone would come out and admit they weren't good?) You'll get to examine the results in a minute.

◆ White space

Okay, campers, time to change another default. Let's create a larger margin of white space between the box and the text. WordPerfect, in yet another display of semantic economics, has employed the same word for two more functions. Imagine all those words they're saving. (I only wish I knew what they were saving them for.)

WordPerfect is insisting on calling both the lines and the white space around the box "borders." I'm tired of numbering words, so let's be rebellious and go with something different. The lines around are borders, the white space around is "space" (the final frontier). To increase the space around the box to a quarter of an inch, type

O .25" [ENTER].25" [ENTER].25" [ENTER].25" [ENTER]

Since we have a graphic, and not text, inside the box, let's leave the inside space the way it is, at 0" all the way around.

◆ Numbering

Now let's play cops and robbers (or Perry Mason) and change the numbering method from numbers to letters, as in "Exhibit-A." Press

F L

We could also have selected any of four options: **O**ff, **N**umbers, **L**etters, or **R**oman numerals (for when you're in Rome). If you press **S**, you can set the second numbering method in the same way. Since I hardly believe in numbering of any kind, I'll leave this up to you.

If you press

C

you can change the caption numbering style. Using the Perry Mason analogy, this is where WordPerfect (or Raymond Burr) would label the graphic "Exhibit A" rather than Figure A. You can call this word whatever you want (including "Balustrade," if you are into stair accessories).

◆ Caption positioning

As we near the end of this odyssey, it's time to put all seriousness aside as we reach another important option. Press

P

to position the caption. You can place it either above or below the graphics box, and either inside or outside the borders. We're talking real borders here, not space: if you put the caption inside and you have a printing border, it will appear inside that printed border. Let's place the caption above the box, and inside the border. Press

A I

◆ Minimum offset

If you've entered a Vertical offset so that a paragraph box prints a certain distance from the top of the paragraph, WordPerfect tries to keep this measurement, unless the paragraph is near the bottom of the page. In this case, WordPerfect will make this offset smaller in order to keep the graphic on the same page as the paragraph. This option allows you to specify how small that offset should be. The default is 0" and so WordPerfect will move the graphic to the top of a paragraph before moving it to the next page.

If you've set 1" as the vertical offset, and don't want the graphic is closer than 1" from the top, enter 1" here. If you don't care, leave it at 0". If you want to ensure that your offset measurement is never reduced, enter some ridiculously high number here. Remember, this number is not the offset, but the smallest number WordPerfect can reduce the set offset to. It won't make the offset any bigger, but it won't allow it to get smaller.

◆ Amazing grays

This is one of the more entertaining options, as it permits you to create a gray background for the box. These backgrounds (below) can cause a graphic (or readout, pull-quote, or table) to stand out from the rest of the page. You can choose any percentage of gray from 0% (white) to 100% (Black). In this case, let's choose 10%. Type

G 10 [ENTER]

◆ LaserJet

A 10% background will be dark enough to be visible, without making text hard to read. You shouldn't use a background darker than 20%, or text will be difficult to read. While 6% is the lightest you can use, it appears identical to 10% when printed.

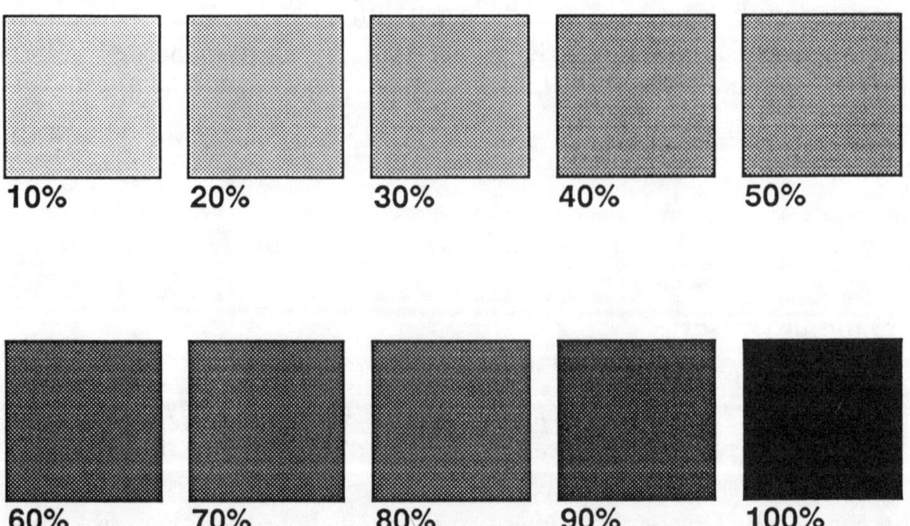

❖ PostScript News
incorporating the Rotated Text Times

PostScript grays are both darker and coarser than the same percentage is on a LaserJet. Even 10% can be too dark. 6% is the lightest gray you can use, but it looks so similar to 10% that I couldn't notice any appreciable difference. Remember that even though laser printer dots seem tiny at 300 per inch, they can be quite obtrusive behind text, especially when printed on PostScript laser printers.

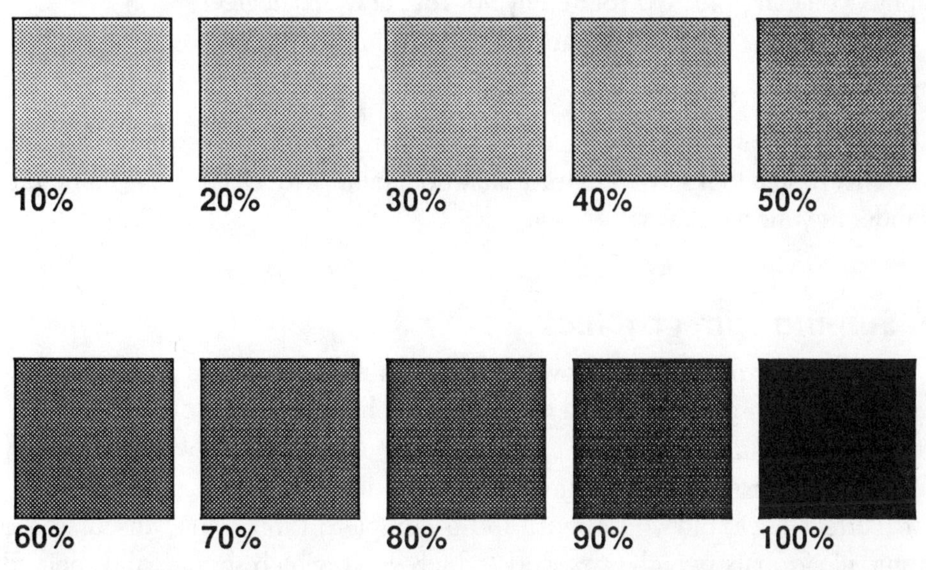

Two more notes for PostScript users: If you choose 100% for the background, set the surrounding borders to None: otherwise, there will be a tiny white line between the border and the background of the box.(This might be an interesting effect when printed on a high-resolution Linotronic typesetter, but on a laser printer it just seems like a mistake).

For reverse type on PostScript printers (white text on a black background): Set the background to 100%. Enter the text inside the box by pressing **E**. Before typing any text, press **ALT-F8 C W [ENTER]** to make the text white. The white text will not appear in View Document, but it will print correctly. LaserJet's can't print white text on a black background. Sorry Charlie—that's another reason why PostScript printers cost three times what a LaserJet does.

Reverse type: white on black

If you are going to print the final output on a Linotronic PostScript typesetter, the gray patterns are much finer, resulting in easier-to-read text. But remember, the quality of the offset printing or photo copying must be high-grade, or the gray backgrounds will look inferior.

For text printed at an angle on PostScript printers: Here's yet another fun (or as chichi New Yorkers say, "important") extra you can tap with a PostScript printer. While LaserJets alone can't print both portrait and landscape text on a single page, PostScript printers can. Using a graphics box with text instead of a graphic, you can print text rotated by 90, 180, and 270 degrees.

Now that we've all but exhausted the possibilities, press

F7

to exit the options menu. Hold onto your hat, it's time to see what this assault on quality design looks like. Go into View document with **SHIFT-F7 V** and take a gander at your handiwork.

❖ *Summa cum graphics*

Believe it or not, you are now familiar with all the graphics commands (excluding lines that are covered ad nauseam in a chapter of their own).

From here on in it's gravy. The rest of the chapter is chock full of corking good fun: how to get around limitations, particulars neither your mother or WordPerfect ever told you about, and a complete (and frank) discussion of graphic file formats (which ones work, which don't, which should, and their advantages and disadvantages).

Full coverage of graphics programs and clip art collections can be found in Chapter 17, *Utility Software,* right next to the lingerie department. While all those lonely male execs scramble to find that chapter, why don't you and I cover a little more graphic ground?

◆ Drop shadows (dark shadows)

I may complain about the Mac, but I'm still a fair kind of guy. There is one graphic design trick popularized by the Mac that I admire. It's called a "drop shadow." This creates a dark shadow (graphic element, not the soap opera) on one side of a picture, providing it with a three dimensional effect (almost as if it's raised above the page and has a shadow). You can achieve a simulated drop shadow with WordPerfect by using the graphic options that we were just playing with.

Make sure the cursor is located ahead of the figure you want to place the drop shadow on.

Go into Graphic options by pressing

ALT-9 F O

Because we read from left to right (at least those of us who are not dyslexic), drop shadows are usually on the right, as if the light were coming from the left. To create a thick drop shadow, we'll going to have single lines on the left and the top and thick lines on the right and the bottom. (See the illustration below for a preview of how it will look when printed.) To make the lines, press

B S T S T [ENTER]

If you want to see how this will appear, go into View Document by pressing

(SHIFT F7 V)

If you want an extra thick drop shadow, type

ALT-F9 F O B S E S E [ENTER]

AquA
RodeO
Libation
for the
Imagination
Freze Dried H_2O
At last, relief for the
sun-drenched masses.
Water, whenever you want it.

◆ Box around the page and format fixing

Don't worry, this is no relation to ring around the collar. At times, a box printed around a page may be warranted (on title pages, report covers, slide presentations, and signs, to name just a few examples).

To accomplish this formidable task without any formid, simply ignore the advice found in the WordPerfect manual. The manual claims that full-page graphics boxes should be used "on a page by itself." Baloney. Salami. Chicken Franks.

Take a look at the Abe Lincoln example in Chapter 4, *Show & Tell,* and you'll see one example of how to use full-page graphics with text. The report cover with the butterfly is another. All you have to do is set wrap to NO.

But let's stand up to authority together so you can blame me if anything goes wrong.

The first step is to jimmy around with the margins; otherwise the text will run into the box around the page. When you create a full-page box, it sizes itself by how the margins are set, we need to make the margins bigger so the box itself will be bigger.

If you already have Left/Right and Top/Bottom margin codes in the file, move the cursor above them (or to the left).

If you don't, you're going to try a technique I use all the time that I call "*Format Fixing.*" This has nothing to do with what happens at racetracks, and is completely legal. What I often do prior to any major changes (like margins) is to enter the current settings as codes. If I'm going to change tabs, I save the tab-line to a code without changing anything, thereby fixing the current settings. (To fix a tab, type SHIFT-F8 L T F7 F7)

To fix any other code, just go to the menu (such as line), select the function, and press return,to accept the current value. Some functions will insert a code, but others, such as justify and hyphenation, will insert a code only if you're changing settings. This means you have to change settings, and then restore them to the way they were, thereby inserting two codes.

In this case we're going to fix the margins, so type

SHIFT-F8 L M [ENTER][ENTER][ENTER] P M [ENTER][ENTER] F7

Now our text won't change, even though we're about to set new margins for the box around the page.

These new margins should be at least .25" wider than their previous setting. We're going to make them .5" wider for this example, leaving plenty of breathing room between the box and the text.

If the margins were Left/Right 1" 1" and Top/Bottom .75" .75", make them Left/Right .75" .75" and Top/Bottom .5" .5".

Remember that most laser printers require at least a .25" margin around the page. Any text or graphics positioned closer to the edge will not be printed. For this example, I'll assume you're using the WordPerfect defaults of 1" all around, and so we'll enter the following

SHIFT-F8 L M .5" [ENTER] .5" [ENTER][ENTER] P M .5" [ENTER] .5" [ENTER] F7

Move the cursor to the left of these new margins by pressing

[LEFT ARROW][LEFT ARROW]

Now it's time for our willful act of defiance! We're going to create a full page graphics box, and turn wrap off. Type

ALT-F9 F C T A V F W N [ENTER]

Are you ready to experience a thrill that your grandparents would never have dreamed of? Check out how it looks in View Document. Press

SHIFT-F7 V

Pretty niftoid, wouldn't you say? As in any other graphics box, you could use Figure Options to make the line around it single (the default, so we didn't need to change it), double, dashed, dotted, thick, or extra thick.

AN AUTOMATIC BOX AROUND EVERY PAGE (and a chicken in every pot): To print a box on each page, put this graphics box in a header, and set the header to print on every page. You may have to fool around with the margins in order for this to function properly. I had the best luck with at least 1" of margin all around the graphics box, and then a 1.25" margin around the page for the text.

Or, just create a paired style that contains large margins and a full page figure with wrap turned off. (Use a paired style so that the margins will automatically return to normal after the Style Off code.) Place this in any position on any page that you want surrounded with a box.

◆ Readout all about it

A readout (also known as a pull-quote) is one of those wonderful multi-purpose design elements that readers love. They reiterate the highlights or essential points of an article, allow you to editorialize in such a way that people don't even notice you're editorializing (taking words out of context), and add to the readability and style of a page. (The term readout is derived from newspaper jargon, while pull-quote comes from magazine jargon. They both have the same meaning.)

With WordPerfect, they aren't even difficult, illegal or fattening. What more could you want, except for fame, fortune, happiness, and perhaps a vacation or two at Robin Leech's (Mr. Lifestyles of the Rich & Famous) expense.

Achieving these minor miracles requires nothing more demanding than creating a graphics box and packing it with text. Who said this desktop publishing stuff was hard?

Because it's such a snap, I've come up with oodles of variations and tips for using graphics boxes as readouts/pull-quotes.

◆ Tip: What font glory?

Don't forget about WordPerfect's default font (SHIFT-F8 D F) because this will also be the default for the readout.

But readouts are almost never the same size, and rarely use the same typestyle as the body text. Readouts are most effective when they contrast the type.

It is acceptable to use the same typeface, but with a different weight. Here's an example: If you use Times Roman/Dutch for the body text, but also want Times Roman/Dutch for readouts, use the italic, or bold italic versions of the font.

It's also proper form to utilize the same font you've used for the headlines, only in a smaller size. With 10 point body text, readouts are generally set with 14-18 point type.

Here are some good fonts to use as readouts with Times/Dutch body text: Times/Dutch italic or bold italic, Helvetica, Helvetica condensed, Avant Garde, Optima, Futura light/oblique/Extra bold, Korinna, Serifa/Glypha.

Here are some bad choices for fonts when you are creating readouts with Times/Dutch body text: Palatino/Calligraphic, Century Schoolbook, Galliard, Baskerville.

◆ Tip: What type glory?

Should you work with a paragraph type box, or a page type box? Or should you use a graphics box at all? Why not use the header or just lines? (For tips about using lines for readouts, see Chapter 13, Lines.)

Using a page type box offers you two advantages: 1) Precise positioning: it's easy to make sure a readout will be at the top or bottom of the page, regardless of where the code is or how the text moves. 2) The ability to create a readout that spans several columns, so that it floats between two columns with text wrapping around all sides. Remember, if you want a page box to print on the top of the current page, the code must also be on top of the page; otherwise, it will print on the next page.

Using a paragraph type box assures that the readout remains close to its associated text. It will automatically resize itself should you change any margins or columns.

If you use any type of graphics box, the options should be set with some sort of "Inside Border Space," generally at least .15". You need plenty of white space between the readout and the body text.

You can also use a header for readouts. If your page design incorporates a large top margin, the header can be used for a headline on the first page, with readouts on subsequent pages. Use a style for the basic header information (this will simplify matters on pages without headlines or readouts). For detailed information about utilizing the header for readouts, see Chapter 10, *Styles*, and a section called "Under the Big Top."

◆ Tip: Don't get out of line

Readouts can be completely enclosed in a box with lines all around it, or contain lines on the top and bottom only. I personally think that lack of lines on the sides appears more elegant, and prefer readouts with lines above and below only.

If you are working with a graphics box, set options for the type of line you want. It's usually advisable for the lines to be of two different weights (i.e., a thick line on top, with a single line on the bottom; an extra thick line on top, with a dotted line on the bottom).

There are two schools of (design) thought as to whether the heavier line should be on the top or the bottom. Either one is okay, so take your pick. See examples on following pages.

◆ Tip: Hey, big letter!

One of desktop publishing's most wonderful features is the freedom of "choice." You don't have to use any lines at all if you don't feel like it. I'm not going to force you, the only ones who might force you are those people you work for, and what do they know?

If lines aren't your scene, you can use lots of extra white space instead, or a raised cap (easy to do, see Chapter 7, *About faces*), or a little black box above and below, or a gray background (no darker than 10%).

The following eight different examples employ the fonts that are built-in to PostScript printers, but they are also available from Bitstream for use with Fontware. Notice how the different typefaces allow for a wide divergence of appearances. In all the examples, remember to set the line height to fixed when you use raised caps; otherwise, WordPerfect will leave extra space below the first line. The line height in these examples is fixed at .22"

❖ *Readout examples*

The first example uses a graphics box only for the drop cap. The top line is entered with **ALT-F9 L H W .1,** and the bottom line is **ALT-F9 L H W .01c G 10**.

Should you feel the urge to exercise, lie down until the feeing passes.
Robert Benchley

Although the examples on these pages have been reduced by 18%, I am going to use the actual point sizes in these explanations. The big S is 36-point Palatino, in a paragraph box .6" wide by .4". The options are set for no lines on all sides, with an outside border space of 0" all around. The rest of the readout is 14-point Palatino italic. Simple and elegant.

The second example (with the two square bullets) is comprised of three graphics boxes. The little squares are user-defined boxes .1" by .1", centered, with options set to **G 100**. The big S is 36-point Palatino italic; the rest is 14-point Palatino italic. Always keep plenty of white space around this type of readout.

■

Should you feel the urge to exercise, lie down until the feeling passes.

■

The third example (with a vertical line on the left side) is a single figure box, with options set for a border of a single line on the left side only, with an inside border of .2" all around. The big S is 30-point Times Roman bold, and the rest of the text is 14-point Times Roman italic. This type of readout works well between two columns, so use a page type box.

S*hould you feel the urge to exercise, lie down until the feeling passes.*

The fourth example (dotted line on top, thick line on bottom) is also a single graphics box, with options set to dotted line on top, thick line on bottom, .1" inside border. The big S is Avant Garde 30-point, and the rest of the text is Avant Garde 14-point. It's amazing how effective a change of fonts can be. The "S" in this font is so different (especially in contrast to the very traditional S of the second readout), that the entire readout has a much more modern appearance. If you make this a paragraph box, and set the horizontal to "both left and right," it will fit perfectly into a column. If you want this to straddle two columns, use a page type box, and have at least .15" of outside border in options.

Should you feel the urge to exercise, lie down until the feeling passes.

The fifth example is a single graphics box, with a dotted border all around, and a .1" inside border. The big S is 30-point Helvetica bold, and the text is 14-point Helvetica Condensed. I find this all very attractive, but I wouldn't use more than one of these on a two page spread, lest they appear too busy. (Don't you think Campbell's should start catering to us desktop publishers and come out with a Helvetica Condensed soup? Mmmmm good.)

S*hould you feel the urge to exercise, lie down until the feeling passes.*

Should you feel the urge to exercise, lie down until the feeling passes.

The sixth example has a single line on the top and left, and thick lines on the right and bottom. The font is Bookman 30-point bold for the S, and Bookman 14-point light for the text. (Didn't that sound frighteningly like the description of a Miss America Contestant? And while we're on the subject, where else do people wear high heels with bathing suits? And who's responsible for that silly combination?)

This example sports double lines above and below, single lines on the left and right. It somehow appears to be academic, if you ask me. The big S is 30-point Times Roman bold, the text is 14-point Times Roman medium.

Should you feel the urge to exercise, lie down until the feeling passes.

The last readout is the most extreme and calls the most attention to itself. It has a classic, yet modern look, a bit wacky, but still elegant. Basically, it's just fun. It's also difficult. It can be a pain if the text moves, because the little black boxes may separate from the main gray box. Careful preview in View Document is required prior to printing. It consists of five, count 'em, five, graphics boxes.

Should you feel the urge to exercise, lie down until the feeling passes.

Robert Benchley

The four black squares are each one user-defined box. I created the first two on top and simply copied them for the bottom two. They are .1" by .1", with options set to **G 100**. The readout itself is contained in a figure box, with .25" inside borders on the right and left, .1" inside borders on the top and bottom, no lines on any side, no outside margin, and gray shading set to 10%. To make the bottom two touch the bottom of the box, I had to use Advance Up .3" (SHIFT-F8 O A U .3"). This example is 14-point Palatino bold (it must be bold, otherwise it would be harder to read), with a big S in Extra Large size.

❖ *Table manners*

It shouldn't come as any great surprise that you can place tables inside graphics boxes (especially since one of the box types is called table). The question is *why* would you want to do this? The answer is fourfold.

- You can set columns, tabs, and engage in any type of complex formatting without worrying about it changing by accident, or by moving it.
- To put a box around tables.
- To put a gray screen behind tables.
- For lack of anything better to do.

But what if you want horizontal lines in the table—after all, wouldn't tables seem naked without them? You can't place graphics inside of graphics, so what's a mother to do? It all has to do with **SHIFT-F8 O U YY,** so that tabs are underlined continuously. Check out Chapter 8, *Paragraphs,* for some glamorous ways in which you can use the normally mundane underline.

❖ *Text in a box*

There are times when you really want a paragraph to stand out, such as when you have a warning such as the following.

> WARNING: Feeding Miracle Whip to children under the age of eight may permanently warp their taste buds so that they will never be able to differentiate between "sandwich spread" and genuine mayonnaise.

Anything of such vital importance should certainly be boxed with lines all the way around, lest your readers miss it. Remember, however, that when you box text, you must first create an option that contains an Inside border space of at least .15". Otherwise, the text inside the box will run into the line around the box and you will be humiliated, or, if you are Japanese, lose face. It would be a pity too, because it's a cinch to avoid. If you were creating a figure box, you would set the option by pressing

ALT-F9 F O I .15 [ENTER] .15 [ENTER] .15 [ENTER] .15 [ENTER][ENTER]

Then you would create the figure box itself by pressing

ALT F9 F C E

and type the text that you want to appear inside. If the text is already available in a file, press **SHIFT-F10** to retrieve the file into the graphics box. (Remember, it can't exceed one page, and WordPerfect won't let you leave the graphics box until you shorten it. It reminds me of one of those horrible French plays, like "No Exit," where the audience is made to feel that there is no escaping the boredom of the play and you get an idea of what hell must be like.)

This text will not appear in normal editing mode. You will only see it when you are in View Document mode, which leads to my next point.

◆ See what you're missing

Text in a box is not visible when you are writing and editing. I find this inconvenient because I can't refer to it. A worst-case scenario has me forgetting it's there and writing it all over from scratch. Since I'm loathe to repeat myself repeat myself, I came up with this solution. When you are finished editing the text inside the graphics box, mark the entire contents by pressing

HOME HOME [UP ARROW] ALT-F4 HOME HOME [DOWN ARROW]

You will now copy this block, so press

CONTROL-F4 B C

WordPerfect will respond by removing the highlighting and saying "Move Cursor; press **ENTER** to retrieve." We're going to move the cursor completely out of the box, so press

F7 F7 [ENTER]

This will create a copy of all text inside the graphics box. Now you can't just leave it there, or it will print *twice* (once here and another time inside the graphics box). So we're going to place this text in an unprinting comment that will display on-screen, but not print.

Block all the text copied from the box by pressing

ALT-F4

(If that didn't confuse you, this will: The vessel with the pestle has the pellet with the poison, the chalice from the palace has the brew that is true.)

To turn this text into a comment, press

CONTROL-F5 Y

To change the comment into regular text, place the cursor below the comment and type

CONTROL-F5 C T

◆ Box text

The one disadvantage of putting a table inside a graphics box is you then have to edit the graphics box in order to edit the text. Here's a procedure to keep the text out in the open, and still print a box around it.

Create a User-defined box, set it for horizontal both left & right, and wrap text around to NO. Set the height of the box for at least .1" larger than the height of the paragraph (or paragraphs) you intend to box. Use the LN marker on the bottom of the screen to calculate the height of the paragraph.

Use a Left/Right indent (SHIFT-F4) to indent the text so it won't touch the box around it. You could also use a paired style to achieve this. The text will superimpose itself on the box, fitting neatly inside. If the paragraph gets longer, you will need to edit the user-defined box and lengthen it too.

There is a disadvantage to this method: if the paragraph moves too close to the end of a page, it may print on one page while the box will print another.

12

Do you want me to draw you a picture?

Graphics file formats

WordPerfect lets you create text, but not graphics. Use a paint or draw program, or a scanner, to create graphics, or purchase already-drawn clip art. If you can't draw a stick figure that at least a four-year-old would be proud of, don't worry. Two agreeable solutions are scanners, which act like a copy machine (only they copy to a file in the computer rather than to another piece of paper), and clip art graphics that others have scanned, or created directly on computer. Both of these can provide professional pictures even for the non-artistic among us.

And so, you get into more than just WordPerfect when you get into graphics. But don't fret, you don't have to get in over your head. If all else fails, WordPerfect includes a program that "grabs" what's on the screen and allows you to enter it into a WordPerfect file.

This chapter will cover the many types of graphics files that WordPerfect can use, some it almost can use, and even some it can't. Chapter 16, *1-2-3 Publishing*, and Chapter 17, *Software*, explore graphics programs in detail, and also cover clip art packages.

❖ *Illustrating*

Before we talk tech, just a reminder that you don't have to use graphic pictures at all. For all of its power, you may never use graphics. If basic typesetting is all you desire, if you never want to do full page layouts, or add graphics of any type, you don't have to use them. No one's keeping score. There won't be a test at the end of the chapter. If you need them, use them; if you don't, don't worry about it (although I have a feeling WordPerfect might entice you into using them).

As with everything else in graphic design, use pictures for a reason, not just as mere ornamentation. It's not a good idea to use pictures if they don't *illustrate* something. Remember the old theatrical adage: don't introduce a gun in the first act if it's not going to go off in the third. In this case, don't use a picture of a cow unless it goes off in the third act—no, no, unless the text is addressing cows, dairy products, or Belgian leather sofas.

Using a picture just because you admire it has some built-in pitfalls. People will spend more time studying the picture and trying to figure out what it has to do with the text, than reading that text and getting the message. If there is no legitimate reason for the picture, people will use their overactive (or underactive) imaginations to come up with one, which is more than likely not what you had in mind.

◆ Illumination

First, you need to understand the differences between a "paint" program and a "draw" program.

Paint programs

A paint program provides you with the same sensation as free-hand drawing does. You paint on the screen as if you were sketching on a piece of paper. You use the mouse, or cursor, to draw lines, circles, and boxes, and then fill them in with various patterns.

Everything is part of a single "painting." If you want to change anything, such as the pattern you've used to fill in a circle, you usually have to erase the circle and start over. You are creating a finished painting that is comprised of many little dots; if you try to increase or decrease the size or the picture, the quality deteriorates, and solid grays can become unwanted tartan plaids.

A Paint-type graphic (Metro)

➻ Draw programs

Draw programs employ the same basic idea of drawing on screen with a mouse, but they treat what you draw in a completely different fashion. In a draw program, whatever you draw is a distinct object. If you draw a circle, and then place a box halfway inside of it, you still have two separate graphic items. You can fill the circle with one pattern and the box with another, and even change the patterns later on. You can control the circle independently from the box, place one on top of the other, and then switch which one is on top. This makes creating (and revising) complex graphics easier than using a paint program.

Drawings do not consist of little dots, as in a paint program, but of shapes—squares, circles, lines, etc. When a drawing is made larger or smaller, it changes sizes perfectly, because the shapes are being re-sized, not the dots. This is known as "object-oriented" graphics (shapes), as opposed to "bitmap" graphics (dots).

The printed output will also appear to be sharper, no matter what it is printed on, because, once again, you aren't dealing with dots, but with shapes. A graphic created in a draw program will print at the highest resolution: from 300 dpi for laser printers, to 2450 dpi on Linotronic typesetters.

Draw programs are best for creating structured, technical, or geometric-based graphics (such as technical illustrations, floor plans, architectural drawings), and presentation graphics. Since Draw programs allow for freehand lines, they can be used for artistic drawing as well, including logos, line art, and visual aids (such as slides, maps, and graphs). The newest draw programs, such as Micrografx Windows Designer and GEM Artline, allow you to mix paint and draw files in a single image; these can be imported into WordPerfect for printing on PostScript printers.

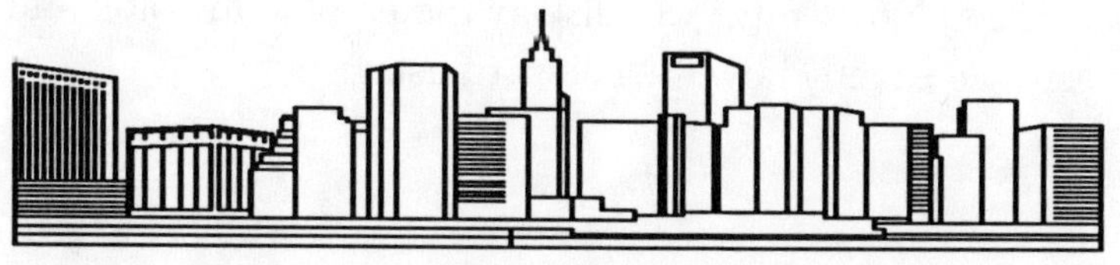

A Draw-type graphic (MGI)

Even if you aren't an artist, you can still produce cleaner, more attractive graphics with draw programs because they employ precise tools that don't demand painstaking skill to master.

Programs that use draw-type files include AutoCAD, Micrografx Designer, Draw and Graph, Harvard Graphics, Lotus Freelance, Lotus 1-2-3, .PIC files, and WordPerfect's own spreadsheet, PlanPerfect.

◆ Lucky 13

Have you ever seen a building with a 13th floor? Think about it. The elevator buttons go from 12 to 14. There's an episode of the *Twilight Zone* in there somewhere, but if you write it, I want to share story credit. Also, "Friday the 13th" inspired the ultimate spoof of horror movies, "Saturday the 14th Strikes Back" (There's nothing really violent or disgusting in this movie—just me, and that's sickening enough. Pop a couple of Pepto Bismol and watch in awe as I try to upstage the rest of the cast.)

Why the discourse about the lucky number 13? Because WordPerfect can read 13 different graphics file types, that's why. If you've ever tried to read a WordStar file or one from Microsoft Word directly, you're aware that almost every word processing program uses a different "file format." This format contains not just the text, but formatting codes for underlines, bold, margins, etc.

Graphics programs file formats have a lot more differences than do word processing programs, and are less standardized as well. But WordPerfect accepts 13 different formats directly, and that provides you with many graphics programs and file formats to choose from.

◆ Local color

WordPerfect can display color graphics on-screen if you have a color monitor. What it can't do is print them, even with a color printer. I would be surprised if WordPerfect didn't add this capability sometime soon, but for the moment you'll have to settle for black and white print-outs of your color pictures.

WordPerfect converts colors to different shades of gray, and, while this is usually accurate, at times the outcome can surprise you. A light color like Yellow may turn out black. If you are using a monochrome monitor (black and white and red all over), View Document will give you a good idea of what the printed graphic will look like. But a color monitor will display the graphic in color, and you will have to print it to see exactly how the colors translate.

Before. This line art comes from the Pictorial Archive series of copyright-free Dover books, and is a fairly straightforward illustration. But when scanned, and edited by my wife Toni in PC Paintbrush, look what happens to those poor unsuspecting geishas.

After. Mere moments later, the geishas have been turned into Mr. Spock and Captain Kirk—complete with pointy ears, raised eyebrows, and Enterprise emblems on their kimonos. Notice their hands now making the familiar Vulcan greeting. Beam me up, Scotty.

❖ Unlucky 13

It would be convenient if it were all that simple, but it's not. Just because a program claims to make files in a format that WordPerfect accepts, the files still may not function as they should; this is because so-called standard file formats are far from standard.

Here is a list of the file formats WordPerfect accepts, including some comments on the programs that create these files, and particular problems inherent in the file format. Hopefully this will help you avoid expensive software mistakes when purchasing graphics software.

◆ Paint formats

PCX

This is the industry standard paint format for MS-DOS computers and is called .PCX format. This format was created by a company called ZSoft, for use with their PC Paintbrush line of paint programs. A variation of this format is called .PCC. Both .PCX and .PCC are totally standardized and work flawlessly.

Many scanners can also save files in .PCX format. PC Paintbrush itself can run a scanner, and then edit the scanned images, such as the ones pictured on the left. Clip art packages are often in .PCX format. Popular programs that create .PCX files include PC Paintbrush, Publisher's Paintbrush, HP Drawing/Charting Gallery, HP Scanning Gallery.

➾ IMG

This is another industry standard, because .IMG (for image) files always work. Popular programs that use this format include GEM Paint, Halo, Halo DPE, SLed. An excellent 3-D charting and graphing program by the name of Boeing Graph also creates .IMG files. (I'm waiting for 4-D graphics: a program that would "channel" the spirit of Leonardo DiVinci, and create charts and graphs without human intervention. I'm not holding my breath, however.)

➾ TIF

Also known as "TIFF," or "Tagged Image File Format." (not to be confused with "Tiff" as in "the bride and groom had a tiff.") This is the newest bitmapped format, and also the least standardized. TIF files can be compressed, and contain "gray scale" information. WordPerfect reads uncompressed TIF files consistently, but compressed TIF files may be erratic. Sometimes it reads them, other times it doesn't. The more compressed they are, the less likely WordPerfect is to read them.

Popular programs that create TIF files include HP Scanning Gallery, GEM Scan, Boeing Graph, HP Drawing/Charting Gallery. SnapShot, from Aldus, creates and edits TIF files obtained from video sources.

➾ PIC

Dr. Halo and Halo DPE are two popular paint programs. They can read and write with their own format, and with .IMG files. Don't confuse this paint-type format with the Lotus 1-2-3 draw-type .PIC format.

➾ MSP

Microsoft Windows Paint is a very limited program included with Microsoft Windows (a "graphics environment").

➾ MAC

Mac Paint is a popular paint program for the Macintosh computer. Macs use 3 1/2 inch disks, but the disk format differs from MS-DOS 3 1/2 inch disks. Because of this, moving files from one machine to another can require a network, modem, or internal hardware board, such as the "MatchMaker" from Micro Solutions. Some companies sell clip art in this format, namely Software Publishing's "PFS: First Publisher Art Portfolios."

PPIC

PC Paint Plus. Another paint program for the PC. Not as competent or popular as PC Paintbrush.

❖ *Draw formats*

CGM

"Computer Graphic Metafile." is potentially the most useful, and troublesome of the line art formats. CGM files are compact, so they display and print quickly. Many programs are capable of creating CGM files.

Unfortunately, despite its reputation as an "Industry Standard," there are so many versions of this format that it is anything but standard.

The only type of CGM files WordPerfect will use are straight line art, black and white. A few programs, such as Harvard Graphics, can include gray patterns, but WordPerfect will convert patterns from some CGM files into unadulterated garbage.

And so, although many programs can create CGM files, not all of them can be used with WordPerfect. A single program may create files that you can use, and others that you can't, depending on what you've included in the files. Even Harvard Graphics can produces some CGM files which WordPerfect uses flawlessly, while others may appear all-black inside WordPerfect. The one cardinal rule to remember is: **ALWAYS CHOOSE PATTERNS, NEVER COLORS.** If a program doesn't offer you a choice, it probably won't work with WordPerfect.

This can be enormously frustrating, so make sure that you can create CGM files with a program, and test them with WordPerfect first. Most graphic editing programs can read a wider variety of CGM files than WordPerfect can; so a program may create a technically perfect CGM file, but WordPerfect still may not read it.

Some popular programs that create CGM files include Freelance Plus, Graphwriter, Harvard Graphics, and PlanPerfect. More explicit directions for using Harvard Graphics with WordPerfect are addressed later in this chapter, and in Chapter 16, *1-2-3 Publishing.*

DXF

"Data eXchange Format" is a format which was standardized by the AutoCAD computer-aided design program. Most CAD software supports this format, but the format itself is limited. Text has a resemblance to stick figures. This was not designed as an artistic format, and so lacks useful features.

To use DXF files, with WordPerfect, you must first convert them by using with the GRAPHCNV program supplied on the Conversion disk. This is the only supported format that WordPerfect can't read directly.

HPGL

Hewlett-Packard Graphics Language was designed for pen plotters. One drawback is that WordPerfect works fine with black and white, or stick-figure graphics, but will not accept HPGL files containing objects filled with patterns. These files are made up of smaller line segments that appear coarse when enlarged, and do not size as well as other line art files. For example, to fill a circle with black, this format packs the circle with countless closely spaced lines. If you enlarge the picture, the individual lines become visible, and no longer appear solid.

If you are having trouble retrieving CGM, you might consider using HPGL, if your graphics program supports it. With Harvard Graphics, some files are compatible with CGM, while others, notably those with patterned background, work most effectively in HPGL format.

If a graphic program can support a HP plotter, simply print the file "to disk," rather than to the printer.

EPS

Encapsulated PostScript may sound as if it's inside a cold capsule, but it's easy to swallow *if*, and only if, you have a PostScript printer.

Because PostScript is a language, these files are actually programs that describe an image to the printer. Some people create these program files themselves, but the more sane among us utilize graphics programs to create EPS files.

WordPerfect will only print EPS files if they are "well-behaved;" in other words, they must conform exactly to EPS specifications.

EPS files do not display on-screen unless they include a .TIF file for a screen image. The .TIF file is used for display only, not for printing. If they don't include a .TIF file (and many don't), nothing will be apparent in either graphics edit, or view document; the graphic will appear as an empty box.

EPS files can contain dazzling special effects, including rotated types, "fountain" fills which contain a smooth progression of gray tones, and even photographs using gray-scale information for high-quality reproduction.

Adobe Illustrator on the Mac is specifically designed to create PostScript files, but PC software such as Micrografx Designer can produce EPS files as well. Harvard Graphics and the spreadsheet Quattro (uno, dos tres...) also create EPS files. If the software you are using doesn't create EPS files, you can attempt to print the file to disk by using the PostScript printer driver, rather than the printer. These files will sometimes function as EPS files.

WPG

Just what the world needs, another graphic file format. This is a new file format devised by WordPerfect Corporation. I am not aware of any programs that create graphics in this format—even WordPerfect's own PlanPerfect creates CGM files.

And so it will be difficult, if not impossible, to edit graphics in .WPG format. In addition, the WPG format can hold both line art and bitmapped files. MGI sells its clip art collection in .WPG format; these are line art files, but if you use the GRAPHCNV program you can convert bitmapped files into .WPG files.

◆ Ivy league tips

Of all the graphics programs I have tried (and believe me, I have tried altogether too many), the one that was consistently compatible with WordPerfect was *Harvard Graphics*, from Software Publishing.

HG offers you plenty of control over how you want your pictures drawn. Here are some tips for creating files that will function effectively with WordPerfect, whether you use CGM or HPGL.

- Always select a fill style of "Pattern" instead of color. While color may be attractive on-screen, WordPerfect tends to print out several different colors as black, and this can be quite unappealing in charts.
- **CGM Files:** Select patterns from the "Printer Pattern" wheel in Appendix F.

- **HPGL Files:** Select patterns from the "Plotter Pattern" wheel in Appendix F.
- **ONLY USE COLOR 1** (white, which prints as black) to print in black, and **SET BACKGROUND COLOR TO 16** (Black, which prints as White) to print in white.

❖ *Grab bag*

If your graphic program does not create files that WordPerfect can use, there is one last resort in the form of a program called GRAB.

This is a "screen grab" program that literally grabs whatever is on the screen, and creates a copy of it on-disk. WordPerfect can then load the disk file into graphics boxes.

There are limitations, however. First, the program doesn't work with all monitors. The most popular graphics systems, including CGA, EGA, VGA and Hercules, are supported, but less popular monitors, such as full-page, high-resolution, or video cards in special modes, are not.

The other limitation is that the resolution of a Grab file is only as high as the screen it was used on. With CGA monitors, that's very low. Hercules, EGA and VGA are higher, but at approximately 72 dpi, these are still relatively low-resolution. These images will appear somewhat jagged when printed full-size on a 300 dpi laser printer, such as the LaserJet. The quality will improve if you print them at a smaller size, but these files are not large to begin with, so reducing them may lead to tiny graphics.

◆ Grab for it

Using this program is quite effortless, as there is only one command: GRAB. Located on the Fonts/Graphics disk, the program can either be run from the floppy, or copied to the hard disk. The program can be in any directory.

To start the program, type

GRAB [ENTER]

The program will display a message, reminding you that the command to grab is:

ALT-SHIFT-F9

It will also tell you that typing:

GRAB/H

will enable you to ask for help with the program. Grab takes up a mere 10K of memory, but it may find itself in conflict with other memory resident programs, such as SideKick.

GRAB only operates in graphics mode, so don't bother trying to grab a screen full of text. When you are in graphics mode, and want to save a copy of the current screen onto a disk file, press:

ALT-SHIFT-F9

If your graphics card is supported, GRAB will emit a two tone chime. Ding-Dong. No, it's not the Avon lady; is simply proclaiming that it is saving the screen picture onto disk.

If GRAB makes a low buzzing noise that sounds as if you answered incorrectly on a game show, don't bother checking behind door number three because you really have lost. This soothing sound indicates that GRAB doesn't support your graphics card in its current mode. If you try all the modes and GRAB still buzzes, well, it's time for Truth or Consequences, and you're getting the consequences.

If you are a lucky winner, GRAB will save the screen in the "default" directory (usually whatever directory you started the graphics program in). However,the graphics program may have changed directories, and so the file might not be where you think.

To ensure that the file goes where you want it, begin the program with: **GRAB/d=C:\WP50**. This forces GRAB to save its files in the WP5 directory. You can specify *any* directory after the "/d=" and GRAB will save its files in that directory.

GRAB calls the first file it saves GRAB.WPG. When you press **ALT-SHIFT-F9** again, it creates a file called GRAB2.WPG. This predictable scenario goes on ad nauseam until you've saved GRAB9999.WPG. If you delete or rename the GRAB files, GRAB will commence renumbering from the beginning. It's often wise to rename these files with something a trifle more descriptive than GRAB894.WPG. Once you've loaded the file into a graphics box, that name will be displayed in Reveal Codes, and you'll know what the graphics box contains, even if you don't have a caption. You can use List Files, **F5** to rename the files.

GRAB has two more options up its sleeve. If you start the program with **GRAB/F=JUNK**, GRAB will name its first file JUNK.WPG, its second JUNK1.WPG, and so on. Of course, you can use any four letters you want; (yes, *any* four letters) this will give your file a more specific name right from the start. You could use a name like **GRAB/F=PIES,** if you were grabbing pie charts from a graphics program, or **GRAB/F=FLEA** if you were grabbing pictures of dogs.

If you use this last option, type

GRAB/R

GRAB will remove itself from memory. You may not be able to remove GRAB from memory until you remove any other memory resident program loaded *after* GRAB.

One sure-fire way to remove GRAB from memory is to turn the computer off, press the reset button (if you have one), or press **CONTROL-ALT-DELETE** simultaneously. Remember to save your work and exit any program (especially WordPerfect) before you utilize any of these options. Otherwise, you may lose material that was not saved to disk.

❖ *Be a convert*

WordPerfect is accompanied by another program for graphics files. This one is called GRAPHCNV (for graph convert), and converts all the supported formats into .WPG files. If you are using files in any format other than .DXF, this program will not be necessary.

If you are using .DXF files, you must first convert them with this program (as WordPerfect doesn't read them directly).

You can use this program in batch mode by using DOS wildcards instead of complete filenames. If you wanted to convert a whole directory containing .DXF files in one swell foop, you would type:

GRAPHCNV *.DXF [ENTER]

WordPerfect will ask if you want to replace all the .WPG files in the current directory. If you answer **N**, the program stops and returns to DOS (maybe it's offended because you didn't agree to its terms). If you answer **Y**, the program is overjoyed and leaps into action. It asks what directory you want the .WPG files to be created in. Press return for the current directory, or specify any other directory you want. When you press **[ENTER]**, the program begins converting files with relish (catsup or mustard).

❖ *Clip art tip*

If you plan to buy clip art (professionally designed graphics on-disk), you can purchase it in several different file formats.

◆ Bitmapped

The most popular file format for clip art is .PCX, with all the advantages and disadvantages of bitmapped files. These files are easy to edit with programs like PC Paintbrush. Even minor editing can customize clip art so it appears less generic and more specific to your individual needs.

As in all bitmapped files however, they will print jagged and look like they were produced on a computer if you enlarge them to excess. Also, any gray patterns in the file may turn into highland plaid patterns. While it might be amusing to argue about what clan these patterns belong to, they are not terribly attractive and distract from the picture itself. But as long as you don't size them too radically, they can be indistinguishable from hand-made artwork.

One other item to check for when purchasing clip art is resolution. Because laser printers usually print 300 dots per inch, clip art at 300 dpi will print sharper than clip art of lesser resolution.

If you shrink low-resolution graphics, they will print as sharply as 300 dpi graphics. A 75 dpi picture printed at one-fourth its original size will look identical to a 300 dpi picture (only smaller).

◆ Line art

There is not nearly as much line art format clip art available; while bitmapped clip art can simply be hand-drawn and scanned, line art clip art needs to be created on a computer. The advantage of clip art in these formats is that it retains its high-quality, no matter what size you print it, or what printer you print it on. Clip art in line art format will print at full resolution on a typesetter with 2450 dpi resolution.

MGI includes 30 pieces of line art clip art on the Fonts/Graphics disk. These files are a small selection from its Publisher's PicturePak series of clip art portfolios. They are available in both .WPG and .CGM formats. As I said, I am not aware of any software that can edit .WPG files. Due to the lack of standardization in .CGM files, you may or may not be able to edit these files with a program that says it can read .CGM files. These .CGM files work beautifully with WordPerfect; it can even rotate, flop, and size them. The .WPG and .CGM files operate identically with WordPerfect, but .CGM files are also compatible with other programs. If you want to purchase the MGI graphics, I would recommend buying the clip art in .CGM rather than .WPG format.

13

Rules to live by

or What's my line?

Graphic designers call them rules, and there are many rules related to these rules. Rules are important in design because they help organize the page and make it easier to read. WordPerfect has two types of rules, horizontal and vertical. These can be used in a wide variety of ways, as you will find out all too soon.

You can place lines between columns (and learn how to have them print automatically on all pages, not just one). You can place them above headlines and subheads, or on separate charts or readouts. Don't confuse these with the Line Draw feature that allows you to draw with the cursor, but does not print with all printers. I'll cover that later in this chapter as well.

Best of all, the lines are blissfully easy to use with WordPerfect. And to prove my point, I shall now attempt to show you everything you need to know about lines, and I won't even have to rely on a translator from the U.N. It's a tall order, and I'll probably spend a half page just hyping what a terrific feat this will be, but I'll bet I can do it. At no time will my fingers leave my hands.

Vertical lines are set to an absolute position on a page. They don't move with text like graphic boxes or horizontal lines. Notice how I've set the width of line with 1w, the thinnest setting possible with WordPerfect.

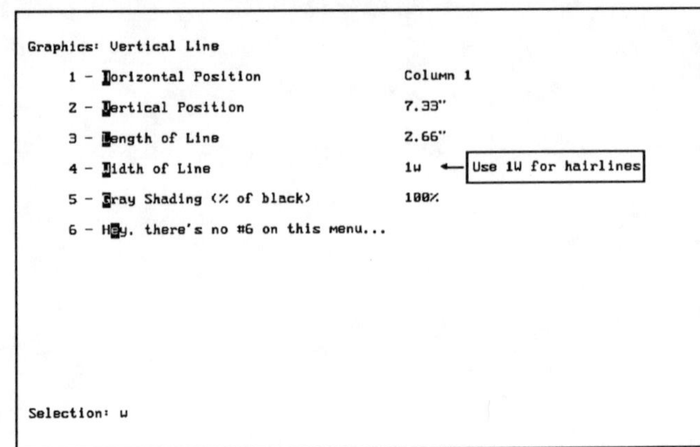

◆ Creating lines

The main command for creating lines is

ALT-F9 L (V or H)

If you follow this with a **V**, you will create a vertical line; if you follow it with an **H**, you will create a horizontal line.

TA-DA!

That's it. With that information alone, you can create a line in WordPerfect. Of course, you'll have to expand your attention span to cover some of the more involved options (having the line print somewhere other than across the width of the page or down the left margin, for example). Or, maybe you just want to grab a sandwich, or go to the bathroom. To learn how to make vertical rules float with text, see Chapter 9, *Columns*.

◆ Horizontal lines

Let's be alphabetical and start with horizontal lines. Press

ALT-F9 L H

You are now staring at the horizontal line menu, a sight that would have been shocking a mere 100 years ago. Today, of course, it's commonplace, and you'll be seeing a lot of it.

If you press return now, you will be asking for a line that runs from the right margin to the left margin (and changes lengths automatically if you change margins). The line will be .01" (or .03c) wide, and 100% black.

```
Graphics: Horizontal Line

     1 - Horizontal Position                Left & Right
     2 - Length of Line
     3 - Width of Line                      0.01"
     4 - Gray Shading (% of black)          100%

Selection: 0
```

Horizontal lines can be set to start at the left or right margin and can be any length or thickness. When they are set to Left & Right (as seen here), they change length automatically if the margin changes.

◆ Line positioning

If you want something other than this default line, you have five choices:

The first is **H** for horizontal position. When you press **H**, you are faced with five options: **L**eft starts the line from the left margin, **R**ight starts the line from the right margin, **C**enter centers the line, **B**oth is identical to the default (it creates a line that travels from the left margin to the right margin), and **S**et position allows you to specify the precise distance you want the line to start from the left end of the paper (not the margin).

For our example, let's center the line. Press

H C

Notice that the length of line is set to 0"; if you were to press return now, you would create a line 0" long (which is a pretty short line). To avoid this embarrassing turn of events, we're going to make the line 3 inches long. To do this, press

L 3 [ENTER]

The next step is to tell WordPerfect how thick of a line to create. In most cases, the default of .01" is just right. It's not too thin or too thick. But we're going to make this a thick line by pressing

W .1 [ENTER]

The last item to decide upon is whether the line will print solid black (the default) or in a shade of gray. Since we seem to be living life in the "lite decade," gray lines are often a lighter alternative to those heavy black lines. Let's make ours a 20% gray line. Press

G 20 [ENTER]

Now let's double check our handiwork. Lines cannot be edited once you've placed them on the page. If you want to change them, you must delete them and put in a new line. To avoid this, let's get it right the first time. The screen should read:

Horizontal Position = Center
Length of line = 3"
Width of line = .1"
Gray Shading (% of Black) = 20%
If it does, press

[ENTER]

A code will be placed in the text. If you want to see the code, press **ALT-F3** for Reveal Codes. The code will look like this: [Hline:Center,3",.1",20%]. This tells you whatever you need to know about the line: it is centered, 3" long, .1" wide, and 20% gray. To finish off the line, press

[ENTER]

Now press **SHIFT-F7 V** to view this on-screen. C'mon, admit it. Isn't that about the prettiest horizontal line you've ever seen?

◆ Tip: Get down (get back up again)

When using a horizontal ruling line, it's often a good idea to have an Advance Down of .1 (SHIFT-F8 O A D .1 F7) before and after the rule, to keep it from getting too close to the text.

Even if you use a hard return before and after the line, the extra .1" adds white space, and keeps the page from looking crowded.

◆ Vertical lines

With horizontal lines under our belt (don't you hate it when those lines dig into your stomach?), let's give our all to creating a vertical line.

But first, a few particulars. Unlike graphics boxes and horizontal lines, vertical lines do not move with text when you edit. They are anchored onto a page in a particular position, either from top to bottom, or at a certain distance from the top at a particular length.

Because of this, they can be annoying to work with, especially if you edit text and paragraphs move but lines don't. I'll have a fix for that later on, but it is vital that vertical lines not move with text.

Vertical lines are most often used between columns of text, and so that's what we're going to create. Your first intercolumn rule, oh isn't this exciting? Someday you'll look back on all of this and smile, or hopefully just pay someone to look back and smile for you.

As Peter Pan says 11,234 times a day at Disneyland, "*Come on everybody, here we goooooooo.*" (Pneumatic clicking noises are heard, a shadow of Peter flits across the wall, and the windows of the nursery open themselves magically to allow a flying sailboat to soar over London—and you didn't even have to wait 45 minutes in line, you lucky stiff.)

◆ Intercolumn rules

Because we're going to create an intercolumn rule, we'll first have to create a column. For more information about columns, see Chapter 8. We're going to leave room for a headline, so press

[ENTER]

until the measurement in the right corner is at approximately **Ln 2.00"**.

To create a two column page, press

ALT-F7 D D .3" [ENTER][ENTER] C

We're now going to create a vertical line that runs from the top of the columns (not the top of the page) to the bottom of the page. Press

ALT-F9 L V

If you were to press return now, you would create a default vertical line .01" (or .03c) wide running from top to bottom of the left margin. But we're not about to settle for that, are we? We're too busy striving for self-enlightenment, self-improvement, and world peace, and we don't want no stinking defaults.

The first item on the menu (the appetizer so to speak) is Horizontal. This is similar to horizontal lines, only different. The difference is that the "Center" choice is replaced with Between Columns. Since that's what we want, press

B 1 [ENTER]

When you press **B**, WordPerfect replies "Place line to right of column:" WordPerfect put the line to the right of that column because you pressed 1. If you had more than two columns on a page, you would have to repeat this command, for each column (except the last one, because a line is not needed at the right margin).

Behind "Door #2" lies **V**ertical. "Full Page" is displayed right now because that's the default. The choices are **F**ull Page, **T**op, **C**enter, **B**ottom, and **S**et Position. These measurements are always set from the margins, not from the edge of the page. Because we want the line to start at the top of the columns, rather than the top, center or bottom of the page, we're going to press

V S [ENTER]

When you press **[ENTER]**, WordPerfect displays your current horizontal location on the page. If you want, you can type a new number here, and the line will start in that position and then print down the page. A more efficient way to use this feature is to be on the line of text where you want the vertical line to start printing. WordPerfect will then calculate the measurement for you.

Length of line is also filled in correctly so that the line reaches from its current position to the bottom of the page. You could enter a different number here if you wanted the line to stop before the end of the page. But you don't want that, do you?

◆ Line width

It's **W**idth of Line time. In the case of intercolumn rules, thin is best, and so leave it at .01"

Don't try it right now, but if you wanted an even thinner line, you would press

L .1W [ENTER]

> ➾ Remember, W's are WordPerfect's internal measurement system (that I can only dream they named after me). There are 1200 W's per inch. If you print onto a PostScript typesetter, you'll see a huge difference (called a "hairline"). If you print to a PostScript laser printer, you'll see a considerable difference. If you have a LaserJet, you'll see a less dramatic but still noticeable difference.

We're going to create an even thinner line by using tiny little dots. We'll do this with the Gray Shading (% of Black) command. Press

G 10 [ENTER]

The vertical line is now complete. Press

[ENTER]

to finish. If you want to admire your handiwork, press **SHIFT-F7 V**.

It would be nice if we could edit lines like graphics, but we can't.

Since I'm not a programmer for WordPerfect, I can't tell you why this isn't possible, but I can offer an alternative.

◆ In lieu of editing lines

Delete the line code (or codes) and create a new one (or ones).

Let's try it. Turn reveal codes on with **ALT-F3**. Move the cursor so that the [Vline:Column 1,2",7",0.01",10%] code is highlighted. Press

[DEL]

The code is gone. Long live the code. Now let's quickly create a thin, black vertical line between the two columns, rather than the extremely light dotted line. Press

ALT-F9 L V H B 1 [ENTER] V S [ENTER][ENTER]

If you use this type of line often, you can create a macro that will produce the same line with just one keystroke. See Chapter 15 for more information about macros.

❖ *The wrap rap*

Text will wrap around graphics boxes, but will not wrap around lines. In other words, the text won't budge if you try to place a horizontal or vertical line to print over it. Therefore, you have to exercise a little more caution when working with lines.

While horizontal lines set to "Left & Right" *will* shorten themselves to keep from printing over graphics boxes, a vertical full-page line can only be shortened by using a top and bottom margin change, or by adding headers and footers.

◆ Creating readouts

This means that if you create a page with a readout in the middle of two columns, and then place a full-page vertical line between the columns, it will print right through the middle of the graphics box readout. This can only be averted by setting two vertical rules. One runs from the top of the column to the top of the graphics box readout, and the other runs from the bottom of the graphics box readout to the bottom of the page.

This isn't too difficult if you move to the lines where the readout begins and jot down the LN measurement from the lower right-hand corner of the screen. Then move to the line where the readout ends, and write down that measurement.

Move to the line on the page where you want the vertical line to begin. Create the first vertical line and press

ALT-F9 L V V [ENTER]

This will tell WordPerfect to insert the current vertical position. Press

L

Here comes the math, so you might want to get out your $5 pocket calculator. (If you can figure this kind of stuff out in your head, you should probably sell your computer and become a card counter in Vegas.) Subtract the measurement at the top of the readout from your current position. This will tell you the length of line you need. Enter this number, then press **[ENTER]**

Now we're going to create the line from the bottom of the readout to the bottom of the page. Press

ALT-F9 L V V S

Enter the measurement of the line where the readout ends. Press

[ENTER]

WordPerfect will calculate the distance to the bottom of the page, and enter it in Length of Line.

The intercolumn rule will now stop at readout box, and continue underneath it, allowing for a thoroughly professional appearance. You are now a horizontal and vertical lines whiz-kid.

◆ Line draw for LaserJets only

While horizontal and vertical lines are codes, lines created with "line-draw" are actual characters. Because of this, they won't print on all printers (notably PostScript printers). The LaserJet II contains a line-draw font built-in that matches the line characters available on all MS-DOS computers. The original LaserJet does not have these fonts built-in, but they're available on cartridge.

One drawback with line-draw and desktop publishing is that line-draw characters are monospaced, while DTP type is proportionally spaced. This is why WordPerfect doesn't recommend using line draw with proportionally spaced type. If you want to, go right ahead, but it's really not worth the trouble. It requires writing all the text, then using line-draw, then going back and inserting tabs so that the lines print as they appear on-screen. You should use horizontal and vertical lines instead, or use graphics boxes to create boxes around text.

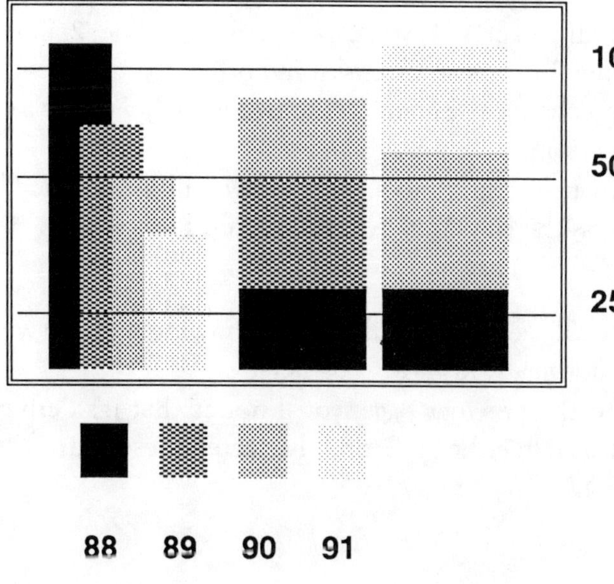

These line-draw characters can be useful for LaserJet users. You can easily create bar charts, such as the one pictured here.

However, these line-draw characters can be useful for LaserJet users. You can easily create presentable bar charts.

Not surprisingly, there are a few tricks involved here. Notice how (in the previous illustration) I never place text on the same line as a line-draw graphic, except at the end of a line. That's a sure-fired and simple way to have line-draw work for you.

LINE HEIGHT: Here's another important point to remember. Because these line-draw characters are part of the Courier 10 pitch PC-8 font, you must set line (fixed) height at .16" in order for the line-draw characters to print as they appear on-screen. Additional line spacing will result in horizontal white gaps between each line of characters, while less spacing will cause the line-draw characters to overlap. Because the line spacing for the entire graph is fixed at .16", it doesn't change even when I add text at the end of a line.

◆ Drawing lines

Okay, kids, what time is it? Why, it's play time! To get into Line-Draw mode, press

CONTROL-F3 L

You now have six choices. If you press **1,** you can draw a single line; **2** allows you to draw with a double line; **3** draws an asterisk (and other characters we'll discuss in a minute); **4** lets you change the character drawn with 3; **5** erases as it moves; and **6** moves without erasing.

Unlike the normal word processing mode, line-draw will automatically create new lines when you press the **[DOWN ARROW]** key. Press

1

Now move the cursor. You'll see that WordPerfect is drawing a line as you move. And WordPerfect will automatically create corners.

If you study the graph on the previous page, you'll notice that it's derived from characters that aren't shown in either 1, 2, or 3. I selected these characters using option 4. So join me, won't you? Press

4

You'll see nine more options displayed here. Press

4

This will select the thick solid-black box. Now when you move the cursor, WordPerfect draws a thick black line. For the graph on page 325, I used five different types of lines: the #2 double line for the box around, and #4, #3, #2 and, #1 within option 4.

◆ Character sets

This is so cute it could make you want to watch a Doris Day movie. Press

4 9 [ALT-3]

Be sure to press the **3** on the keypad, not the 3 under the "#," or F3. A precious little heart will appear, and now, when you move the cursor, WordPerfect will draw a line of hearts. Use the cursor to design a heart like this:

Write a syrupy-sweet message underneath it and send it off to mother. (Who knows?—she might get off your back. On the other hand, she might want to move in with you.)

For a complete list of the IBM-PC character set, see Chapter 7, *Fonts.* You can use any of these characters by pressing

4 9

Then hold down the **[ALT]** key and Press the number of the symbol you want.

The mysterious option 9 allows you to draw with any character included in the 12 character sets. Because only the IBM-PC character set offers you WYSIWYG, those are the only characters I can recommend. However, if you do want to utilize special characters, you can use the Compose feature, **CONTROL-2**. Special characters will appear on-screen as a small square box, but will display properly in View Document. But remember: the character can't print if it's not available in the printer.

➺ Style tip

For a safer and simpler line-draw, create a "line-draw" paired style. This should contain a font change to the Courier PC-8 font, and a fixed line height of .16" before the [Comment].

Use the Line-Draw feature, then use **ALT-F4** to block the line-draw graphic, and apply the "Line-Draw" style. Now no matter how you change the body text, the line-draw graphics will be in the right font with the correct leading.

➺ Grids

Many graphs include a "grid" to help the viewer relate to the height of bars. The grids on the line-draw chart is yet another in the grand tradition of surreptitious work-arounds. You cannot create horizontal grid marks with line-draw and still have continuous vertical bars.

The secret is in the lowly underline. That's right. All I did was leave line-draw, then underlined the segments of the line-draw graphic where I wanted a horizontal grid. Pretty simple. Pretty nifty. Pretty sneaky.

◆ Idiosyncracies

As wonderful as WordPerfect's line feature is, it still has its idiosyncrasies. In Chapter 6, *Measure,* you (hopefully) read about achieving the thinnest possible line by entering the measurement in centimeters instead of inches. .01c gives you a hairline, while .01" gives you a line three times thicker.

But there are other little peculiarities as well. For anyone familiar with a page composition program, WordPerfect's inability to print ruling lines on all pages can be frustrating. But rather than simply complain about the situation, I've come up with some ways to get around it. (Well, *someone* has to.)

◆ Automatic rules

There are two solutions to the non-automatic intercolumn rule dilemma. The first is an efficient method that will put ruling lines on any page. The second seems rather complicated, but once you've set it up, it provides the entire document with a consistent design. And both can be used together as well.

Using a single style, you can instruct WordPerfect to place rules between several columns. If the document has two columns, WordPerfect will print rules between column 1 and column 2; if you have three columns, WordPerfect will print rules between columns 1, 2, and 3. (If you have only one column, there's no such animal as an intercolumn rule, and so WordPerfect will print the rule in the right margin).

◆ Rules: Open

[Vline:Column1,Full Page,9.53",.01"100%][Vline:Column2,Full Page,9.53",.01"100%][Vline:Column3,Full Page,9.53",.01"100%]

Because these rules are set to "full page," they will adjust their length in accordance with the margins on the page, and headers and footers. But remember: these vertical lines will only stop for headers and footers, not for headlines or readouts.

❖ *Under the big top*

One of the advantages of WordPerfect is that all the features seem to mesh together. This next pointer combines styles, headers, and vertical ruling lines to create a pleasing page design, with a large top margin for headlines and pull-quotes, and automatic vertical ruling lines on every page. Best of all, thanks to the design of the page, you don't have to ruminate about turning column rules on or off.

This is vaguely reminiscent of a Catch 22 because you can't enter column definitions into headers or footers, and you can't place intercolumn rules unless columns are turned on. But "O blood type" that I am, my little brain churned away until I conjured up a solution.

You'll need the following styles:

TOPPER PAIRED
[L/R Mar:1",1"][T/B Mar:1",1"]
[Comment]
[AdvToLn:2"][Col Del:3,1",3",3.25",5.25",5.5",7.5"][Col On]
{*Use a distance between columns of .25"*}
[Just on][Hyph On]

HEADER:OPEN
[AdvToLn:1.7"][VLine:3.15",2",8",0.01",100%]
{*Use the Horizontal Set command, and type in the number 3.15". Use the Vertical Set command, and type in the number 2"*}
[Vline:5.35",2",8",0.01",100%]
{*Use the Horizontal Set command, and type in the number 5.35". Use the Vertical Set command, and type in the number 2"*}

The first header contains the following:
[Font:Dutch 30pt]Headline{*Whatever headline you want*}
[Font:Dutch 14pt][HRt]
[Flsh Rt]Subhead[C/A/Flrt]
{*Created when you press [ENTER]*}
[HRt]
[Flsh Rt]Subhead2[C/A/Flrt][HRt]
[Open Style:header]

The header has 1" worth of space built-in for text. That text can be a headline, or, on later pages, a pull-quote. The Header Open style contains an advance command (so it's in exactly the right place, no matter what the leading or how much text you've used) and then rules, set to print between the columns.

There are a few points you need to remember about headers.

WordPerfect automatically takes the height of headers and footers into account when it is calculating the number of lines available for text. If you are using this method, the headers must always be the same length, hence the [AdvTo-

Ln:1.7"] code. If the headers change length, the bottom margin of the page may print off the paper.

In addition, a header can't print on the top of a page unless it's either the first code on the page, or located on a preceding page. If you place a header in the middle of page 1, it will only take effect on page 2.

Also, if you put text in the header, it will repeat on every page until WordPerfect hits another header code. This means that unless you want the headline or pull-quote to print on every page, you should place another header code in the text. A header only has to contain the header style, so you don't have to worry about complicated formatting.

If you want neither a header nor a readout in the extra 1" top margin, create a blank header containing only the header style. *Do not discontinue or suppress headers*. Again, this will alter the bottom margin of the page and may cause text to print off the bottom of the page.

◆ Readouts and pull-quotes in style

Remember when we discussed using graphics boxes for readouts? I know, you're probably still reeling from the excitement, but you'd better brace yourself. We're now going to accomplish the same task by using paired styles. This method has its advantages and disadvantages.

The main advantage of this system is that the actual text of the readout appears on-screen with the rest of the text. You don't have to go into a graphics box to edit it. The main disadvantage is that you can't put these readouts between two columns because the readouts aren't in graphics boxes and text won't wrap around them. A readout created with this method will be the width of whatever column it's in.

This type of readout is popular and accepted, so don't envision it as just some kind of shortcut—it's attractive, and works just as efficiently as graphics box readouts.

This style consists of several elements: ruling lines above and below, space above and below the ruling lines, and a block protect (because readouts should never be interrupted by pages or columns). See Chapter 11, *Graphics,* for some examples of readouts.

◆ **Readout: Paired**

[Block Pro:On][AdvDn:0.1"][HLine:Left & Right,6.5",0.01",10%][HRt][AdvDn:0.1"][VRY LARGE][Comment][AdvDn:0.1"][vry large][Hrt][HLine:Left & Right,6.5",0.1",100%][AdvDn:0.1"][Block Pro:off]

In this example, I use a dotted line above the readout, and a thick line underneath it. You can create the lines at any thickness and at any percentage of gray you want.

◆ **Table setting**

In Chapter 9, *Columns*, I showed you how to make horizontal lines in tables. Because you may not have read that chapter, I'm going to repeat myself (in slightly condensed form) here.

The only rules for using underlines as rules in tables are:

- You must use tabs so that tables line up on the page as they do on-screen.
- You must set underline to print under spaces and tabs. Accomplish this by typing: **SHIFT-F7 O U Y Y F7**
- You cannot use bold and italic type on an underlined line. Each font has its own underline character (isn't that interesting?), and the underline will not look continuous. (The bold or italic underlines will print a bit lower than the regular underline).

❖ *Forms-a-plenty*

Forms. You can't live with them, you can't shoot them. WordPerfect's Workbook presents a complex procedure for creating relatively simple forms. Here's a simple method for creating complex forms.

This all hinges on one elementary function: underlined tabs, the very same function you employed for horizontal rules in tables.

On the opposite page is an example of a fill-in-the-blanks form.

WIN A FABULOUS TRIP TO
LAS CRUSAS NEW MEXICO
IN THE DEAD OF SUMMER!

First: ______________________ **Last:** ______________________
Address: ____
City: ______________________ **State:** ______________________
Zip: ______________________

Personal Information: You must enter this to be eligible.
Age: ______________________ **Shoe Size:** ______________________

IQ: _ **Color:** ☐ **Blue,** ☐ **Green,** ☐ **Beige,** ☐ **Eggshell,** ☐ **Puce**

In 100 words or less, please tell us why you should win this unbelievably fabulous prize:

____
____
____
____

Leave one space (yes, a space) after the word and before the horizontal line. This prevents them from running into each other. They still align because all the tabs end in the same place. Don't ask why, it works. If you want several lines of the form to align, you *must use tabs, not spaces, for the underlines.* (I've typed that phrase so many times that my keyboard is wearing out on the letters u-s-e t-a-b-s).

The ballot boxes are a simple graphics box trick. Read all about it in Chapter 10, *Styles.*

◆ Dotted or dashed vertical lines

What, you say WordPerfect doesn't have these? And you're going to let that stop you? Ha! Where there's a Will-Harris there's a way, or in this case, ways.

You have two choices for dotted vertical lines. The first is easiest. Simply set the width of the vertical line to .01", and the Gray Shading (% of Gray) to 10%. This will give you a very thin gray line. This line may not always display in View Document, but it will print.

The second choice is also the procedure used to create vertical dashed lines. You don't actually create lines at all, you create graphics boxes. We're going to create an *intercolumn vertical dashed line.*

For this example, the dashed line will run down the center of the page, as an intercolumn rule for two columns. Let's quickly set up the columns (normally you would have already done this, and so this step is not mandatory for creating dashes or dotted vertical rules). Press

ALT-F7 D D .3" [ENTER] [ENTER] C

Here are the steps (we're going to be using a user-defined graphics box, but you could use any of the four types).

1. Set figure options so that you have a border on only the right hand side by pressing

ALT-F9 U O B N A N N

2. Create a User-defined box. You can place a Page type box exactly on the page. A Paragraph type box will float with the text. If you want an intercolumn rule, you must use a Page type box, and that's what we'll use for this example. We also want to turn WRAP OFF, so that it won't push text aside. Press

ALT-F9 UC WN TA VF H 4.25" [ENTER] SB .01: [ENTER] 9.25" [ENTER] [ENTER]

This vertical line code can also be put into a style or a header, allowing you to use it on every page.

What's Horizontal, Doc? You can produce horizontal dotted or dashed lines by using these same tips. Dotted lines can just be .01" 10% gray, but dashed lines require a graphics box.

◆ On-screen graphics ruler

Here's a rather esoteric trick, that should give you a better idea of the size relationship between on-screen View Document and the real world. If you've ever seen a page composition program, you'll know that they have on-screen rulers to simplify working with pages.

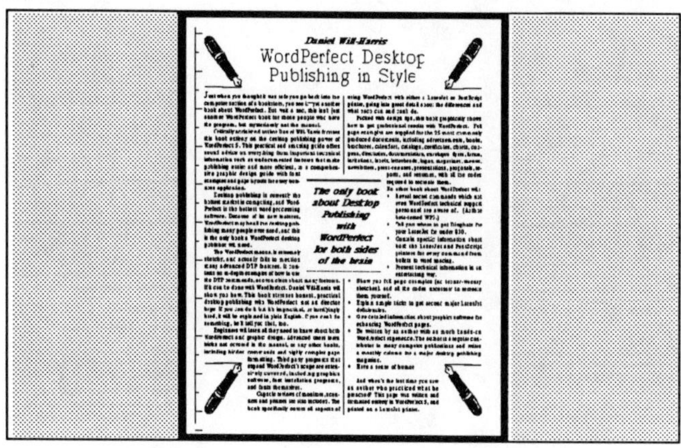
Daniel Will-Harris
WordPerfect Desktop
Publishing in Style
The only book about Desktop Publishing with WordPerfect for both sides of the brain

These on-screen rulers help you perfect a page by letting you see on-screen distances. You can create these visual aids with a paired style.

Using this method, the on-screen ruler will appear when you are in View document, with tick marks every half inch. *Use this for reference purposes only, and remove it before you print the final draft.*

You will want to create this all within a style. You create a style by pressing

ALT-F8 C N Ruler [ENTER] C

For more information about Styles, check out Chapter 10, "Styles."

Yes, this looks complex, but you don't have to enter all the codes manually. Create the codes, then block and copy everything underlined *12 times.*

[T/B Mar:0.25",0.25"][L/R Mar:0.25",1"]

[VLine:0.25",Full Page,10.5",0.01",100%] [HLine:Left,0.2",0.01",100%] [AdvDn:0.5"] [HLine:Left,0.1",0.01",100%] [AdvDn:0.5"]

[Comment][AdvToLn:0"]

The [Adv] code moves WordPerfect back to the top of the page. If you don't use this command, the ruler will appear on a line by itself, and this defeats the whole purpose.

14

Printing

Off the screen and onto the page

Some day my prints will come, some day, da dum dum dum... Despite what those clever folks at Hewlett-Packard might say, that song was not written about laser printers. While the final print-out is the final step in desktop publishing (unless there are minor revisions, and there always are), it's one of the simplest operations.

I was going to assume that you had chosen the correct printer and then created a file. But a woman wise beyond her years (my wife Toni) once told me to "never assume anything," and I will follow her advice.

We will cover printer installation and all the options involved with printing. Remember: you have to use **SHIFT-F7 S** in order to select the proper fonts for your printer. If you don't, you will be using WordPerfect's standard printer, which has *no* font options. Bo-ring.

❖ *Let's start at the very beginning*

A very good place to start. Lest you think I'm channeling the spirit of Oscar Hammerstein (again), there are some basic steps you must follow before you print (or even write) a document.

To access any printer command, press

SHIFT-F7

Before you burn up your laser printer, you need to use this command to set up your document for that printer.

This is the print menu, window on a wonderland of desktop publishing. (Gag me with a laser beam, what a sickening caption.) Actually, this menu is the place for printing, viewing, selecting and editing printers.

```
Print

     1 - Full Document
     2 - Page
     3 - Document on Disk
     4 - Control Printer
     5 - Type Through
     6 - View Document
     7 - Initialize Printer

Options

     S - Select Printer                  HP LaserJet Series II
     B - Binding                         0"
     N - Number of Copies                1
     G - Graphics Quality                High
     T - Text Quality                    High

Selection: 0
```

◆ Installing a printer

If you still haven't installed a printer, it's now or never. Press

SHIFT-F7 S A

A list of printers will appear if you have any of the three WordPerfect ".ALL" files on your disk. I'm going to assume that you're using a LaserJet (or compatible). In this case, you'll need the file called WPRINT1.ALL. If you copied it to the same directory as the program, a list of printers will appear. If you didn't, put the floppy disk into Drive A: and press

O A: [ENTER]

Move the cursor down to the specific LaserJet model you are using. (If you are using a compatible and have at least 512K of memory, select the LaserJet +.

```
Print: Select Printer

  Bodoni-o-do
  Dragon
  Dutch
  Futura
  Galliard
  Gumby/Pokey
  Goudy
  Goudy - Hammersmith 18, 36
  Hammersmith
  Headlines
  HP - Melior
  HP Helv - Boring
  HP LaserJet Series II
  Koosh Ball
  Korinna - FW
  Melior/Optima - FW
  Palatino
  PostScript 2 (Dingbats in User 12)
  PS Beta (Has the great condensed Times/Helv missing in release)
* QMS PS Jet Plus /800 II/810
  Zulu

1 Select; 2 Additional Printers; 3 Edit; 4 Copy; 5 Delete; 6 Help; 7 Update: 1
```

WordPerfect allows you to access countless printers. I use a separate printer for each font family. (SHIFT-F7 S)

You should only select that model if the printer's manual specifically states that it's compatible with the LaserJet II. Press

[ENTER]

WordPerfect will now suggest a file name for the printer. You can type a new name for the file as long as it ends with .PRS. If you want to use WordPerfect's name, Press

[ENTER]

WordPerfect will display a screen containing "Helps and Hints" about the printer you've selected. This also informs you that LaserJets cannot print landscape graphics. If you want a printout of this, make sure that the printer is turned on, and press **SHIFT-[PrtSc]**. If you are using a LaserJet, the page will not eject automatically. You will need to press the on-line key on the printer, then the form feed key, and then the on-line key again.

```
Select Printer: Edit

     Filename                             GOU-HAM.PRS

   1 - Name                               Goudy - Hammersmith 18, 36

   2 - Port                               LPT1:

   3 - Sheet Feeder                       None

   4 - Forms

   5 - Cartridges and Fonts

   6 - Initial Font                       Goudy Roman 11pt (ASCII) (Port) (FW)

   7 - Path for Downloadable              A:\
         Fonts and Printer
         Command Files


Selection: 0
```

Printer Edit (SHIFT-F7 S E) lets you set defaults for each printer, including name, port, sheet feeder, forms, fonts, initial font, and the location of downloadable soft fonts.

To leave this screen, press

F7

WordPerfect now displays another menu (menus, menus everywhere and not a byte to eat). Now you can change the name of the printer (for your reference only), change the port the printer is attached to, select a sheet feeder, select fonts, choose an initial font, and tell WordPerfect where the downloadable fonts are located.

◆ Any port in a storm

Since you are only installing one printer, leave the name as it is. As I've said many-a-time before, try to use a Parallel connection to the printer if at all possible. If you have one parallel port, this will be LPT1; if you have two ports, it could also be LPT2. If you need to change the port, press **P**, and then the number of the port you'll be using.

◆ Sheet-Feed me, Seymore, feed me

Unless you have a LaserJet 500+, Mannesman Talley 910, Kyocera F series, or Dataproducts LZR-1230, or optional sheet feeder, do not select any other sheet feeder. If you do, you may find a strange letter at the top of every page that shouldn't be there.

◆ True to form

WordPerfect is set up with four forms: Standard, Legal, Envelope, and Letter. If you regularly use some odd-sized form, you can enter its specifications here. Once you do, you can simply select that form and avoid entering all sorts of dimensions whenever you create a file. Don't bother to set up custom forms unless you are going to use them frequently.

◆ Fonts-a-plenty

Time to select your fonts. The LaserJet supports the complete set of Hewlett-Packard soft fonts (sold separately). If you have installed Bitstream Fontware (available for free by calling WordPerfect) and created fonts, they will be listed here. Move down the list of fonts and press * on the fonts you want when you in-

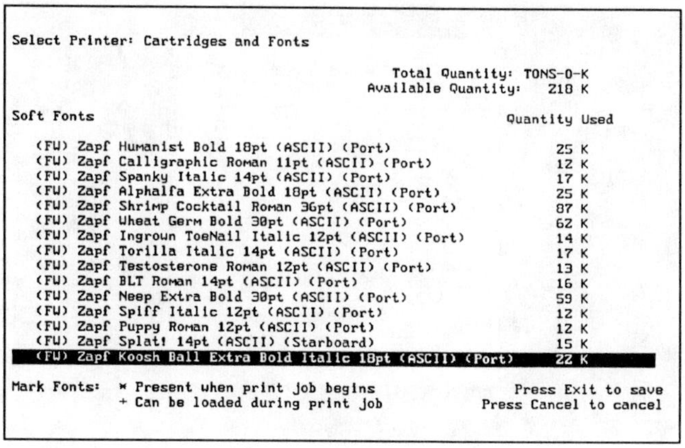

```
Select Printer: Cartridges and Fonts

                                        Total Quantity: TONS-O-K
                                    Available Quantity:    210 K

Soft Fonts                                                Quantity Used

   (FW) Zapf Humanist Bold 18pt (ASCII) (Port)                  25 K
   (FW) Zapf Calligraphic Roman 11pt (ASCII) (Port)             12 K
   (FW) Zapf Spanky Italic 14pt (ASCII) (Port)                  17 K
   (FW) Zapf Alphalfa Extra Bold 18pt (ASCII) (Port)            25 K
   (FW) Zapf Shrimp Cocktail Roman 36pt (ASCII) (Port)          87 K
   (FW) Zapf Wheat Germ Bold 30pt (ASCII) (Port)                62 K
   (FW) Zapf Ingroun ToeNail Italic 12pt (ASCII) (Port)         14 K
   (FW) Zapf Torilla Italic 14pt (ASCII) (Port)                 17 K
   (FW) Zapf Testosterone Roman 12pt (ASCII) (Port)             13 K
   (FW) Zapf BLT Roman 14pt (ASCII) (Port)                      16 K
   (FW) Zapf Neep Extra Bold 30pt (ASCII) (Port)                59 K
   (FW) Zapf Spiff Italic 12pt (ASCII) (Port)                   12 K
   (FW) Zapf Puppy Roman 12pt (ASCII) (Port)                    12 K
   (FW) Zapf Splat! 14pt (ASCII) (Starboard)                    15 K
   (FW) Zapf Koosh Ball Extra Bold Italic 18pt (ASCII) (Port)   22 K

Mark Fonts:  * Present when print job begins              Press Exit to save
             + Can be loaded during print job           Press Cancel to cancel
```

Select Printer Cartridges and Fonts (SHIFT-F7 S E C F) is how you tell WordPerfect which fonts you want to use with each printer. These particular fonts are only available for those with a warped sense of humor.

itialize the printer, and + on the fonts you want downloaded each time you print. See Chapter 7, *About faces,* for more detailed information about installing fonts.

- Number 1 Font: After you have selected the fonts for a printer, you can select the font that WordPerfect will use as the default. This will become the initial font for any document using this printer, unless you specifically change it.
- A Better Mousetrap: If you are using downloadable fonts, **P**ath is the place to inform WordPerfect of their whereabouts.

Once you've filled WordPerfect in on all the particulars, press

F7 S

If you have selected downloadable fonts with an *, press **I** now and WordPerfect will download them. If you marked them with a +, WordPerfect will download them automatically each time you print.

◆ View Document—Take a gander at this

No, don't print. Not just yet. If you do, you'll be missing out on one of WordPerfect's snazziest tricks: View Document. This feature displays the finished page on-screen, almost exactly as it will print.

As if that weren't enough, it's such a snap that even a child could do it (a cat could do it, for that matter, if it stepped on the right keys). Press

SHIFT-F7 V

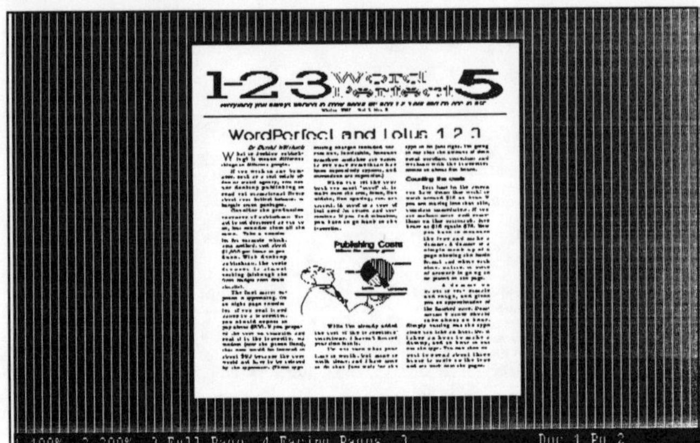

View Document in Full Page view.

- Full Page: Before your very eyes, a page will appear in living black and white (or in living color, if you own a color monitor). You can view the page at four different zoom levels. The default is Full Page. Unless you have a full page display like the Genius, or a high-resolution monitor like the WYSE, you will not be able to read the text.
- Changing pages: At any zoom level, you can press **[PgDn]** or **[PgUp]** to move from page to page. You can also use **[HOME][HOME][UP ARROW]** to move to the first page, and **[HOME][HOME][DOWN ARROW]** to move to the end of the file. Don't forget: when you press **CONTROL-HOME**, WordPerfect moves to whatever page number you enter.
- Full Size: For a closer look, press **1** for "100%." This is approximately 100% of full size, although it may be slightly smaller or larger depend-

View Document in 100% view. This is actual size, although the size varies depending on the kind of graphics your computer has.

View Document in 200% view. This is twice actual size.

ing on the monitor. You will not see the entire page on-screen unless you have a full-page monitor.

- For a better view: You can move around the page by using the cursor keys. The gray + key moves you down one screen at a time, the gray - key moves you up a screen at a time. **[HOME] ARROW]** moves you to the right side of the screen, **[HOME] [LEFT ARROW]** moves you to the left side of the screen.
- Larger than Life: Zoom in even closer by pressing **2** for a view that is twice as large as life.
- Two, two, two pages in one: Pressing **4** gives you a "facing pages" view, so you can look at left and right pages simultaneously. If you are creating a book, magazine, or newsletter (where the pages are printed back

View Document in Facing Pages view. See two pages at once, on-screen. Many people never know this particular brand of excitement.

to back and "face" each other when open), this will provide you with an accurate representation of how the pages will appear.

WordPerfect has three on-screen fonts: a serif for Dutch/Times fonts and the like, a sans serif for fonts like Swiss/Helvetica, and a typewriter font for Courier-like fonts. These fonts are in a file called WP.DRS, located on the Fonts/Graphics disk. If you are not seeing all three, you may have installed WPSMALL.DRS (on the WordPerfect 2 disk), which only contains the typewriter-like font. If you want to see all three (and it's recommended because it gives you a better idea of the page's appearance), copy WP.DRS to the same directory containing the WordPerfect program.

◆ Initial reaction

If you have selected fonts using an *, you will need to use the Initialize command **SHIFT-F7 I** before attempting to print. This will download any font marked with an * in **SHIFT-F7 S E C**.

If you forget to do this, both the LaserJet and PostScript printers will substitute Courier for any fonts you didn't download. These pages will be unusable, and you will have to initialize before printing again.

Unlike many programs, where you must stop and wait and wait and wait until the fonts are downloaded (which can routinely take five to ten minutes, depending on the number and size of fonts), WordPerfect can download fonts in the background while you continue to write and edit.

You don't have to wait for WordPerfect to finish initializing before you start to print other files. These files will be put in the "print que" and will print automatically *after* all fonts have been downloaded.

When you press **I**, WordPerfect clears all the fonts that are currently in the printer's memory—only the fonts that are currently downloading will be available.

If you consistently forget to initialize the printer and download the fonts, you might try marking them with a +. WordPerfect will then download them every time you print, and you will get so tired of waiting for them that you will mark them with a * and put them in the printer for baby and me.

◆ Selecting pages to print

Okay, *now* we can burn up that laser printer with those masterful pages of yours. You've installed a printer, selected it, created a file, and now you want to see it on paper.

Of course, you will need to select the pages to be printed.

- To Print the current page: Press **SHIFT-F7 P**
- To Print the entire document: Press **SHIFT-F7 F**
- To Print a block of text from the screen: If you have the file on-screen, move the cursor to where you want to start printing and press **ALT-F4**. Highlight all the text you want to print and press **SHIFT-F7 Y**.
- To print several pages from the screen: Move the cursor to the first page you want to print, and press **ALT-F4**. Highlight all the text (you might want to use CONTROL-HOME to jump to the last page you want to print), and press **SHIFT-F7 Y**.
- To print selected pages: If you are printing from List Files, or from Document on Disk, once you've selected the file, WordPerfect will ask: "Page(s): (all)." If you press return, WordPerfect will print the entire document; if you need only specific pages printed, type in the correct page numbers.

Here's an example: If you wanted pages 10 and 14 printed, you would type **10,14**. If you wanted pages 10 through 14 printed, you would type **10-14**. Typing **10-** would print from page 10 through the end of the file. **-10** would print from the beginning to page 10. You can even combine these: **3,7,9,10-14,25-** would print pages 3, 7, 9, 10 through 14, and 25 to the end of the file. You can only select pages in this way if you are printing from List Files or Document on disk.

- List Files is convenient in that you can print many files at once. Press **F5**, move to the file you want, and press **P**. WordPerfect will ask you which pages to print. Follow the examples above. You can move to as many different files as you want and press **P**, adding them to the print que.

◆ Mysteries of printing from disk

Whenever you print a file from disk WordPerfect checks to see if the file was formatted with the same printer that is currently being used in Document 1 or Document 2.

If the file was not formatted with this printer, WordPerfect displays this message, "Document not formatted for current printer, Continue? Y/N?" In other words, if you print this file now, it will not be reformatted, but it will be printed with a different printer's format (which may not have the same fonts or abilities).

This shouldn't matter too much if you're working with a draft copy. WordPerfect will try to find substitute fonts (more about this later) and use whatever it thinks is best.

If you want the file to print exactly as you formatted it, you should answer **N** for no. You will then either need to select the printer used for that file and make it current, or load that file and print it from screen (which will perform the same function automatically).

◆ Checking printer status

How can you tell what WordPerfect is printing, how many copies it's printing, and where it's printing them to? With Control Printer, that's how. Press **SHIFT-F7 C** to access the Control Printer menu. This will: tell you what job number is currently printing; tell you the status of the print job (Initializing); tell you that the printer is not accepting characters; tell you the type of paper and paper tray being used; and confront you with suggestions or out and out demands: Check cable, make sure printer is turned on and tell you the current page and copy being printed.

This is also where you can control the print que and cancel print jobs.

◆ Print que and cancelling printing

"Your call will be answered in the order it was received..." I don't know about you, but I don't put a lot of stock in that kind of talk.

But with WordPerfect, you can believe it. Its sophisticated "print que" will let you line up a list of files to be printed. WordPerfect will print these in order, one after another, without any intervention from you. This is a very convenient way to churn out printed material.

This requires no great effort from you. Every time you tell WordPerfect to print, it adds that job to its list of files. If it's not currently printing anything, then there's no que, and it just prints the file. But if it is currently printing, WordPerfect adds it to the list, and gets to it in "the order received."

If you have a long list of files to print, and need something printed out quickly, put the print job on the list, and then press **SHIFT-F7 C R**. WordPerfect will ask which job you need to rush. Press the number beside the print job. WordPerfect will ask if you want to interrupt the file that is currently printing. If you do, press **R**. If you can wait until the job is done, the file will move to the second spot on the list.

◆ Jane, stop this crazy thing!

What should you do if you are printing and paper begins to fly out of the printer or, even more exciting, jam? Go to Control Printer, go directly to Control Printer, do not pass GO do not collect $200.

The simplest way to stop printing is to press **C** for cancel. WordPerfect will ask which print job you want to cancel. Type in the number and press **[ENTER]**. If you want to cancel all print jobs, press **C * Y**.

Remember, however, that most laser printers have very large buffers. You can tell WordPerfect to stop, but it may have already sent several pages to print. In this case, you will have to have it out with the printer directly.

If you are using downloadable fonts, do not turn the printer off to clear its memory, as you will have to load all the fonts again. If you are using a LaserJet II, press the **ON-LINE** button (to take the machine off-line). Then press and hold down the **Continue/Reset** for about five seconds until the word "RESET" appears on the LCD. You can then press the **ON-LINE** button again. Any fonts downloaded with * will still be in the printer's memory.

> ➜ Stop it! If you have some kind of tragic printing accident, such as a paper jam, you should just stop the print job, not cancel it. To do this, press S.

WordPerfect will stop printing, and a message will advise you to press **G** when you want to resume printing. Fix the jam (ooh, that toner's messy and sometimes even dry-cleaning is a dismal failure), and then press **G**. WordPerfect will ask you to enter the page number it should resume printing on.

Want a fast printout of your page? Set WordPerfect's Graphic Quality feature (SHIFT-F7 G) to Medium (150d dpi), Draft (75 dpi), or Do Not Print. When you're ready for a final printout, select High (300 dpi).

```
Print

     1 - Full Document
     2 - Page
     3 - Document on Disk
     4 - Control Printer
     5 - Type Through
     6 - View Document
     7 - Initialize Printer

Options

     S - Select Printer                    Zoom-o-matic
     B - Binding                           0"
     N - Number of Copies                  1
     G - Graphics Quality                  High
     T - Text Quality                      High

Graphics Quality: 1 Do Not Print; 2 Draft; 3 Medium; 4 High: 4
```

❖ Quality, not quantity, or memory for faces

Laser printing can be a slow affair. Laser printers generally print 300 dots per inch. That entails a lot of dots, a lot of information, and a lot of time. When you are proofing pages, you don't need high-quality print jobs, you need everything to work as quickly and efficiently as possible.

You may not have much memory at your disposal if you have an older LaserJet, but you still may want to print graphics. And if you have a PostScript printer, you are probably well aware that they are notoriously slow at printing bitmapped graphics. Draft printing works with all laser printers, both LaserJet and PostScript. That's when WordPerfect's Quality options come in handy. Pressing **SHIFT-F7 G** allows you to determine the sharpness of printed graphics.

- Tartar: If you choose **N** for "Do **N**ot Print," WordPerfect prints the type, but none of the graphics, pictures, or lines. This is the most expedient method when you just need to check the text. But it can be difficult to visualize what the page will look like without any graphics. Do Not Print will also suppress graphics from View Document. This can save you time if you're using bitmapped graphics, which often take a while to display on-screen. (If the graphics don't appear in View Document, and you can't figure out why, this is probably the reason.)
- Rare: If you want a rough idea of the page's appearance, select **SHIFT-F7 D** for graphics in Draft mode. Graphics will print at 75 dpi, or a quarter of 300 dpi quality. They take up a quarter of the memory, and about a quarter of the time to print. This is very useful for draft copies (in desktop publishing, it's not unusual to print many draft copies).

- Medium: Press **SHIFT-F7 G M** to reach the next plateau. This medium resolution is 150 dpi, or half the quality of 300 dpi. If you have a LaserJet + or LaserJet II with no additional memory, this will be the highest setting you can use when printing a full page of graphics.
- Well Done: High-Res graphics can be yours by pressing **SHIFT-F7 G H**. These are full 300dpi babies, sharp and slow.
- Text Quality: Although WordPerfect uses these same four settings for text, only two of them work with laser printers: Do **N**ot Print and **H**igh. If you set this to Draft or Medium, WordPerfect will still print high-quality text, because downloadable and PostScript fonts are always 300 dpi.

❖ *Extras extras, read all about it*

Two more extras we haven't covered yet are Binding Width and Number of Copies. Number of copies is basically self-explanatory. If you want three copies of a page, pages, or document, press **SHIFT-F7 N** and enter the number three.

What's not so self-explanatory is that WordPerfect will send three entire copies to the printer, in order. Laser printers can create any given number of copies from a single page of data automatically, and this expedites the printing of multiple copies. However, WordPerfect sends the entire page, pages, or document for each copy you print.

If the pages are to be bound into book or magazine format, the area between left and right pages is referred to as the "binding margin." Because books and magazines rarely lie flat, it's wise to leave extra space in this area, so the reader doesn't miss anything.

WordPerfect's binding margin feature adds extra space to the right side of left pages, and the left side of right pages. It accomplishes this by shifting the entire left page to the left, and the entire right page to the right by the amount you enter here. For example: if you had .5" margins on both sides, and entered a binding width of .25, the left page would have a left margin of .25" and a right margin of .75", while the right page would have a left margin of .75" and a right margin of .25".

This is simple enough, but you must remember to enter this number before you print, as this setting is not saved with the file. And, once you set it, this number will be in effect for whatever you print until you reset it or leave the program.

◆ Change printers and dance

What should you do if you create a file with, say, Dutch/Times and Swiss/Helvetica fonts, but decide you want to print it with Goudy Old Style and Futura?

Good question, glad you asked. You press **SHIFT-F7 S**, move the cursor to the printer that accommodates those fonts, and press **[ENTER]**. WordPerfect will do its best to match the fonts you've chosen with the new ones it has available. If the same typeface is available, it will use it. If not, it will substitute another font with similar qualities. If you select Palatino but the new printer driver only has Dutch/Times and Swiss/Helvetica, WordPerfect will choose Dutch/Times because it is a serif font. Avant Garde would become Swiss/Helv.

While WordPerfect is fairly proficient at substituting fonts, it's certainly not perfect. In one test, I took a file that had been created using Korinna on a LaserJet and printed it on a QMS PostScript printer. WordPerfect selected Zapf Chancery as a substitute for Korinna. While this might have been a proper choice technically, the serif styles and other attributes, resulted in a frankly hilarious appearance. My wife said it looked like a romance novel should look. Well, who cares if it's terribly hard to read? It looks very "gothic."

This is why it's always a good idea to go into a file and ascertain what fonts WordPerfect has chosen. You can search for font changes by typing: **F2 CONTROL-F8 F F2**.

If you're not happy with a font substituted by WordPerfect, delete the font code, and add the one you want using **CONTROL-F8 F**.

◆ Foolproof substitutions

These translations will be almost foolproof if you keep each typeface in a separate printer file. If you created it with Dutch/Times and want to print it with Korinna, simply select the printer containing Korinna fonts by typing **SHIFT-F7 S**. Since WordPerfect has nothing to choose from but Korinna it can't make a mistake in the translation; all it has to do is match the point sizes.

If you have hyphenation on, remember to press **HOME HOME [DOWN ARROW]** so that WordPerfect can re-hyphenate the file with the new font.

◆ Worst case scenario

When you save a file in WordPerfect, the name of the printer file you used is included in that file. This tells WordPerfect what printer to use the next time you edit the file.

If WordPerfect can't locate that file, it will automatically reformat the file in accordance with the last printer you used. This is replete with all the potential problems related to WordPerfect font substitution.

If the printer file has vanished for whatever reason (you deleted it accidentally, someone you hate deleted it for you, your dog ate it), the best course of action is to recreate it. That means reinstalling the printer from the WordPerfect disk. If you used Fontware, you will want to go into Cartridge and Fonts using **SHIFT-F7 S E C**, and mark them for downloading.

If you used Fontware fonts but no longer have the .ALL file, you will need to have Fontware remake all the fonts you want to use (as there is no other way to include them in the .ALL file without purchasing a third party font installation program such as SoftCraft or Glyphix).

If you merely renamed the printer file, or possess another file that utilizes the same fonts, select that printer *before* you load the file. WordPerfect will inform you that it can't find the correct printer, but will then use the current printer (containing the same fonts) and life will be just hunky-dory.

◆ High (quality) anxiety and "printing to disk"

You can print absolute, top-o-the-line typeset pages with WordPerfect. While most laser printers are 300 dpi, typesetters are generally 600, 1250, or 2450 dpi.

The typesetters that WordPerfect can drive are called "Linotronic," from the famous typesetting company, LinoType. These typesetters use the PostScript language (the same language employed in PostScript laser printers, such as the QMS 800 series, or Apple LaserWriter).

These huge machines also cost from $30,000 to $50,000, and require connections to running water, so they're probably not items you can afford or get onto a desktop.

However, you can rent time on these machines at "Desktop Publishing Service Centers." These ancillary businesses perform a variety of high-end tasks, such as Linotronic typesetting. You give them a PostScript file and about ten bucks (per page, usually), and they give you a fully typeset page of the highest quality typesetting.

I once told someone about this and he said, "I don't know if it's worth having to drag my computer across town and hook it up to their big machine." I didn't laugh in his face, I simply told him what I'm going to tell you now.

It's not done with wheelbarrows or mirrors, but with a feature called "printing to disk." Instead of having WordPerfect send information from the computer to a printer, it sends it to a file on a disk.

Once you have this file on-disk, you can forget about WordPerfect and print it wherever you want. This differs from saving a file as an ASCII or generic file; those files only contain text. These files contain all the formatting and printer codes that are necessary to print the file.

We'll assume that you'll be printing the file on a PostScript typesetter, and so you'll need to install the printer driver called "Apple LaserWriter," or "QMS PS Jet Plus /800 II/810."

You will need to select this printer before working on the file. This driver includes many different PostScript fonts that can be selected in sizes from 1 to 1199 point, in 1/10th of a point increments.

Once the PostScript printer is installed, you need to edit the configuration. To do this, press

SHIFT-F7 S

Move the cursor to the PostScript printer and press

E

Printing-to-disk is the latest craze. This allows you to print to a file instead of a printer. You can then use this file to print the file on a remote printer.

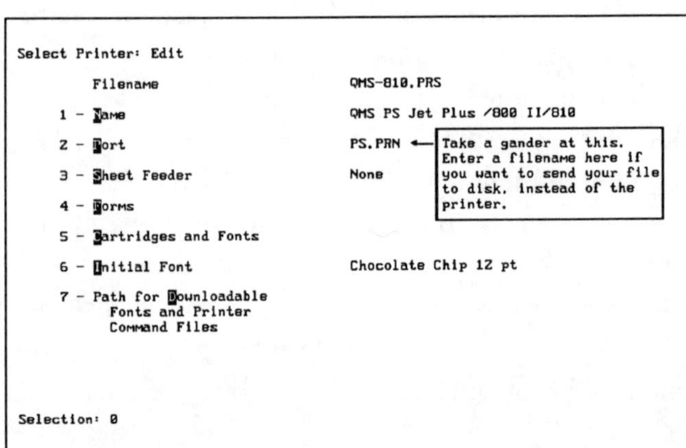

Now all you have to change is "Port." Press

P O

WordPerfect asks for the "Device or Filename." Since you want to create a file, you will type a filename here.

PS.PRN F7 F7 F7

You are now at the print menu. If you press **P** for a single page, or **F** for the entire document, WordPerfect will create a file on disk containing the exact same material it would otherwise send to a printer.

Each time you print, WP will send the output to the file you have named, overwriting any previous print job. If you have several different files to print, remember to rename the print file after you print so that WordPerfect won't erase the previous print job when it prints again.

When you want to print to a printer again, instead of to a file, press

SHIFT-F7 S E P

Press the number that corresponds to the printer port and then:

F7 F7 F7

WordPerfect will now print to a printer, rather than to a disk.

◆ Gimmie proof

All this inevitably leads to our next question: What if you want to print to a PostScript typesetter, but don't have a PostScript laser printer? How do you "proof" the pages—print them for an approximation of the document's appearance?

Simple, mi amigo. First: Save the file to disk. Then press

SHIFT-F7 S

and move the cursor to "LaserJet" printer. Press

S D

This will select the LaserJet printer, and then instruct WordPerfect to print a "document on disk."

WordPerfect will respond that "Document not formatted for current printer, Continue? Y/N?" Answer: **Y**

WordPerfect will then print the file using whatever printer is current for the document you are in. The document will not be reformatted, and all line breaks will be as they were. WordPerfect will substitute the font and, whether it's similar or not, will space all the words and letters correctly.

Proofs such as this often don't look very attractive, but, they are precise, and let you know where line and page breaks are going to occur. For most proofs, this is more than adequate.

❖ *Living color*

Color laser printers. I'd give it a year or two until color laser printers become affordable. Right now you could count the number of color laser printers on one hand. The same hand you chew on as you wonder how many convenience stores you'd have to knock over to afford one of your very own. The only color laser printer I am familiar with is the QMS ColorScript 100. If you've got $26,000 burning a hole in your pocket, you can get one fabulous machine.

This PostScript printer has all the standard PostScript typefaces, 8 megabytes of memory and a 20 megabyte hard disk for downloadable fonts. It uses a thermal transfer process that takes color from waxy sheets and puts it on the page at 300 dpi. The results are truly dazzling.

But while WordPerfect can print text in color (CONTROL-F8 C), and even display graphics in color, version 5.0 cannot print graphics in color. I'd bet money it will in version 5.1 (whenever that appears), but right now, you'll get colorful type, and black and white graphics.

◆ See spot color, see spot color run

Spot color is a term referring to the use of color on a page. This doesn't use full four-tone color, but the addition of a second color on the page. The page is run through an offset printer once for black, and then once again for an additional color. This is not a fancy technique, but it does add areas of color on a page, which can add visual impact.

Using WordPerfect's "Graphics Quality" and "Text Quality" features, you can print out two pages for each single page: one for black text, and another for the graphics in a second color.

This only requires changing the printer settings. For the text elements press

SHIFT-F7 G N

This will set the graphics to "Do Not Print." The page will include text, but not graphics.

Once you've printed the text portions of the page, press

SHIFT-F7 T N

This sets text to "Do Not Print" and only prints the graphics. When you're finished, don't forget to set the print mode for both text and graphics in a single pass. Press

SHIFT-F7 T H G H

When you take your publication to an offset print shop, keep the related pages together. Indicate the text pages are to be in black, and the graphics pages for color. Because spot color doesn't always involve high tolerances, you need to watch the alignment of the black and color; it can be a little bit off, one way or the other, so have the printer take extra care.

❖ *Tidbits*

◆ A few additional morsels to chew on

- FACING PAGES WARNING: This is a rather bizarre and confusing tip. If you want to produce facing pages with a large outside note margin, read on. If you are easily confused, skip it.

At last, a practical use for backwards thinking. In most book and magazine designs, the binding margins dictate that the inside margin be larger than the outside. But in some designs, the outside margin is wider than the inside margin. This design is employed when you want to create a publication with room for the reader to make notes, and also for certain aesthetic impact.

Usually you can't do this with WordPerfect. What you can do, however, is fool the program, as long as you don't use automatic page numbers. On the first page of the document, use this command:

SHIFT-F7 P O E

This command "forced" WordPerfect to create an odd page when you press **O**, and an even page when you press **E**. The first page is usually an odd page, but today it's going to be even.

For a design like this, you will need both a wide margin (so that the binding isn't reduced to nothing) and a wide binding margin. Press

SHIFT-F7 L M 1.5 [ENTER] 2 [ENTER] F7

to create left and right margins of 1.5" each. Now change your binding margin to .5" by pressing

SHIFT-F7 B 5 [ENTER]

This will add an additional .5" onto the binding, and remove .5" from the other margin. We forced the first page to be an even page and so, the wide margin will be on the right, or the outside edge of the page, rather than in the middle at the binding.

Of course, the problem with this system is that the page numbers are going to be incorrect. Page 1 will say page 2, because WordPerfect still thinks of it as a left hand page, while you're going to use it as a right hand page.

But as long as we've come this far, let's take one additional step. Place an added .25" margin at the bottom of each page if you are going to want a footer, or put an additional .25" at the top for a header. Now print out all the pages sans page numbers (but don't let them get out of order).

Now create a file consisting of nothing but a footer (or header). Put the pages you printed back into the printer, and run them through again to print the footer or header. Now page 1 will say page 1, instead of the Page 2 WordPerfect thought it was.

I told you it was bizarre, and sometimes the paper crinkles, so use it only as a last resort.

◆ Disk space and temporary files

Each time you print from the screen, WordPerfect creates a file on-disk that contains the information to be printed. This is so WordPerfect will know what to print if you change anything while the file is printing, or move to another file.

These files take up disk space. If you are printing a single page, they use the amount of room that the single page takes, and if you are printing an entire file, they take the space of that entire file. WordPerfect deletes these files when the print job is finished, so they don't clutter up the hard disk.

The reason I'm bothering with all this is that if you live on the hard disk borderline as I do, these files can sometimes fill the hard disk, albeit temporarily. You finish typing, try to save a file and—whoops, no disk space. Gee, there was a couple hundred K just a few minutes ago... This problem can be especially severe if you are working with floppies. WordPerfect saves them to whatever directory is current, and so if you have a hard disk and are working with a floppy, it can save them there as well.

Of course, there is one way around all this. If you print files from disk, using either List Files (F5) or Document on Disk (SHIFT-F7 D), WordPerfect won't need to create a temporary file. Printing the files from disk, especially if they are large, is the best way to avoid the horrors of a full hard disk.

◆ May I? Yes, you might

All printers have limitations, and WordPerfect is very forthright about telling you what it can and can't do with certain printers. For example, PostScript printers don't support the line-draw feature, and LaserJets can't print graphics in landscape mode.

You can see precisely what the limitations of the printer are by pressing:

SHIFT-F7 S

Move the cursor over to the name of the printer you are using (there may only be one) and press

F3

A screen chock full of information about the printer driver will appear, and you can determine which features are supported and which aren't. To exit, press

F1

Laserjet

By far the most important limitation is WordPerfect's inability to print graphics onto a LaserJet when you are printing in landscape mode (the paper is wide rather than tall).

If you have chosen a landscape page format with SHIFT-F8 P S T, you should not even attempt to place graphics in a graphics box. WordPerfect will not print graphics correctly in landscape mode. If you try, you'll get some awfully strange results. I have yet to find a way around this drawback. WordPerfect may change all this, however, so you might want to give their tech support number a call.

➻ PostScript

WordPerfect supports all the fonts built-into PostScript "Plus" printers, but only supports seven Adobe downloaded type packages. This too will pass, when the new fonts are added. WordPerfect will send you an update if you call tech support. Call me a nag, but don't forget that PostScript printers can't support the Line-Draw feature.

❖ *Organization tips*

◆ A font for all season or I left my font in San Francisco or How to organize fonts and have thin thighs in 20 minutes

When you start amassing a huge assortment of fonts, you realize that you don't want them lumped together in a single printer file. Your printer probably doesn't have enough memory, and you probably don't have enough time or patience to download them all at once. Not only that, but good design sense suggests that you should never (never say never) use too many different typefaces all at one time.

Since I have more varieties of typefaces than there are grains of sand on the beaches of Hawaii, I create a separate printer driver for each font family, or for certain combinations.

Right now I have 20 different printer drivers on my hard disk. When I go to select a printer, I have 20 to choose from, all of which were spawned from a single LaserJet driver. All but one is for the LaserJet. And each one for the LaserJet contains a single typeface, such as Korinna or Futura, or a tasteful combination of the two, such as Dutch and Swiss, or Futura and Bodoni. While my .ALL file contains all my fonts, I only use a selection of them for each printer file.

I create them by going into printer selections with **SHIFT-F7 S**. Then I move the cursor to the file I want to duplicate (in this case the LaserJet II driver), and press **C**. WordPerfect asks for a name for the new driver, and even offers a suggestion. You can use it, or, as I do, enter a new name corresponding to the fonts it will contain. The driver named KORINNA.PRS contains Korinna fonts. It's one less detail to tear your hair out over.

I name each printer file specifically, so I don't have 20 "HP LaserJet Series II" printers with no clue as to which fonts each one supports.

Before I create a document, I select the printer driver containing the fonts I want to use. I press **SHIFT-F7 S**, move the cursor over to the printer I want, and press **[ENTER]**.

I then press **I** immediately so that WordPerfect will start downloading the fonts while I am writing and editing the file. The fonts are all downloaded by the time I'm ready to print.

The other advantage to this system is that changing fonts becomes fast and accurate. Select a new printer with **SHIFT-F7 S** and all the fonts are changed.

◆ Not lots-o-disk space

If you are always low on disk space, you can download fonts from floppies. Yes, it's true—take it from a hard disk space miser like myself. The trick is that they must all fit on a single floppy disk, otherwise WordPerfect will stamp its feet and give you two choices, you can cancel the initialization (or print job), or you can start over (which isn't much help if the fonts aren't there). If you have 1.2-megabyte floppies, or the new 1.44-megabyte baby floppies, you should be able to cram quite a few fonts onto a single floppy. If you have 360K floppies, you will only be able to store smaller sizes.

◆ Subculture

If you are creating a document with multiple chapters, and multiple WordPerfect files, you should be familiar with the Subdocument feature. This feature allows you to create a "master document" that will automatically combine many different files so that page numbering will be automatic throughout the entire document. It can also create tables of contents, indexes, tables of figures, tables, boxes, etc.

The subdocument feature consists of only three commands. The first command, **ALT-F5 S**, allows you to insert a filename that WordPerfect will call a "subdocument". The second, **ALT-F5 G E**, directs WordPerfect to "expand" the document. WordPerfect looks at each subdocument code and retrieves the file it names until it has one colossal file that holds all the files. The third and final command, **ALT-F5 G O**, instructs WordPerfect to "condense the file," or to write all the files (and any changes you may have made in them) back to their original filename.

There is only one cautionary note regarding this feature. Once you've expanded a file, *do not remove any of the subdoc codes* that appear on-screen like comments. If you do, WordPerfect will not be able to condense the file correctly, and several files may be saved under one filename. Nothing will be actually lost, but the files will contain more or less text than they originally did.

❖ *Printer notes*

◆ Wait until dark (or light)

Does the output from the printer appear dark and heavy? Or too light? Most printers have a darkness control, and this can make a world of difference in the way type appears.

With the LaserJet II (or any Canon-based printer), the lightness control is *inside* the top of the printer. Press the big button on the top of the printer and the top will pop up. (If you're cheap, it's a great way to entertain the kids.) If you look straight down into the printer, the Light/Dark control (usually a green wheel) is located in the left front corner. This wheel will probably be set at 5, for medium. A setting of 9 is very light, and 1 is very dark.

Most typesetting fonts look best at 7 or 9, because the lightness makes them appear sharper. On the other hand, jagged edges are more obvious when the type is sharper. Extra toner can be used by setting the printer to 3 or 1. This toner melts around the edges, filling in the jagged edges. However, it also makes the type look heavier, and on typefaces with a small x-height (the height of a lower case "x"), the insides of a letter such as "e" can get filled in.

In general, you should set the printer to medium if you are going to use the laser printer pages as originals. Setting the printer to light also offers an additional plus: it saves toner and prolongs the life of the printer cartridge. The only negative is that blacks will not be as dark and solid; this is fine for reproduction, but may be inadequate for originals.

"Camera ready" pages (for photocopying or offset printing), should print at a light setting, at 7 or possibly 9. The lighter black should not give you any problem and should print as solid, dark black.

◆ Toner hell

If you use LaserJet II, or any other printer based on a Canon engine, you know how wonderfully simple these printers are to maintain. The toner, drum, and most of the moving parts are in a single enclosed cartridge. There's never any toner mess (unless you let the piece of tape that covers the toner stick to you), and it's an efficient and pleasant system.

But if you have a printer based on the Ricoh engine (Ricoh, IBM, TI, Destiny, Acer), then you know the horrors of spreading toner all over the place.

This is just a helpful hint about what to do if you get toner on yourself.

NEVER WASH IT OFF WITH HOT WATER!!!!!

Since toner is designed to melt (that's how a laser printer works; it melts the toner onto the paper, not unlike a Tuna Melt but not as tasty), it will also melt onto your hands.

Use cold water and soap. If it gets on your clothes, chances are, it's there to stay—but wash them in cold water anyway. Desktop publishing may be a lot of things but it should not be dirty.

15

Keys to success

Macros/Soft Keyboard

No, *Macros* are not a new Chef Boy-ar-dee product comprised of pasta in o-shapes. Nor are they the macaroni equivalent of McNuggets, and whatever you do, don't confuse them with macrame. And soft keyboards are not designed by Claes Oldenberg (the famous soft sculpture artist), are not squishy, have nothing to do with frozen yogurt, and of course, are not *hard*ware at all.

Macros allow you to do a lot by doing a little. By just pressing one key you can type your entire address, or change fonts, or search and replace countless variables in a single bound.

I've already covered a wide variety of applications in which macros can be used. Review those chapters for information about 1-2-3, converting underlines to italics, converting underlines to styles, dashes, fonts, graphics, indents, lines, paragraph numbering, quotation marks, spreadsheets, or styles.

This chapter will offer some helpful macro tips (to prevent a macro from wreaking havoc with a file), and will also cover some useful but little-known macros included with WordPerfect. In addition, we'll throw in some miscellaneous macros, and fill you in on WordPerfect's "Soft keyboard" feature (this allows you to modify the function of any key on the keyboard).

❖ *Basics*

Recording macros is a breeze. Just press

CONTROL-F10

WordPerfect will ask for a name by saying "Define Macro." A name can be any eight letters, or **ALT** and any one letter (letters only, no punctuation, numbers, or function keys). WordPerfect will then ask you to type a description of the macro you want to record. You can type a line of text, or just press return.

From then on WordPerfect will record whatever you type and each and every command.

To save the macro, press

CONTROL-F10

There are two ways to playback the macro. If you typed ALT and a letter, just press ALT and that letter, and the macro will run. If you typed a name for the macro, press

ALT-F10

and then type that name.

Normally, you won't see anything while a macro is running, but while recording a macro you can type **CONTROL-PgUp D Y** and WordPerfect will display this macro. It's a kick to watch WordPerfect working by itself, but remember that macros run much slower with display on. Don't turn this feature on if you're in a rush, or recording a complex macro. If you want WordPerfect to pause so that you will be able to type, press

CONTROL-PgUp P

Now the macro will stop whenever it encounters this pause, and will restart when the **[ENTER]** key is pressed.

If you never do any more than this, macros can save you a lot of time and tedium. If you never want to do any more than this, skip to "Undocumented Boon Again."

```
Macro: Edit

      File            UNDZITAL.WPM

  1 - Description     WP underline to WP italics, excitement personified

  2 - Action

    {IF}{STATE}&512~
    {Reveal Codes}{ELSE}{END IF}{DISPLAY OFF}{Search}{Underline}{Search}
    {Block}{Search}{Underline}{Underline}{Left}{Backspace}{Search}{Font}
    ai{Backspace}n{Backspace}y{Macro}undZital{Enter}

Selection: 0
```

Recording macros is easy, but editing them requires technical understanding.

◆ Macro editing (for the macro-nically inclined)

If you're in an adventurous mood, you can now edit this macro. To do this, type: **CONTROL-F10** and type the name of a previously recorded macro (or press ALT and a letter). WordPerfect will point out that "BLAHBLAH.WPM" is already defined (of course, it will substitute whatever name you entered for Blahblah). You now have two alternatives, you can **R**eplace the macro (record a new one from scratch) or you can **E**dit the macro.

To edit the macro, press **E**

WordPerfect displays the macro in a window, and presents you with two choices. You can **D**escribe the macro, or you can change the **A**ction of the macro. Let's try the latter. Press **A**

You're now deep in the bowels of the macro. You can change whatever you like, and even add new commands or text. You can also mess something up if you're not careful. If you do change something accidentally, press **F1 Y**.

When editing a macro, commands appear in bold, surrounded by curly brackets like this: **{Search}** refers to the F2 key. Text that you typed (including letters such as Y and N in response to prompts from WordPerfect) appears as normal. Spaces appear as little dots.

You can move around the macro using normal cursor keys. Function keys, however, will not perform their usual function, and will place a code in the macro instead.

Inserting cursor movements: You will need to change modes if you want to add a cursor movement code, such keystrokes as ESC, F1, F7 or [ENTER]. Pressing **CONTROL-F10** again will put you in code mode. Now any key you press will insert its code into the macro. You can't leave the macro by pressing F1, F7, and ESC as you normally would. In addition, the cursor keys will place cursor movement codes in the file, but will not move you through the macro.

To get out of this mode, press **CONTROL-F10** again.

◆ Special macro commands

WordPerfect's macros are actually an entire programming language. Wait, don't run screaming from the room; you don't have to learn how to program them (although you can if you're so inclined). These commands tell WordPerfect whether reveal codes is on or off; they can also pause the macro, display messages on the screen, make the computer beep, wait for a specific amount of time. You name it, a macro can do it (if you can figure out how).

You access these commands by pressing **CONTROL-PgUp**. A small window pops up from the top right-hand corner of the macro window. You can either use the cursor to scroll down the list, or press the first letter of the command to jump to that command. To leave this window, select a command and press **[ENTER]**, or press **[ESC]**.

We're going to use a few of these commands to create fail-safe macros later on, but fear not, we're not going to dwell on the subject for long.

Get me out of here: to leave the macro editor, press

F7

if you want to save the macro, or

F1

if you want to abandon any changes you may have made.

◆ Undocumented boon again

If you read Chapter 10, this is all old hat. But because it's not covered in the manual, and is essential for creating macros that call styles, I'm repeating myself (for your benefit).

When you create macros that call styles, don't press ALT-F8 and move the cursor to the style you want. If you do, the macros will no longer work when you add or delete styles, because they rely on cursor movements to select the correct style. There will be more, or fewer styles, and the cursor may move to the wrong style.

WordPerfect includes a feature to solve this problem, but WordPerfect's manual neglects to mention it.

The feature is none other than our friend "name search," a feature found in almost every list WordPerfect presents. List Files, Base Font, all of these have N on the menu. You press it, type the name you are searching for, and WordPerfect jumps to the name that matches what you type. Style offers this feature as well, although it's not on the menu (possibly because there's no room for it).

Still, even if the authors of the manual at WordPerfect didn't think it was important enough to acknowledge, *we* know it's important, don't we? In fact, it's indispensable when you are creating macros.

Whenever you create a macro that uses a style, use the Name Search feature instead of moving the cursor to the style you want. Then, no matter how many styles you add or delete, the macro will still call the style you want.

◆ Big Tip #2

Some macros will run differently, depending on whether Reveal Codes is on or off. When you are deleting codes, WordPerfect will ask if Reveal Codes is off, but will not ask if it's on.

This can lead to problems if you create macros where you want to search for one code and replace it with another. If you forget to turn it off, the search and replace will not function, and you'll have a lot of extra characters in the file. This messes up spelling and garners complaints from sticklers who believe that "the" should be not spelled "they." These same people know that even WordPerfect's wonderful spell check program can't find errors like this (because "they" is a word, too).

There are two solutions to this dilemma, and each involves editing the macro once you've recorded it. It's no great thrill entering complex macro codes in each of your files, and so we're going to use a macro that comes with WordPerfect, hidden deep inside a soft keyboard. (Oh boy, we get to do it all at once. Isn't this going to be fun? Say yes, who knows, it might be. You'll never know unless you try.)

First we'll get the WordPerfect macro, then record another macro that converts underlines into italics (without the need for a style), and finally combine the two together into a fail-safe macro.

OK, time for some macro merriment. Get out the "Conversion" disk and copy a file called "Macros.wpk" to your WordPerfect directory. If at any time during this procedure you don't understand what I'm doing, play along anyway. No one but you will know that you're hopelessly lost and confused.

Now we're going to edit this keyboard file and save one of the entries as a macro. Press

SHIFT-F1 K

Move the cursor to "Macros" and press

E

(If you don't see Macros listed, you may not have copied the file correctly, or may have neglected to tell WordPerfect where to look for keyboard and macro files. To tell WordPerfect where to look, press **ESC L K** and type the directory where you want macros and keyboard files to reside.)

You're now presented with a long list of keys on the left, and definitions on the right. The cursor should be on "ALT-E," and conveniently, this is what we want. Press

S

to save this as a Macro. WordPerfect will ask you to "Define Macro," which is its own round about way of asking for a filename. Why it doesn't just come out and ask for a filename is not ours to ponder. In that we're going to use this macro to save us from ourselves (for those times when we forget to turn Reveal Codes off), let's call it ALT-S for "Safety." Press

ALT-S [ENTER]

We delve into all this keyboard jazz later in the chapter, but for now, let's get outta here. (A prime tidbit of information: 80% of all Saturday morning cartoon shows contain the line "Let's get outta here!!!" I should know. I wrote for a couple. Other popular lines (in descending order) include, "Let's Go!!!" "(terrified) Whadda we do now!?!" "I've got an idea!!!" "Not again!!!" "Hold it right there!!!" "Yaaaaaooooowwwwwww!!!" "I've heard of ____, but this is ridiculous!!!" and my personal favorite, "And then the world will be mine!!!" Notice how all sentences must end in exclamation marks, preferably three of them. I hope you found this aside entertaining, educational, and at least as informative as the "Cheers and Jeers" section in *TV Guide*.

Let's get outta here! Press

F1 Y F1 F1

Now you have this macro called ALTS.WPM. All WordPerfect macros end in .WPM, which stands for "WordPerfect Macro" (and not for "Words Per Minute," or "Wealthy Pinhead Movement," as previously and erroneously reported in the *National Enquirer.*) To run this ALT-key macro, all you need to do is press ALT-S.

This macro will turn Reveal Codes off automatically. The next time you record a macro, press **ALT-S** after you've named and described it. That will insure that reveal codes will never be a problem in your macros again.

Bear with me as we create a macro to turn all underlines into italics.

◆ Underline to italics macro

Underlines become Italics right before your very eyes

If you already have a document with underlines, and you want to typeset these as italics, you can search and replace underline codes and replace them with italic codes. It's easy, but not very straightforward. Don't confuse this with a similar example in Chapter 10, which creates a style to let you easily change underlines to italics, or the macro in the same example which lets you use that style in a single keystroke.

Okay, I admit it. I've got this thing for turning underlines into italics, what can I say? But it is one of those items you may find yourself using on a daily basis. You're right, I did state earlier that "WordPerfect automatically prints underlines as italics." But it only does that when italics are not available (and even then it may get confused and uses another font's italics instead of underlining the current font). Are you *happy* now?

The major advantage of all this is that you only have to do it once, one single underline to one single italic. After that, the macro will do it all for you, over and over again, without getting crabby. It will automatically run through an entire file and change all underlines into italics.

Are we ready? Good. Since you now know the basics for creating a macro, I'm going to give you all these keystrokes in one big lump (and if you skip ahead now, you won't be hurting anyone but yourself).

This macro works by searching for an underline, turning block on, searching for the closing underline (which extends the block to cover the entire underlined area), applying italics, and then deleting the underline. The macro then calls itself, searches for the next underline, and keeps calling itself until it can no longer find another underline. Gee, wouldn't this be painfully dull if you had to do it by hand? Remember, as in all macro's, don't press the **[ENTER]** key unless you see the word **[ENTER]**. And don't put in any spaces, except where you see a ^. And *make sure reveal codes is* OFF. Okay, here goes.

CONTROL-F10 UND2ITAL

[ENTER]turn ^ underlines ^ to ^ italics[ENTER]

CONTROL-PgUp D Y ALT-S F2 F8 F2

ALT-F4 F2 F8 F8 [LEFT ARROW][BACKSPACE] F2

CONTROL-F8 A I [BACKSPACE] N [BACKSPACE] Y

ALT-F10 UND2ITAL [ENTER]

CONTROL-F10

Okay, you now have a macro that will turn underlines into italics. Because you pressed ALT-S (a macro we had created to turn Reveal Codes off), you don't have to worry about whether Reveal Codes is on or off.

Now let's run this macro. You should really test it on a file you've already saved, so that if for some reason it doesn't work, you won't lose anything important.

First, turn reveal codes on, to verify that it works. Next, find a file with lots of underlines, or put some underlines in your file. Now start the macro by pressing

ALT-F10 UND2ITAL [ENTER]

You can now see every step the macro makes, because we turned display on when we were recording it. Unfortunately, this really slows it down. If you get tired of watching the macro do its thing, rerecord the macro but do not type **CONTROL-PgUp D Y.** (This was the command that we used to turn display on). The default is "display off," so unless you press **CONTROL-PgUp D Y,** WordPerfect will not show a macro as it is running.

◆ A more technical way to do the same thing

If you are going to utilize this macro on long files, you might want a quicker (albeit more technical) method to convert underlines into italics. When WordPerfect has to call the other macro, it takes extra time whenever the macro is run. This procedure uses simplified macro programming features to enable it to run faster. Create a macro as usual, and then go in to edit it. Add the following commands

{IF}{STATE}&512~

{Reveal Codes}{ELSE}{END IF}

These commands instruct WordPerfect to check if Reveal Codes is on. If it is, WordPerfect will turn it off; if it's off, WordPerfect will leave it off.

◆ True typographic quotation marks

Some people are real sticklers about typographic quote marks. I'm not one of them, although I do feel they add an extra touch that takes laser printing one step closer into the realm of typesetting.

Don't let the apparent complexity of this macro fool you. It took all of two minutes to create, and you can use it over and over and over until you become sick and tired of word processing in general and move to a small island in the South Pacific to paint naked natives.

But who wants to enter CONTROL-V 4,32 [ENTER] by hand whenever they want a quote (on a PostScript printer). And who wants to enter " or " instead of " (when they have LaserJets). Meanwhile, people read your rough draft in Courier and keep asking, "What are those strange marks?" until you want to throttle them, scream, or force-feed them lots of diuretics.

This is a relatively simple macro that searches for the first quote mark and turns it into a ", and then replaces the next " with a." Unlike other macros, this method will not mess up a file if you happen to have a mismatched set of quotes.

The macro works by finding all the quote marks preceded by a space, a tab, indent, double indent, or a hard return. These would be the opening quote marks. Once it has searched and replaced through your file three times, it then converts all other quotes into closing quote marks.

Of course, if you want to use " for inches, then you'll have to enter them as some other code in your document (perhaps a ~), and then replace them with regular inch marks.

I'm going to present two variations of this macro. The first one is for LaserJet users, and uses ' ' ' ' for double quotes. I found this to be so effective that no one has even noticed these quotes (although a few people thought there was too much space between them).

For PostScript users, the macro will replace " marks with **CONTROL-V 4,32** for authentic opening quotes “, and **CONTROL-V 4,31** for authentic closing quotes”. These will not appear as quote marks on-screen, but as little black boxes. It's a bit disconcerting initially to see text with all these bullet-like characters, but you get used to it. If you can't stand to see them on-screen, use the LaserJet method; the printout is almost identical, although the real quote marks are closer together.

A word of warning. This macro won't find a quote mark directly preceded by a code, and so if you ever have a bold, italic, underline, or other WordPerfect code before a quote mark, you should search and replace it manually. Of course, underlining or italicizing text in quotes can be redundant, but you need to execute these changes before running this macro.

I've tested this macro on a number of files and they all performed perfectly, but none of my quote marks were preceded by a WordPerfect code. You can't always remember if you've placed a code before a quote mark, but it's the one obstacle that this macro can't overcome. Once you've run this macro, any quote mark that didn't fit into the opening quote mold (preceded by a space, tab, indent, double indent, or hard return) becomes a closing quote, and they can be hard to find.

Always save your file before running a macro like this. Then if there is some kind of problem, you can exit the current file without saving, and retrieve it from disk.

LASERJET QUOTE MACRO: (Don't press the space bar unless you see ^)

CONTROL-F10 QUOTE [ENTER] Turn ^ " ^ marks ^ into ^ real ^ quotes [ENTER]

[HOME][HOME][UP-ARROW] ALT-F2 N ^ " F2 ^ “F2

[HOME][HOME][UP-ARROW] ALT-F2 N [TAB]" F2 [TAB]“F2

[HOME][HOME][UP-ARROW] ALT-F2 N [ENTER]" F2 [ENTER]“F2

[HOME][HOME][UP-ARROW] ALT-F2 N F4" F2 F4“F2

[HOME][HOME][UP-ARROW] ALT-F2 N SHIFT-F4" F2 SHIFT-F4"F2

[HOME][HOME][UP-ARROW] ALT-F2 N " F2 "F2

POSTSCRIPT QUOTE MACRO: (Don't press the space bar unless you see ^)

CONTROL-F10 QUOTE [ENTER]

Turn ^"^ marks ^ into ^ real ^ quotes [ENTER]

[HOME][HOME][UP-ARROW] ALT-F2 N ^" F2 ^ CONTROL-V 4,32 [ENTER] F2

[HOME][HOME][UP-ARROW] ALT-F2 N [TAB]" F2 [TAB] CONTROL-V 4,32 [ENTER] F2

[HOME][HOME][UP-ARROW] ALT-F2 N [ENTER]" F2 [ENTER] CONTROL-V 4,32 [ENTER] F2

[HOME][HOME][UP-ARROW] ALT-F2 N F4" F2 F4 CONTROL-V 4,32 [ENTER] F2

[HOME][HOME][UP-ARROW] ALT-F2 N SHIFT-F4" F2 SHIFT-F4 CONTROL-V 4,32 F2

[HOME][HOME][UP-ARROW] ALT-F2 N " F2 CONTROL-V 4,31 [ENTER] F2

❖ *Outlines (for anyone who writes)*

Most of the tips in this book have been meant for people who want to desktop publish, this one is meant for people who want (or have to) write.

As I've learned (the hard way), the real key to writing is organization. It's almost impossible (or at least extremely difficult) to write a long and involved manuscript, be it a novel or a manual, without some sort of outline.

I wish that some clever teacher in school had come up with a way to make outlining fun. I hated it and everyone I knew hated it. The only thing worse was sentence diagramming.

If you already use outlines, you'll appreciate this tip. If you don't, try to get the hang of them, because like them or not, they're a tremendous help. My outline for this book was 30 pages long. I didn't sit down and write a 30 page outline, but every time I had an idea of any kind (an occurrence that merits a celebration around here, complete with chocolate chip cookies), I would write it down in the outline, in the proper chapter, or at least in what seemed like the proper chapter at the time.

When I actually sat down to write this book (which I did in about 90 days—90 very long days), I reviewed the outline and expanded upon my ideas. I wouldn't have been able to remember them otherwise, and this book would have been a mere pamphlet.

◆ Automatic paragraph numbering & non-printing comments

Two of WordPerfect's most useful tools for outlining are automatic paragraph numbering, and non-printing comments. All of these can be enhanced with macros (or at least that's the excuse I'm going to use for addressing them here).

Let's start with automatic paragraph numbering. **SHIFT-F5 P [ENTER]** inserts an automatic paragraph number. Now you'll never have to manually renumber your lists after you make changes (which you always do).

Once you put one of these little babies into a file, you'll see a number on-screen that resembles any other number. But when you remove one of these numbers, all the rest of them renumber themselves. But wait, there's more. These numbers also change their format, depending on what tab stop (or level) they're on. When you tab one in, or backspace one out, they change format, and the rest of the list renumbers. Chalk another one up for outlines.

WordPerfect gives you four standard numbering methods (Paragraph, Outline, Legal, and Bullets), and create one of your own design called "user-defined."

But that's not good enough for me, and it shouldn't be good enough for you either. We're but a mere step away from the 1990's. We want more automation! More, more, more! (Enough already.)

In any event, a simple macro will insert a number and indent the text. Now the numbers are "outdented" and the outline is easier to read. Because I use this macro a lot, I've made it an **ALT-KEY** macro, and called it ALT-P for paragraph number. Here it is. Press

CONTROL-F10 ALT-P automatic paragraph numbering [ENTER]

SHIFT-F5 P [ENTER] F4 CONTROL-F10

If you don't love this macro, you should have your head examined, or you should forget about it and get on with the rest of your life; one or the other.

◆ Fill in the blanks or connect the dots

My next little tip for the writer, would-be writer, or has-been writer involves WordPerfect's non-printing comments. These appear on the screen but not on the page. In other words, they melt in your mouth, not on your keyboard.

Once you've created this divine outline, you're going to use it as a... um... outline. But not just an ordinary run-o-the-mill outline, but a super outline! (How's that for hype?) This outline will appear on-screen, but not print. Each heading of the outline will appear in glorious color (if you have a color monitor), or in glorious black and white (if you have a black and white monitor). No one will ever know that you needed assistance each and every step of the way; they'll just know that what you wrote seems, um... not terrible, not bad at all, pretty good, well, better than they expected.

This macro will take each entry in an outline and turn it into a comment, right before your awestruck little eyes. It's almost too wonderful to believe (unless you've seen Microsoft Word's outliner, which doesn't require this type of maneuvering to be effective. WordPerfect's outlining will hopefully be better the next time around. Who said that?)

Because this macro is fun to watch, we're going to turn display on. Well, not just because it's fun. This macro can't determine when it reaches the end of the outline, and it keeps trying to turn nothing into a comment. Soon WordPerfect will start beeping at you about every second, and will continue to do so until the cows come home. To stop this electronic tantrum, press **F1**.

Are we ready?

CONTROL-F10 OUT2COMM Turn outline into comments [ENTER]

ALT-F4 [ENTER] CONTROL-F5 Y [ENTER]

ALT-F10 OUT2COMM [ENTER] CONTROL-F10

Now all you need to do is look at the comment, type anything you can think of on the subject, and then press the **[DOWN ARROW]** key so you are under the next comment.

Now you see them, now you don't department: If you get sick of seeing the comments, you can set WordPerfect so they won't appear on-screen, but will still be in the file. Press **SHIFT-F1 D D N F7**. When you want to see them again, type **SHIFT-F1 D D Y F7**. Better yet, create two macros: one called *No Comment* (the type of macro the Reagan administration used so frequently), and another called *Comment*. *No Comment* tells WordPerfect not to show comments, while *Comments* tells it to go right ahead and show them.

NO COMMENT MACRO:

CONTROL-F10 NOCOMMENT [ENTER] Turn off comments [ENTER]

SHIFT-F1 D D N F7

COMMENT MACRO:

CONTROL-F10 COMMENT [ENTER] Show comments [ENTER]

SHIFT-F1 D D Y F7

◆ Revision markers or the Mrs. Samuel Clemons macro

Comments can also be used as a revision marker. Most documents require a seemingly endless progression of minor changes, and these markers will indicate who changed what and when. You can use this macro anywhere; it doesn't have be on a blank line. WordPerfect will insert this comment in the middle of a sentence, between two letters, anywhere you want.

If you want to be doubly sure about what has changed, use one of these markers at the beginning of the revised text, and another at the end. Then the revised text will be surrounded by revision markers.

The comment looks like this:

↓May 23, 1989 - 2:06pm - (Your Initials Here)↓

While you cannot search for text that is inside a comment, you can search for comments, and in this way move quickly from one revision to another.

Once again, this macro seems complicated, but you'll only need to type it once. WordPerfect won't allow you to use its automatic date feature within a comment, and so the macro will have to do all the text, block it, and then turn it into a comment.

I call this macro ALT-C for comment. I've made it an ALT-macro because I use it frequently. Here's the macro to create the revision marker. **ALT-25** means that you should hold down the ALT-key and press 25 on the keypad. When you see (Your initials here), type your own initials:

CONTROL-F10 ALT-C Revision marker [ENTER]

ALT-25 SHIFT-F5 F CONTROL-END 3 1, 4 - 8:90 [ENTER]

T (Your initials here) ALT-F4 SHIFT-F2 ALT-25 SHIFT-F2

SHIFT-F2 SHIFT-F2 [LEFT ARROW] CONTROL-F5 Y

❖ *On-screen calculator*

While WordPerfect's math feature is powerful, it isn't always convenient. There is an on-screen calculator that comes with WordPerfect though, and it's great for handling those all-important desktop publishing measurement calculations.

The only drawback to this clever calculator is that it uses whole numbers only, no decimals. An easy way around this is to multiply everything by 100 before you enter it. (Oh no! Now he's asking me to do math to enable the computer to do math. Will this madness never cease? *No, the madness will never cease; get used to it.*)

This is easier than it sounds if you remember elementary school math. All you have to do is move the decimal two places to the right. Here's an example: 1.47 becomes 147, .24 becomes 24, 10.5 becomes 1050. Basically, just leave out the decimal point. That's not so tough, is it?

I find this on-screen calculator much more convenient than having to look all over my desk for my pocket calculator only to find that the batteries are dead. You might too. Of course, this is a very long, complex, and involved macro, but you don't have to type it in. Just save it as a macro from the WordPerfect keyboard file called Macros.WPK on the Conversion disk. Here's how to do it.

Press

SHIFT-F1 K

Move the cursor to "Macros"

E

Move the cursor to CTRL-C

S CALC [ENTER] F1 y F1 F1

Now, let's try the calculator. Press

ALT-F10 CALC [ENTER]

The calculator should appear on the left side of the screen. Use it as you would a regular calculator. If you want to insert the total into the text, press the **SPACE BAR**. This will also remove the calculator from the screen. Press **C** when you want to clear the totals, and **F1** or **F7** will get you out of it.

◆ Temporary fonts

Another simple-to-use (but extremely complicated to create) macro lets you insert a "temporary" font. When you are in block mode, this macro will assign any new font you choose to the block, then return to the base font. When not in block mode, this macro inserts two font codes: the new font you've selected, followed by the base font. This allows you to temporarily switch to a new font, and then return to the base font.

An important note: this macro does not involve styles. Therefore, if you should change base fonts, the "base font" placed in the text by this temporary macro will still be the previous base font. If you plan on making many changes, it's always wise to use styles, even if the style contains nothing more than a single font change. That way, the Style Off code will always contain the current base font.

As with the Calc macro, you save this macro using the WordPerfect keyboard file called Macros.WPK on the Conversion disk.

SHIFT-F1 K

Move the cursor to "Macros"

E

Move the cursor to CTRL-F8

S ALT-F [ENTER] F1 y F1 F1

◆ **Let's try it out. Press**

ALT-F

Notice that a new item has been added to the menu. To use it, press **T**. This will operate just like the regular font key, except that instead of just entering one code, this macro will insert two: the font you've just chosen, followed by the current base font.

I don't recommend using this macro in your soft keyboard file, as it appears in Macros.wpk, because it will then act as a substitute for your normal CONTROL-F8 key. As a result, you will be unable to search for fonts, and will have difficulty selecting fonts within other macros, and just generally complicate your life.

❖ *The hard facts about the soft keyboard*

WordPerfect's soft keyboard feature is tremendously powerful. It's akin to attaching macros to any key on the keyboard. Well, almost any key. You can't redefine the following by themselves: the 5 on the number pad, Shift, Control, ALT, Caps lock, Num Lock, Scroll Lock, or Sys Req. This Sys Req key is only included on your keyboard if you have an AT. (I still lie awake nights trying to decide if this key has any practical benefit).

Soft keyboards let you customize WordPerfect in any way you like. I grew up with WordStar, and so I use the WordStar Control-key cursor movement keys. I also use Control-B for block, Control-W for the thesaurus, and Control-L for search (or look). I use other WordStar commands as well, such as Control-G for delete character, Control-T for delete word, and Control-Y for delete to the end of the line.

I'm not suggesting that you should set up your keyboard in this manner. Still, because these commands are so firmly entrenched in my mind after years of use, and because I'm a touch typist, I find these faster and easier to work with than WordPerfect's usual commands.

I also carry this .WPK file with me for those times when I might be working with another person's WordPerfect. That way I can still use my own commands, even on someone else's computer. All I have to do is copy my keyboard file into their WordPerfect directory, select it using **SHIFT-F1 K**, move the cursor to my keyboard file, and then press S.

I'm going to show you how to create a new keyboard for yourself, and then offer you a couple of keyboard entries I find useful for desktop publishing.

◆ Keyboard definitions

Start by pressing

SHIFT-F1 K C

WordPerfect will ask for a filename. Why not be terribly unoriginal, type in your own initials as a filename, and press

[ENTER]

You will now see a screen which is totally blank except for a menu running along the bottom. You can create a keyboard definition by pressing **C** and then the key you want to redefine. If you have already created macros and want one or more of them to become a new definition for any key, press **R**, the key you want to redefine, and then type the name of the macro. The macro will now be copied into the keyboard file.

First, let's create a definition from scratch. For this example, we're going to modify F8 so that it will insert a code for italics rather than underlines. If you often use italics, this is much more efficient than typing **CONTROL-F8 A I**.

```
Keyboard: Edit

  Name: GUMBALL

  Key                 Description                                  Macro

  Alt-I               italics                                         11
  Alt-O               Entire Gettysburg Address                       17
  Alt-F               "Temporary" Font addition to menu               15
  Alt-J               Change "Love Boat" Scrpt to MurderSheWrote      18
  Alt-X               Start Coffee Maker                              14
  Alt-N               Clear trashy novel from screen                  16
  Alt-M               Show WPDPiS file instead                        13
  Ctrl-Num *          Standard Calvin & Hobbes Fan Letter
  Ctrl-PgUp           Print "Nuke Mary Hart" motto                    10
  Ctrl-A              word left
  Ctrl-J              Joke Generator
  Ctrl-C              page down
  Ctrl-D              Right
  Ctrl-E              up
  Ctrl-F              word right
  Ctrl-G              delete
  Ctrl-H              screen left                                    4

Key: 1 Edit: 2 Delete: 3 Move: 4 Create:  Macro: 5 Save: 6 Retrieve: 1
```

The Soft Keyboard feature allows you to make any key on the keyboard do whatever you want.

Now we're going to give a short description of what the key will do, and then change that function. Follow me by pressing

C F8 D Italics [ENTER] A

Notice that it says {Underline}. We're going to change that function. Press

[DEL] CONTROL-F8 A I F7 F7

Once you save and select this keyboard, pressing **F8** will give you italics instead of underlines. If you use underlines and italics equally, you might want to put italics onto CONTROL-I. Follow the same procedure as you did using F8, except now when WordPerfect asks which key to define, you press CONTROL-I. Here it is; press

C CONTROL-I D Italics [ENTER]

A [DEL] CONTROL-F8 A I F7 F7

Inserting cursor movements: if you want to add a cursor movement code, such as ESC, F1, F7, or [ENTER] to a keyboard definition, you need to change modes. Pressing **CONTROL-F10** again will put you in code mode. Any key you press now will insert its code into the macro. F1, F7, and ESC will not get you out of the macro as they normally would, and the cursor keys will place cursor movement codes in the file, rather than move you through this macro.

To get out of this mode, press **CONTROL-F10** again.

Here's another keyboard definition. This one calls the Und/Ital style that you learned how to make in Chapter 10. You could have F8 call this style, but since we've done F8 to death, let's make this ALT-U.

C ALT-U D Underline/Italic Style [ENTER]

A [DEL] ALT-F8 N UND [ENTER] O F7 F7

When you're satisfied with all your keyboard definitions, press

F7

to save the keyboard file. Check to see if the cursor is in the keyboard name you just created, and press

S

to select that keyboard. You can work with as many keyboard files as you want, and simply switch between them. If you want to return to the original WordPerfect keyboard quickly, press

SHIFT-F1 K 0 F7

◆ A little something for ex-WordStar aficionados only

Once a word processing junkie, always a word processing junkie. I'm an ex-WordStar addict, but now I get my fix with the hard stuff—WordPerfect. Even so, I'm still addicted to how you can move the cursor in WordStar without taking your hands off the typing area and moving them to the cursor pad.

If you're a touch typist, you will find the WordStar cursor diamond is the absolute greatest way to move the cursor. It's not mneumonic, but it does make sense once you study the arrangement of the keys on the keyboard.

It was invented because at one time not all computers had cursor keys. What a wacky computer world we once lived in (as if we still don't). The only way this tip relates to desktop publishing is that it can make your life easier, and that's what desktop publishing is supposed to do to.

Here (in rapid succession so that we don't bore those people who wouldn't touch WordStar with a 10 foot keyboard) is the cursor diamond.

Create or edit the keyboard of your choice. Note: [-] is the WordPerfect Screen Up key, [+] is the WordPerfect Screen Down key. Type the following

C CONTROL-**E** D UP [ENTER] A [DEL] CONTROL-F10 [UP ARROW] CONTROL-F10 F7 F7

C CONTROL-**X** D DOWN [ENTER] A [DEL] CONTROL-F10 [DOWN ARROW] CONTROL-F10 F7 F7

C CONTROL-**S** D LEFT [ENTER] A [DEL] CONTROL-F10 [LEFT ARROW] CONTROL-F10 F7 F7

C CONTROL-**D** D RIGHT [ENTER] A [DEL] CONTROL-F10 [RIGHT ARROW] CONTROL-F10 F7 F7

C CONTROL-**C** D DOWN SCREEN [ENTER] A [DEL] CONTROL-F10 [+] CONTROL-F10 F7 F7

C CONTROL-**R** D UP SCREEN [ENTER] A [DEL] CONTROL-F10 [-] CONTROL-F10 F7 F7

C CONTROL-**F** D WORD RIGHT [ENTER] A [DEL] CONTROL-F10 CONTROL-[RIGHT ARROW] CONTROL-F10 F7 F7

C CONTROL-**A** D WORD LEFT [ENTER] A [DEL] CONTROL-F10 CONTROL-[LEFT ARROW] CONTROL-F10 F7 F7

16

1-2-3 Publishing

Uno, dos, tres, WordPerfecto cinco

Lotus 1-2-3 is unequivocally the single most popular piece of PC software in the world. WordPerfect is the most popular word processing software in the world. So it's natural to assume that the two are able to work together. Sure they do, but like Ethel Merman and Ernest Borgnine, or Sylvester Stallone and Brigitte Nielson: so badly that most people give up after a brief time.

WordPerfect can't read 1-2-3 worksheets directly, and 1-2-3 print files are incompatible with proportional fonts. WordPerfect can read 1-2-3 graphs, but these are neither very attractive or interesting, two of the primary reasons why you'd use graphs.

Odds are good that if you need to create any kind of financial report, you will be using 1-2-3 with WordPerfect. It's also a fair bet that you'll run into some rather frustrating situations trying to get the two to work together (especially when you start using proportional fonts for desktop publishing).

What's a person to do? Problems in transferring data from one program to another are easily avoided if you know what they are. Relax. Have a pickle, turn down the lights and enjoy this 1-2-3/WordPerfect horror story.

The most obvious task you'll need to do is move numbers from the 1-2-3 file into the WordPerfect file. The most obvious problem you'll encounter is that WordPerfect can't read 1-2-3 "worksheet" files. If you try to do this, you'll wind up with something like this:

^@^@^@^H^@^@^@^C^@^@-^@^B^@^@^@^X.

Gee, that doesn't look anything like next year's sales projections, and unless the folks in your company are extremely nearsighted, they may sense that something is amiss.

So you're pretty distraught, but then this colleague tells you he knows how to do it. No sweat, he'll explain it to you over lunch. Over the salad he says, "Print the 1-2-3 file to disk. It's easy. Hey, pass the crackers, will ya? Oh yeah, then you just press"

/PF [ESC][ESC] C:\wp50\123.prn

This instructs 1-2-3 to print the file to disk rather than to the printer, and to send the disk file to a file called 123.prn in the \WP50 directory. "Of course, you could give this file any name you wanted," he tells you, smugly expecting you to pay for his lunch in return for this priceless advice. You just wish he would remove that piece of radish between his teeth.

"Now you need to tell 1-2-3 which part of the spreadsheet to print," he says. "If you want to print it all, type the following:"

R [HOME] . [END] [HOME] [RETURN]

"Gee," you think, naively, "This isn't so bad." "Oh, one more minor detail," he says. "Press"

O M L 0

M R 240

M T 0

M B 0

O U

Q

This procedure told 1-2-3 that you wanted the file to start at the left margin, print 240 characters wide with top and bottom margins of 0, and to print an unformatted, straight ASCII file.

We're having some fun now. But since your friend is probably getting tired of telling you what to do, he'll probably forget to tell you to press

G Q

Does this means that some guy in an expensive Italian suit is going to appear on-screen and shoot you a withering glance? No, the command has nothing to do with a men's fashion magazine. You merely told 1-2-3 to Go, and then Quit from the print menu.

"Lo and behold," your friend tells you, "the spreadsheet is in a form that WordPerfect can read." And just think, it only took 46 keystrokes and one lunch.

While WordPerfect can technically read this file called C:\wp50\123.prn, you should load WordPerfect and retrieve the file using the Text In option of List Files.

There it is, on your screen, just like your friend promised between bites of saltines. But why did that guy make such a fuss about this in his WordPerfect book? Geez, everything is such a production with him.

And then you print the file using Times Roman/Dutch 10 point, and you see this:

Jan Feb March April May
June
Roger 0.50 0.55 0.83 1.24
1.86 2.78
Crusader 0.70 0.77 1.16 1.73
2.60 3.90
Bugs 0.30 0.33 0.50 0.74
1.11 1.67
Ricochet 1.10 1.21 1.82 2.72
4.08 6.13
Peter 0.10 0.11 0.17 0.25
0.37 0.56

Instead of this:

	Jan	Feb	March	April	May	June
Roger	0.50	0.55	0.83	1.24	1.86	2.78
Crusader	0.70	0.77	1.16	1.73	2.60	3.90
Bugs	0.30	0.33	0.50	0.74	1.67	1.67
Ricochet	1.10	1.11	1.82	2.72	4.08	6.13
Peter	0.10	0.11	0.17	0.25	0.37	0.56

Gee, who can we take out to lunch next week? Of course, the mess on the previous page was caused by creating columns with spaces instead of *tabs.*

Fear not! You didn't cough up $21.95 for naught. You're about to learn what you couldn't learn anywhere else (even if you bribed someone with a really nice Italian lunch): how to get that pesky 1-2-3 file to print correctly in WordPerfect while using proportional fonts.

You also have a choice of dressings, House Honey Mustard, or Bleu Cheese... Sorry, I was temporarily distracted. You have a choice of two methods to accomplish this task. The first is free (and so naturally requires more of your time), the second costs about 100 bucks, but is worth it if you use it often.

◆ Do it yourself 1-2-3 conversion

There are a few drawbacks to this method, but what the heck, it's free, so you can't expect everything. Well, you can expect it, but you'll probably be disappointed. It works, and that should be enough for you. If you ask for perfection, people are only going to brand you as an obsessive-compulsive troublemaker or call you an ingrate.

The first method is a two-step, not to be confused with a Polka. You must first properly format the 1-2-3 worksheet for conversion, and then you will use a WordPerfect macro for the rest.

Go into 1-2-3 and insert an additional column between each existing column with

/WIC

Repeat this for each column. Fill these new columns with exclamation marks (!). If your worksheet is 20 lines long, you can enter 20 !'s quickly by placing the cursor on the first one, then typing:

/C [ENTER]

Move to the last line in the column and press

[ENTER]

This will fill the column with !'s. Repeat this for each of the new columns you added. Move to any cells containing spaces in labels, and edit them with

F2

Replace any spaces in words with an _ character, like this: Rabbit_Industries_Inc. Consult the print-to-disk instructions at the opening of this chapter.

◆ **Rabbit_Industries: If_It's_Fuzzy,_It's_Rad**

!!Jan!Feb!March! April! May! June

Roger!0.50!0.55!0.83!1.24! 1.86! 2.78

Crusader!0.70!0.77!1 16!1.73! 2.60! 3.90

Bugs!0.30!0.33!0.50!0.74! 1.11!1.67

Ricochet!1.10!1.21!1.82!2.72! 4.08! 6.13

Peter!0.10!0.1 1017! 0.25!0.37! 0.56

Load the file into WordPerfect, and create the following Macro (to save you time whenever you convert a file). *The space character is shown in this example as a ^. When you see a ^, press the space bar.* Press

CONTROL-F10 123 [ENTER] convert 123 print file [ENTER]

ALT-F2n ^ F2 F2

[HOME][HOME][UP ARROW]

ALT-F2n_ F2 ^ F2

[HOME][HOME][UP ARROW]

ALT-F2n! F2 [TAB] F2

CONTROL-F10

This macro first removed *all* spaces from the file (because 1-2-3 uses spaces between columns when it prints to disk). Then it replaced all underlines with spaces, and finally it replaced all !'s with Tabs.

And voila, faster than you can say "I want my money back," the file is formatted and ready for WordPerfect. Once you've created the macro, you can use it over and over again by pressing

ALT-F10 123 [ENTER]

- **Set those tabs:** Now all you need to do is set **decimal** tabs. If all the columns are the same width, it's a pushover: measure one column on-screen using the measurements in the lower right-hand corner of the screen. Set the tabs to be equally spaced. Remember: **SHIFT-F7 L T [HOME][HOME][LEFT ARROW] CONTROL-END 0,.75** (or whatever increment you want to use) will set equally spaced tabs across the page.

If the columns have different widths, it becomes a bit more involved. Because on-screen appearances can be deceiving, here's a quick way to print out the data so you can measure it on paper.

Set the left and right margins to .25 (the smallest allowed with laser printers). If you are working with a very wide spreadsheet, choose a landscape orientation for this print out so the spreadsheet will not be broken up when it prints. Print the page and find the longest column. Measure it and set tab spacing to be slightly larger than that width, or measure each column individually and make notes for tab settings.

◆ High class conversion

If you resented having to mess up the spreadsheet with exclamation marks and underlines, then you're going to have to shell out 99 bucks for a program called "*Corel Tabin.*"

This program can take a plain 1-2-3 print file filled with spaces, and convert it so that it uses tabs instead. The file can then be immediately loaded into WordPerfect using the Text In/Out feature of List Files.

In addition, if you tell *Tabin* the point size of the font you're using, it will analyze the file and offer you suggestions about where you should set the tabs (what a time-saver this can be with big spreadsheets).

Corel Tabin is the most sophisticated spreadsheet conversion program available because it enables you to change any or all of its options. It does not require strict adherence to formatting rules, as some other spreadsheet convertors do. It's also remarkably fast. In my tried and true tests, it never took more than 15 seconds to convert a file.

No other program provides such a high degree of control and customization. *Tabin* allows you to change its configuration file to specifically tailor any aspect of the program's conversion. If you are using foreign currencies, *Tabin* allows you to use European punctuation for commas, instead of periods. The French use spaces instead of commas, and *Tabin* can automatically format in this way as well. You can place the currency marker before or after the numbers, line them up, or remove all but the first and last in a column.

Overall, *Tabin* is the most powerful and versatile program in its class, and an excellent value. (The address for Corel is located in the Appendix, along with the addresses for all the other programs mentioned in this chapter.)

❖ *Making the numbers look like a million bucks*

Now that you know the basics, here are some advanced tips for making the spreadsheet look its best.

- **Use a style sheet:** You use larger headings in the text, so why not in the spreadsheet? Create a paired tag called headings, and use the Size Large or Very Large (**CONTROL-F8 S V**) command. Embolden the important points. If you are going to mix type sizes on a line (the titles here are larger than the numbers), you should use fixed line height so that the line spacing will be even.

	Jan	**Feb**	**March**	**April**	**May**	**June**
Roger	0.50	0.55	0.83	1.24	1.86	***2.78***
Crusader	0.70	0.77	1.16	1.73	2.60	***3.90***
Bugs	0.30	0.33	0.50	0.74	1.67	***1.67***
Ricochet	1.10	1.21	1.82	2.72	4.08	***6.13***
Peter	0.10	0.11	0.17	0.25	0.37	***0.56***

- **Separator Rows:** Most spreadsheets contain "separator rows," rows of dashes or equal signs to segment the spreadsheet into readable chunks.

But standard dashes and equal signs can appear rather clunky when you start typesetting the spreadsheet:

Jan Feb Mar April May

==
======================

In addition, because all of this doesn't line up on-screen, it's difficult to see where these lines really end. In this example, the equal signs stop a few characters after "April," on-screen, while they print as two lines.

The solution to this problem is simple: delete the rows of dashes or equal signs, and replace them with WordPerfect graphic lines. Since most separator rows run from the beginning to the end of a line, create a "left & right" like this:

ALT-F9 L H [ENTER]

If you want to stop the line at the last column, move the cursor to the right of the last word and note the measurement. Subtract the left margin from that number, and you will have the correct length of line you need. Create a left aligned line by pressing

ALT-F9 L H H L

Then press **L** and enter the length you just calculated.

Jan	Feb	Mar	April	May

You won't be able to use graphic lines if you want to place the spreadsheet into a graphics box. In this case, underlines will create a solid line. The larger the type size, the thicker the line.

- **Titles:** When using graphics (our next subject, oh boy, I'll bet you can't wait), don't use the fonts of your graphics program for titles. The fonts will either be stick figures (1-2-3) or limited in type variety (Harvard). WordPerfect allows you to put captions inside rather than outside the graphics box.

This allows you to produce handsome titles that match in the rest of the text. The results improve the appearance of both the text and graphs. To do this, set graphics box options as follows:

ALT-F9 F O P A I [ENTER]

◆ Problem # 2 - Crummy graphs

Now you've got this top-notch, typeset presentation, and you decide to use a graph created in 1-2-3. It looks like this:

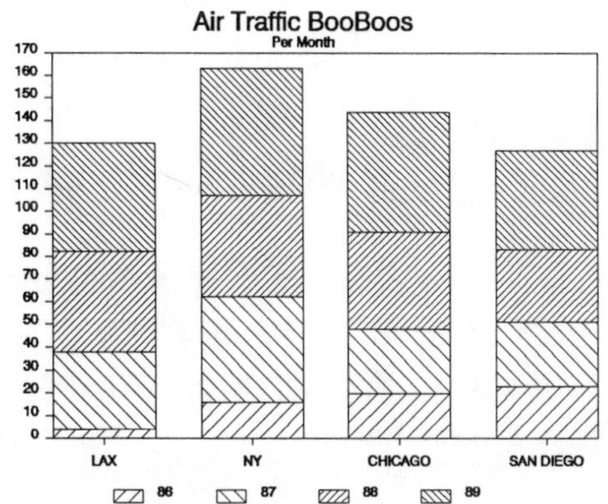

A 1-2-3 Graph saved as Black & White

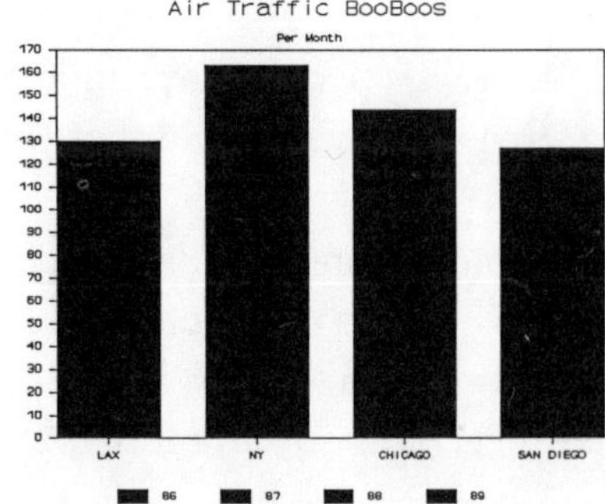

A 1-2-3 Graph saved as Color

If you've ever seen Mr. T, then this graph isn't the ugliest thing you've ever seen. Even so, it certainly doesn't live up to the quality of the typesetting that WordPerfect usually produces. It's the chart equivalent of a stick figure. This graph was created and saved in 1-2-3 as a color graph. When saved as black and white, the patterns filling the slices are even less even, and the pie is not very effective.

This graph would be more than satisfactory for casual documents, but is not recommended for important proposals, or presentations.

➾ **ASKEW:** One way to add interest to these otherwise insipid graphs is to employ WordPerfect's rotate feature so that instead of the graphics just sitting on the page like a lox, they are angled.

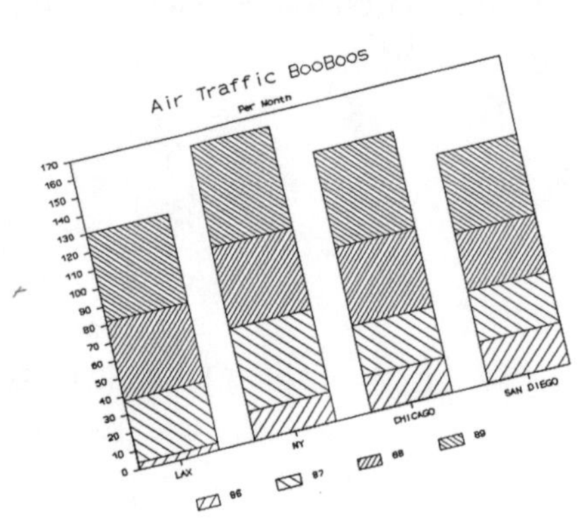

This technique should not be used recklessly: one might conceive of it as the DTP equivalent of television's Batman (where the camera shot scenes at wild angles). It grabs attention, adds interest and visual energy to the page, but it's far from traditional, and even a bit on the whimsical side. It looks as if you just threw the charts down on the page, and left them wherever they landed. You either love this or you hate it.

It's important to angle the graphs enough so that the effect looks intentional; otherwise, people may think that you pasted it up by hand and simply did a lousy job. I also recommend that you turn borders off; otherwise, the graph just appears crooked in a straight box.

If you have more than one graph on a page, place each of them at a different angle to accentuate the haphazard look. I have a feeling that this "Da-Da" look is going to be the new hot trend over the next few years. It happens whenever the real world becomes so surreal that mere parody falls flat.

◆ Baking a better pie (chart, that is)

Depending on your budget, you can convert your charts into a finished product that can range from attractive to spectacular. I'm going to cover three (or four) different ways to turn ordinary 1-2-3 charts into extraordinary graphics for use with WordPerfect.

- Secret of the Universe. The one magic maxim to remember when creating any kind of CGM or HPGL graphs is: *SAVE IT IN BLACK AND WHITE OR PATTERNS*, not in color. (They don't call me the master of subtlety for nothing.)

◆ LaserGraphics

Let's begin with the simplest and least expensive method, a program called LaserGraphics from SoftCraft. This program belongs to a package called LaserFonts. The entire package contains a font installation program called LaserFonts Manager; this can install any HP compatible soft font, as well as create outline and shadow versions of any font.

LaserGraphics contains a program called CNVRTPIC that takes a standard 1-2-3 pic file and turns it into a .PCX or .TIF file. It will also use any soft fonts (including FontWare) in place of 1-2-3's stick figure type. Since the files it creates are bitmapped, the graphs can contain attractive even tones of gray (rather than the sometimes dizzying patterns of black and white .PIC files). They also take up a lot more disk space, and require more time to print. LaserGraphics doesn't add all that much to pie charts; in fact, they don't look much different than standard .PIC files (although the bar charts look extremely different, and definitely improved).

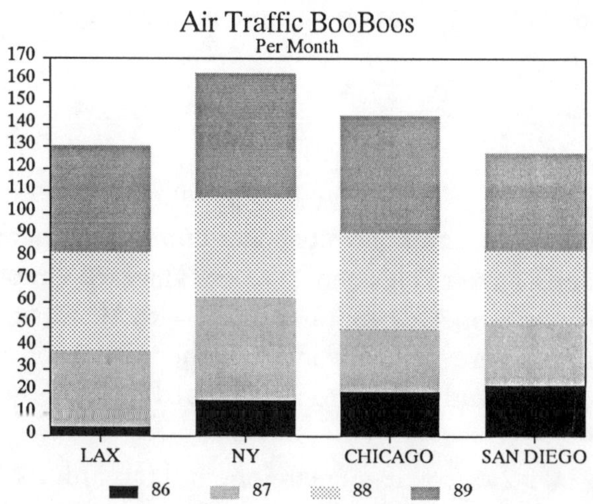

LaserGraphics gives you an assortment of simple gray tones that seem elegant without being flashy. This program allows for clear, easy to read graphs, for those special occasions when you actually want the reader to learn something.

Instead of a sickening array of patterns (which can actually make the bars look as if they are bent), LaserGraphics gives you an assortment of simple gray tones that seem elegant without being flashy. Simple yet baroque. Most importantly, LaserGraphics allows for clear, easy to read graphs, for those special occasions when you actually want the reader to learn something.

There is only one caveat: Because these are bit-mapped graphics, the gray patterns in particular do not scale well. LaserGraphics lets you specify the exact size of graph you want to produce (from 1" to 10"). It's important to have at least an approximate idea of the graph's size before you create it in LaserGraphics. If you know the exact size, so much the better. Your final printed graph will always improve by conforming to the original size of the graphic.

LaserGraphics is about as difficult as typing:

GRAPHMW AIR-BAR.PIC OUTPUT:AIRBAR.PCX

Typing that line took me all of 5 seconds (I'm a fast typist, and a bad one at that), and the program needed approximately 1 minute to process the file. LaserGraphics will save files in either .PCX or .TIF format (although the .PCX files usually require only 10% as much disk space). The .PCX files are normally about 30K, while the .TIF files are about 250K. When the .TIF files are loaded into a graphics box, they use the same amount of space as the .PCX files; aside from that, they take up a lot more room and offer no other advantages.

The LaserFonts package, including LaserGraphics, costs $180, a fairly small price to pay for convenient font installation, with genuinely easy and much improved graphics. (For the address of SoftCraft, and all the programs mentioned in this chapter, see the Appendix.)

◆ Harvard Graphics

Come on, admit it. You always wanted an Ivy league education, if for no other reason than to learn all the ins and outs of white collar crime. Whether you went to Harvard or not, you don't have to be a genius to use Harvard Graphics from Software Publishing. Harvard works exceptionally well with WordPerfect. It virtually allows you to change whatever you want (whether the graph uses colors or patterns), and provides you with all the tools you need to properly import a graph into WordPerfect.

If you can create a graph in 1-2-3, you can create one in Harvard. Even if you can't, you can create one in Harvard. All you have to do is answer a whole bunch of questions. And in case it didn't register the first time, the most important answer is:

ALWAYS CHOOSE PATTERNS, NEVER COLORS

Before proceeding any further, however, you must set up what's called the "VDI" (Virtual Device Interface). Although you have to install this separately from the program, installation is still automatic. (Just a note to avoid confusion: Harvard refers to .CGM files as "Metafiles" as in metamorphosis).

The VDI interface uses what's called "Device Drivers;" these are automatically loaded into the computer when it starts up, and so take up memory. Depending on the version of DOS, these will take up different amounts of memory. On my 286 computer, the VDI used 50K of memory, a rather large chunk. If you are working on long WordPerfect files, or files with lots of graphics, removing the VDI when you're not using it, will leave more memory available for WordPerfect. You can do this by renaming a file called CONFIG.SYS that contains the VDI information.

There are two more important options you need to set, options that I spent far too long trying to decipher. Once you get the hang of them, they're a breeze. But believe you me, after *days* spent agonizing over this kind of crud, you begin to appreciate it. Don't bother searching for this in the manual, it's not there.

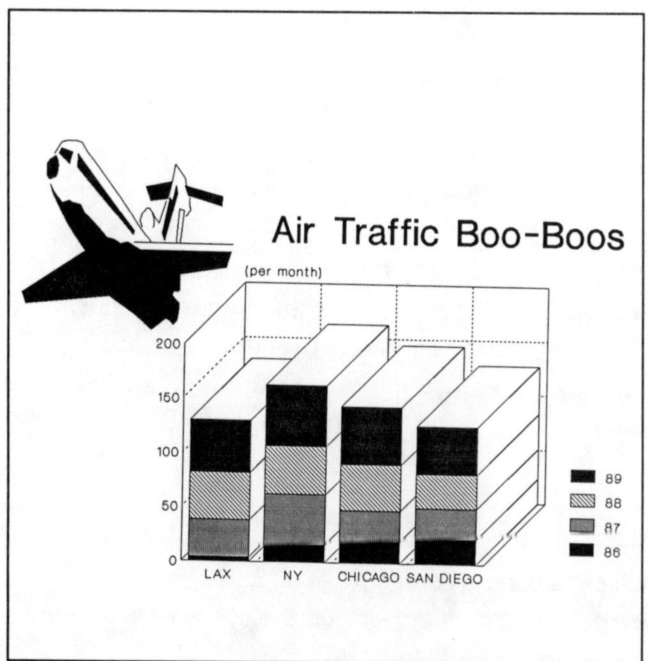

Harvard Graphics creates truly "wow-inspiring" graphics, complete with clip-art and 3D effects. All it takes it a little time, and enough sense to SAVE IN BLACK AND WHITE AND PATTERNS ONLY. I don't think one can repeat something important too many times.

- **ONLY USE COLOR 1** (white, which prints as black)
- and **SET BACKGROUND COLOR TO 16** (black, which prints as white)

When asked if you want to **USE HARVARD GRAPHICS FONTS** when converting to a metafile, always answer **Y**. Otherwise, you will wind up with stick figure letters. The Executive (Swiss/Helvetica) and Square Serif fonts look the best. The Roman is sketchy, as is the Script and Gothic.

Harvard comes with a large assortment of clip art, and will import CGM files using its separate "Meta2hg" program. You might also consider purchasing an option package, such as "Business Symbols" (more cute clip art to distract people from the figures in the graphs) and "Designer Galleries" (which allows you to plug your own numbers into a large assortment of pre-designed graphics. Or, if your numbers aren't so hot, why not just use theirs?)

Harvard lets you save graphs in .CGM, HPGL, and .EPS formats. I find that .CGM is by far the most compact (about 1/4 of the size of EPS), the fastest to draw on-screen, and the fastest to print. CGM is line art, and so you can scale it to any size and it will still print at the highest resolution. If you will be using a PostScript typesetter, CGM will print quickly (and cost you less) while offering you the sharpest output possible.

Harvard reads and extracts graph information from 1-2-3 .WKS and .WK1 files. Or, if you find some of 1-2-3's commands ridiculous (as I do), retrieve only the data from the 1-2-3 file so that you don't have to retype all those numbers.

Harvard even includes a spell checker so you don't make embarrassing errors in front of those very same people you spent all this time desktop publishing to impress.

Naturally, graphs this attractive are going to require more time to create (not to mention another program to learn). The graph with the butler took me about 30 minutes to create, but since it was the first graph I produced, I didn't think that was too bad. My next graph took about 20 minutes, and now I can make one in about 10 minutes. (I should make a graph showing how fast I can create a graph.)

It takes some doing, but once it's done, WordPerfect and Lotus 1-2-3 can make beautiful music together. The graph and logo on the opposite page were created with Harvard Graphics and printed on a QMS-PS 810.

1-2-3 WordPerfect 5

Everything you always wanted to know about WP and 1-2-3 but had no one to ask...

Winter 1989 - Vol 1. No. 3

WordPerfect and Lotus 1-2-3

By Daniel Will-Harris

What is desktop publishing? It means different things to different people.

If you work in any business, such as a real estate office or travel agency, you can use desktop publishing to send out promotional flyers about your hottest listings, or bargain travel packages.

Consider the production expenses of publishing. Try not to get depressed as you do so, but consider them all the same. Take a newsletter for example, which, using the old method, cost about $1,000 per issue to produce. With desktop publishing, the costs dropped to almost nothing (although the Oreo budget rose dramatically).

The first major expense is typesetting. On an eight page newsletter, if you sent typed pages to a typesetter, you should expect to pay about $300. If you prepared the copy on computer and sent it to the typesetter via modem (over the phone lines), that cost would be lowered to about $80 because the copy would not have to be retyped by the typesetter. (These typesetting charges included corrections, inevitable, because somehow mistakes are easier to see once something has been expensively typeset, and corrections are expensive.)

When you get the copy back you must "proof" it, to make sure the text, fonts, line widths, line spacing, etc. are correct. (A proof is a copy of text used for review and correction.) If you find mistakes, you have to go back to the typesetter.

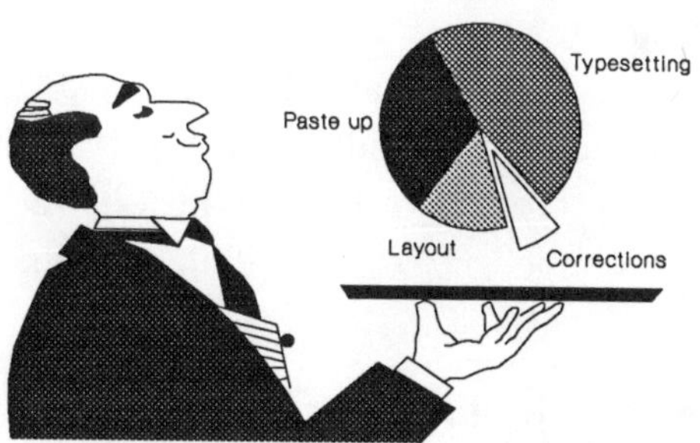

While I've already added the cost of the typesetters' corrections, I haven't figured your time into it.

I'm not sure what your time is worth, but mine is worth plenty, and I have more to do than just wait for the type to be just right. I'm going to say that the amount of time spent proofing, correcting and working with the typesetter comes to about five hours.

Counting the costs

Your time (or the person you have doing this work) is worth around $15 an hour. If you are making less than this, complain immediately. If you are making more, spill something on this paragraph. Five hours at $15 equals $75. Now you have to measure the type and make a dummy. A dummy is a simple mock-up of a page showing the basic format and where each story, picture, or piece of artwork is going to be placed on the page.

A dummy on paper is very simple and rough, and gives you an approximation of the finished page. Dummying eight pages should take about an hour. Simply cutting out the type alone can take an hour. So, it takes an hour to make a dummy, and an hour to cut out the type. You can then expect to spend about three hours to paste up the type and art work onto the pages.

Harvard lists at a pricey $395, but we're not the type that pays retail, are we? The street price (through mail order, and discount software stores) is approximately $200.

◆ Lotus Freelance

From the people who gave you 1-2-3, here comes Lotus Freelance Plus. This graphics program reads Lotus Worksheets and PIC files, and also created CGM and HPGL files that WordPerfect can read. The program even employs the 1-2-3 style of moving bar menus, so 1-2-3 users will feel right at home.

Freelance allows users to dress up charts with fonts, symbols, designs, and, true to its name, freehand graphics. The program combines several functions to let you create various types of charts and graphics. You can combine and modify text, lines, circles, rectangles, slices, polygons, arcs, and arrows, in whichever way you like. The program also includes a number of design tools: fonts, fill patterns, and a symbol library.

Freelance's graphic editing is more powerful than Harvard's; CGM files can be read into the program directly, letting you illustrate and enhance charts with clip art. Freelance is excellent for editing CGM clip art. It imports the file not as a single picture, but in individual pieces, which allows you greater control over line art graphics. This means that you can both use and abuse clip art, forcing it to conform to your exact specifications. The zoom feature lets you zoom in on even the tiniest detail, and so the editing control of this program is noteworthy.

However, the charts are not nearly as exciting as those made by Havard. You can't explode pie slices, and there are no 3-D effects. Also disappointing is that when creating a CGM metafile, the built-in Freelance fonts are not exported, leaving you with stick figure type. If you create an HPGL plotter file, the fonts are exported, but the file is larger and doesn't scale as well.

◆ Get some Perspective, junior

There's not too much you can depend on in this world, but rest assured that a graph from Perspective Junior will never bore anyone. Confuse them, maybe; distract them, probably; give them a queasy stomach, possibly; impress them, most assuredly. If you are seeking a whole new dimension in graphics, consider the Perspective Jr., a program from Three/D/Graphics that creates genuine 3-D graphs.

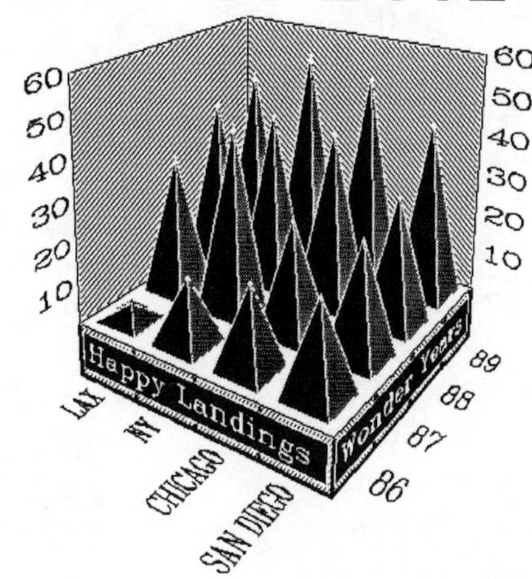

Perspective Junior produces flashy, though sometimes obtuse graphs. They are retreived into WordPerfect as .IMG paint-type files.

Perspective Jr. reads 1-2-3 files directly, and so there's no need for retyping. It also creates .IMG and .TIF files, so you can add these little dazzlers right into your WordPerfect document. Since these are bit-mapped files, they will not scale as well as CGM files, but they look beyond compare. They have depth, they have graph types no one outside a university has ever heard of, but most importantly, they have *sizzle.*

Perspective Jr. includes 180 (count 'em, 180) different fill patterns, some the likes of which you've never seen before. As well as a huge variety of gray tones, there are push pins, fish scales, squares, circles, diamonds, random patterns resembling wood grain, and a few patterns that can only be described as "wall-paper-like" from the 1930's to the 1950's.

To use Perspective Junior, just save the files as "Picture" files by pressing

F3 F2 F5

Perspective Jr. knows what kind of picture file to create by the extension (last three letters after the period) that you add. .IMG will create a GEM paint file, and .TIF will create a TIFF file.

Perspective Junior creates image files that are 4.16" wide and 3.15" high, and so it's best to use them at their actual size. If you do want to make them larger or smaller, use whole increments (half, or three quarters as big, or one and a half or two times larger). That enables the patterns to size smoothly.

PC Paintbrush lets you create cute graphs (the kind I decry in this book). But what can I say? It's fun, and there are times when you want cute. What's more, PC Paintbrush is perfect for editing scanned images, and great for customizing clip art, such as this cash register from the Metro Image Base.

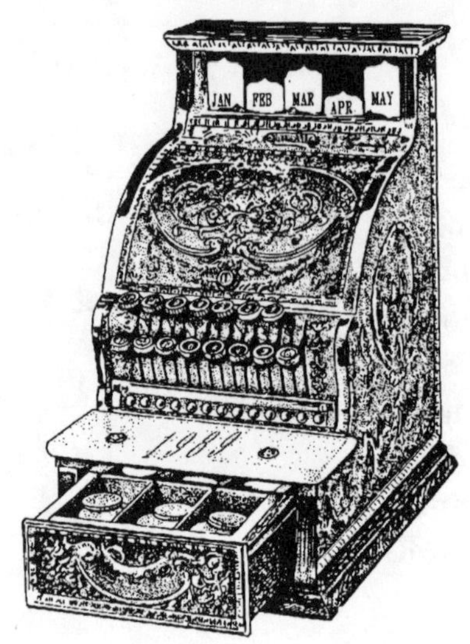

◆ PC Paintbrush Plus

PC Paintbrush is the best paint program for the PC. So what does this all have to do with 1-2-3 graphics, you ask? Plenty, I answer. PC Paintbrush Plus contains a feature called "Chart Interpreter" that can read 1-2-3 PIC files and convert them into ZSoft's .PCX format (which WordPerfect reads directly).

Although .PCX files are bitmapped, take up more space and don't scale as well as PIC files, they provide you with much more flexibility for editing. .PCX is *the* standard bitmapped format for PC's, and so there's a wide range of clip art available in this format. You can enhance graphs with clip art or scanned images (since the program supports scanners directly), and like LaserFonts, obtain attractive even gray tones in bar charts.

It's also easy to create those cutesy kind of graphs that I have spent so much time decrying. While they aren't suitable for all occasions, they are suitable for framing. They can be especially effective for less formal documents, such as newsletters (where regular charts and graphs may come across as too formal and off-putting. See the example with the cash-register graph).

In addition, PC Paintbrush is a truly fun piece of software. It's not unlike an electronic Etch-A-Sketch, but with more control. It's easy to spend hours drawing, or if you can edit clip art, give the Mona Lisa a moustache, whatever you find enjoyable. After all, desktop publishing should be fun, even if it is work.

MORE or less

Arts & Letters & WordPerfect 5

Arts & Letters gives you the power to create headlines which are really graphics. These can be sized like any other graphics, and allow you to break the standard LaserJet Plus type size limit of 30 point.

◆ Artsy smartsy

Arts & Letters is another program that gives you the power to enhance 1-2-3 .PIC files. The major advantages here are A&L's high-quality typefaces, and large library of clip-art. A&L automatically replaces 1-2-3's stick figure type with any of its fonts. Any type in A&L can be outlined, shadowed, compressed, expanded or rotated to any angle. At times, simply enhancing the text of a graph will greatly improve its appeal.

The graphs themselves are not substantially improved for LaserJet users who must make do with striped graphics similar to standard .PIC files. Trying to use color yields only black and white. PostScript users can obtain a full range of gray tones through ESP files.

A&L saves CGM files in black and white only. If you have a PostScript printer, A&L converts its files into EPS, and these files can include gray patterns. Otherwise, you'll use the black & white .CGM files created by A&L.

Text manipulation is excellent, with 15 high-resolution typefaces (unfortunately, only two of these are serif fonts, similar to Times Roman medium and bold). Another 17 typefaces are optional and cost $25 each. These display faces range from a version of "Broadway" to "Quadrata." These fonts can be rotated to any angle, can be filled with a variety of patterns and gray tones (which only show up with PostScript printers), and can also be outlined or reversed.

Unfortunately, due to the un-standard nature of CGM, files appear different in WP than they do in A&L. WordPerfect causes white fill patterns to become black, and vice versa. As a result, you must reverse everything, and this can be annoying. The utility program that solves this problem for Ventura does not work with WordPerfect. Computer Support Corporation, the manufacturers of Arts & Letters, has told me they are working with WordPerfect on the problem.

Still, A&L is a practical program, especially for people who have limited printer memory, but want giant headlines and/or special type effects. The clip art and type effects are excellent, and the program is simple to use.

◆ Future graphics

While Harvard and Freelance are fine, they don't hold a candle to what Micrografx's Windows Graph Plus can do. Windows Graph runs, not surprisingly, under Windows, but doesn't seem sluggish like most Windows programs. It's more intuitive than Harvard and Freelance, and supports a wider range of monitors (including full-page screen, such as the MDS Genius) and printers.

As I write this, however, the only way to get these remarkable graphics into WordPerfect is with EPS files. That's fine for people with PostScript printers, but LaserJet users are out of luck.

Micrografx has announced a new utility to convert their files into the CGM format (which WordPerfect can use). The program will be bi-directional, and include batch processing to convert groups of files automatically. In that I've yet to be disappointed by any of Micrografx's software, I imagine this convert program will work as advertised. If so, Windows Graph will be a sensational graphics partner for WordPerfect.

◆ The low-priced spreads

Some people use word processors for a living, while others use spreadsheets. Individuals who use word processors instantly recognize the differences between WordPerfect and "El Cheapo/WP." Individuals who use spreadsheets know the difference between 1-2-3 as compared with the low-priced knock-offs.

But spreadsheet addicts are content to use "El Cheapo/WP," and word processing junkies are happy to use one of 1-2-3's lower priced competitors. They may not have all of 1-2-3's features, but they cost less than half as much (in one case 1/5 as much), and roughly perform the same function: crunch numbers.

(No one ever calls word processing "Word Crunching;" probably because while numbers crunch, words turn to a kind of mush if not handled very carefully.)

In the grand old spirit of cheapness, we present the "Michael Dukakis Balanced Budget Award" to two 1-2-3 clones: VP Planner Plus, and Words and Figures. Both these programs are keystroke-identical to 1-2-3; if you can use 1-2-3, you can use either of these. VP Planner plus reads 1-2-3 files (either .WKS or .WK1). Words & Figures reads only the older .WKS files. Each of these produces .PIC files that can be imported directly into WordPerfect (or into other graphics programs, such as Harvard and Freelance). 1-2-3 costs $495 (the same as WordPerfect), VP Planner Plus costs $179, and Words & Figures costs $99.

In all cases, 1-2-3's graphs are superior to the other two programs, but in some cases by only slight margins.

Pies: Charts by 1-2-3 and VP Planner Plus are quite similar, with 1-2-3's being denser and rounder. Words & Figures' pie is frankly pathetic: no fill (even though it was saved as Black and White) and no exploded slice; what's more, the pie isn't very round and the words aren't in the right location.

Bars: But the WAF bar chart is almost identical to the 1-2-3 chart (although the bars are slightly thinner, and there are fewer tick marks on the left-hand scale). The VP Planner Plus bar chart is the thinnest, and lacks top and side rules (you might like this; it does allow for a somewhat cleaner look, especially when the entire graphics box is boxed).

The moral of this story is that if you don't know the difference, don't pay the difference.

❖ *Performance tips for power users*

If you're a whiz at software, but know zilch about hardware, you may not be aware of two words that can make your computer seem like it's running at double speed. No, these words are not "Mush, Mush!" but "Buffers and Files."

Without delving into pedantic detail, lets just say that DOS isn't all that bright. It has one small bookshelf for a file, and when that shelf gets too full, it has to pile everything on the floor. Later, it then wastes a lot of time looking for whatever it needs. (Of course, I don't mean to infer that *you* are not bright if your work place is like this. Mine, unfortunately is, but you'd think a computer would be a little more organized than we scatterbrained humans are.)

Anyway, the magic words "Buffers and Files," will provide you with more working room for the computer. These words don't give you more memory (in fact, they give you a little less), but they do let DOS perform more functions in a shorter amount of time. It's like adding bookcases; they take up space, but allow for a more useful and organized room.

(Forgive me if this sounded like a bedtime story, but what the heck? Try it on your kids and see if they start cleaning up their room. I suggest you add dinosaurs to the story. Kids love them, and you can infer that because dinosaurs weren't organized and didn't clean up their rooms, they lost their allowances and TV privileges, became extinct, and are now powering cars and other internal combustion engines.)

So how do you use these magic words? First let's see if your computer already contains them. Press

CONTROL-F5 T R C:\CONFIG.SYS [ENTER]

If you do not have this file, WordPerfect will say "Error: File Not Found." If you do have this file, it will appear on-screen. This file should begin with the lines:

Buffers=20

Files=20

If it contains the words "buffers and files," with numbers larger than 20, leave it as it is. If the numbers are smaller, or are simply not there, type them (as above) at the top of the file to create the first two lines.

Don't change any other information contained in this file; it may contain information about a mouse, scanner, and other peripherals. Save the file by pressing

CONTROL-F5 T S C:\CONFIG.SYS [ENTER]

These changes will not take effect until you turn the computer off, and on again. You can also use **CONTROL-ALT-DELETE** to reset the computer. (Make sure you exit WordPerfect before using CONTROL-ALT-DELETE.)

Harvard Graphics Normal Size

Harvard Graphics 100X 40Y

Harvard Graphics 50X 100Y

Harvard Graphics Normal Size

❖ *Parting shots for LaserJet users*

Those PostScript people can get pretty uppity, what with their giant fonts, outlines, shadows, rotated text. But once again, ingenuity (and software) can triumph over hardware.

Here's one more way to use that copy of Harvard Graphics (or any other program that saves in acceptable CGM format, such as Arts & Letters) to add jazzy logos or headlines to your pages (including outlines, shadows, huge sizes, and compressed or expanded text). This method also exceeds the 30 point limit of the LaserJet Plus and standard Series II printers. You can see examples of this in Chapter 4, *Show & Tell.*

Begin with a new empty chart. Don't enter any data, just go immediately to the main menu and press **F7.** Select either the Executive or Square Serif fonts (the other fonts will work, but won't be as attractive and will not let you create outline or shadow effects).

Next, go to Draw/Annotate. Select **Add Text,** and then press **F8** to set Text Options. Here you can select the size of text, and can also choose between solid, outline, or shadowed. Change whatever you like, but the color should always be **1** for White, which prints Black. (If you're skimming this book, you'll have no idea why white would print as black, but that'll teach you a lesson for not reading every chapter in order.)

When you've set your options, press **F8** again to start typing. Remember that this text will be a graphic in WordPerfect; you won't be able to edit it, so get it right here.

Save the file, and then export it to a "Metafile." Load this file into a graphics box as a .CGM file. You can now size it, stretch it, compress it, rotate it. This text takes up as much memory as any graphic, but not nearly as much as a large downloadable font; it also offers more versatility. In addition, this is the only method for printing both portrait and landscape text on the same page.

And you'll have fun, fun, fun 'till her daddy takes the T-bird away. Goodnight, Chet. Goodnight, David. There's nothing like mixing show biz metaphors (add two parts alliteration and one part onomatopoeia) to help end a complex chapter.

❖ *Putting it all together*

Now you know the truth about 1-2-3 worksheets and 1-2-3 graphics, and it's time to put them all together. What report could be complete without a financial statement? Here are all the codes for the following example.

◆ Financial Statement Funny Business

Experience Level: ***Intermediate***

- **Fonts:** Bitstream Swiss 12pt, Bitstream Swiss Extra Compressed
- **Graphics:** Harvard Graphics
- **Printer:** Hewlett-Packard LaserJet II

Notes: Tabs work differently with math on. Math doesn't work properly with leader tabs (you can make some *serious and costly* errors this way). Tabs don't automatically change from normal (or math) to leader; they must be removed and replaced (you can use search and replace for this). The pies have wrap turned off, so they can overlap slightly. This allows them to be larger. The dates under the pie charts are captions.

```
[T/B Mar:1",0.5"][Tab Set:4.75",5"][L/R Mar:1.25",1"]
[Usr Box:1;PIE87-2.CGM;]<TA VB HML SW 2.25 WN>
[Usr Box:2;PIE88-2.CGM;]<TA VB HMC SW 2.25 WN>
```

Funny Business Productions

1989-1990 Financial Statement

Assets:

Joke Library	$14,797,119.82
Rumor Mill	69,455.99
Whoopee Cushion Factory	45,211.16
Joy Buzzer Franchise	999,321.09
Collection: Stars' Hangnails	291,778.99
Total Assets	**$16,202,887.05**

In Development:

Agnes of Dog	$320,234.11	Shocker: A girl discovers a mysterious litter of puppies
The Pirate Caterer	12,350,000.00	Rollicking Broadway-bound musical comedy, full of food-services humor.
My Mother the Virgin	4,222,900.01	Sit-Com on fall schedule. Ogilvy & Mather pegs this for sure hitdom.
Unauthorized Autobiography	411,432.11	Autobiography of an amnesiac, won in fierce bidding war.
Total Development	**$17,304,566.23**	

Debts:

Junk Bonds	$4,555,006.01	All Ted Turner's fault.
Junk Food	655,991.08	Those Oreos really add up.
Just Plain Junk	43,621.09	Lots of stuff from K-Tel.
Chinese Junk	14,214.06	For promotional tour.
Total Debts	**($5,268,832.24)**	

Funny Business Bottom Line — $28,238,621.04

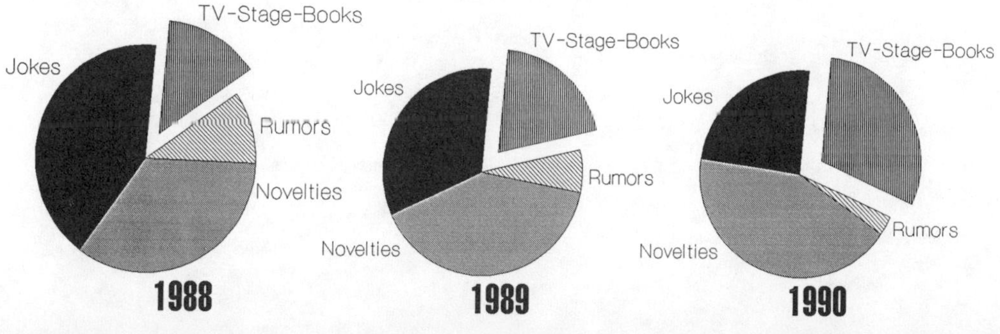

[Usr Box:3;PIE89-2.CGM;]<TA VB HMR SW 2.25 WN>

[Font:Swiss Extra Comp Roman 30pt (ASCII) (Port) (FW)]

Funny Business Productions[Flsh Rt]

[Font:Swiss Extra Comp Roman 18pt (ASCII) (Port) (FW)]

1989[-]1990 Financial Statement

[Font:Swiss Roman 12pt (ASCII) (Port) (FW)][C/A/Flrt][HRt]

[AdvUp:0.1"][HLine:Left & Right,6.25",0.1",100%][HRt]

[HRt]

◆ *Paired Style for Subheads:*

[Font:Swiss Extra Comp Roman 18pt (ASCII) (Port) (FW)] [Comment]

◆ *Paired Style for Total Lines:*

[AdvDn:0.1"][BOLD][Comment][AdvDn:0.1"][HLine:Left & Right,6.5",0.05",20%]

◆ *Paired Style for Grand total:*

[HLine:Left & Right,6.5",0.01",100%][HRt][AdvDn:0.1"]

[Font:Swiss Extra Comp Roman 18pt (ASCII) (Port)(FW)]

[Comment][AdvDn:0.1"][HLine:Left & Right,6.5",0.05",100%]

17

Coordinating your accessories

Utility software programs

Many useful utility programs have sprung up around desktop publishing programs. For novice desktop publishers, predesigned style sheets can be a big help. They contain many practical tips about the basics of graphic design and show how to quickly modify a style sheet. Users load in their own text and graphic files, and can instantly tailor any element of the page layout to fit their individual document.

◆ Designer Disks

➔ Will-Harris Designer Disks, Box 480265, Dept B, Los Angeles, CA 90048 $35.95 mail order only—not available in stores

As a tutorial for graphically design impaired new WordPerfect users, "Will-Harris Designer Disks" explain and demystify some of the program's more intricate functions, and illustrate proven design techniques to help users quickly produce attractive, effective documents. Culled from the examples in Chapter 4 of this book, the style sheets serve as templates for newsletters, manuals, catalogs, directories, and many other applications. Designed for use with both LaserJet compatibles and PostScript printers, "Designer Disk 5," containing 30 style sheets, is available by mail order only.

❖ *Third party font installation*

◆ Fontware

- Bitstream Fontware, Athenaeum House, 215 First Street, Cambridge, MA 02142 800-522-3668 $195 per package

Bitstream deserves a lot of credit for supplying us WordPerfect aficionados with high-quality fonts for free. In the past, users have had to pay dearly for Bitstream fonts, but now an installation kit and two fonts are included free with WordPerfect. I might normally be suspicious of a company that apparently gives away fonts in order to hook you into buying more, but buying Fontware is never a mistake.

If Dutch (Times Roman) and Swiss (Helvetica) suit your applications, then there's nothing more to buy. As with all Fontware kits, you can create fonts in sizes from 3 to 144 points for LaserJets and compatibles, as well as PostScript printers.

But once you start using Fontware, how can you resist buying Goudy Old Style, Zapf Humanist, Korinna, Hammersmith (Gill Sans), or Futura (including the ever-popular Extra Black)? And how long will it be before you succumb to the childhood catch phrase "collect 'em all!" (each sold separately, of course). Each package contains either four weights (medium, italic, bold, and bold italic) of a single font such as Palatino, or four special fonts packaged to be used as display faces only, such as Headline Package No. 1: Cooper Black, University Roman, Cloister Black, and Broadway.

Fontware does have a couple of flaws. You can't use it to install fonts from any other manufacturer. Some people might ask "why would you want to," and the answer is, because as good as Fontware is, other vendors have typefaces Bitstream doesn't (although they are constantly adding new fonts). Also, you must create fonts individually for each piece of software. If you have Ventura and

WordPerfect, you will need twice the fonts, twice the disk space, and twice the time to create them.

But trying to install fonts unassisted in WordPerfect can be a nightmare even for the technically inclined, and a near impossibility for almost everyone else. Three third party programs ride to the rescue to let you install fonts from any manufacturer.

◆ LaserFonts

➺ SoftCraft, 16 N. Carroll St. Suite 500, Madison, WI 53703
(608) 257-3300 Manager, Font Effects $95 each; LaserFonts & LaserGraphics $180; Word Processor Pack $595; Spin Font $95

The best of the bunch is SoftCraft's LaserFonts Manager. This reasonably-priced program installs any soft fonts for WordPerfect, including the Fontware fonts. If you've already made the fonts, and for some reason don't have your .ALL file, the LaserFonts Manager will reconstruct it for you. You can also use any Fontware fonts that you may have created for other programs.

The program is similar to "WYSIfonts," SoftCraft's font installation program for Ventura and PageMaker. Whether mouse or menu driven, it's both quick and easy, even for the occasional user.

If you have an eccentric font (not listed in the long list of font names), the LaserFonts Manager lets you enter any pertinent information so that it can be installed correctly, and called up by name from within the word processing program.

The installation for WordPerfect is particularly, shall we say, entertaining. WordPerfect has built-in commands for outlined and shadowed characters, and so LaserFonts Manager includes a portion of SoftCraft's Font Effects power. It will create shadowed or outlined fonts of *any* bitmapped font automatically, and install them so they will be instantly accessible in WordPerfect.

The LaserFonts Manager fully supports automatic kerning for the finest-looking output with any font. And it lets you install special effects fonts you design yourself, using the full version of Font Effects.

It provides an on-screen preview of font appearance during selection (supporting CGA, EGA, VGA, and Hercules), includes complete support for all symbol sets (including user-defined sets (no small feat with WordPerfect 5), and installs any font in either portrait or landscape orientation, creating landscape fonts when necessary. I dare say the next release will offer "shampoo carpet" and "deep fat fry" features as well.

The LaserFonts Manager also enables you to use SoftCraft's own $15 per disk fonts in a wide variety of styles. These are the most inexpensive quality fonts I know of, and include hard-to-find fonts such as Hebrew (Serif and Sans Serif), Cyrillic, Phonetic, and even sign language for the hearing impaired.

The Manager also installs Fontware fonts created with SoftCraft's own Fontware installation program. This program has an advantage over the free Bitstream installation program because you can choose your own symbol sets from the 560 character Bitstream character set, and oblique fonts, as well as compress or expand them.

The LaserFont Manager can even handle unusual fonts such as Weaver's DB (Dingbats) for LaserJets (the only Zapf Dingbat-like font I can find for LaserJets). These fonts use the standard ASCII character set, and require two font sets to include the entire Dingbat typeface. Each set costs $29.

Even if you have limited memory, these entertaining little symbols can add a lot of fun, spice, and whimsy to publications. With these fonts, WordPerfect LaserJet users will be one up on WordPerfect PostScript users who can't access the Dingbats which are built into PostScript printers.

If you also want to improve the appearance of Lotus 1-2-3 .PIC files, a LaserFonts & LaserGraphics package includes several programs to enhance graphs.

For the most comprehensive font control available in word processing programs, you might consider SoftCraft's "Word Processor Pack." This includes the installation program, a Bitstream Fontware typeface package of your choice, and Font Effects (to create your own special effects, not just outline and shadow).

The package also includes an infinitely useful program called Spin Font, which takes any Bitstream font and lets you set it in paths, such as arcs and circles, and at angles. The program creates a .TIF file containing the finished text. You can also set headlines that exceed the normal 30 point limit of the LaserJet Plus and standard Series II.

To accomplish this, you would have Spin Font create a .TIF file of the headline (with no angle, so that the text is straight), and insert it into your document as a graphic. If you distorted the graphic, you could compress or expand the type as well.

◆ Glyphix

➺ Swifte International, Ltd., P.O. Box 5773, Wilmington, DE 19808
(800) 237-9383 Set of four typefaces $99

If your documents do not require the highest quality fonts, for less than half the price of a single new Bitstream typeface, you can purchase four typefaces, and the Glyphix system, making some revolutionary features available at a fraction of the cost.

Glyphix can take a single 50K font and create fonts in all weights and italics, from 3 to 60 point, *as you print*. It's almost like having PostScript, but it costs a whole lot less. Glyphix also includes special effects such as slanting, widening, narrowing, stripes, and grayed type. Swifte says that Outline and Shadow effects are forthcoming.

Glyphix only downloads the specific characters you are going to print, rather than the entire font, and so saves hardware, disk space, and even printer memory. The Font Manager monitors the amount of memory remaining in your printer, and can swap Glyphix fonts in and out of the printer to optimize memory usage on each page. Glyphix offers font managers for both WordPerfect and Microsoft Word. These managers let you mix scaleable Glyphix fonts, soft fonts from any manufacturer, and cartridge fonts.

At present, there are four Glyphix packages, including book and display faces. Glyphix is memory resident and takes up roughly 60K of memory. It is the most economical way I know of, both in terms of software and hardware, to have a varied selection of fonts.

◆ Font Effects

➺ SoftCraft, 16 N. Carroll St. Suite 500, Madison, WI 53703
(608) 257-3300 $95

LaserJet owners often feel like supporters of Jimmy Carter. There are lots of them out there, but for a long time they were soundly ignored. There are many more LaserJets around than there are PostScript printers, but PostScript printers garner all the attention. This might be because Hewlett-Packard is notoriously stingy with review units, or because it takes a little more effort to get LaserJets to do some of the flamboyant things PostScript printers do.

One spectacular alternative is a program called Font Effects. Talk about value for money—it can take any LaserJet compatible font and add shadows, create outlines, and stripe or fill them with gray or checkered patterns. This program creates some of the finest special effects I've seen for LaserJet fonts. You can create unlimited special effects on fonts, and they all appear razor sharp.

Let's say you need a font with narrow characters—a "condensed" font. You don't have to buy another font. You simply modify the old font with Font Effects to make it half as wide. Or perhaps you need a short, wide font. With Font Effects, you can create a new font which is just as wide, but only half as tall, or the same width and taller, whatever you want. These variations allow you to use more words in a headline, and give you a greater degree of flexibility from the fonts you already own. The jagged edges often associated with resizing bit-mapped fonts are not a problem thanks to a remarkable "Fillet" function which fills in rough edges.

EFFECTS

But we're not through yet. Font Effects gives you inverted or reverse fonts which can print white on black. White type on a black background may be more difficult to read than black on white, but it can also attract attention and add visual interest to a page. Font Effects will reverse most type up to 24 point. (Actually, Font Effects will reverse any size type, but because the LaserJet Plus limits the size of any single font, it won't print an inverted 30 point font.) The LJ Series II with added memory does not have this limitation, but with the standard 512K, large reverse fonts may not fit in memory. (Turn kerning off if you're going to use any of these reverse fonts.)

Font Effects does another trick I like: it creates "gray" letters, with the gray ranging from a smooth medium tone, to a very coarse checkerboard light gray. You can even combine these special effects, creating narrow, outline, shadow, slanted, 22 point fonts. You can change a font as often as you like. The process itself takes anywhere from about one minute for smaller fonts, to as long as 10 minutes for resizing and filleting large fonts.

Font Effects provides 15 different features with which to modify type, and they can all be utilized in endless variations. The effects include outlining, filling with patterns, contouring (also called "inline," in which a white line is formed just inside the outside edge of characters), stripes, checkerboard, shades of gray, shadow, drop shadow, reverse, box, widen, narrow, embolden, slant, and fillet.

Font Effects is a great means of enhancing the type you already own, and can create distinctive fonts for logos, banners, advertisements, stationery, report covers—any circumstance in which big, flashy type is appropriate. For sensational-looking LaserJet fonts, Font Effects can't be beat. To ease installation with WordPerfect, see the review of the LaserFonts Manager (on a previous page).

➻ At long last keytops

If you produce computer documentation of any kind, keystrokes are a must. You also know how hard it is to find something that looks like a keytop, and looks good. I've known people who've gone to the extreme of designing key shapes, having them reproduced in rub-on sheets, and rubbing them on the finished pages.

But now there's hope (at least about this). At my urging, SoftCraft, pioneers in computer typesetting, developed a new font for LaserJets and compatibles called "Keyboard," or "Keytops," or something like that. Anyway, all you have to do is look at them to know they're going to be useful.

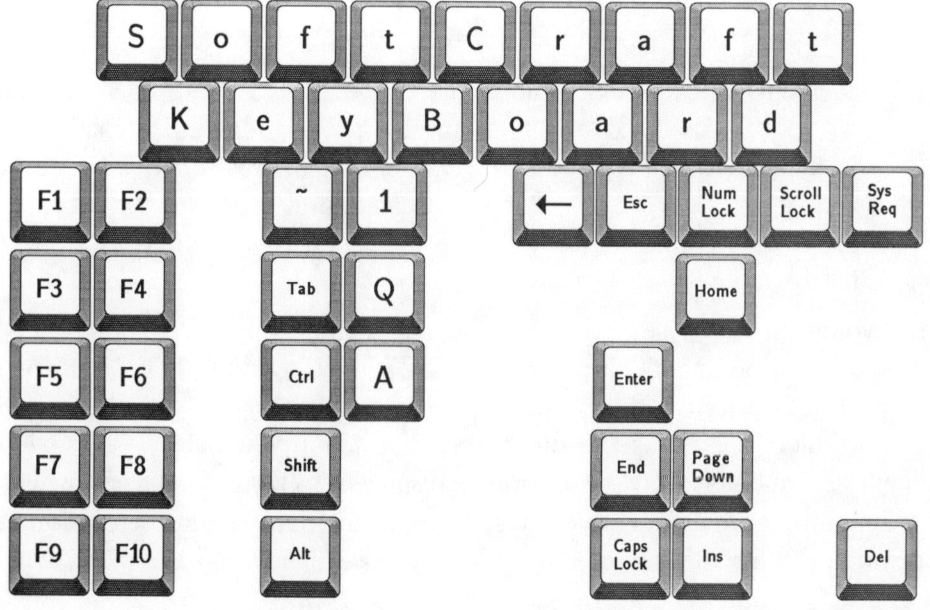

You'll also need SoftCraft's LaserFonts to install the font for WordPerfect, but this font will vastly improve the look of documentation. Details haven't been set about which sizes will be available, or what they will cost, but if you produce documentation, you are going to want to get your hands on a set of these babies.

When complete, the set will include all the keys on the keyboard, including the entire upper and lowercase alphabet, and all numbers and symbols. Hooray!

The only reason I didn't use them for the keystrokes in this book is because they were still in development, and not ready by my production deadline. I'm planning on using them in my next book though (and it's not even going to be about computers).

- Owners of the original LaserJet, see Chapter 18, page 440, for a new and unusual selection of fonts on cartridge from UDP.

◆ Additional soft font vendors

- Weaver Graphics, Fox Pavillion Box 1132, Jenkintown, PA 19046 (215) 884-9286 LJ Fonts $29.95

Weaver makes great dingbats for LaserJet users. The complete set costs $60, and is a good way to add visual interest to documents. They sell all their fonts by individual weight, such as Times Roman Italic, so you can buy exactly what you want. Each weight includes sizes from 6 to 30 point, and costs $29.95.

- DigiFonts, Inc., 528 Commons Dr., Golden, CO 80401 (800) 242-5665, (303) 526-9435 DigiDuit Installation program and 8 typefaces $89.95; additional typefaces, $29.95 per disk (of about 8). Complete library of 271 typefaces, $369.95. Installation programs for WordPerfect, Ventura, Windows/PageMaker, and Microsoft Word, $20 (each).

If you want the biggest type library at the smallest price, DigiFonts will be your choice—around $460 buys a whopping 279 typefaces. DigiFonts uses their own proprietary font format, but the fonts are quite good. While not all DigiFonts' faces are as good as Bitstream's, the quantity and selection is overwhelming, containing scores of decorative display faces not available elsewhere.

Generating DigiFonts is very fast, even faster than the latest version of Fontware, and installation into WordPerfect is automatic. What's more, Digi-

Fonts can automatically create outline and shadow fonts of any typeface, and other special effects such as pattern fills are also included. As an added bonus, all DigiFonts typefaces are compatible with Corel Draw.

If you want big type, but have little printer memory, DigiFonts will allow you to create fonts which contain only the characters you're going to use. This can save so much memory that you can actually print huge type, even with 512K.

Here's an example: a 72 point font in a normal US character set can take as much as 400K. Obviously that's not going to fit into the 380K available on the LaserJet II. But if all you want is a headline which reads "WAR DECLARED!" you really only need eight characters. A font with only those eight characters takes 43K and easily fits into memory.

If you use other programs that need downloadable fonts, such as Ventura or PageMaker, DigiFonts will install the same fonts into all these programs. This means you only need one copy of the fonts on your hard disk, and this can save you megabytes of disk space. DigiFonts even maps characters correctly into the complex WordPerfect character set (and the character sets of the other programs as well).

❖ *To clip art, or not to clip art*

By this time you should know that WordPerfect combines text and graphics. If this revelation is coming as a big surprise, you need professional help. Find a parade and join it.

Most people have no great trouble producing text (everyone thinks they're a writer), but fewer people consider themselves artists. Even with the array of graphics programs available, the old adage "Garbage in, garbage out" still applies. I find it much easier to "draw" in a draw program than a paint program, because I can combine basic geometric shapes and come up with something vaguely recognizable.

If you've got a scanner, the world is your clip art. But remember that graphic images are covered by the same copyright laws that words are. Dover Publications sells a huge line of reasonably priced books filled with copyright-free illustrations of everything from Renaissance and Victorian artwork to Art Nouveau and Art Deco designs (write or call for a catalog: Dover Publications, 31 East 2nd St., Mineola, NY 11501; (516) 294-7000). These images you can scan to your heart's content. Don't however, scan material from a book (particularly THIS book) or magazine and expect to distribute it without infringing on someone's copyright.

If you don't have a graphics program, or a scanner, but still want to include art on your pages, electronic clip art is your best bet.

I've used and can recommend the following clip art packages. Since taste and style are always subjective, I suggest you obtain catalogs from the following companies, and choose the ones that match your style.

◆ Object oriented clip art

These packages use draw-program-type line art format, and will always print a sharp image, no matter what the size. In addition, they always print at the highest resolution possible.

◆ Publisher's PicturePak

July

➡ Marketing Graphics Incorporated
4401 Dominion Blvd. Suite 210
Glen Allen, VA 23060-3379
(804) 747-6991
$99.95 per set, or all three for $250

The clip art included with WordPerfect is derived from this three-set collection of clip art.

Each collection has a different business theme: Executive & Management, Finance & Administration, and Sales & Marketing. They may sound dull, but they aren't.

These files are available in .WPG, .CGM, or .PCX format. Unless you plan to edit them in a paint program, I recommend the .CGM format.

These graphics are simple, but extremely attractive and up to date. I find them very useful. (Pictured: Wave & Typewriter.)

◆ ClickArt

⇴ T/Maker, 1973 Landings Drive, Mountain View, CA 94043 (415) 962-0195 $129.95 per set

If you own a PostScript printer, you might be interested in T/Maker's ClickArt EPS files.

These are Encapsulated PostScript files, and so can take advantage of PostScript's special effects. They do not display on-screen, however, and will not print on a LaserJet, or any other non-PostScript printer.

Each set of EPS files includes 180 images. The designs all tend to be emphatically modern. (Pictured: Grapes & Wine bottle.)

◆ Bitmapped clip art

The next three packages all sell their wares in bitmapped, or paint format. These clip-art packages allow you to use a program such as *PC Paintbrush.* to manipulate the clip art (change its size, add text, invert it, stretch it, etc.). Remember: most bitmapped graphics can't be enlarged much or they get jagged.

◆ ClickArt

⇴ T/Maker, 1973 Landings Drive Mountain View, CA 94043 (415) 962-0195 $69.95 per set

These pieces of clip-art are lively, but low-resolution (only 75dpi). This means you must use them in small sizes or they will get a severe case of the jaggies. Sets include symbols, holidays, and "lifestyles." Each set contains from

13 to 21 files; each file consists of anywhere from 1 to 25 different images. Since there are so many images in one file, you will need a graphics program such as PC Paintbrush to edit them for use with WordPerfect.

◆ PC Quik Art

PC Quik Art, 394 S. Milledge Ave.
Athens, GA 30606
800-543-1779 $59.95 per set

PC *Quik-Art* uses the graphic library of the large paper clip art company, SCW Services. PC Quik-Art tends to resemble the graphics found in newspapers advertisements, simple but useful. They include many attractive images, cleanly and professionally rendered (some of them are quite amusing). PC Quik-Art is available in packages categorized by subject matter, and is a convenient way to enhance your pages with graphics. These graphics tend to be very traditional and, at times, old fashioned. Each image is in its own file, and so you can use them directly with WordPerfect. However, they are low-resolution, so use small sizes, or say hello to the jaggies.

◆ Desktop Art

Dynamic Graphics, 6000 N. Forest Park Dr., Peoria, IL 61656
800-255-8800 $75.95 per set, multiples are discounted

Desktop Art is the electronic wing of Dynamic Graphics, another large clip-art company. At last count there were eight art-on-disk packages, including Business, Four Seasons, Graphics & Symbols, Sports, Education, Artfolio, Health Care, and Borders and Mortices. The style of these packages ranges

from ultra-modern to traditional. They include realistic line illustrations, cartoony-type drawings, and decorative elements.

While the art itself is excellent, the packaging leaves something to be desired for WordPerfect users. A paint program such as PC Paintbrush is a virtual necessity for using Desktop Art, because so many images are contained in a single file. You need to go into the paint program and save the image you want to a separate file. Unfortunately, you cannot crop these images adequately from within WordPerfect. The collections are discounted if you order more than one.

◆ Metro Image Base

➻ Metro ImageBase, Inc., 18623 Ventura Blvd., #210
Tarzana, CA 91356 800-843-3438 $145 per package

A late entry into the electronic clip art fray, Metro obviously has learned from the mistakes of its predecessors. To begin with, each file has a single image, and so you don't need a paint program to edit them before you can use them. Next, each file is very large, often over 100K; even though the files are bit-mapped, they offer high resolution and print a sharp image, even on Linotronic typesetters.

The three packages I've examined each consisted of five high-density disks. Since these disks hold 1.2 megabytes, you'd be right to assume that you were getting 3.6 megabytes of art. But the art on these disks is "arced," which means that *each disk* really contains about 4 megabytes of art.

I'm not one to buy anything artistic by the pound (or megabyte) but the sheer size of the art tells you how sharp it's going to be on the printed page.

Most importantly, the art is wonderful. This is the most modern, most attractive clip art I've seen for computers. The best thing you can say about clip art is that it doesn't look like clip art, and Metro Image Base art doesn't.

Each package contains 100 images. Fourteen packages are now available, including Newsletters, Business Graphics, Art Deco, Four Seasons, Reports, Borders and Boxes, Exercise and Fitness, Nine to Five, Food, Weekend Sports, Team Sports, Computers, People, and Travel. This clip art is extremely varied and of very high quality.

❖ *Graphics programs*

Here are a few graphics programs not covered in Chapter 16, *1-2-3 Publishing.*

◆ SLED

➺ VS Software, P.O. Box 6158, Little Rock, AR 72216 (501) 376-2083 $149.95

Sled is a fascinating hybrid of a paint program—a graphics power tool. The name stands for "Signature/Logo Editor" but that's a misnomer, because SLED is capable of far more than that. Not only can you perform the normal paint-type functions, but you can insert 300 dpi bitmapped fonts into your graphic, edit fonts as if they were graphics, and read and write images in not only .PCX and .IMG formats, but as downloadable fonts for use with word processing programs.

SLED's most useful and unique feature is the manner in which it allows you to manipulate bitmapped type. You can enlarge it, reduce it, bolden or lighten it. You can write the font back to its original file, create a new file, or apply the new type as part of a graphic. I don't know of any other program for the PC that allows you to use high-res fonts directly in a graphic, or manipulate them in such immediate, graphic ways.

If you have a LaserJet and desperately want reversed type, SLED can either create an entirely new reversed font from your downloadable fonts (which will print correctly on a LaserJet), or can create just a headline, or character in reversed type. SLED also lets you incorporate any LaserJet bitmapped fonts into a PostScript-printed page by saving them as paint files.

But unless you have CGA, EGA, or Hercules graphics, you're out of luck. Overall, SLED is a very handy program, especially when you want to play with bitmapped type.

◆ Hot Shot Graphics

⊷ SymSoft, P.O. Box 4477, Mountain View, CA 94040 (415) 941-1552 $245

Anyone who's ever written, or even glanced at a software manual, recognizes the importance of screen dumps. I like to imagine that Bette Davis was really talking about software when she uttered the immortal line: "What a dump!" Hot Shot, an overnight sensation because of its ability to convert any text screen into a screen dump, is worthy of accolades, real or imagined.

While Hot Shot was confined to text screens, Hot Shot Graphics can create a screen dump of text or graphics. HSG includes all of Hot Shot's text screen editing features, including a paint program. While other programs can perform screen dumps (namely PC Paintbrush's Frieze utility and Halo's Grab), HSG is an entire system specifically designed to capture, edit, convert, and catalog screen dumps.

HSG's own format is compact: a 7K CGA screen dump converts into a 16K .PCX file. Conversion requires approximately 30 seconds per dump, and you can convert to .PCX, gray scale .PCX, TIFF, Encapsulated PostScript, or "printer-ready" format. You can scale as you convert, so normally tiny and distorted CGA screen dumps wind up looking great.

HSG includes all the original Hot Shots annotation features for text screen, and a paint-type program for editing graphics screen dumps. The graphic editor doesn't function in CGA mode (although it will display graphics in CGA). HSG edits both its own files, and .PCX formatted files. The paint program includes a fine selection of tools for curves, lines, circles, and squares, but will only fill in black, white, or one of 16 colors. If you use lots of screen dumps, HotShot Graphics will introduce you to a new artform.

❖ Style programs

- Grammatik III, Reference Software, 330 Townsend St. #135, San Francisco, CA 94107 800-872-9933, 415-541-0222 $99
- RightWriter, Rightsoft Inc., 2033 Wood St., Suite 218, Sarasota, FL 33577 813-952-9211 $99

You need help. We all do. Good editors are few and far between. Unless my copy editor, Steve Paymer, happens to be available, what are you going to do? Even with Steve's eagle eye, it's easy to make mistakes while making his expert (not to mention comical) corrections.

Two pieces of software can help. Grammatik III and Rightwriter are two excellent grammar and style checking programs.

Everyone seems to be waiting for the day when a computer can actually proofread your text. Sure, computers can locate spelling errors, but they can't tell you if you should have used the word "their" or "they're." Grammatik III now uses "artificial intelligence" to pinpoint incorrectly used homonyms like its/it's, and transpositions such as form/from. It doesn't catch everything, but it has improved at finding some of those mistakes which spell checkers may miss. This so-called intelligence is surprisingly smart: and it often finds sentences that are missing a word, mismatched tenses, and lots of other boo-boos which, if uncaught, make you look like an idiot (when you're really only human—or is that redundant?). It's amazing, and genuinely helpful.

Grammatik is most effective in digging up cliches, improper punctuation, and, especially, improper use of the passive voice. The greatest advantage of Grammatik (one of the first style programs on the market) is that it's interactive. When Grammatik encounters what it deems to be a problem, it stops and presents you with several options. You can ignore the problem entirely (I've always been a firm believer in ignoring one's problems entirely), ignore a particular word or phrase, disregard a specific type of problem entirely, or, if you are able to accept criticism from a machine, have the program mark the problem in your file, or edit the problem right then and there.

The ability to edit within Grammatik means that its comments are fresh in your mind, and changes are easier to apply. Grammatik also offers extensive on-line help. If you don't understand a comment by the program, press F1 and a detailed explanation of that problem type appears. Some explanations run for four screens, and so whatever you need to know is right there in front of you.

I appreciate how Grammatik allows you to turn off any features you don't need. I usually turn off the "mixed-caps" feature, because so many computer-related names use mixed caps (*WordStar*, for example).

RightWriter is most proficient at discovering long, complex sentences, and this is exceptionally important if you want to avoid long, rambling sentences, like this one that I am writing right now.

RightWriter offers an optional package called *Rightwords* consisting of additional dictionaries which are already set up for specialized users. When you use these dictionaries, the program recognizes words specific to your field, and doesn't lower your "strength index" because you've used them. The package includes dictionaries for business, electronics, computers, navigation, communications, weapons system controls (I use this one frequently), shipboard mechanical and electrical systems, and aircraft equipment. You can also create your own dictionaries.

Some people buy both programs and then double check their files. If I had to choose just one, I'd probably buy Grammatik, because of its new features and interactive mode. It's a learning tool, as well as a writing tool. It seldom ceases to amaze me that a machine can find so many mistakes. But don't throw away your proofreader just yet.

◆ VCACHE - VOPT - VKETTE - VTOOLS

Golden Bow Systems, 2870 Fifth Avenue, Suite 201, San Diego, CA 92103 (619) 298-9349

$59.95 VCACHE & VKETTE together; $59.95 VOPT; $49.95 VTOOLS

Just a quick mention of a couple of programs which I simply find indispensable. VCACHE is an excellent disk cache program that utilizes conventional, extended, or expanded memory. It's the best disk cache I've used. VOPT is a disk cache specifically for floppies. Since I never have enough hard disk space, I store and download my fonts on floppies. VKETTE doubles the speed of this process and quickens the pace of all floppy-related functions.

VOPT is a remarkable program that prevents your files from being scattered about your disk. Both the *Mace* and *Norton* utilities possess this ability, but only VOPT can polish off this procedure in all of 30 seconds a day.

VOPT only moves the files that are not contiguous (not the entire disk, as Mace and Norton do). I put VOPT in my "autoexec.bat" file, and whenever I turn on the computer, it toils away, keeping my hard disk efficient. The resulting difference in performance is tremendous.

VTOOLS is a collection of handy little utility programs that make dealing with files easier. It allows you to find files anywhere on your hard disk, move files, change the date on files, compare two files, and perform many other bothersome tasks.

These little programs can make a big difference in how your system works. I for one, couldn't live without them. (Okay, I could probably live, but I'd do a lot more whining and complaining and everyone around me would probably wish I was dead.)

◆ Less is more - LaserTORQ

➺ LaserTools Corp., 3025 Buena Vista Way, Berkeley, CA 94708
(800)-346-1353 $99

If you've got a LaserJet Plus, or Series II with 512K, you may have tried to print a full page of graphics at 300 dpi and found you couldn't. One solution is a program called LaserTORQ. Actually a "print buffer," it receives data as quickly as a laser printer, and then doles it out to the printer in the background, while you continue to work.

LaserTORQ's "Optimization" feature can compress graphics to take up to 60% less space in the printer's memory. In my test, a graphics file which overflowed the LaserJet's memory and printed on two pages, printed perfectly on one page when optimized. Optimization does not function with downloadable fonts, and the difference will only be apparent on desktop published pages if many graphics are involved. PostScript printers do not require (and cannot use) optimization.

18

No desktop is an island

Hardware options

While you may have used previous versions of WordPerfect on floppies, the desktop publishing features in this version require a hard disk. For some of you, this may mean purchasing a new computer.

While WordPerfect runs fine on an XT, if you're serious about desktop publishing, you might want to consider an AT or compatible. These run at least four times faster than XT's, and the performance improvement is dramatic, saving a lot of time in View Document and in printing.

You can use at least 640K of memory, Hercules or EGA compatible graphics and monitor, and the largest hard disk you can afford—at least 20 megabytes (downloadable fonts take up enormous amounts of disk space).

Here are some AT compatibles I've tried and can recommend: the Victor 286 and WYSE 286 (both used for the production of this book), and the computers made by AST, Compaq, Dell, Epson, MultiTech, and even IBM. I especially love the keyboard on the Victor, with its big return key and function keys on the side. It also works perfectly with everything I've tried: graphics cards, big screen monitors, scanners, and printers.

Don't let anyone sell you more computer than you need, though. Don't be pressured into buying a PS/2 or any other computer unless it will perform the tasks you plan on using the computer for better than a regular AT.

The most important point to remember when purchasing a computer is to get one with a good warranty. Also, you need to determine that the company you buy from (the dealer or mail-order operation) will still be in business for the length of the warranty. Be careful about buying low-cost clones with no recognizable brand names—you get what you pay for.

❖ *Screen tests*

If you are happy with your current computer, you may still want to purchase a larger monitor, or one with better resolution. A big screen monitor can save you time when formatting by giving you a much better idea of what your finished pages will look like when they are printed.

"What-you-see-is-what-you-get" really hits home to anyone who has spent long hours working with graphics for desktop publishing (DTP) while staring at a computer screen. Without a high-quality high-resolution monitor, what you see is often fuzzy, and what you get is often dizzy. As graphics play an ever-increasing role in WordPerfect computing, high-res and full page monitors are also becoming increasingly important.

Neither EGA nor Hercules (the current PC graphics standards) deliver very high-resolution or display more than about a third of a page at a time. Even the Mac, known as a graphics computer, has a monitor with resolution only a little higher than the PC standards, and one which is often inconveniently small.

By comparison, the WYSE 700, the smallest and least expensive of the high resolution displays, shows a full page in View Document with four times the resolution of Hercules graphics—in other words, it's four times as sharp.

Larger monitors, like televisions, aren't necessarily superior. Because the resolution of a monitor is independent of its size, a bigger monitor isn't always easier on the eyes. Think of it this way: 350 lines on a 12-inch monitor will be closer together and sharper than 350 lines on a 14- or 19-inch monitor. Characters and images on the smaller monitor appear sharper. All the monitors covered here come with their own high-res graphics cards.

I'm going to examine two of the most popular monitors here, each representative of its type. The first is a true full page portrait monitor—it shows 66 lines of text, and a full page in View document (practically life-sized).

◆ MDS Genius

⊷ Micro Display Systems, 1310 Vermilion St., Hastings, MN 55033
612-437-2233, 800-328-9524 Resolution: 736 x 1008 pixels;
pixels per inch: 100 x 100; screen size: 8" x 11";
image area: 7.5" x 10.5", one year warranty, $1795

One of the first, and possibly best known full-page monitors for the PC was the MDS Genius. This offers complete compatibility with all text-based programs. The Genius display is the only full-page monitor supported by WordPerfect, and the one I used while writing this book.

You can view up to 66 lines of text on the Genius, and that's more than a full page of type. While 66 lines is standard, utility programs that come with the monitor can change the spacing of lines to display up to 82 lines per screen. Remember that even 66 lines is more than a normal page of text, making the Genius an excellent monitor for writers, editors, and users with large spreadsheets.

Surprisingly, the display fills all 66 lines with more speed than many regular 24-line monitors. Text can be displayed black on white, white on black, or even double height.

The Genius also offers the widest software support of any large screen, and so you can use it with a wide variety of graphics software; *PC Paintbrush, HALO* and *AutoCAD* all possess the Genius display on their install menus and this simplifies installation because no additional software drivers are necessary. The Genius is so popular that it is often the first large monitor new programs support.

The Genius has a resolution of 100 dots per inch. Because it displays 100 dots both horizontally and vertically, the pixels are considered square, delivering a more accurate display of the printed page.

The Genius screen is so sharp that you can easily read the page in View Document mode (except in facing pages mode). In full-page, details appear which are invisible on EGA or Hercules. In 200% mode, every detail, no matter how small, is clearly visible. The Genius is tall and narrow, however, and in facing pages mode, the pages are not much larger than on a standard screen.

The Genius full-page display emulates IBM monochrome and CGA—at the same time. The top half of the screen is monochrome, and the bottom simulates CGA, so the monitor is compatible with a great deal of graphics software which doesn't support its full-page, high resolution mode. Programs such as *1-2-3* and *Symphony* can display their worksheet on the top half of the screen, and their graphs on the bottom half. The CGA mode does not work with all programs, however.

Overall, the Genius is a versatile doubly-useful monitor that enhances both graphics and text-based software. If you do a lot of writing or word processing, the full-page Genius can be an effective time-saver. Despite the $1795 price tag, this is no longer a luxury, but a means of reducing the number of test prints, and improving your overall word processing and desktop publishing capabilities. Once you get used to 66 lines of text and a full-page View Document that you can actually read, it's difficult to imagine writing or editing with anything else.

◆ WYSE 700

➺ WYSE Technology, 3571 N. First St., San Jose, CA 95134
800-GET-WYSE Resolution: 1,280 x 800 pixels;
pixels per inch: 125 x 105; screen size: 12" x 9";
image area: 10.1" x 7.6"; one year warranty, $999

The WYSE 700 is not a true "full-page" monitor. It's a large, 15" high-res monitor that displays 25 lines of text, just like any other monitor, but with extremely high resolution in View Document mode. The Wyse's strength is its relatively low price and its relatively high resolution.

As well as high-res View document mode, the Wyse functions in high resolution mode with GEM, Ventura Publisher, Windows, PageMaker, PC Paintbrush, HALO, AutoCAD, 1-2-3, Symphony, and most other graphics and CAD packages. If software doesn't specifically support the Wyse's high-res mode, the monitor is compatible with CGA. While CGA still has low resolution, it *looks* better on the Wyse than on regular CGA monitors.

Any text-based program (including word processing programs) can be used, and will offer exceptionally large and sharp characters. Text programs' display will only appear as white characters on a black background, not black characters on a white background.

The Wyse has a wide screen that displays facing pages in a larger size than any other monitor I know of. You can actually read the type, and you just can't do that on most monitors (except in 200% mode). This may be the best value among high-resolution monitors for anyone who wants higher resolution and a medium size display area.

❖ *Laser printers*

◆ QMS-PS 810

⊸ Quality Micro Systems, P.O. Box 81250, Mobile, AL 36689
205-633-4500 $5,495

When comparing laser printers, it somehow seems natural to associate them with cars. To begin with, they cost as much as cars did just a few years ago, and they inspire the same kind of loyalty, frustration, and joy in their owners.

With that in mind, meet the QMS PS-810, the Rolls Royce of PostScript printers. Its parallel port and fast 68000 processor make it the fastest PostScript printer for PC users. The LaserWriter NTX, even with its faster 68020 processor, would be far slower because it lacks a parallel port, and serial connections are slow. The QMS has parallel, serial and AppleTalk ports, 2 megabytes of memory, and exact Diablo and LaserJet emulations. It offers every feature you'd want in a luxury printer, including a price higher than most others.

The 810 uses the excellent Canon SX engine that is small, quiet, truly easy and inexpensive to maintain. Most importantly, it provides the finest print quality of any 300-dpi laser printer (especially when the darkness control is set to 7 or 9). Solid blacks and crisp type are consistent throughout the long life of the toner/drum cartridge.

The QMS has a LaserJet emulation mode for your software that doesn't know from PostScript (or for pages with paint-type files that take forever to print with PostScript). The QMS, like all printers with Canon engines, is almost completely silent when not printing—there is virtually no noise, not even from the fan. This may seem trivial, but a quiet work space is always desirable and appreciated by others.

The paper path is perfectly straight, and so the machine practically never jams, except occasionally on two-sided, or manually fed pages. When it does, the top opens so far that it's always a simple task to clear the jam. Thick envelopes run through the machine smoothly, and the "face-up" tray in the back stacks them neatly. The drum even covers itself (it's shy and modest) when you open the printer top, so you won't accidentally scratch it when clearing any infrequent paper jams.

In general, the QMS PS-810 is the premier PostScript printer for PC users in every aspect: type quality, speed, reliability, convenience, and cost of operation. But then, you get what you pay for, and you pay a premium for the QMS.

◆ NEC LC 890

→ NEC Information Systems, 1414 Massachusetts Ave., Boxborough, MA 01719 (617) 635-4400 $4,795

If the QMS is a Rolls Royce, the NEC is more like a Nissan. It gets you where you're going, offers lots of little convenience features, but just doesn't have as much style, speed, or reliability.

The NEC has a host of benefits going for it. First, its list (and street) price is lower than most other PostScript printers. It comes standard with 3 megabytes of memory, a full megabyte more than many other PS printers. The blacks are solid, and it has PostScript, as well as excellent LaserJet and Diablo emulations. It can be easily be equipped with two paper trays and so it is efficient for office use. It has serial, parallel, and AppleTalk ports, and a convenient LCD control panel mounted on the front, with no knobs or dip switches in the back.

However, even though this printer has more memory than the QMS, it's not nearly as fast.

The printer comes with two paper trays, so you can utilize letterhead in one and second sheet in another. Each tray holds 200 sheets, and the output is face down and collated. The 890 can handle envelopes, and output them face up in the front of the printer. But there is no tray for them, and they'll fall to the floor unless you devise some kind of holding contraption.

The print quality is acceptable, and the blacks are solid, but the results are not as impressive as those achieved by a Canon SX engine, such as the LaserJet, or QMS PS-810. Type from the NEC appears noticeably heavier, even on the lightest setting; it also seems more jagged and not as sharp as type from the QMS. "Toner fuzz" is often apparent around the edges of characters, and pages lack the crispness you find on the QMS.

Three other complaints come to mind. The fan is loud, and this is a consideration when you want to leave the machine on all day. Canon-based printers are practically silent, but the NEC is louder than a floor fan I have in my office. This can be uncomfortable when you use downloadable fonts and don't want to turn the printer on and off repeatedly.

Paper jams are another annoyance that occur with more regularity than with Canon printers because the paper path is not as straight, and the way paper sits in the hoppers encourages paper curl, and dust. The cover of the printer does not open very wide, which makes removing a jam, or getting inside the printer at all, difficult.

Still, the 890 is $800 less than the QMS, contains more memory, and provides acceptable print quality. It's not a Rolls, but it does get you there.

❖ *LaserJets and compatibles*

While there are many brands of laser printers, they are all based on engines from a few companies. Canon produces the engines for their own company, HP, QMS, and Apple. Canon engines can print up to eight pages per minute. Ricoh produces two different engines for themselves, TI, Acer, Okidata, AST, Destiny, Epson, Quadram, and others. Ricoh's large engine (which I don't recommend) prints as many as eight pages per minute. Their small engine prints as many as six pages per minute. Kyocera produces their own engine, which is also used by Mannesmann Tally. It prints as many as 10 pages per minute. NEC makes their own engines which can print as many as eight pages per minute.

I say "as many as" because this rating is based on printing the same page repeatedly. The printers are quickest when you send a file once, then tell the printer to create several copies of it. If you ask for several copies in WordPerfect, WordPerfect repeatedly sends the file for each page, so these "as many as" figures are not very accurate when working with WordPerfect.

Personally, I prefer Canon engines, because they are easy to set up and maintain, and they are economical. In my experience, you can actually print 4,000 pages on a single drum/toner unit that costs about $99. Other printers I've tried ran out of toner after only a few hundred desktop published pages, and their toner cost $30.

Canon engines produce the best print quality and are also the quietest. If you think all laser printers are quiet, you should take a listen to some like the AST TurboLaser. I turned on this Ricoh engine printer and my wife Toni ran into the room, ecstatic. She thought I'd finally bought a washing machine.

I used a LaserJet II and a QMS PS 810 for all the material in this book because I admire their capabilities more than the others I've tried. You, however, will have to decide for yourself.

There are several points to bear in mind. Don't buy a particular brand of laser printer just because it's inexpensive. I've been witness to some really unpleasant machines that were loud, had terrible print quality, used a lot of toner, and jammed often. I won't say the brand name, but the initials are "C. Itoh Jet Setter" (my wife spells this AST Turbolaser).

To achieve WordPerfect perfection, you need a laser printer that is either LaserJet or PostScript compatible. Some LaserJet emulations are excellent, such as the Mannesmann Tally. Others are close, but no cigar. Close often isn't close enough, and so I'd recommend you test the printer of your choice with WordPerfect and whatever fonts you want to use. Cart all your disks down to the dealer and check it all out very carefully. Choosing the wrong laser printer can be an expensive mistake.

If you need a printer with two paper bins, look into the NEC LC-890, LaserJet 500 Plus, QMS PS 800 Plus, or Mannesmann Tally 910.

◆ Some items to consider when choosing a printer

- What does it emulate? How good is the emulation?
- If it has fonts built-in, are they identical in width to those available for LaserJets or PostScript printers? WordPerfect supports many laser printers, but Bitstream fonts will only work with LaserJet compatibles and PostScript printers.
- How much memory does it contain? The LaserJet has 512K standard, and is expandable to 4 megabytes. The Okidata only has 640K, and that limits the amount of graphics you can use.
- Can you expand the printer? How much does more memory cost? Can you add PostScript?
- Can you use cartridge fonts, and if so, are they identical to the LaserJet fonts?
- Can it print on envelopes? This is a more important consideration than you might think. Not all printers can. You really can print envelopes efficiently in WordPerfect, so don't overlook this. Canon engines can print on envelopes. The small Ricoh engines can, the large Ricoh engines can't. Kyocera and NEC printers can.
- How much are consumables, and how long do they **really** last?
- How loud is the fan?
- How long is the warranty?
- How fast does it **really** print? When a printer claims to print eight pages per minute, that refers to eight copies a minute, not eight originals. Some printers are faster than others, even though they have identical ratings.
- Does the printer have a parallel port? If not, it's going to require a lot more time to print with WordPerfect.
- Print out a solid black page. How solid is the black? Is it even? Is it dark? Is it blotchy?
- Print out a gray screen that fills the page. Is it even, or does it become lighter and darker around the edges?

◆ Hewlett-Packard LaserJet

➺ Peripherals Group, 16399 West Bernadino Dr., San Diego, CA 92127 619-592-8182 $2,695

The LaserJet is the standard by which all non-PostScript printers are measured. It's small, quick, quiet, and (amazingly) competitively priced. While the list price is higher, I often see them advertised for around $1,700. As with all Canon engines, the print quality is unsurpassed. The blacks are black, and text is sharp and crisp. The printers are easily expandable with HP memory or less expensive third party add-ons. There are many font cartridges available (the best being the Z, which is copied at about a third of the price by UDP, reviewed on page 440 of this chapter). You can use two cartridges at a time, and envelopes print just fine.

If you want to add PostScript, The Laser Connection produces a board that fits into a computer and adds PostScript to the LaserJet. This costs $2,500, more than the printer itself, but taking into account the price of the printer, it's still less expensive than other PostScript printers. This is one machine that grows and matures with you, rather than becoming outdated.

The LaserJet has a 16-character readout which presents specific error messages in plain English—much easier to understand than the idiot lights or cryptic numeric codes found in some other printers. You can select fonts and paper orientation from the front panel, and there are no dip switches; all settings are performed using a menu system on the readout. The Series II is covered by a full one-year warranty, considerably better than many manufacturers' standard 90-day warranty.

All in all, the Series II keeps the LaserJet in the forefront of laser printers. With its competitive price, it doesn't even have to cost more to purchase a LaserJet. While other printers come standard with more memory, you can expand the Series II memory with a simple plug-in card for a comparable price.

If you need to print on both sides of the paper, the LaserJet's sibling "IID" can pull it off. The IID will automatically print on the first side of the paper, then turn around and print on the back. This is a great feature for anyone who uses the laser printer as their final output device. No more collating—it's all automatic. The IID uses the same fonts as the II, but will also rotate fonts automatically, so you no longer need to create landscape fonts (this saves disk space). The IID also has no limit on the number of fonts which can be in memory at one time. The IID comes with two paper trays so you can fill one with letterhead and the other with blank paper for the second sheet. Or, if you're printing a big job, use you can both to hold up to 400 sheets of paper at once (if you print on both sides, that means 800 pages). An optional envelope feeder is also available. The IID comes with more fonts than the II, and includes a font cartridge with Times Roman and Helvetica. All this makes the IID a versatile printer for those heavy-duty offices where sharing a printer between several computers is necessary.

◆ PDP 1-2-4

⊸ Pacific Data Products, 6404 Nancy Ridge Dr., San Diego, CA 92121 (619) 552-552-0880 1-2-4 Memory board from $295 to $1795

The only problem with HP's memory upgrades is that they aren't upgradable. If you buy the one-megabyte board and then need more memory, you have to toss it and buy the two-megabyte board. This can get expensive. Pacific Data Products, the makers of the low-cost font cartridge, *25 in 1,* have a memory upgrade system that makes sense. You can purchase their *1-2-4 Board* with no memory, then keep adding as much as 4 megabytes. If you buy it with memory installed, you only save about $50 off HP's price, but because you can keep adding memory, you really save money when you want to upgrade.

◆ LaserMaster LX6

⊸ LaserMaster Corp., 7156 Shady Oak Rd., Eden Prairie, MI 55344 (612) 944-6069; LX6 Professional (with 4 megabytes of memory) $3,995; LC2 $2,395

What's the fastest way to get WordPerfect to print twice as sharp? The LaserMaster LX6 Professional printer controller board. The LX6 can print 600 x 300 dots per inch on a standard LaserJet II, double the resolution of a standard LaserJet. Everything from type to gray scale images look twice as good, with a print quality which rivals typesetting machines costing $10,000 more.

The LX6 is capable of almost all of PostScript's type tricks, including scaling a single outline font from 3 point to 1200 point, rotating type, printing white on black, outline fonts, etc. The only thing the LX6 doesn't do with type is make you wait around for it. The LX6 consists of a board which fits in any XT, AT, or 386 compatible computer. Connected to the optional I/O port of the LaserJet II (or IID) via a modular "telephone-like" cable, installing the board and software takes about 30 minutes, with the software installation being almost completely automatic. The LX6 is also extremely fast, usually able to print a full eight pages a minute, as fast as the LaserJet's engine will allow. It also supports the LaserJet IID's duplex printing. The LX6 uses any standard Bitstream Fontware typeface, so there's a good library of high-quality fonts to choose from. The system uses all Bitstream font "hints" to create fonts on-the-fly that are just as sharp as bitmaps.

The LX6's 35 fonts are the same as those found in PostScript "Plus" printers. They are all "PostScript width-compatible," so it's possible to "proof" pages on the LX6 and then send them to a Linotronic for final printing while still retaining correct character and line spacing. While the LX6 is versatile, it is not PostScript compatible, so you cannot print EPS files directly (but they're working on it).

For anyone who wants to use their laser printer as a final output device, the LX6 is going to produce the sharpest pages I've seen come from a desktop laser printer. The LX6 and a LaserJet II together cost only around $5,700, the price of a quality 300 dpi PostScript printer, and almost $10,000 less than the price of a Varityper 600. A six-megabyte version of the board costs $5,995 (the additional memory is important for duplex printing). A network option is available for $995.

The LX6 is a realistic and reliable way to produce high quality type and graphics. If you use WordPerfect and need the best quality output at the lowest cost, there is currently no competition for the LX6. If you can't cough up four big bills for the LX6, LaserMaster offers the LC2, another LaserJet add-on board which gives you almost all of the LX6's advantages. The LC2 comes with the same 35 typefaces as the LX6 (or a PostScript printer), but it doesn't print 600 dpi, and you have to create bitmapped fonts for smaller sizes (for speed and quality). The LC2 is still fast, uses all Bitstream Fontware fonts, and scales fonts to any size.

LaserMaster is one company that's always coming up with something new. Call and see what else they have up their sleeves (and tell them I sent you).

◆ Big fonts in little cartridges

➾ UDP Data Products, 1309 Laurel Ave., Manhattan Beach, CA 90266
(213) 545-5767 Desktop Publishing Font Cartridges $379 each

An excellent new line of font cartridges from UDP contains fonts in sizes larger than ever before available on cartridge. A Times Roman-like font in sizes from 8 to 30 point is on one cartridge, and the same sizes in a Helvetica-like font are on another. These cartridges contain 512K worth of fonts, and are a boon for anyone who uses WordPerfect on a network, doesn't want to spend time downloading fonts, or wants to save the memory fonts normally take so they can print more graphics.

Appendix

Design Glossary

Alley. The space between columns of type on a page. See **Gutter.**

Alignment. Designation regarding the ends of lines of type, such as flush right, flush left, justified, or centered.

Ampersand. Name of the type character "&," used in place of "and."

Artwork. Images, including charts and photos, prepared for printing. It can refer to whatever is meant to be reproduced, whether it be a drawing, photograph, or text, and is treated as an artistic element on the page.

Ascender. The part of a lowercase letter that rises above the body of the letter, as in b, d, f, h, k, l, and t.

Baselines. Invisible lines where the bottom of each character rests.

BF. Copyreader's abbreviation indicating that the copy should be set in boldface type.

Bleed. Printing that extends off the edge of a sheet or page after trimming.

Block. A standard paragraph in which the first character of the first line is not indented. Block paragraphs also contain a blank line between paragraphs.

Blurb. A short summary of a book's contents to be used on the jacket copy. May also refer to a longish caption or a short block of text treated as a **readout.**

Boards. In traditional printing, the typeset copy is pasted up on a board. In desktop publishing, if you are not going to use a laser printer for your final output, you may still need to employ paste up boards for the printer to use in preparation for duplicating.

Body copy. The bulk of text in a publication. The stories and articles are the body of your publication. Headlines are not body copy, as they are set in *display type.*

Boldface. A heavier, darker version of a regular typeface.

Boxed. Matter enclosed by rules or borders.

Bullet. A large dot used as a graphic element in body copy.

Byline. A line telling the reader who wrote the article. Usually follows the headline and comes before the body copy, but can also appear at the end of an article. The byline is usually set in boldface type.

Camera Ready Copy. Finished pages prepared for the printer's camera. The camera is a *copy* camera, which photographs pages so that they can be used with the printing press. The whole idea behind desktop publishing is the ability to produce these completely ready-to-go-to-the-printer pages.

Capitals. The large letters of the alphabet. Also know as "caps" or "uppercase letters."

Captions (or Cut-lines). Sentences or paragraphs of descriptive text accompanying illustrations. They are usually set in a different style of type (often italics or boldface) to distinguish them from body copy.

Characters. Individual letters, figures, punctuation marks, etc., of the alphabet.

Clay-coated paper. A paper with an especially smooth surface, recommended for use in laser printers because the ink doesn't smudge on it. It is heavier than regular copy paper, and so can easily be sprayed with adhesive or glued with rubber cement for manual pasteup.

Clip art. Illustrations, usually black and white, which can be used without securing permission from the artist or paying royalties.

Columns. Vertical rows of text. The purpose of a column is to make reading easier by keeping lines of text shorter, while still allowing you to use a lot of text on a page.

Comp. The abbreviation for *comprehensive,* an accurate layout displaying type and illustrations in position on a page. Mainly used in advertising agencies to show clients various different layouts.

Condensed type. Narrow version of a regular typeface.

Copy. All the text on your page. Available in various flavors, the most plentiful of which is body copy.

Deckhead or deckline. The lines following the headline and preceding the byline, usually imparting more information about the article. See **Headline and Subhead.**

Descenders. The part of a lowercase letter that falls below the body of the letter, as in g, j, p, q, and y.

Display type. Type set larger than body copy (which is usually about 10 or 12 point), for headlines, readouts, etc. Attention-grabbing display typefaces are employed for effect in advertisements, promotional materials, etc.

Drop cap. Display letter that is inset into the text. May also be raised.

Dummy. A type of blueprint for page layouts. You mark off sections of a page where stories or artwork will be placed later. Dummies are a quick and efficient way to decide what will go on each page.

Editing. The process of checking copy for fact, consistency of style, spelling, grammar, and punctuation prior to typesetting.

EM. A printer's unit of measurement, refers to the width of the letter "m," used for inserting white space in a line of type.

EN. Another printer's unit of measurement, also refers to the width of the letter "n," used for inserting white space in a line of type. Sometimes called a "thin space."

Family of type. All the typestyles of available typefaces (roman, italic, bold, condensed, expanded, etc.).

Flop. *Howard the Duck* (sorry, Steve); To turn an image over so it faces the opposite way. This is usually done with portraits so that they will face the correct way on the page. A mirror-image.

Folio. Page numbers.

Font. Complete assembly of all the characters (upper and lowercase letters, numerals, punctuation marks, etc.) of one size and one typeface. Special characters (those not in a font), are called "pi" characters (bullets, arrows, stars, etc.).

Footer. Text appearing at the bottom of a page, such as a page number or chapter title, etc.

Formatting. The process of designing pages on the computer.

Galley. A long sheet of typeset text not yet in page format, often used to proof text.

Graphics. Art and other elements (including type) used on a page as a visual statement.

Grid. An arbitrary geometrical pattern that divides the area of the page into horizontal and vertical shapes (columns).

Gutter. The blank space where two pages meet at the publication's binding, or the blank space between columns of type.

Hairline. A fine line or rule, the finest that can be reproduced in printing. The next largest size in many systems is a half-point line, followed by a one-point line.

Halftone. The process of reproducing photographs so they can be printed on a large press. Photos have a "continuous-tone" that are converted into a "halftone" by photographing the original through a fine cross-line screen. This is necessary for quality reproduction of the photos, and is performed at the printers' before plates are produced for printing.

Hanging Indent (Outdent). A style in which the first line of copy is set full measure, and all the lines that follow are indented.

Hard copy. Type which is printed on a piece of paper, as opposed to type on the screen of a computer. It is useful to print out a hard copy of a page as a rough draft for proofing before you print out a final version.

Header. A line of text (such as the title of a publication, name of article or chapter), appearing at the top of a page.

Headlines. Lines of type (set in a display type, a larger size than body copy), telling readers what the story or article is about. They are often accompanied by subheads (or deckheads), which are smaller headlines. Also abbreviated as "hed."

Hung initial. Display letter set in the left-hand margin.

Indent. An indented paragraph is the most common style. The first line of each paragraph is indented, usually 3 or 5 spaces, with no blank lines left between paragraphs. The indent can be longer or shorter, depending on the effect you want.

Initial cap. The first letter of a body of copy, set in a display type for decoration or emphasis. Often used to begin each chapter of a book, it may be either dropped into a paragraph or raised above it.

Insert. A separately prepared and printed piece which is inserted into another printed piece or a publication.

Italic. Letterform that slants to the right: *Italics appear like this.*

Jumphead. The headline appearing above an article continued from another page. The jumphead may only contain one or two words of the original headline.

Jumpline. The line which is to be continued from the end of a column of text, stating the page the article jumps to. Also at the top of the column, under the *jumphead,* stating where the article was continued from.

Justified type. Lines of type that align on both the left and the right of a column's full measure.

Kerning. Adjusting the space between letters so that part of one letter extends over the body of the next. Kerned type is more pleasing to the eye.

Kicker. The words positioned just above the headline. Usually in a smaller typesize, flush left, sometimes underlined. Also called a "teaser."

Landscape. A horizontal page, printed so that the width of the page is greater than its height. A vertical page is called *portrait.*

Layout (or Make-up). The placement of all elements, including text and graphics, on a page. Layout is the design process, and **make-up** involves the physical paste-up of the elements. In desktop publishing, layout is also referred to as *page composition* or *page processing.* A layout specifies the sizes and styles of type, the positions of illustrations, spacing, and general style.

Leading (pronounced ledding.) The term originates from a time when thin strips of lead were inserted between lines of type to achieve proper spacing. Leading determines the amount of white space between lines of type, and can be expressed as "10/11," or "10 on 11,"(10-point type with 11-point leading).

Letterspacing. Adding space between individual letters in order to fill out a line of type and improve appearance.

Ligatures. A ligature refers to two connected characters, like "ff" is when typeset, or the "ae" in *Encyclopædia Britannica.* Kerned pairs of letters, such as the "ff" and "fi," may fit closely together enough so as to resemble ligatures, but most software doesn't support them (since they are not included in many fonts).

Line drawing. Any artwork created by solid black lines, usually with pen and ink.

Linotron. Trade name for phototypesetting machines and systems manufactured by Mergenthaler Linotype.

Logotype. "Logo" for short. Two or more type characters joined together for use as a trademark or company signature. Can also refer to any type and artwork combined to represent a single graphic element or distinctive symbol.

Lowercase. The small letters, as opposed to the capitals.

Measure. The length of a line of type, normally expressed in picas, or in picas and points.

Mechanical. The camera-ready pasted up assembly of all type and design elements located in exact position on artboard or illustration boards; instructions for the platemaker are contained either in the outside margins or on an overlay.

Modem. Short for modulator/demodulator, this is a device used to transmit data from one computer to another, via telephone lines. Utilized in desktop publishing to send files to a typesetter for higher quality.

Non-repro blue. A type of light blue pencil used especially for marking camera-ready copy or paste-up boards because the marks will not reproduce when photographed.

Oblique. Roman characters that slant to the right. Not true italics, but similar.

Offset printing. A system which uses special printing plates created directly from photographs of the original pages. Your camera-ready copy is used as the original page.

Outdent. Text on the first line of a paragraph which prints to the left of the paragraph margin.

Orphan. The first line of a paragraph stranded at the *bottom* of a column or page. This is undesirable and should be adjusted whenever possible. See also **Widow.**

Page composition. Identical to layout. The design and placement of all the elements on a page. Also called *page processing.*

Pagination. The process of putting pages into consecutive order. In page composition programs, **batch pagination** is a process in which text is automatically flowed onto pages in consecutive order. Some programs require you to **paginate manually** by using a mouse to place the text on each page individually.

Pasteboard. Laminated chipboard utilized for paste up.

Paste-up. The process of placing the type and graphic elements on the pasteboard in preparation for camera-ready copy. When the paste-up is completed it is called a *mechanical.*

Photomechanical. The complete assembly of type, line art, and halftone art in the form of film positives. Used for checking proofs and monitoring the production of printing plates.

Pica. A typographic unit of measurement equal to one-sixth of an inch. Column width is measured in picas.

Pi characters. Special characters of a font, such as arrows, bullets, stars, copyright symbols, etc. as: ® © ™ ⇐ ⇒.

Point. Smallest typographical unit of measurement, approximately 1/72 of an inch. Type is measured in terms of points, the standard sizes being 6, 8, 10, 12, 14, 18, 24, 30, 36, 42, 48, 60, and 72 point.

Portrait. A vertical page, printed so that the width of the page is less than its height. A horizontal page is called *landscape.*

Press run. The length of the printing run, or the number of sheets to be printed.

Printing plate. A surface, usually composed of metal, that has been treated to carry an image. The plate is inked, and the ink is transferred to the paper by a printing press.

Production artist. A person who performs paste up.

Proofreader. A person who checks for accuracy by reading type that has been set against original copy. Proofreaders may also read for consistency, fact, and style.

Proofs. A trial print or sheet of printed material that is checked against the original manuscript, and then subsequently used for corrections.

Raised cap. Display letter that is set above the text. The "R" at the beginning of this entry is a raised cap. May also be dropped into the text.

Readouts (or callouts or pull quotes). A readout is a section of text which is set apart from the body copy for use as a graphic element. It pulls out an important quote or statement from the text, and is set in a larger typesize than the body copy. Readouts are not headlines or sub-heads, but are most often duplicates of sentences or paragraphs of body copy used for emphasis. However, readouts can also contain sentences or paragraphs that are *not repeated* in the body copy.

Ream. A unit of measure for paper of any size: 500 sheets of paper.

Reverse type. Type that drops out of the background and assumes the color of the paper. Normally white type on a black background.

Rules. Black lines, used for a variety of effects, including borders and boxes. They come in a range of thicknesses *weights* that are measured in point sizes, the thinnest of which is called "hairline." Rules may be dotted, dashed, or contain a number of lines of various weights.

Rulers. Measuring devices which help you place *rules* (lines). On the computer screen, rulers are used as electronic measuring devices.

Running head or foot. Title or other information at the top or bottom of every page of a publication.

Sans serif. Without serifs. A clean, modern typeface, such as Helvetica (Swiss).

Scanner. A device, connected to a computer, which can convert a typewritten page or artwork (such as a photograph or line drawing), from the printed page into data which is compatible with the computer.

Serifs. The curves and flourishes at the ends of letters. Times Roman (Dutch) is a serif typestyle.

Sidebar. A shorter story than the primary one it supports, containing specific information relating to one aspect of the main article. Used to highlight a particular point, or present related or background information.

Signature. A printer's term referring to a single sheet of paper with several pages printed on each side. The sheet is then folded into "booklets" from which books and magazines are assembled. One fold creates a four-page signature, two folds, an eight-page item.

Subheads. Can be placed directly after a headline or above certain paragraphs, highlighting a specific area of body copy. Subheads stand out, and help the reader find specific topics.

Text. The body copy on a page or in a book, as opposed to the headings.

Thumbnails. Small, rough sketches used to explore designs for page layout.

Typeface. Used interchangeably with *typestyle.* A typeface is a font, such as Times Roman. Typeface can also refer to a type family designation, such as bold or italic.

Type family. A range of typeface designs that are all variations on one basic style of font. A family is usually made up of roman, italic, and bold faces.

Typestyle. Used interchangeably with *typeface.* A typestyle indicates a particular font, such as Optima.

Typography. The art and process of working with and printing from type.

X-height. A typesetting term used to represent the height of the main body of the lower case letters of a typeface, excluding the ascenders and descenders.

White space. Refers to the blank space that frames or sets off text and graphics. Also called *negative space.*

Widow. A relative of the orphan: the last word or line of a paragraph that stands alone at the top of a page or column, separated from the rest of the paragraph. This is undesirable and should be corrected whenever possible.

Wordspacing. Adding space between words to fill out a line of type and improve appearance.

WYSIWYG. What You See Is What You Get (printed.) Pronounced "wissywig" or "wizzywig," depending on how you pronounce *Caribbean.* Refers to the ability to display a close representation of the printed page on the computer screen.

Read More About It

There are several books that deal specifically with desktop publishing, and a few of them that address both design and electronic publishing techniques. Here are a few of the best.

◆ Desktop Publishing

Desktop Publishing With Style, a *complete guide to design techniques and new technology for the IBM PC*, Daniel Will-Harris (And Books), 1987. This practical and amusing overview offers sound advice on all MS-DOS software, hardware, and graphic design. Includes in-depth coverage of fonts, printers, paint and draw programs, scanners, utilities, graphics cards, and monitors. Replete with design tips, it graphically shows how to achieve professional results with Ventura, PageMaker, and the big three word processors, and includes over 45 full page examples of newsletters, reports, flyers, etc. $21.95.

LaserJet Unlimited: *How to get the most from your Hewlett-Packard LaserJets,* Ted Nace and Michael Gardner (Peachpit Press), 1988. Packed with up-to-the-minute information, this book covers everything you ever wanted to know about LaserJets—utilities, compatibility, typesetting techniques, and tons of tips and tricks. An indispensable tool for all LaserJet and Series II owners. $24.95

◆ Graphic Design

Mastering Graphics, Jan White (R. R. Bowker), 1983. An excellent book for serious students of design; it details the principals of design and layout in clear, concise terms. Those who produce newsletters, brochures, and many other publications will appreciate the many examples and understandable way in which the material in this book is displayed. $29.95.

Editing By Design, Jan White (R. R. Bowker), 1982. A useful book for the editor who wants to learn more about communicating effectively in print. Also helpful for the art director who wants an improved understanding of how to effectively present written material. Covers all the basics, including type specifications, cropping photos, and numerous design alternatives. The author spent 22 years as an art director for major magazines and what he doesn't know about graphic design isn't worth knowing. $34.95.

Graphic Design For The Electronic Age, Jan V. White (Watson-Guptill), 1988. The subtitle for this book is "the manual for traditional and desktop publishing," but the emphasis is on graphic design, rather than desktop publishing specifics. No particular software or hardware is referred to, although electronic typographic considerations are dealt with extensively. This book draws on material from several of White's other informative and useful books, and is well worth the price. If you can only afford of White's books, this is the one. $34.95.

Graphic Idea Notebook: *Inventive techniques for designing printed pages,* Jan V. White (Watson-Guptill), 1980. Another work by the master of the genre, Jan White. With this book, transforming ordinary material into provocative publications looks easy. A book to stimulate your imagination and open your eyes to the many possibilities by which you can enhance your publications with special handling of graphics. $22.50.

Graphics Handbook, Howard Munce (North Light), 1982. A book about design not written by Jan White? How did this wind up in here? Well, this is a good book, too. Not as detailed as White's, but excellent for the beginner. This book attempts to take the fright and mystery out of the design and preparation of simple printed pieces, and it really does simplify some of the mechanics. Generously illustrated with hundreds of graphic examples of the most popular applications. $14.95.

◆ Typography

Rookledge's International Typefinder, *the essential handbook of typeface recognition and selection* by Christopher Perfect & Gordon Rookledge (PCB International) 1983. An absolute classic. Although essential is an appropriate word, the subtitle could easily have been "the *perfect* handbook of typeface recognition," because that's what it is. The volume is well-structured, dividing 700 typefaces into a logical progression, and highlighting the special identifying characteristics of each font. For anyone interested in type, this book is an Aladdin's cave, full of wondrous treasures. $24.95.

Photo Typography, Allan Haley (Scribner's Sons), 1982. The author is a vice president at ITC (International Typeface Corporation), and his book offers valuable guidelines and insight into effective typesetting and design standards. If you need more in-depth information about specific fonts, including their history, distinct characteristics, and usage, read this book. $18.95.

The Art of Typography: *Understanding contemporary type design through classic typography,* Martin Solomon, (Watson-Guptill) 1988. This book explores aesthetic elements, and contains numerous examples to illustrate attractive composition and design. Includes a variety of problem-solving ideas and a comprehensive directory of typefaces. $29.95.

Designing With Type, *a basic course in typography,* by James Craig (Watson-Guptill). Often used as a textbook for design students, this manual thoroughly examines five popular typefaces and demonstrates how they can be applied to a multitude of publications. Also includes a type gallery of over 120 faces. The author has written several other books about design and typography, and is well-equipped to share his vast knowledge with readers. $24.95.

Decorative Letters, *Copyright-free designs,* Carol Belanger Grafton (Dover Publications), 1986. Over 800 decorative letters of the alphabet to add spice to a variety of publications. For standard LaserJet users, these ornamental letters are especially effective when used as large dropped or raised capitals. $3.50.

◆ Producing Newsletters

Slinging Ink, Jan Sutter (William Kaufman), 1982. All about newsletters, from start to finish. $12.95.

Editing Your Newsletter, Mark Beach (Van Nostrand Reinhold), 1983. Practical information on the writing, editing, design, and layout of newsletters. $18.50.

◆ Offset Printing

Getting It Printed, Mark Beach (Coast to Coast), 1986. A how-to book on working with print shops and graphic artists, with an emphasis on the basics of getting the job done. $29.50.

Printing It, Clifford Burke (Wingbow Press), 1972. Written by a printer, this books offers sound advice on how to get a print shop to produce a publication to your satisfaction. $12.95.

◆ Periodicals

Personal Publishing, a Hitchcock publication. This monthly magazine is a must for desktop publishers. Full of useful, detailed, practical how-to articles, and the latest trends in this ever-growing field. Subscriptions are $24 a year; P.O. Box 3019, Wheaton, IL 60189.

Step-By-Step Graphics, published by Dynamic Graphics. This magazine is jam-packed with informative articles about specific design techniques, with special focus on how to improve the visual communication process. High quality and comprehensive. Subscriptions are $42 a year for six bimonthly issues; Step-By-Step Graphics, 6000 N. Forest Park Dr., Peoria, IL 61614-3592, 800-255-8800.

U&lc, *International Journal of Typographics,* published by the International Typeface Corporation. *Upper and lower case* is published four times a year, and this tabloid always contains an eclectic mix of information about type, design, and all matters artistic. Free subscriptions are available from U&lc Subscriptions, 2 Hammarskjold Plaza, New York, NY 10017.

The WordPerfectionist, monthly newsletter of the WordPerfect Support Group. The aim of this publication is to provide help and guidance to users of WordPerfect. In that it is not affiliated with WordPerfect Corp. and extremely user-friendly, a healthy mix of information is achieved. This newsletter will help you keep up with WordPerfect's metamorphases and idiosyncrasies. Subscriptions are $36 a year from The WordPerfectionist, P. O. Box 1577 Dept. DTP, Baltimore, MD 21203 or call (800) USA-GROUP.

WordPerfect, the Magazine, published by WordPerfect Publishing. This monthly magazine features articles about business, professional, and industrial applications for WordPerfect, as well as covering third-party products and services. Daniel Will-Harris writes a regular column on desktop publishing topics, and many feature articles. Subscriptions are $9 for six issues, $15 for a year, or $24 for two years. WordPerfect Publishing, 288 W. Center St., Orem, UT 84057.

◆ WordPerfect

Instant Access Guide to WordPerfect 5.0, by Michael Seif and Karen Rockow (Price/Stern/Sloan), 1988. If you need additional information on WordPerfect's basic commands and functions, I can recommend no better step-by-step guide. We served as editors for this book, and worked closely with the authors to insure that this be a quick and efficient reference. The book takes a visual approach by using screen graphics, key symbols and cross-referencing of minimal text to show people how to learn to use the program. With its bright blue cover and spiral binding, the book is very helpful for the new user, and also the infrequent user who needs a quick refresher. ISBN 0-89586-725-7 $14.95

—*Toni Will-Harris*

Product Directory

Arts & Letters
Computer Support Corporation
15926 Midway Road
Dallas, TX 75244 (214) 661-8960

Perspective Junior
(formerly Boeing Graph)
Three/D/Graphics
860 Via de la Paz
Pacific Palisades, CA 90272
(213) 459-8525

Cambridge Computer Z88
Sinclair Systems
424 Cumberland Ave.
Portland, ME 04101
(207) 761-3700

ClickArt
T/Maker, 1973 Landings Drive
Mountain View, CA 94043
(415) 962-0195

Corel Tabin & Draw
Corel Systems Corporation,
1600 Carling Ave., Ottawa, Ontario
Canada K1Z 7M4 (613) 728-8200

Desktop Art
Dynamic Graphics
6000 N. Forest Park Dr.
Peoria, IL 61656 800-255-8800

DigiFonts
528 Commons Dr.,
Golden, CO 80401
800-242-5665, (303) 526-9435

Font Effects
SoftCraft, 16 N. Carroll St.
Suite 500, Madison, WI 53703
(608) 257-3300

Fontware
Bitstream, Athenaeum House
215 First Street
Cambridge, MA 02142
800-522-3668

Genius Full Page Display
Micro Display Systems
1310 Vermilion St.
Hastings, MN 55033
612-437-2233, 800-328-9524

Glyphix Fonts
Swifte International, Ltd.
P.O. Box 5773
Wilmington, DE 19808
800-237-9383

Grammatik III
Reference Software, 330 Townsend
St. #135, San Francisco, CA 94107
800-872-9933, (415) 541-0222

HALO DPE

Media Cybernetics Inc., 8484 Georgia Ave., Silver Springs, MD 20910 800-446-HALO

Harvard Graphics

Software Publishing Corporation, P.O. Box 7210, 1901 Landings Drive Mountain View, CA 94039-7210 (415) 962-8910

Hewlett-Packard LaserJet

H-P Peripherals Group, 16399 West Bernadino Dr., San Diego, CA 92127 (619) 592-8182

HiJaak

InSet Systems, Inc., 71 Commerce Dr., Brookfield, CT 06810 800-828-8088, (203) 775-5866

Hot Shot Graphics

SymSoft, P.O. Box 4477
Mountain View, CA 94040
(415) 941-1552

LaserFonts

SoftCraft, 16 N. Carroll St. Suite 500, Madison, WI 53703 (608) 257-3300 Also LF Manager, Font Effects, LaserFonts & LaserGraphics, Word Processor Pack, Spin Font

LaserMaster LX6, LC2

LaserMaster Corp.
7156 Shady Oak Rd.
Eden Prairie, MN 55344
800-LMC-PLOT

LaserTorq

LaserTools Corp.
3025 Buena Vista Way
Berkeley, CA 94708
800-346-1353

LJ Fonts

Weaver Graphics
Fox Pavillion Box 1132
Jenkintown, PA 19046
(215) 884-9286

LaserPlus

Hammermill Paper
1540 E. Lake Road, Erie, PA 16533
800-242-2148

LaserUltra

James River Corp., 356B Sewall St.
Ludlow, MA 01056
800-451-5501, 800-521-5035

Lotus 1-2-3, Freelance

Lotus Development Corporation
55 Cambridge Parkway,
Cambridge, MA 02142
800-345-1043

Metro Image Base Clip Art
Metro ImageBase, Inc., 18623
Ventura Blvd., #210
Tarzana, CA 91356 800-843-3438

NEC LQ 890 PostScript Printer
NEC Information Systems
1414 Massachusetts Ave.
Boxborough, MA 01719

PC Paintbrush Plus
Zsoft, 450 Franklin Road, #100,
Marietta, GA 30067
(404) 428-0008

PDP 1-2-4 Memory Board
Pacific Data Products
6404 Nancy Ridge Dr.
San Diego, CA 92121
(619) 552-552-0880

PC Quik Art
PC Quik Art
394 S. Milledge Ave.
Athens, GA 30606
800-543-1779

Publisher's PicturePak
Marketing Graphics Incorporated,
4401 Dominion Blvd. Suite 210,
Glen Allen, VA 23060-3379
(804) 747-6991

QMS-PS 810
Quality Micro Systems
P.O. Box 81250, Mobile, AL 36689
(205) 633-4500

Ricoh PC Laser 6000
Ricoh Corporation, 155 Passaic
Ave., Fairfield, NJ 07006
(201) 882-2000

RightWriter, Rightsoft Inc., 2033
Wood St., Suite 218
Sarasota, FL 33577
(813) 952-9211

Toshiba T-3100
Toshiba America, Inc.
Information Services Div., 2441
Michelle Drive, Tustin, CA 92680
800-457-7777, (714) 730-5000

SLED
VS Software, P.O. Box 6158
Little Rock, AR 72216
(501) 376-2083

VCACHE - VOPT - VKETTE - VTOOLS
Golden Bow Systems, 2870 Fifth
Avenue, Suite 201, San Diego, CA
92103 (619) 298-9349

Victor 286
Victor Computers, 380 El Pueblo Road, Scotts Valley, CA 95066
(408) 438-6680

VP PLanner & VPP Plus
Paperback Software International, 2830 Ninth Street
Berkeley, CA 94710

Will-Harris Designer Disk 5
Designer Disks
Box 480265, Dept B,
Los Angeles, CA 90048
Available by mail order only—not sold in stores

Windows Graph
MicroGrafx Inc.
1820 North Greenville Ave.
Richardson, TX 75081
(212) 234-1769

WordPerfect
WordPerfect Corp.
288 West Center, Orem, UT 84057
800-321-5906

WordPerfect Classes
Simply Wordperfect
P.O. Box 491155
Los Angeles, CA 90049

Words & Pictures
Lifetree, 411 Pacific Street,
Monterey, CA 93940
(408) 373-4718

Writer Series Font Cartridges
GNU, 100 Hilltop Road, Box 414,
Ramsey, NJ 07446 (201) 825-1222

WYSE 700 Monitor
WYSE Technology, 3571 N. First St.,
San Jose, CA 95134 800-GET-WYSE

❖ *Further communications*

- If you would like to send me examples of what you are producing with WordPerfect, I would be happy to take a look at them and offer suggestions for improvement, or answer questions—I like hearing from readers.

  If you want a reply, be sure and enclose a self-addressed stamped envelope, though. Write to me at:
  DWH, Box 480265, Dept. Q, Los Angeles, CA 90036

i Index

!

A

B

C

D

G

H

I

S

U

V

Z

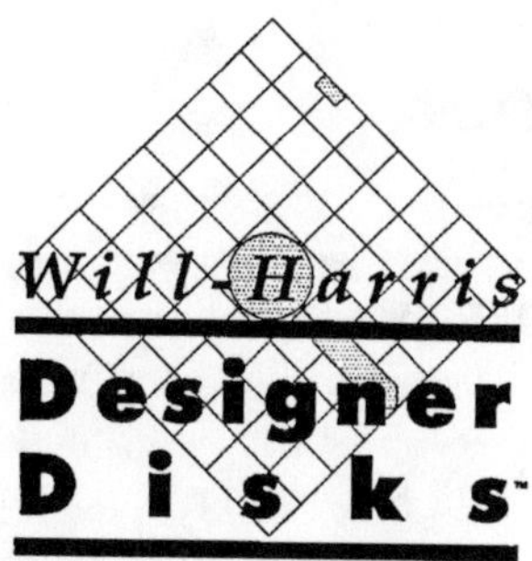

Style Sheets for WordPerfect 5 & Ventura Publisher

Will-Harris Designer Disks offer Style Sheets for use with WordPerfect 5 or Ventura Publisher—already set up and ready to go. The WordPerfect style sheets duplicate all of the examples in this book (including text). Disk 5 will help you utilize proven design techniques to quickly create attractive, effective documents.

Designer Disks can save you time in getting started, and they illustrate many of WordPerfect's trickiest and most powerful features. In no time you can tailor any element of the page layout to specifically suit your application, and get results of a high-priced professional designer without the high price.

You receive the *Style Sheets* with the formatting information and codes in place, ready to use. When ready, remove the text from the files and load in your own text and graphics. *Designer Disks* will print on any printer WordPerfect 5 or Ventura Publisher supports.

Designer Disk 5 for WordPerfect

WordPerfect Style Sheets for three newsletters, two catalogs, documentation, a book, resume, proposal, flyer, price list, pamphlet, invoice, financial statement, form, outline, overhead, sign, magazine, resume, advertisement, report cover, calendar, menu, invitation, storyboard, promotional pieces, and letterhead stationery. $35.95

For Ventura Publisher

The *2-Disk Ventura Publisher Designer Duet* contains the most requested and popular style sheets for use within Ventura Publisher, and comes to the aid of *everyone* who needs to publish *anything.*

Designer Duet (Disk 1 & 2)

Ventura Style Sheets for four different newsletters, two books, two pamphlets, two program guides, a catalog, manual, price list, magazine, brochure, annual report, leaflet, program guide, presentation, storyboard, postcard, menu, cookbook, and recipes. Also contains a Style Sheet for Forms with complete instructions about how to use databases to mail merge within Ventura. $49

Disk 3

Ventura Style Sheets for a tabloid-size newspaper, standard letter-size newsletter, magazine, price-list catalog, three-fold two-sided flyer, and HPLJ-compatible envelope and labels. $39

Order Form (Prices include shipping)

________	copies of WordPerfect Disk 5 @ $35.95 each	$________
________	copies of Ventura "Designer Duet" (Disks 1 & 2) @ $49	$________
________	copies of Ventura Disk 3 @ $39 each	$________
________	copies of Ventura "Designer Trio" (all 3 disks) @ $84	$________
	subtotal	$________
	California residents add 6% sales tax	$________
	Total	$________

Please enclose a check or money-order made payable to: "Designer Disks." (Sorry, no credit card or phone orders.) Send to: Designer Disks, Box 480265, Dept. B, Los Angeles, CA 90048 (Not affiliated in any way with Peachpit Press)

About the book

This entire book was written and edited in WordPerfect 5. I started with a beta version, and worked my way through many upgrades. The body text is set in Bitstream Fontware Goudy Old Style. The headings, subheads and keystrokes are Hammersmith, Bitstream's Fontware version of Gill Sans. The diamond subheadings are Bitstream Zapf Dingbats, currently available with the LaserMaster CAPCard (but not retail Fontware packages).

All pages were printed 8 1/2 x 11", and reduced by 18 percent (to 82% of their original size). This improved the quality of the type and graphics. For speed, the final printing of the book was accomplished with a LaserMaster CAPCard and a Hewlett-Packard LaserJet II. The pages were printed on James River LaserUltra paper, and Hammermill LaserPlus paper.

A QMS-PS 810 was used for proofing everything in the early stages of the book, when it was one of the few printers WordPerfect supported. Later it was used for the PostScript example pages in Chapter 4, *Show & Tell.* All of those examples are documented as to what specific fonts, graphics programs, and printers were used to produce them.

The computers used for writing and producing the book were a Victor 286 (AT compatible), WYSE 286 (AT compatible), and Toshiba T3100 (portable AT compatible). The monitors were the full-page MDS Genius, WYSE 700, and Toshiba plasma display, all of which are supported in high-resolution graphics modes by WordPerfect.

Screen shots were created with Hot Shot Graphics (SymSoft) on the WYSE, and Halo DPE (Media Cybernetics) on the Genius. I also used HiJaak for graphic file format conversions. I used a Cambridge Computer Z88 (a one and a half pound portable computer with 512K memory) for taking notes on those rare occasions when I was allowed to leave the house.

We ate a lot of Stouffer's frozen food during the preparation of the book (otherwise we might not have had any hot meals). We also ate altogether too many Entenmann's chocolate chip cookies, and let our Panasonic answering machine insulate us from the rest of the world. I had a Caframo fan constantly blowing in my face, lest I overheat (this saved my wife Toni the horror of finding me in a puddle on the floor, something which would have ruined the inlaid parquet).

I sat on a genuine Balans chair (you know, the backless pretzel-shaped things, where your knees rest on little pads), and Toni used a very lovely (but totally inappropriate) Italian pine shell-backed chair from the Spiegel catalog. We both had frogs covered in William Morris fabric from Liberty's of London on top of our monitors to provide amusement after those 18-hour sessions with WordPerfect.

One last note: You would not be reading this book if it were not for the special people at Peachpit Press. They make hard work worthwhile.

—DWH

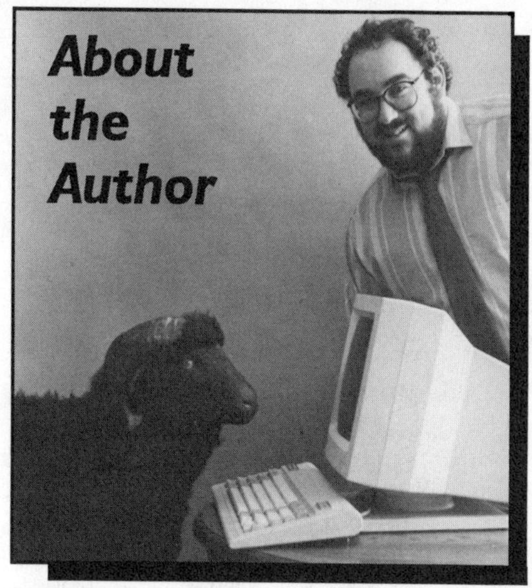

What's a nice comedy writer like Daniel Will-Harris doing in a field like this—computer books—the ultimate techno-snooze? Well, his first computer book, *Desktop Publishing With Style,* received much popular and critical acclaim, and if you can make a computer book entertaining and informative, the future is yours.

Daniel has always been interested in any form of communication, from finger painting to being editor-in-chief of his college paper. It was on that paper that he met his first (and hopefully only) wife, Toni, who is responsible for the art direction of his books, and that last parenthetical. They live in L.A. with their pet sheep, Selsdon.

For many years Daniel worked as a writer for television and the musical theater. When he discovered what computers offered a writer, he was hooked, and has been a slave to technology ever since. He has written for many magazines, which led to his current predicament: he writes a monthly column for *Personal Publishing* magazine (on a deadline that pops up with frightening regularity).

Daniel paid his dues for many years as contributing editor for a best-selling line of computer books by Peter A. McWilliams. Daniel and Toni also desktop published the camera-ready pages of Peter's most recent book, *The Personal Electronics Guide,* for Prentice Hall, and they recently edited a series of computer books for yet another publisher.

As a past writer of technical manuals and user guides, Daniel enjoyed the many free trips to Japan (from where he's schlepped home a lot of those little pastel plastic gee-gaws). He's also in great demand as a lecturer, and to conduct seminars about desktop publishing and writing with a computer—yes, he knows it's tough work being the leader in the desktop publishing/graphic design field, but someone's got to do it. After so much experience with computers, it was a natural step to start his own consulting firm, and become a parasite of the rich and famous. As a consultant, Daniel deals primarily with people in the entertainment industry and the media, such as Robert E. Lee, William F. Buckley, Gene Roddenberry, Hanna-Barbera, and Time/Design, headquartered in Denmark (more free trips). Just so you know, he feels that name dropping, if used judiciously, is a virtue.

You don't do all that schmoozing with celebs for nothing, so it should come as no surprise that he's served as a consultant on many feature films, most recently for *Half Moon Street* director Bob Swaim. Living proof of the "it's all who you know school," he's also appeared in several motion pictures, including *Love Letters,* with Jamie Lee Curtis, and *The Mae West Story,* with Ann Jillian. He's just completed a featured role in an as yet untitled movie starring Ray Walston (My Favorite Martian), and (everyone's favorite Bad Seed), Patty McCormack.

In his spare time, Daniel likes to collect anything art deco, or stuffed, and to get away for dinner at his favorite restaurant in Belgium. His greatest ambition is to have some spare time within this decade.

CODE	KEYSTROKE	COMMAND
[ ]	[HOME] [SPACE]	Hard Space
[-]	-	Hyphen
-	CONTROL-	Soft Hyphen
[/]	F1	Cancel Hyphenation
[AdvToLn]	SHIFT-F8 O A I	Advance to Line
[AdvUp]	SHIFT-F8 O A U	Advance Up
[AdvDn]	SHIFT-F8 O A D	Advance Down
[AdvRgt]	SHIFT-F8 O A R	Advance Right
[AdvRgt]	SHIFT-F8 O A R	Advance Right
[Align]	F6 (or [TAB] with decimal or right tabs}	Tab Align
[Block Pro]	ALT-F4 SHIFT-F8	Block Protection
[BOLD]	F6	Bold
[C/A/FlRt]	(Automatic after Center, Align or Flush Right	End of Tab Align or Flush
[Center Pg]	SHIFT-F8 P C	Center Page Top to Bottom
[Cndl EOP]	SHIFT-F8 O C	Conditional End of Page
[Cntr]	SHIFT-F6	Center
[Col Def]	ALT-F7 D	Column Definition
[Col Off]	ALT-F7 C	End of Text Columns
[Col On]	ALT-F7 C	Beginning of Text Columns
[Comment]	CONTROL-F5 C C	Document Comment
[Color]	CONTROL-F8 C	Print Color for Font
[Date]	SHIFT-F5 C	Automatic Date/Time Function
[Decml Char]	SHIFT-F8 O D	Decimal/Thousands Separator-character
[EXT LARGE]	CONTROL-F8 S E	Extra Large Print
[Fig Opt]	ALT-F9 F O	Figure Box Options
[Figure]	ALT-F9 F C	Figure Box
[FINE]	CONTROL-F8 S F	Fine Print
[Flsh Rt]	ALT-F6	Flush Right
[Font]	CONTROL-F8 F	Base Font
[Footer]	SHIFT-F8 P F	Footer
[Force]	SHIFT-F8 P O	Force Odd/Even Page
[Form]	SHIFT-F7 P S	Form (Printer Selection)
[Header]	SHIFT-F8 P H	Header
[HLine]	ALT-F9 L H	Horizontal Line
[HPg]	CONTROL-ENTER	Hard Page Break
[HRt]	[ENTER]	Hard Return
[Hyph On]	SHIFT-F8 L Y O	Hyphenation
[HZone]	SHIFT-F8 L Z	Hyphenation zone
[->Indent]	F4	Indent
[->Indent<-]	SHIFT-F4	Left/Right Indent
[Index]	ALT-F5 I	Index Entry
[ITALC]	CONTROL-F8 A I	Italics
[Just On]	SHIFT-F8 L J Y	Right Justification On
[Just Off]	SHIFT-F8 L J N	Right Justification Off
[Just Lim]	SHIFT-F8 O P J	Word/Letter Justification Limits

CODE	KEYSTROKE	COMMAND
[Kern]	SHIFT-F8 O P K	Kerning
[L/R Mar]	SHIFT-F8 L M	Left and Right Margins
[LARGE]	CONTROL-F8 S L	Large Print
[Ln Height: Auto]	SHIFT-F8 L H A	Leading/Line height auto
[Line Height: #"]	SHIFT-F8 L H F	Leading/Line height Fixed
[<-Mar Rel]	SHIFT-[TAB]	Left Margin Release
[Open Style]	ALT-F8	Open Style
[Ovrstk]	SHIFT-F8 O O C	Overstrike Preceding Character
[OUTLN]	CONTROL-F8 A O	Outline Font
[Par Num]	SHIFT-F5 P	Paragraph Number
[Par # Def]	SHIFT-F5 D	Paragraph Numbering Definition
[Pg Num	SHIFT-F8 P N	New Page Number
[Pg Num Pos]	SHIFT-F8 P P	Page Number Position
[REDLN]	CONTROL-F8 A R	Redline
[Set Fig Num]	ALT-F9 F N	Set New Figure Box Number
[Set Tab Num]	ALT-F9 T N	Set New Table Box Number
[Set Txt Num]	ALT-F9 B N	Set New Text Box Number
[Set Usr Num]	ALT-F9 U N	Set New User-Defined Box
[SHADW]	CONTROL-F8 A A	Shadow Font
[SM CAP]	CONTROL-F8 A C	Small Caps
[SMALL]	CONTROL-F8 S S	Small Print
[SPg]	(Created automatically)	Soft Page Break
[SRt]	(Created automatically)	Soft Return
[StkOut]	CONTROL-F8 A S	Strikeout
[Style On]	ALT-F8	Styles/Paired
[Subdoc]	ALT-F5 S	Subdocument (Master Documents)
[SubScpt]	CONTROL-F8 S B	Subscript
[Suppress]	SHIFT-F8 P U	Suppress Page Format
[SuprScpt]	CONTROL-F8 S P	Superscript
[T/B Mar]	SHIFT-F8 P M	Top and Bottom Margins
[Tab]	[TAB]	Tab
[Tab Opt]	ALT-F9 B O	Table Box Options
[Tab Set]	SHIFT-F8 L T	Tab Set
[Table]	ALT-F9 T C	Table Box
[Text Box]	ALT-F9 B C	Text Box
[Txt Opt]	ALT-F9 B O	Text Box Options
[UND]	F8	Underlining
[Undrln]	SHIFT-F8 O U	Underline Spaces/Tabs
[Usr Box]	ALT-F9 U C	User Box
[UsrOpt]	ALT-F9 U O	User Box Options
[VLine]	ALT-F9 L V	Vertical Line
[Vry Large]	CONTROL-F8 S V	Very Large Print
[Wrd/Ltr Spacing]	SHIFT-F8 O P W	Word and Letter Spacing
[W/O On]	SHIFT-F8 L W Y	Widow/Orphan Protect On
[W/O Off]	SHIFT-F8 L W N	Widow/Orphan Protect Off

More from Peachpit Press...

Ventura Tips and Tricks, 2nd Edition

by Ted Nace

This latest release of Peachpit's unique, easy-to-use resource covers Version 2.0 of Xerox Ventura Publisher, including both the base version and the Professional Extension. Like the best-selling first edition, it's loaded with tips, tricks, hints, shortcuts, and all-around good advice. You'll find sections on Ventura's basic structure and underlying concepts, how to assemble the hardware system that's right for your needs, how to organize your hard disk, and how to create and format illustrated documents. A "Special Topics" segment holds a miscellany of information: how to add more fonts, improve hyphenation, speed up output, overcome memory limitations, and import screen shots and PostScript illustrations into Ventura.

LaserJet Unlimited, Edition II

by Ted Nace and Michael Gardner

This new, updated edition of the definitive guide to the Hewlett-Packard LaserJet offers concise, authoritative information and hands-on advice on every aspect of HP's popular family of laser printers, including the LaserJet series II. *LaserJet Unlimited* covers the use of the printer with word processors, spreadsheets, databases, and desktop publishing programs, as well as special subjects like font-editing programs, form design systems, and utilities for printing labels and envelopes and creating screen shots. A section on hardware explains the various upgrade options available for the LaserJet, such as the JetScript PostScript controller and the LaserMaster CAPCard. The appendices include a complete table of font cartridge selection codes, a table of PCL Printer Language commands, and a comprehensive font directory.

Order Form:

Mail to Peachpit Press or call 415/527-8555 to order direct—all orders are backed by an unconditional 90-day return privilege. Dealers: please ask for quantity discount schedule.

Quantity	Item	Unit Price	Total
	LaserJet Unlimited, Edition II	$24.95	
	Ventura Tips and Tricks, 2nd Edition	22.95	
	WordPerfect 5: Desktop Publishing in Style	21.95	
		Subtotal	
		Tax	
		Shipping/handling	
		Total	

Tax of 6.5% applies to California residents only.
U.S. shipping (UPS): $3.50 first item, $.50 each additional. UPS 2nd day is $7.00 first item, $1 each additional.
Canadian shipping (air mail): $5.00 first item, $1.00 each additional.
Overseas shipping (air mail): $10.00 each item.

Name	
Company	
Address	
City	
State	Zip

Check ____ Visa ____ MasterCard ____ COD ____

Card Number	
Card Holder	
Expiration Date	Phone Number

PEACHPIT PRESS
1085 Keith Ave.
Berkeley, CA 94708
415/527-8555